federalism andpolitical community

Essays in Honour of Donald Smiley

federalism andpolitical community

Essays in Honour of Donald Smiley

edited by David P. Shugarman
and Reg Whitaker

broadview press

Canadian Cataloguing in Publication Data

Main entry under title
Federalism and Political Community

Bibliography: p.
ISBN 0-921149-42-5

1. Federal government — Canada. 2. Smiley, Donald V.,
1921-   . I. Shugarman, David P., 1943-   . II. Whitaker,
Reginald, 1943- . III. Smiley, Donald V., 1921-   .

JL27.F43 1989   320.971
C89-093687-0

broadview press   in the U.S. broadview press
P.O. Box 1243   269 Portage Rd.
Peterborough, Ontario   Lewiston, NY
K9J 7H5   Canada   14092   USA

CONTENTS

INTRODUCTION

HISTORY AND ITS CONSEQUENCES

THE ROLE OF THE STATE IN CANADIAN LIFE

POLITICAL COMMUNITY AND POLITICAL TRADITIONS

THE CONSTITUTION AND THE CHARTER
OF RIGHTS

MASS COMMUNICATION AND POLITICS

DONALD SMILEY AND THE STUDY OF FEDERALISM

POSTFACE

APPENDIX

INTRODUCTION

SMILEY'S PEOPLE

David P. Shugarman and Reg Whitaker

For over three decades Donald Victor Smiley has been one of the leading scholars and teachers in Canadian political science. In the quintessential Canadian field of federalism, the always controversial area of constitutional politics, and the relatively new area of interest in the ideas which underlie political institutions and practices, he has been an especially influential figure. Nobody who is seriously devoted to the study of the "federal condition" (to use one of Smiley's apt phrases) has been able to ignore his numerous publications or avoid grappling with the ideas he has continued to generate over a long and very distinguished career. Textbooks, monographs, essays, scholarly and popular articles, commentaries and studies commissioned by governments and public interest organizations make up an impressive contribution to Canadians' understanding of their political community, and one that will surely last.

Underlying Don Smiley's long years of scholarship and writing is a deep commitment to the standards and traditions of the scholarly community, both in Canada and abroad, and a deep, even passionate commitment to the political community of the country in which he was born and to which he has devoted his many talents and energies over the years. In both cases, there is the same strong faith in the value of freedom: free institutions and free people pursuing their goals without arbitrary interference from either the state or powerful interests, but with maximum tolerance for the diversity of goals and beliefs among fellow scholars and citizens. The liberal ideal is always fragile and difficult to realise but Don Smiley in his life and work has exemplified it.

It is not only in his work but in his person that Don Smiley has left his mark on a generation. As a teacher and as a colleague he will be long remembered. Whether conducting a graduate seminar, participating in one of the innumerable scholarly conferences to which he has been devoted, or simply engaging with seemingly inexhaustible gusto in discussions about politics and life, he has enlivened and stimulated all with whom he has come in contact. It can be said of him, as it can be said of a very few, that he has always remained young, interested in and open to new ideas, and is always ready to revise and reformulate his own.

In 1989, Don Smiley formally retired as Professor of Political Science at York University, where he had taught for the last decade and a half of his career. As a tribute to him and a mark of the respect in which he is held by York and the Department of Political Science, a very successful *festschrift* had been organized in his honour in the spring of 1988, under the title of 'Federalism and the Quest for Political Community'. The present volume arises out of that conference.

As organizers of the conference, we were struck by the warmth of the reception we received from all those we contacted to participate. All were delighted with the idea of a conference in honour of Don Smiley and were willing, indeed, eager to prepare papers for presentation. A few who had previous commitments expressed great regrets over their inability to participate. It became apparent to us that over his long career, Don had made innumerable friends and many appreciative colleagues and students. Even those who were in disagreement with this or that position welcomed the opportunity to join in the intellectual debate.

Although, as more than one participant at the conference put it, we are all 'Smiley's people', the papers presented here attest to the special kind of influence Smiley has had on Canadian political science. He has never been the sort of scholar who founds a 'school' and spawns followers. This indeed would be antithetical to his liberal ideal of scholarship, to the free play of ideas and to a tolerant, diverse community of scholars. As a teacher he has never tried to fit his students into a mold, but rather to spark in them the same kind of love of debate and exploration which has always burned so brightly in his own mind. 'Smileyism' is not a doctrine, or a claim to truth, but a way of approaching the world. In their very ideological and intellectual diversity, the papers in this volume offer the best tribute to Smiley's influence on Canadian political science.

The conference and the preparation of this volume of essays have involved the support and participation of many people and organizations, which we are pleased to acknowledge. Peter Meekison and Henry Mayo both contributed personal reminiscences of Don as teacher and as student which very much entertained and illuminated a banquet held as part of the conference. Ralph Heintzman, William Lederman, Thomas Courchene, and Leo Panitch all gave papers to the conference which, for various reasons, we were regrettably not able to include in this book. Eugene Forsey, J.E. Hodgetts, and Paul Fox were unable to attend at the last minute but sent their good wishes. Gerard Bergeron, Daniel Latouche, and David Cameron were unable to attend due to previous commitments but expressed their regrets. The essays in this volume by David Bell, Stephen Clarkson, Stefan Dupré, and Ian Greene were not able to be presented at the conference but we are pleased to present them here.

Support was generously granted to the enterprise by the Social Sciences and Humanities Research Council of Canada, through their Aid to Scholarly Conferences program. York University was especially helpful, offering both financial and institutional support from the following: President Harry Arthurs; the Dean of Arts, Tom Traves; the Faculty of Arts Committee on Research Grants and Scholarships; Noli Swatman, Executive Officer of the Office of Research Administration; the York Ad Hoc Fund; the Dean of Graduate Studies, Sandra Pyke; the Robarts Centre for Canadian Studies, and our own Department of Political Science, especially through the good graces of our former Chair, Robert Drummond and our former Administrative Assistant, Jean Bowers. Special mention should be made of two graduate students, Andrea Demchuk and Paul Rynard, who provided excellent and unstinting assistance in the preparation of this book, both of an administrative and an editorial nature. Rynard was also invaluable in assisting in the organization of the conference.

Last, but certainly not least, mention should be made of Don Smiley himself who, despite his great modesty, was not only the inspiration for the conference and this book but was invariably helpful and polite as we put him through the various paces required for bringing the project through to reality. Don's own speech to the banquet honouring him was characteristically thoughtful and moving in its affirmation of the fundamental values for which he has always stood. We are proud to include it here.

This volume is, we believe, a fitting tribute to a great scholar in a form which he himself will best appreciate. Leading political and legal scholars grapple with some of the great issues animating the Canadian political community in the late twentieth century. This is what Smiley's people do, and this, along with his own valuable writings, is Don Smiley's legacy to Canada and its scholarly community.

HISTORY AND ITS CONSEQUENCES

THE ORIGINS OF CO-OPERATIVE FEDERALISM

Garth Stevenson, Brock University

The expression "co-operative federalism" arose in the United States in the 1930s and spread to Canada after the Second World War, attaining the peak of its popularity in the 1960s. (Subsequently, of course, it has been replaced in this country by the term "executive federalism," which was first developed and popularized by Donald Smiley.) Apart from its normative aspects, the concept of co-operative federalism, in both the United States and Canada, was intended to emphasize the growing prominence of intergovernmental relations as a result of the expanding role of the state and the resulting difficulty of maintaining a rigid distinction between the fields of activity which the constitution assigned to the two levels of government. Implicit in the concept was the assumption that prior to the New Deal in the United States, and prior to the postwar development of the Keynesian welfare state in Canada, the two levels of government in both federations had pursued their respective tasks in virtual isolation from one another. With little or no overlap between the responsibilities of the two levels of government there was little need for intergovernmental relations involving either politicians or administrators. All that was needed was for the Supreme Court, or in Canada's case the Judicial Committee of the Privy Council, to maintain the jurisdictional boundary between the two levels by periodically striking down statutes that exceeded the constitutional powers of the legislature that enacted them.

Some time after the term co-operative federalism had become popular, Daniel Elazar's research demonstrated that the supposedly classic variety of "dual federalism" had not corresponded closely with reality, even at the time when its virtues were being extolled in numerous decisions of the Supreme Court of the United States. Instead, Elazar showed that the federal government and the states began to collaborate in performing a variety of shared or overlapping functions almost as soon as the Constitution came into effect, and that such supposedly modern phenomena as conditional grants and jointly administered programs had emerged even before the Civil War, let alone the New Deal.[1]

In Canada the accepted orthodoxy regarding the early history of federalism is somewhat different from the orthodoxy which Elazar refuted in the United States, but parallels it in certain respects. All students of Canadian federalism know that John A. Macdonald deliberately rejected many features of an American model which he believed had contributed to the breakdown that led to the Civil War. Instead, Macdonald designed a more hierarchical kind of federalism, largely based on the ideas of Alexander Hamilton, which was intended to subordinate the provinces to the central government by such means as the declaratory power of Parliament, the disallowance of provincial legislation, and the extensive powers of the federally-appointed lieutenant-governor. In addition, the provinces were made dependent on federal subsidies, which the British North America Act optimistically assumed could be fixed forever at the level specified in Section 118. This model of "quasi-federalism," as K.C. Wheare later called it, thus implied intergovernmental relations of a kind, in contrast to the American model, which appeared superficially to imply an absence of interaction between the two levels of government. However, the Macdonaldian concept of intergovernmental relations seemed to make the provinces no more than the passive recipients of decisions made unilaterally in Ottawa, and thus had little in common with the complex pattern of intergovernmental collaboration that had characterized both North American federations in recent decades.[2]

Intergovernmental relations in the modern sense would thus appear to have been no more necessary in Macdonaldian federalism than in the federalism of the nineteenth-century United States as it was understood prior to Elazar's revisionist interpretation. Macdonald's Canada would seem to have shared with the nineteenth-century United States the essential conditions for the practice of "dual federalism": a constitutionally entrenched division of legislative powers, a relatively limited role for the state, and a judiciary willing and able to prevent either level of government from trespassing on the other's field of jurisdiction. In fact the distribution of legislative powers in the B.N.A. Act was more detailed and apparently more rigid than that provided for in the Constitution of the United States, so that the need for intergovernmental collaboration would perhaps seem to be even less in the Canadian case.

There is, however, a provision of the B.N.A. Act that until recently has attracted little attention, and that is an exception to the general rule that powers are exclusively assigned to either Parliament or the provincial legislatures. This exception is, of course, Section 95, which provides that either the provincial legislatures or Parliament may legislate in relation to agriculture and to immigration, but that provincial laws shall have effect only insofar as they are not "repugnant" to the terms of any Act of Parliament. Perhaps few have stopped to consider why these two subjects, and only these two, should have been concurrent fields of jurisdiction, in a constitution that carefully enumerated no less than forty-six other fields of jurisdiction which it assigned exclusively to either Parliament or the legislatures. Fewer still have examined the intergovernmental relations to which Section 95 gave rise during the early years of Canadian federalism.[3]

To the modern mind agriculture and immigration may seem like a random juxtaposition of two unrelated subjects both of which, for unrelated and equally mysterious reasons, could not be exclusively assigned to either level of government and were thus shared between them. This is an understandable error now that more than half of the foreign-born population resides in the three largest metropolitan areas of Canada. In 1867, by contrast, agriculture and immigration were closely related subjects. The circumstance that made British North America attractive to immigrants was its supply of more or less unoccupied land that could be used for agriculture. Land was a means of absorbing immigrants and immigrants were a means of occupying the land and developing the country. Although manufacturing was beginning to develop, and although the older staples of fur, fish, and timber were still significant, Canada was primarily an agricultural country in 1867, and was expected to remain so. Confederation, followed by expansion to the west, was expected to make the country larger, in area, population, and what we would now call GNP, but not to cause a qualitative change in the character of its economy. Canada wanted immigrants, and the most desirable immigrants were considered to be farmers, who would increase the cultivated acreage of the country, produce exportable commodities, and provide traffic for the railways and markets for indigenous secondary industries.

Both agriculture and immigration were thus subjects of great importance, a fact that seemed to argue for placing them under the jurisdiction of Parliament. On the other hand the original provinces retained (or in the case of Ontario and Quebec were given) ownership of crown land, which was the principal instrument of policy in relation to both agriculture and immigration. Section 95 must be read in conjunction with Section 92:5 ("The Management and Sale of Public Lands belonging to the Province ...") and Section 109, which confers ownership of "All Lands, Mines, Minerals and Royalties ..." These provisions unavoidably gave the provinces primary responsibility for both agriculture and immigration. Yet in contrast to mining and forestry, both agriculture and immigration were too important to be left exclusively to the provinces. There had to be a federal role, but it could not be as exclusive as the federal role in relation to banking, interprovincial transport, or fisheries. Section 95 was the response to this set of circumstances.

Section 95 must also be read in the light of Canadian experience with immigration before 1867, as well as the experience of the United States. Public policy towards immigration can have two objectives: to attract immigrants or to exclude them. The two objectives are not mutually exclusive, since there may be a desire to attract some kinds of immigrants and to exclude others, or to attract them at some times and to exclude them at others, or to attract them to certain parts of the country and to exclude them from others. In the United States, as of 1867, there was not much in the way of explicit policy regarding immigration. The country had such an abundance of land and resources, as well as political freedom and social mobility, that little effort was needed to attract immigrants from Europe. Insofar as effort was needed, it was largely provided by private enterprise, particularly the transatlantic shipping companies. On the other hand, there was not much politically effective support for excluding immigrants from the United States until late in the nineteenth century. Thus Congress took little interest in the subject, and did not legislate regarding immigration until as late as 1882, when a measure restricting the immigration of Chinese was adopted.[4] Before that time anyone, at least in theory, could enter the United States. The reception of immigrants and their absorption into the community was left to state, local and private initiatives, particularly in the Atlantic seaports where most immigrants then arrived. Perhaps in part because of this localized administration, immigrants tended to remain in the rapidly industrializing northeastern states, where they filled the needs of the manufacturing industries for cheap labour.[5] The task of populating the western frontier was largely left to native-born Americans, mainly of Anglo-Celtic ancestry and Protestant religion. This pattern of settlement, as well as the tendency of immigrants to avoid the South (where industrialization was limited and blacks provided the cheap labour) is still reflected in the ethnic and religious composition, not to mention the political culture, of the different states.

In all of these respects Canada's experience, before (and after) Confederation, was very different. In particular, the laissez-faire approach of the United States was inappropriate to Canada's needs, and this fact was recognized long before Confederation. Canada could not assume that immigrants would be attracted to its shores, because it had to compete with a generally more attractive destination: the United States. The United States had more land and resources, a higher standard of living, more political democracy and social mobility, and a better climate. Some immigrants came to Canada initially because it was slightly closer to northwestern Europe, making the ocean passage cheaper and less perilous, but most of those attracted for this reason soon moved on to the United States. Canada had to abandon laissez-faire in immigration policy in order to maintain, and still more in order to improve upon, its proportionate share of the North American population. As early as 1841, before responsible government was achieved and four decades before the United States Congress took any action regarding immigration, the United Province of Canada adopted legislation to create a fund for defraying the cost of moving indigent immigrants from the port of entry to their destinations, and of supporting them until they found employment.[6]

On the other hand, Canada had incentives to adopt exclusionary policies also. Canada was a part of the British Empire, and in relation to other colonies it was not very far from the British Isles. For both of these reasons there was a well-founded suspicion that Canada was used by the United Kingdom as an outlet for unwanted elements of that country's population, without much regard for either the interests of Canada or those of the immigrants themselves. The struggle for responsible government was in part a struggle for the right to control entry into Canada. The Imperial government did not acknowledge that right until 1848, after the influx of Irish famine victims had persuaded most Canadians as well as the Governor General (Lord Elgin) that controls were essential.[7] The first of several statutes imposing restrictions on entry was adopted in that year. Five years later the government of the United Province took over control of the immigration agencies in Quebec City, Montreal, Ottawa, Kingston, Toronto, and Hamilton. These offices had previously been operated by the Imperial government. Significantly, after 1853 they reported to the Minister of Agriculture.[8]

Apart from measures to support immigrants and measures to exclude them, there was a third strand of pre-Confederation policy that gives some credence to the "merchants against industry" interpretation of Canada's development. A statute adopted in 1850 was designed to encourage immigrants bound from Europe to the United States to use the St. Lawrence route as a means of getting there.[9] This of course was the converse of the traditional goal of directing American exports of agricultural produce through the St. Lawrence system. The same boats that carried produce downstream could carry immigrants upstream. At the time of Confederation about four out of every five immigrants who were recorded as arriving in Canada continued on, within the same calendar year, into the United States.[10] Despite this fact, about one-sixth of Canada's population was foreign-born at the time of the first Dominion census, almost exactly the same proportion as today.[11]

Confederation, from a central Canadian perspective, had the practical consequence that the existing functions of the colonial state had to be distributed between two levels of government, federal and provincial. For reasons already suggested, agriculture and immigration could not be given exclusively to either level. The United Province of Canada had a department and minister of agriculture, and the successor governments of Quebec, Ontario, and the Dominion all established such departments immediately. Like their predecessor in the United Province, all of these departments had responsibility for immigration as well. The appropriate division of responsibilities between the two levels of government would have to be discovered through trial and error. Common sense suggested, however, that the control of entry into Canada would be a responsibility of the Dominion, particularly since it was closely associated with Section 91, subsection 11, "Quarantine and the Establishment and Maintenance of Marine Hospitals." Canada had already experienced epidemics of infectious disease caused by immigrants arriving from the British Isles, and this was one reason why the United Province had demanded the right to control entry in 1848. Virtually all immigrants arrived at either Quebec City, Montreal, or Niagara Falls, and control of entry at these points was not difficult, but there was no feasible way to control the movement of persons between Quebec and Ontario.

The provinces would play a significant role, however, in efforts to attract immigrants and in assisting them after they arrived, particularly if the immigrants were farmers and intended to settle on the public lands. Prior to Confederation, according to Hodgetts, Canada had seemed resigned to a situation in which most "immigrants" continued on to permanent homes in the United States.[12] After Confederation this situation was frequently deplored and efforts were made, with some success, to correct it. The more upbeat mentality created by Confederation itself and the anti-American sentiments stimulated by the Fenian raids and the termination of Reciprocity probably contributed to this change, at the same time as the resumption of railway building on a large scale increased the demand for labour.

The desire to attract immigrants was shared by the federal and provincial authorities after 1867. Ontario, then as now, attracted the largest share of the immigrants who remained in Canada; in 1871 it accounted for 75 per cent of the foreign-born persons enumerated by the census. Quebec and New Brunswick apparently wished to increase their share of immigration, and both had large areas of unoccupied land that they considered suitable for agriculture, some of which would be made more accessible by the building of the Intercolonial Railway. Nova Scotia, which had the smallest foreign-born population of the four provinces, appeared relatively uninterested in immigration, perhaps because of its relatively high (by North American standards) density of population. At the federal level, interest in immigration is suggested by the fact that the House of Commons established a Standing Committee on Immigration and Colonization at its first session.

Logically enough, and in characteristically Canadian fashion, the first question with which this committee concerned itself was the appropriate division of responsibilities between the Dominion and the provinces. In its first report the committee expressed the view that the word "colonization" in its title was not appropriate, since the subject fell under provincial jurisdiction. The committee dispatched letters to Sir John A. Macdonald and the premiers of the four provinces, requesting clarification of the meaning of Section 95 as it applied to immigration. Neither Macdonald nor the premiers of Quebec and New Brunswick bothered to reply, while the premier of Ontario replied that the question had not been discussed by his government. The only substantive reply, oddly enough, came from the Attorney General of Nova Scotia, who was trying to extricate his province from Confederation, but his reply was no more than an elementary explanation of the meaning of the repugnancy clause. In its report the standing committee referred to Sections 92:5 and 109 of the B.N.A. Act and concluded that:

> The clauses seem to place every interest in connection with the public lands and their settlement beyond the purview of this Committee, and to limit their inquiries and supervision of immigration matters simply to the sanitary arrangements for the reception of immigrants, the management of the existing agencies, and the transit of immigrants within the Dominion.[13]

Despite this conclusion, it continued to be known as the Standing (or Select) Committee on Immigration and Colonization for many years thereafter.

Even before this report, in November 1867, a question was asked in the House of Commons regarding the government's plans, if any, to encourage immigration. Sir George Cartier replied that the government favoured immigration but would require co-operation from the provinces.[14] Two weeks later Dr. Charles Tupper (who did not enter the cabinet until 1870) introduced a motion requesting the correspondence between the Dominion and provincial governments on the subject of immigration. Macdonald replied that he thought the only correspondence to date was of a purely formal character.[15] A motion similar to Tupper's was moved in the Senate the following year, and led to a somewhat longer debate than had taken place in the Commons. Most of the senators who participated lamented the fact that Canada was less attractive to immigrants than the United States. Senator David Macpherson, who later served in the second Macdonald government as Minister of the Interior, blamed this fact on the provinces, since it was they who controlled the public lands. The Dominion government could do nothing to compete with the free land that was available in the United States. In reply, Senator Wark of New Brunswick noted that his province had adopted a statute making land available to settlers at a price of twenty cents an acre.[16]

A few months afterwards, in September 1868, Premier Pierre Chauveau of Quebec proposed that a federal-provincial conference be held in order to clarify the responsibilities of the two levels of government regarding immigration.[17] No federal-provincial conference, on any subject, had yet taken place, but the idea may have been suggested by the conferences at Charlottetown, Quebec and London that had led to Confederation. Chauveau's suggestion was accepted by the federal government in an order-in-council, which also appointed the Minister of Agriculture, J. C. Chapais, as the "delegate" of the Dominion. Chapais selected 29 October 1868 as the date for the opening of the conference, and invitations were sent to the four provinces.

The conference took place in Ottawa and lasted for two days. Since the Prime Minister of Canada and the premiers of Quebec and New Brunswick attended, as well as an additional minister from each, it was effectively a "first ministers" conference, an indication of the importance attached to the subject. Ontario, however, was represented only by the minister and the deputy minister of agriculture. Nova Scotia, not much interested in immigration and still attempting to withdraw from Confederation, was not represented at all. Despite Nova Scotia's absence, the conference was more fruitful than most of those that have occurred in Ottawa more recently. The delegates were able to agree on eleven recommendations regarding the allocation of responsibilities between the two levels of government, as follows:

1. The Dominion, described in the conference minutes as "the General Government," would establish and maintain an immigration office in London, and possibly other offices in the British Isles.

2. The Dominion would also establish and maintain at least one immigration office in continental Europe.

3. The Dominion would defray the expenses of quarantine stations at Quebec City, Halifax, and Saint John. (No mention was made of Niagara Falls, which had been an important port of entry for immigrants since the completion of the international railway bridge more than a decade before the conference. Presumably the delegates had confidence in the quarantine arrangements at the Port of New York.)

4. The Dominion at its own expense would maintain immigration offices at the eight principal cities of Canada: Halifax, Saint John, Quebec, Montreal, Ottawa, Kingston, Toronto and Hamilton. It will be recalled that these offices, except for the two in the Maritimes, had been taken over by the United Province of Canada from the Imperial Government in 1853.

5. The Dominion government would request funds from Parliament each year to cover its expenses regarding immigration.

6. The provinces agreed to establish an efficient system of offices for the reception of immigrants within their borders, and as much as possible to pursue liberal policies regarding the settlement of their uncultivated lands.

7. Each province could, if it so desired, appoint its own immigration agents in Europe and elsewhere, and the Dominion promised that all such agents "shall be duly accredited by the General Government."

8. Each province agreed to keep the Dominion government and the Dominion's immigration agents overseas informed of the province's policies regarding colonization and settlement.

9. To avoid disappointing would-be immigrants, no province would alter its colonization policies without "due and reasonable" notice. If possible any changes in policy should be made during the winter (which was when legislative sessions usually took place) and remain in effect throughout the following summer (which was when most immigrants arrived.)

10. Dominion-provincial conferences on immigration would take place four times each year.

11. Each of the governments agreed to introduce whatever legislation would be required to carry out its commitments.

The Dominion government embodied these terms in an order-in-council, and copies were sent to all provinces, including Nova Scotia, with the request that the provincial governments indicate in writing their formal acceptance of the agreements. All four replied although Nova Scotia, which was in the process of negotiating "better terms," indicated via the Lieutenant-Governor that for financial reasons it was not in a position to co-operate. New Brunswick expressed second thoughts about the feasibility of sending a delegate to Ottawa every three months (the Intercolonial Railway was not completed until 1876) and stated that it would not require any legislation to carry out its commitments, but it accepted the other terms. Quebec and Ontario accepted the agreements without reservation.[18]

Undeterred by New Brunswick's reservations, the Dominion summoned another conference to be held in March 1869, at which it was hoped that the provinces would supply information regarding their efforts to attract immigrants. Although all four provinces agreed to supply the information, only Ontario was willing to attend a conference at this time. Nova Scotia again pleaded financial stringency, Quebec excused itself on the grounds that its legislature would be in session at the time of the conference, and New Brunswick simply replied that attendance would not be convenient.[19] The conference nonetheless took place, with only Ontario and the Dominion in attendance. Ontario was represented by its Provincial Secretary, while Chapais again represented the Dominion. At this conference Ontario agreed to supply the Dominion with any information about the province which it would like prospective immigrants to have, and also agreed to pay the transportation costs for indigent immigrants from the port of entry to the place in Ontario where they wished to settle. A report on this conference was sent to the other three provinces in the hope that they would agree to do likewise.[20] By the time the St. Lawrence opened for navigation in 1869 the Dominion had appointed immigration agents in London and (for some unknown reason) Antwerp. It also had established immigration offices at Halifax, Saint John, and Miramichi (New Brunswick) in addition to the six existing offices in central Canada. All immigration agents, both at home and abroad, were instructed to co-operate with the provinces in distributing information supplied by the provincial governments and in directing immigrants towards the places where the provincial governments wished them to settle.[21] Ontario had its own immigration agent in London and had printed posters and leaflets, in German as well as in English, to direct prospective immigrants towards the province. Quebec reported that it was considering the appointment of immigration agents in Britain and Europe and that the legislature had voted a sum of $12,000 for the support of immigration over a period of eighteen months. New Brunswick reported that it had no department of agriculture and "as yet" no agents overseas, but that it had immigration agents at Saint John and other locations in the province. Nova Scotia did not submit a report on its immigration efforts, such as they were, although it had promised to do so.[22]

The Dominion government carried out one of its pledges by introducing the Immigration Act, which received royal assent on 22 June 1869.[23] The preamble to the act referred to the concurrent jurisdiction conferred on the two levels of government by Section 95, and also to the Dominion-provincial agreements of October 1868, which were summarized. The Act itself stipulated that the Dominion would maintain immigration agents and offices in London and in the eight major cities of Canada. Additional offices in Canada, the British Isles and Europe could be opened "if the government so decides." The immigration agents were empowered to spend funds granted to them by a "Local Government" for the purpose of assisting immigrants who intended to settle in the province concerned. The remaining provisions of the Act resembled those previously in effect, which the Dominion had inherited from the old Province of Canada, and which were now repealed. They included the imposition of a tax on ships carrying immigrants, based on the number of persons landed, provisions to protect the passengers from various kinds of exploitation and inconvenience that might be imposed upon them by ship's captains and others, and the imposition of fines on captains whose ships were overcrowded or who picked up additional passengers after leaving the original port of embarkation. There were also provisions empowering the government to control the entry of "paupers" or of the mentally and physically handicapped.

Not long after the adoption of this legislation a Canadian immigration office was opened in Dublin. The provincial governments were officially informed of this fact, and were invited to supply any information that might be of particular interest to prospective Irish immigrants.[24] In response, Ontario inquired whether agents had also been appointed in Northern Ireland, Scotland, and continental Europe. The Dominion supplied the name and address of its agent at Antwerp, but indicated that there were none in Northern Ireland or Scotland.[25] An agent in Belfast was appointed shortly afterwards, probably as a result of this exchange.[26] About one out of every ten Ontario residents at this time had been born in Ireland, and most of these Irish immigrants were Protestants from the north. Irish immigrants in Quebec and the Maritimes, by contrast, were predominantly Catholics.

A third federal-provincial conference on immigration took place in October 1869. John A. Macdonald and J. C. Chapais again represented the Dominion, and Premier Pierre Chauveau represented Quebec, while Ontario sent its Minister of Agriculture, John Carling, and his deputy. (Carling would later hold the Agriculture portfolio in the federal government from 1885 to 1892; the present headquarters of the federal department, and the Ottawa street on which it is located, are both named after him.) Neither Nova Scotia nor New Brunswick sent delegates to this conference, although Nova Scotia for the first time provided a report of its activities in the field of immigration. Despite the presence of two first ministers, the conference seems to have been a somewhat perfunctory ritual. The most interesting item of business considered was a proposal from a Mr. Brown of Scotland who offered to write a pamphlet extolling Canada's virtues for Scottish emigrants in return for a grant of a thousand acres of good agricultural land. Since the Dominion had no land to grant, the proposal was referred to the provinces, but none expressed any interest.[27]

The reports by the provinces on their activities indicated that Ontario was continuing its active publicity campaign, and had produced a second edition of its pamphlet describing the opportunities for immigrants in the province. Counting both editions, 100,000 copies of the pamphlet had now been printed. Ontario had also produced posters in English, French, and German. Copies of the poster (presumably the English edition) were said to have been displayed, with the permission of the Imperial Government, in every post office in England. Nova Scotia had entered the field, on a much more modest scale, by producing its own pamphlet of which 200 copies were given to the Dominion authorities for distribution. Quebec was said to be contemplating posters and pamphlets of its own, and also to be still considering whether it should appoint its own immigration agents in Europe. New Brunswick apparently submitted no report.[28] Ontario's efforts seemed to be productive, since it attracted 92 per cent of all the immigrants who settled in Canada during 1869. However, three out of every four immigrants who passed through Canadian ports in that year were bound for the United States.[29]

Another federal-provincial conference on immigration took place in October 1870, lasting for three days.30 No less than eight members of the Dominion cabinet attended, including Sir John A. Macdonald. Christopher Dunkin, who had replaced Chapais as Minister of Agriculture (and who had attended the first immigration conference in his previous capacity as the Provincial Treasurer of Quebec) was the only federal minister present on the final day. Chauveau and Carling again represented Quebec and Ontario respectively, and New Brunswick sent a minister as well, although Nova Scotia was not represented. The conference heard speeches by Canada's immigration agent in London and by several British visitors with an interest in promoting emigration, including an Anglican vicar and a Catholic priest. Premier Chauveau described Quebec's efforts to promote immigration, including a pamphlet of which it had produced 50,000 copies in English and 30,000 in French. He denied allegations that the small number of immigrants settling in Quebec (there had been only 503 in 1869) reflected a lack of enthusiasm on the part of the province. Chauveau urged greater efforts to attract immigrants from continental Europe, saying that Belgians in particular were good settlers who "would assimilate well with the people of Quebec." Earlier in the day Thomas White, who had served briefly as the Ontario immigration agent in London, had described the Dominion agency in Antwerp as a waste of money.

Chauveau's government was apparently sincere in its support for immigration, for it had recently appointed provincial immigration agents at Quebec City and Montreal to assist new arrivals and encourage them to remain in Quebec rather than continuing onwards to Ontario or the United States.[31] Soon after the conference Quebec appointed its own immigration agent for continental Europe, based in Paris. The Colonial Office provided the Quebec agent with letters of introduction to the British ambassadors in various European capitals. However, the Colonial Secretary subsequently complained to the Governor-General that the order-in-council appointing the Quebec agent should have been transmitted by way of Ottawa, rather than being carried to London by the agent himself.[32]

The next federal-provincial conference, in September 1871, was the first at which the new provinces of Manitoba and British Columbia were represented, in addition to all four of the original provinces. At Dunkin's suggestion the agenda was not confined to immigration; the conference also considered the necessity of harmonizing provincial laws in relation to statistics, another subject that fell under his jurisdiction as Minister of Agriculture. Dunkin was apparently the only federal minister who attended this conference. Chauveau again represented Quebec, accompanied by three of his cabinet colleagues, and the premiers of New Brunswick and Manitoba were also present. British Columbia was unable to send a minister (the journey from Victoria to Ottawa then took about two weeks) but the cabinet delegated a private citizen who "was about to visit Canada on private business" to act on its behalf. This delegate was instructed by the Provincial Secretary, to attend regularly, provide information, participate in the discussion, but not make any commitments on behalf of the province.[33]

This conference reaffirmed, in a somewhat revised form, the understandings regarding the division of responsibilities between Dominion and provinces that had been arrived at in 1868. Having acquired the former territories of the Hudson's Bay Company, including Manitoba, the Dominion now had public lands of its own. It committed itself to pursue a liberal policy of colonization in Manitoba and the Northwest Territories, and also to disseminate information regarding those areas for the benefit of would-be immigrants. The unrealistic and unnecessary commitment to hold conferences four times a year was abandoned, having been honoured more in the breach than in the observance. Instead the delegates agreed that conferences would be convened from time to time if requested by one or more provinces or without such request, on the understanding that there would be one conference during each session of Parliament.[34] Dunkin left the cabinet a few weeks after this conference and was replaced by J.H. Pope, also an anglophone from the Eastern Townships.

Apparently no federal-provincial conferences took place during the remaining two years of the first Macdonald government. However, this period, for all of which J.H. Pope was Minister of Agriculture, saw two significant innovations in the practice of co-operative federalism, both related to the subject of immigration.

The first of these concerned responsibility for the costs of transporting immigrants from the port of entry to their ultimate destination. The practice of subsidizing transportation from Quebec City to points west actually predated Confederation. Partly because many of the persons thus subsidized appeared to be bound for the United States, the Dominion government restricted the practice in 1868, but did not abandon it entirely. Railway fares at that time were considerably higher, in relation to prices and other incomes, than they are now, so immigrants who were clearly without funds, and who gave some evidence that they intended to stay in Canada, might still expect to have their fares paid by the Dominion government.[35]

Since most of these assisted immigrants went to Ontario, and since the province shared in the constitutional responsibility for immigration, the federal government began to suggest that Ontario should bear some or all of the cost. As noted above, Ontario agreed to this in March 1869 when it was governed by John Sandfield Macdonald, a political ally of Sir John A. Subsequently Sandfield Macdonald may have had second thoughts, for a year later his government agreed to a British-inspired scheme for exporting teen-aged boys to Ontario only reluctantly and on condition that the overland transportation costs be fully covered by the Dominion.[36] There was logic in Ontario's reservations, because the province did not particularly want immigrants who were unable to support themselves. In any event the federal government had a more obvious interest in preventing the accumulation of indigent immigrants in Quebec City, a place not noted for its friendliness to immigrants of any description.

In 1872, however, Edward Blake's Ontario government agreed with the federal government on a compromise that was, in effect, a shared cost program. The Dominion would pay the railway fares initially for immigrants travelling between Quebec and Ontario, but at the end of the year it would bill Ontario for two-thirds of the costs which it had incurred in doing so. This arrangement covered railway fares between the port of entry and any of the major cities of Ontario where there was a Dominion immigration agent. Transportation costs from that point to the ultimate destination, which would probably be less than a hundred miles away, were exclusively a provincial responsibility.[37] In July 1873 Ontario paid the Dominion the sum of $18,160.53, representing its two-thirds share of subsidized fares for the first year that the program was in operation.[38] Quebec signed a similar agreement for the sharing of transportation costs between Quebec City and Montreal.

The second innovation in 1872 was possibly a *quid pro quo* for the first, although there is no direct evidence of this. For the fiscal year 1872-73 Parliament voted a sum of $70,000 to assist the provinces in their efforts to encourage immigration. The original intention was for only the four original provinces to receive a share of this grant, but subsequently the cabinet diverted $5000 out of the original appropriation to British Columbia, which also (unlike Manitoba) controlled its own public lands.[39] In the following year another $70,000 was voted for the same purpose. In each year Ontario received $25,000, Quebec $20,000, Nova Scotia and New Brunswick each received $10,000, and British Columbia was given $5000.[40] Using the term loosely, this might be considered the first conditional grant in Canadian history, although the conditions were certainly not very rigorous. The Deputy Minister of Agriculture admitted to the Select Committee on Immigration and Colonization in 1873 that, "We do not receive regular reports of the operations of the Provincial Governments. Their jurisdiction in immigration matters is by law perfectly independent."[41] Nonetheless, if it was not quite a conditional grant, it was certainly a shared-cost program, as was the arrangement for covering immigrants' railway fares referred to above.

The House of Commons was apparently not satisfied with the Deputy Minister's interpretation of the constitution, for in April 1873 it passed a motion requesting information on how the provinces had spent the money granted to them for immigration purposes. Letters were dispatched to the five provinces concerned requesting the information and replies were received from British Columbia, Nova Scotia, and Quebec. Only British Columbia's reply is still in the archives. It shows that the province spent its $5000 on salaries for immigration agents at London and San Francisco, renting offices at both locations, and publishing a "prize essay," which presumably extolled the virtues of the province and was used as publicity material.[42] San Francisco may seem an odd choice of location, but the normal way of reaching British Columbia in those days was to cross the United States by rail and then travel by ship from San Francisco to Victoria. In the circumstances, it is surprising that anyone went there at all.

In November 1873 Sir John A. Macdonald resigned as a result of the Pacific Scandal and the Governor-General called upon Alexander Mackenzie to form a Liberal government. These dramatic events coincided with the beginning of an economic depression, in Canada and the world, which lasted for two decades. From 1866 through 1873 the number of immigrants who settled in Canada had increased substantially from year to year, but in 1874 it declined by twenty per cent, the first such decline since Confederation.[43] The Mackenzie government's response to the economic crisis was to reduce expenditures wherever possible, and the immigration program was an early victim of this strategy. No funds were voted by Parliament to assist the provinces with immigration in 1874, or thereafter.

While testifying before the House of Commons committee on immigration and colonization in 1874, the Deputy Minister of Agriculture was asked to explain the respective duties of Dominion and provincial immigration agents, and replied as follows:

> The Dominion special agents have no connection with the provincial agents, and I cannot tell the Committee what are the duties of the latter. The Local Governments have independent jurisdiction on the subject of immigration under the Union Act. But it is also to some extent joint; and as a matter of fact the permanent agents of the Dominion at every point aid the Provinces in as far as they can, the interests being common.[44]

The discontinuance of the federal grant, and the decline in the number of immigrants, seems to have caused provincial governments to question whether they should continue to spend as much on promoting immigration, or whether more economical arrangements were possible. At Ontario's suggestion a federal-provincial conference to consider this question was summoned in November 1874, apparently for the first time in three years.[45] It was presided over by the federal Minister of Agriculture, Luc Letellier de St. Just, who would provoke a serious consitutional crisis as lieutenant-governor of Quebec less than four years later by dismissing the provincial government. Prime Minister Mackenzie and two other members of his cabinet also attended the immigration conference, as did representatives of Ontario, Quebec, Nova Scotia and New Brunswick. Even the Governor-General, Lord Dufferin, made a brief appearance. The Nova Scotia delegation was headed for the first time by the Premier, William Annand, who had been elected in 1867 on a pledge to seek the separation of Nova Scotia from the Dominion.

The conference was called at the suggestion of Ontario and generally agreed, according to Letellier's subsequent report:

> ... that separate and individual action of the provinces in promoting immigration, by means of agents in the United

Kingdom and the European continent, led not only to waste of strength and expense and divided counsels, but in some cases to actual conflicts, which had an injuriously prejudicial effect on the minds of intending emigrants.

It also unanimously adopted a fourteen-point memorandum, which may be summarized as follows:

1. The federal Minister of Agriculture would control and direct promotion of emigration from the United Kingdom and Europe to Canada.

2. Independent provincial agencies would be discontinued.

3. Each province could appoint a sub-agent who would be accommodated in the Canadian government's offices in London.

4. Provinces could employ special agents "or other means" to encourage emigration.

5. All provincial sub-agents or special agents would be under the direction of the Agent-General of Canada, who would receive instructions from the Minister of Agriculture.

6. Provinces would pay the salaries of any sub-agents or special agents whom they appointed.

7. The Dominion undertook to encourage immigration in any possible way, including the subsidization of ocean transport.

8. The Dominion would use its London office to disseminate information about the provinces and their resources.

9. Each province would supply the London office with copies of its statutes and of all public documents and maps printed since Confederation.

10. The London office should be accessible to persons from any province, as a source of information.

11. The provinces would contribute as follows to the cost of maintaining the London office: $5500 per annum from Ontario, $2000 from Quebec, and $1000 from each of New Brunswick and Nova Scotia. If British Columbia and Prince Edward Island decided to adhere to the agreement, they would contribute amounts to be agreed upon. (No mention was made of Manitoba.)

12. The Dominion would pursue a liberal policy regarding the settlement of the crown lands in Manitoba and the Northwest.

13. These arrangements would last for five years, and for a further five if no notice was given to discontinue them.

14. The proposals would be binding on any provincial government that subsequently confirmed its acceptance of them.

By February 1875 all four of the original provinces had confirmed their acceptance of these arrangements, which were embodied in a Dominion order-in-council. The House of Commons Select Committee on Immigration, in its annual report, welcomed the new arrangements. It also reported the following exchange between a member of the committee and the Deputy Minister of Agriculture:

Question: Were not the provincial governments always adverse to yielding up their privileges on the subject of immigration?

Answer: Yes, they always showed the greatest reluctance to give up any of the concurrent powers conferred on them by the Act of Confederation, but it was seen during the last year that the employment of Provincial and Dominion agents in the same places, not only led to waste of strength, but in some cases to actual conflict of opinion, which was bewildering to intending immigrants, and therefore injurious. It was the perception of this fact that led to the memorandum of agreement to which I have referred, at the Conference in November last.[46]

Another question concerned the agents who would continue to be paid by Ontario, although ostensibly subordinate to the authority of the Dominion.

Question: But don't you suppose that they will recognize in their masters those who pay them, and is there not danger of conflict of authority?

Answer: They will, of course, look to the Ontario Government, which employs and pays them, but if that Government places them under the direction of the Dominion authorities, there will be that much centralization.[47]

Ontario's initiative which led to the acceptance of these arrangements was doubtless a consequence of the close alliance between the Mowat and Mackenzie governments. Premier Annand of Nova Scotia may have had an additional motive for agreeing. In May 1875, six months after the conference, the Mackenzie government appointed him as Canada's Agent-General in London, an office whose authority was increased by the new arrangements. (Brian Mulroney's appointment of Lucien Bouchard, another former separatist, as Ambassador to France was not without precedent.)

By 1875 provincial interest and involvement in immigration policy was declining, but this was true of the federal government as well. John Lowe, the Deputy Minister in the federal Department of Agriculture, informed a British M.P. with whom he corresponded that the public pressure to reduce spending on immigration was being felt by both levels of government. "The Ontario Government has felt its effect and it has literally swept away its Immigration Department at Toronto," he reported. Because of the economic crisis, he added, "mechanics" (or in other words the working class) were "crying out to stop immigration." Either in response to this sentiment or simply to save money, Lowe said that he had been ordered (presumably by his minister, Letellier) to stop advertising for immigrants at once.[48] Immigration continued to decline from the peak which it had reached in 1873. By 1881 there were actually fewer foreign-born persons in Quebec, Ontario, and the Maritime provinces than there had been a decade earlier.[49]

Although the provinces no longer received grants for their immigration programs from the Dominion, and although their immigration offices outside of Canada had been absorbed into those of the Dominion, they continued to be involved in this field of concurrent jurisdiction. As David Spence, the official who administered Ontario's immigration program, told the House of Commons Committee on Immigration and Colonization in 1877: "the Ontario government leaves the general question of immigration to the Dominion Government, and...confines its efforts to the bringing out such immigrants as are in special demand in Ontario."[50]

Furthermore, the provinces still contributed financially to two aspects of the Dominion's immigration efforts: the upkeep of the London office (in accordance with the decision of the 1874 conference) and the transportation costs of immigrants after they arrived at the port of entry. In the case of Ontario and Quebec the latter item was governed by the agreements which both provinces had signed in 1872, providing for reimbursement of two-thirds of the costs incurred initially by the Dominion. The Maritime provinces had never signed such agreements, although New Brunswick paid the local transportation costs of immigrants after they left the main line of the federally-owned Intercolonial Railway. Payments from the provinces covered about a quarter of the Dominion's total expenditures on immigration in 1877, and the provinces' expenditures on their own immigration and colonization programs were in addition to this amount.[51]

These early experiments in co-operative federalism ended after Sir John A. Macdonald returned to office in October 1878. Annand, the Liberal and former Nova Scotia separatist, was promptly dismissed as Canada's Agent-General in London, to be replaced by Sir Alexander T. Galt with the new title of High Commissioner. Apparently in retaliation for this change, Nova Scotia terminated its financial contribution to the Dominion office.[52] Instead, it appointed Annand himself as its own Agent-General in London, a position he occupied until his death in 1887. The agreement to share the costs of the London office with the provinces expired in 1880 and was not renewed by the Macdonald government.

Meanwhile the Joly government in Quebec, which had been imposed on the province by Letellier in his bizarre coup a year earlier, gave notice in 1879 that it would no longer contribute to the overland transportation costs of immigrants.[53] Ontario continued to do so for certain classes of immigrants (agricultural labourers, their families, and female domestic servants) but in 1882 it also discontinued its contributions.[54] The provinces still pursued policies of colonization, particularly in Quebec where the subject had strong ideological overtones and where there was a Minister of Colonization until as late as 1962, but immigration was increasingly perceived as a federal responsibility, regardless of what the constitution might say on the subject.

Macdonald's National Policy lessened the provincial role in immigration in two ways. By industrializing the two central provinces, it ensured that most immigrants who settled in those provinces after 1878 would live in the cities, and thus the link between immigration and colonization was broken. Secondly, and far more significantly, the construction of the C.P.R. opened a vast new field for agricultural immigrants on the northwestern prairies. Federal immigration policy adopted as its first priority the need to populate the Northwest. Since the federal government controlled the public lands in that region until the closing of the agricultural frontier was officially recognized in 1930, there was no reason for provincial involvement, even if provincial governments had existed, which they did not in Saskatchewan and Alberta until 1905.

The significant role that the provinces once played in immigration policy, as well as the real origins of co-operative federalism, have thus been almost forgotten. Although there had been six federal-provincial conferences between 1868 and 1874, there were no more until 1906, when Sir Wilfrid Laurier summoned one to consider the revision of statutory subsidies. Similarly, shared-cost programs, which Macdonald's first government had pioneered in 1872, were not proposed again until 1912, when the Borden government attempted to provide financial aid for provincial highways.

In recent years Quebec's concern with its declining birthrate and its declining share of the Canadian population has led that province to take a renewed interest in immigration. Successive federal governments have responded with the Cullen-Couture agreement and with the Meech Lake Accord, which includes a political agreement with Quebec on sharing responsibility for immigration as well as a constitutional amendment that would give such agreements the force of law and would allow other provinces to conclude them if they so wish. None of this is either unprecedented or contrary to the letter and the spirit of Canada's constitution. Whatever the fate of the Meech Lake Accord may be, the Macdonaldian origins of co-operative federalism deserve to be recognized.

Notes

1 Daniel J. Elazar, *The American Partnership* (Chicago: University of Chicago Press, 1962).

2 For an example of the orthodox interpretation see Gerard Veilleux, *Les Relations Intergouvernementales au Canada 1867-1967* (Montréal: les presses de L'université du Québec, 1971), especially 17-25.

3   A partial exception is W. H. McConnell, *Commentary on the British North America Act* (Toronto: Macmillan of Canada, 1977), 304-305.

4   Loren Beth, *The Development of the American Constitution 1877-1917* (New York: Harper and Row, 1971), 28.

5   See the testimony of Peter O'Leary in Canada, House of Commons, *Journals*, Volume 12, appendix no. 2 (1878), 35.

6   Province of Canada, *Statutes*, 4-5 Victoria, chapter 13.

7   J. E. Hodgetts, *Pioneer Public Service* (Toronto: University of Toronto Press, 1956), 240-246.

8   Ibid., 40.

9   Province of Canada, *Statutes*, 13-14 Victoria, chapter 4.

10 House of Commons, *Journals*, Volume 2, appendix no. 7 (1869), 11.

11 Canada, census of 1871, Volume 5, 28.

12 Hodgetts, *Pioneer Public Service*, 255-256.

13 Canada, House of Commons, *Journals*, Volume 1, appendix no. 8 (1867-68), 1.

14 House of Commons, *Debates*, November 25, 1867, 131.

15 House of Commons, *Debates*, December 9, 1867, 221.

16 Senate, *Debates*, May 7, 1868, 256-260.

17 NAC, RG6, Vol. 312, file 573.

18 House of Commons, *Journals*, Volume 2, appendix no. 7 (1869), 1-5.

19 NAC, RG6, Vol. 312, file 640.

20 NAC, RG6, Vol. 313, file 723.

21 NAC, RG6, Vol. 313, file 768.

22 House of Commons, *Journals*, Volume 2, appendix no. 7 (1869), 6-10.

23 Statutes of Canada, 1868-69, chapter 10.

24 NAC, RG6, Vol. 315, file 932.

25 NAC, RG6, Vol. 315, file 938.

26 NAC, RG6, Vol. 318, file 34.

27 House of Commons, *Journals*, Volume 3, appendix no. 5 (1870), 12.

28 Ibid., 2, 13.

29 Ibid., 8-9.

30 NAC, RG17, Vol. 2395 (unnumbered file) contains a complete account of the proceedings.

31 NAC, RG6, Vol. 321, file 264, Belleau to Howe, 25 May 1870.

32 NAC, RG6, Vol. 327, file 704, Kimberley to Dufferin, 15 March 1871.

33 NAC, RG6, Vol. 329, files 866-867.

34 NAC, RG6, Vol. 330, file 927.

35 Canada, *Sessional Papers*, Volume 8, part 8, no. 40, appendix no. 1 (1875), 1-2.

36 NAC, RG6, Vol. 317, file 1016.

37 Canada, *Sessional Papers*, Volume 8, part 8, no. 40 (1875), xviii-xix.

38   NAC, RG6, Vol. 338, file 222.

39   NAC, RG6, Vol. 335, file 1359.

40   Canada, *Sessional Papers*, Volume 8, part 8, no. 40, appendix no. 1 (1875), 6.

41   House of Commons, *Journals*, Volume 6, appendix no. 7 (1873), 5.

42   NAC, RG6, Vol. 338, file 150.

43   Canada, *Sessional Papers*, Volume 8, part 8, no. 40 (1875), v.

44   Canada, House of Commons, *Journals*, Volume 6, appendix no. 7 (1873), 15-16.

45   Canada, *Sessional Papers*, Volume 8, part 8, no. 40, appendix no. 1 (1875) contains a complete account of the proceedings.

46   Canada, House of Commons, *Journals*, Volume 9, appendix no. 4 (1875), 8.

47   Ibid., 6.

48   NAC, RG7, Vol. 1665, Lowe to Jenkins, December 11, 1875.

49   Canada, Census of 1881, Volume 4, 14-15.

50   House of Commons, *Journals*, Volume 11, appendix no. 6 (1877), 55.

51   House of Commons, *Journals*, Volume 12, appendix no. 2 (1878), 14.

52   House of Commons, *Journals*, Volume 13, appendix no. 1 (1879), 14.

53   House of Commons, *Journals*, Volume 14, appendix no. 3 (1880), 7.

54   House of Commons, *Journals*, Volume 17, appendix no. 6 (1883), 26.

THE CONCEPT OF REGION IN CANADIAN POLITICS

Janine Brodie, York University

Introduction

In his most recent volume on Canadian federalism, *The Federal Condition in Canada*, Donald Smiley exhorts political scientists "...to banish the term region from our vocabulary and speak instead of province." And Smiley provides sound reasons for amending our conceptual approach to spatially-based politics in Canada. First, there is little agreement about what the term "region" actually means. Although it is frequently encountered in both Canadian political discourse and analysis, the term is both "loosely" or "imprecisely" defined. Second, Smiley argues that the "province" is a preferable analytic category in the study of spatial politics because it has a "concrete and unambiguous existence" which delineates a "very large number of social and economic groupings."[1]

Few can take issue with Smiley's critical assertion that political scientists desperately need to reformulate their conceptual approach to the enduring questions of uneven economic development and territorial politics in Canada. Hindsight, for example, shows that the plethora of liberal theories of regional economic development, which guided the federal government's responses to regional disparities in the 1960s and early 1970s, misinterpreted the underlying causes of uneven economic development, and completely ignored, at a theoretical level, the explicitly political dimensions of the phenomenon. Similarly, the neo-conservative approach, popular in the "market-driven" political rhetoric of the 1980s, is fraught with conceptual and empirical ambiguities which render it little more than a prescription for regional euthanasia. In the meantime, the revived Canadian political economy school has avoided analysis of the spatial dimension of Canadian politics in its unwavering search for an adequate class-based theory of the Canadian state. In sum, none of the mainstreams of Canadian political science has been particularly successful in explaining the profoundly spatial dimensions of the Canadian political economy or Canadian politics.

These obvious conceptual and theoretical shortcomings in the study of Canadian regionalism, however, do not necessarily dictate that the term should be banished, as Smiley suggests, from our vocabulary or thinking. Instead, this paper argues that much of the confusion in the literature about transprovincial and sub-provincial spatial politics can be traced back to fundamental assumptions about regional definition and integration—that is, how a region is defined and how it is proposed that regions relate to one another and to the nation-state of which they are a part.[2] Moreover, by drawing on the work of Innis, Fowke and Smiley, it attempts to show that the spatial dimension of the Canadian political economy and politics can be best understood as a shifting and relational phenomena which are directly linked to the cumulative effects of overarching state developmental strategies or "National Policies."

Thinking About Regions

Most observers of Canadian politics agree that regionalism is a "profound and fundamental" feature of Canadian life.[3] Canadian politics revolves around persistent and divisive conflicts about the spatial distribution of economic development, state activity, living standards, governmental services, and political power. And, unlike the experience of other advanced capitalist countries, spatially-based conflict in Canada has not disappeared as the pace of development accelerates. Canadians think about the country in terms of cross-provincial spatial partitions and they are constantly bombarded with messages suggesting that these divisions have political relevance.[4] Indeed, references to region are so familiar and pervasive that we have accepted these divisions as natural and self-evident without ever questioning why we have come to think of the country in these terms or what meanings these spatial abstractions actually convey.

Most studies of regionalism in Canada explore regional differences. They begin with predefined geographic units, increasingly the ten provinces, and measure differences in the location of attitudes or things. Political scientists, often working within the behaviouralist tradition, for example, have examined the spatial distribution of attitudes and behaviours as evidence of regional political cultures.[5] Political economists, in contrast, usually map the spatial distribution of objective indicators of economic well-being such as personal income and unemployment rates as evidence of regionalism.[6] The description of subjective and objective differences across geographic units, however, does not explain what a region is or how regional differences evolve and persist.

Smiley correctly points out that there is a great deal of confusion associated with the term region in Canadian politics. Matthews, in turn, argues that much of this confusion arises from the fact that four distinct terms—region, regional differences, regionalism, and regional disparities—are often used unconsciously and interchangeably in Canadian political science and sociology.[7] The first term, region, refers to a geographic unit. It is, as Stevenson argues, "a territorial entity having some natural and organic unity or community of interest that is *independent* of political and administrative boundaries."[8] The term "region" suggests a sameness within a geographic space which separates or differentiates it from some other geographic space. To designate a region, then, is to simultaneously assert differences: regions are only regions in relation to other geographic spaces. But, by which criteria do we most appropriately partition geographic space in terms of similarities and differences?

Richard Simeon has suggested that there are countless criteria for designating regions and that the selection of these criteria is largely artificial and arbitrary. In an oft-cited article, he concludes that "regions are simply containers...And how we draw the boundaries around them depends entirely on what our purposes are: it is an *a priori* question, determined by theoretical needs or political purposes."[9] Simeon is correct, of course, from a strictly positivist perspective. Any high school atlas demonstrates the multiplicity of partitions that can be imposed on geographic space, with each line of demarcation signifying similarities within and differences without. Regions can be defined in terms of topography, climate, land use, and demography to name a few common criteria for regional definition. And, all of these criteria signify regional *differences* which can be used to describe geographic space.

Yet granting Simeon his point does not solve the problem of regional definition for us. Most of these analytic distinctions are "quite irrelevant to the phenomena which Canadian scholars and writers are attempting to explain when they invoke the concept."[10] More to the point, the spatial dimension of Canadian politics involves more than sterile analytic distinctions, drawing lines on a map, and searching for empirical regularities in the location of things, attitudes, and behaviours. Regions in Canada have concrete political and social dimensions which are deeply embedded in our collective historical experience: they are much more than arbitrary intellectual constructs.

Regionalism and regional disparities, the other two terms in Matthew's spatial vocabulary, explicitly acknowledge the social and political dimensions of the phenomenon. Matthews, reflecting his sociological background, defines regionalism as a socio-psychological factor which involves identification with, and commitment, to a territorial unit.[11] Regionalism, from this perspective, is a state of mind which unites a community with a sense of common identity. Yet, this definition does not explain why these loyalties should, in and of themselves, structure political conflict. Breton is much more specific about the political dimension of regionalism. He argues that regionalism is an inherently political phenomenon because economic, political, and cultural interests are defined and articulated in spatial terms. It is an interpretation of social relations that "leads to the identification of circumstances and events related to the condition of a territorial entity, and partly a process whereby these circumstances and events become political issues."[12] Regionalism structures *political conflict around the distribution of resources across geographic space.*

The term "regional disparities" refers to differences in the distribution of resources and development across geographic space. As Matthews correctly observes, the expression of *differences* (such as unemployment rates) as *disparities* also is an expressly political process. When a region is declared to be "in disparity when compared to other regions," it is "not merely a declaration that certain differences exist among the regions but a judgement about the *meaning* and implications of such differences."[13] It is a judgement which gives substance and form to political conflict and it sets an agenda for remedial action to which governments in liberal democracies often must respond.

The concepts of regionalism and regional disparity are at the heart of the spatial dimension of Canadian politics. Politics is judged to be about "place" instead of "people" prosperity and therewith, conflict revolves around the allocation of power and resources across geographic units rather than, for example, among social classes. It emphasizes relationships in geographic space in which some territorial units gain or lose in relation to other territorial units. The spatial dimension of Canadian politics thus evokes two primary research questions: first, why does development occur unevenly in geographic space; and second, how does the fact of uneven spatial development translate into spatially-based political conflict?

Canadian political scientists have provided many different (and often inadequate) answers to these two primary research questions—answers which reflect their particular approach to regional definition. There are primarily two analytic procedures for defining regional boundaries—the *formal* and *relational* methods.[14] Each method, in turn, promotes specific assumptions about the nature of regional integration or how regions relate to one another and to the nation-state.

Regional Definition and Integration

We have already seen that there are numerous ways to determine a formal region. They are designated by homogeneity or similarity in features which distinguish them from contiguous areas.[15] Typically in the past, students of Canadian history and politics have relied uncritically on environmental criteria for designating regions. Canadian regions have been defined by a similarity in physical features and climate and separated from other regions by prominent topographical features. The familiar designation of Canadian territory into the Atlantic, Central, Prairie, Pacific, and Arctic regions is a product of this approach.[16]

Unfortunately, the environmental approach to regional definition often slides unconsciously into an environmentally deterministic explanation for regional differences, assuming, incorrectly I believe, that a common environment gives rise to common political, social, and cultural characteristics. We are often told, for example, that the "laws of nature" have endowed Canada with distinct regional entities which constitute an enduring and formidable obstacle to the achievement of a national identity and national unity.[17] The Task Force on National Unity, which reported in 1979, for example, argues that "Canadian unity has always had to struggle against physical barriers which divide its territory."[18]

Students of Canadian politics are very familiar with arguments asserting the environmental origins of regional disparities and conflict. While these explanations seem plausible and politically neutral, two observations necessarily undermine their reliability. The first and most obvious point is that regionalism is not a universal political expression. Other countries which are similarly divided by geography and topography are not divided by political conflicts over the allocation of resources across space or, at least, to the same degree of intensity and persistence. The United States is an obvious example. Why does "the land" produce these social and political consequences in some countries and not in others? Equally important, the environmental approach for designating regions, and the formal approach generally, does not incorporate the temporal dimension of regional conflict. It constructs a regional configuration which is as rigid and timeless as the physical features to which they are tied.[19] Yet, we know that regional conflict, like the contours of uneven development, have changed dramatically over time. Both of these observations, then, lead to the conclusion that regionalism is social rather than natural in origin and that its dimensions are temporally fluid.

More recently, distinguished Canadian political scientists, such as Smiley, Simeon, Breton, and others, have defined regions in terms of the formal boundaries of federalism. They argue that in order for regional grievances to become mobilized politically, they must have an institutional focus and that provinces now provide such a focus. The Task Force on National Unity also endorsed this view, arguing that provincial political institutions are the primary frameworks through which regional populations can organize and express themselves.[20]

Provinces have been prominent actors in spatial politics in recent years and, according to some criteria for regional definition, region, and provincial boundaries do coincide.[21] These observations, however, do not mean that there are ten distinct regions in Canada whose boundaries perfectly coincide with provincial ones. This "institutional" definition, in fact, presents us with as many conceptual problems in the study of regionalism as it appears to resolve. First, by reducing regional boundaries to the institutional boundaries of federalism, researchers run the attendant risk of explaining spatial politics as the product of institutional imperatives and rivalries. While the environmental determination of regions often falls into the trap of explaining regionalism as a product of nature, the provincial determination often attributes spatial politics to institutional factors, especially the bureaucratic and constitutional forces operating within the provinces themselves and to inter-governmental conflict. Regions become provincial societies where, according to

Alan Cairns, "their sources of survival, renewal, and viability may well lie within themselves and in their capacity to mould their environment in accordance with their own governmental purposes."[22] The provincial formula thus reduces regions to institutional actors with boundaries as rigid and permanent as constitutional jurisdictions. And characteristic of most formal definitions of regions, the sources of difference are located within the units themselves. Regionalism loses its conceptual distinctiveness because it is forced into the conceptual strictures of federalism.[23]

The formal approach of defining regions as provinces also misrepresents and obstructs our vision of regional politics. While it is obvious that provincial governments have been vocal in the past two decades, it is equally clear that the major conflicts in this period reflected divisions between not individual but *groups* of provinces, especially producing and consuming provinces.[24] In addition, the argument of the provincialists that provincial governments are the only institutional mechanisms which now channel regional protest is difficult to support empirically. Provincial governments are not now, nor were they in the past, the only political institutions through which spatial politics has been expressed in Canada. The federal party system, for example, was one of the first vehicles for regional movements and, throughout the 1970s, it was deeply divided on a spatial dimension. Similarly, regional coalitions are formed and battles are fought out daily within federal party caucuses, in the federal courts, in the federal bureaucracy, and in the media. The problem of equating provinces with regions is that it necessarily conceals these real and widespread manifestations of trans-provincial (and equally, sub-provincial) spatial politics.

As I described in detail elsewhere, the procedure employed for designating a region is usually accompanied by a particular perspective on regional integration; that is, how regions relate to one another and to the nation state.[25] Implicit in the institutionalist approach, for example, is the assumption that regional tensions can be reduced through institutional reform.[26] The formal approach, however, is most often accompanied by what have been termed *theories of regional self-balance.*[27] Numerous theories fit into this genre including the liberal staples, neo-classical economic, developmental, and growth pole explanations for uneven economic development. While, on the surface, these appear to be quite distinct approaches to the regional question, they all share similar fundamental orientations toward the phenomenon. All are concerned with the question of regional disparities; they begin with pre-specified regions and, in varying degrees, they locate the source of underdevelopment within the formal boundaries of the region itself. Regional underdevelopment is attributed to such factors as the forces of nature which provide an inadequate resource-base or an inhospitable climate, insufficient entrepreneurial skills among local capitalists, over-population, lack of infrastructure, or an unskilled workforce to name a few of the regional deficiencies which have been identified by theories of regional self-balance.

The fit between formal regional designations and theories of self-balance, admittedly, is not altogether a perfect one. Some of these theories do recognize some outside interferences acting on the underdevelopment of a spatial unit. Courchene, for example, argues that federal subsidies are one among many factors disturbing the local market's equilibrium and the developmental approach recognizes federal policy as a factor contributing to the historical pattern of regional disparities.[28] Importantly, however, all of these approaches seek to remedy disparities by changing the depressed region itself. In other words, their approach to regional integration is to "change the victim" and not its underlying relationships with other spatial units or the state. Because the sources of a region's underdevelopment are located within the region, the nation-state stands outside the region and, if it intervenes, it is limited to putting things into the region such as grants and incentives or luring things out such as population.

In many ways, theories of regional self-balance suffer from an empirical illusion. Regional disparities are manifest at a sub-national level: certain areas within a country clearly can be seen to have more or less of the factors considered necessary for economic development. But this does not necessarily mean that such differentiation is *produced* by mechanisms and processes confined to the subnational level. This is where uneven development appears but its causes may just as well be dominantly the product of mechanisms operating at a national or international scale.[29] Theories of regional self-balance exclude this possibility from their analysis and thus from their prescriptions for change.

Other criticisms can be levelled against theories of regional self-balance: 1) they confuse cause and effect, treating the symptoms rather than causes, 2) they are technocratic and ahistorical, and 3) they assume that governmental responses themselves are devoid of political and class biases.[30] As important, they address only one of the primary questions invoked by the phenomenon. They provide what are in my view partial and misleading answers to the question of why economic development occurs unevenly in geographic space but ignore the equally relevant question of how uneven development translates into spatially-based politics. In other words, inherent in theories of regional self-balance is the tendency to depoliticize an enduring and explicitly political dimension of the collective Canadian experience.

The other approach to regional definition has been variously termed relational, functional, polarized, and dualist. It differs from the formal procedure in a number of ways but, most fundamentally, it does not propose concrete regional boundaries which isolate one region from another. Nor is it primarily concerned with discovering similarities and differences in the distribution of things in geographic space. Instead, as the above terms imply, regions are seen as part of an interconnected whole in which one regional configuration is largely a function or an expression of another. Regions, in other words, are not arbitrary constructs but *effects* or consequences of historical relationships. Following this account, regions are shaped and *reshaped* by political, social, and economic linkages which connect geographic space in relationships and interdependencies.[31]

Thinking about regions relationally may be unfamiliar to many of us but it opens many new perspectives on the spatial dimension of Canadian politics not offered by the formal procedure. First, this perspective de-emphasizes geography and nature in the determination of regional boundaries. Regions are the product of historical experience, human organisation, and social interaction. From a relational perspective, then, regions are fundamentally social creations. Second, this perspective encourages us to think about regions not as being fixed in geographic space but, instead, as fluid phenomena whose boundaries change as their interrelationships change. Third, it enables us to study regionalism synchronically and diachronically, that is, at a given time and across time. Finally, this approach is compatible with the study of subprovincial or subregional relationships. In sum, it is a much more demanding approach which obliges us to identify the forces or linkages which alter relations among territorial entities and thereby reshape them.

A relational perspective also demands an alternative approach to the question of regional integration. In brief, it demands a theory of *regional imbalance* because it locates the causes for the uneven development of a region in its relationships with other regions or social forces. In other words, regional integration is characterized by interdependence, if not exploitation. This is an explicitly political approach to the study of regionalism and is most often, although not always, associated with the work of political economists, dependency theorists, and radical political geographers. It is also an approach which is deeply rooted in Canadian economic history and political sociology. Innis's staples theory, the metropolitan-hinterland thesis, dependency theory, and some neo-Marxist applications all argue that regions are defined by their relationships rather than by their internal elements. These relational approaches differ considerably in terms of the forces or linkages that they identify as defining regions and regional integration but essentially they fall into two distinct streams—the dualist and capital accumulation approaches. We turn first to the dualist perspective on regional definition and integration provided by Innis, the metropolitan-hinterland school, and dependency theorists.

Regions From a Relational Perspective

We begin our survey of political economy's contribution to the study of uneven development and spatial politics with Harold Innis's staples theory.[32] Obviously, it is impossible to do justice to Innis's work here. Most important for our purposes, however, is his point of departure—namely, that the Canadian political economy can only be understood in relation to its unique historical antecedents.[33] He argued that it was defective thinking to attempt "to fit the phenomena of new countries into the economic theories of old countries."[34] The experience of North America was simply different from that of Europe. It came into contact with the old world only after capitalism had emerged as the dominant model of production and social organisation. The key to understanding the pattern of Canadian development then was to trace how the invasion of European culture and the price system left its imprint on a geography which previously corresponded to the non-capitalist forms of social organisation of the aboriginal peoples.

Innis, like Marx, was acutely aware that geography is continuously shaped and reshaped by explicitly historical and social forces such as the organisation of production and new technologies.[35] According to Innis, the new white settler colonies of North America were, by definition, economically weak and were forced to engage in staples trade with a series of imperial centres, first France and then Britain and the United States, in order to obtain necessary material and technological goods. The form and location of economic activity *within* these colonies, however, was determined by the centre's demand for staple products. The exploitation of a series of staples—fish, fur, timber, wheat, and minerals—meant that different areas of the country developed at different times as the demands of the centre as well as technology and transportation made them accessible. The spatial distribution of economic activities in new countries, in other words, developed *in relation* to old countries.[36]

Innis argued that the succession of staples exploitation explained much more of Canadian history than simply the location of economic activity at any given period.[37] Each staple was also characterized by specific patterns of settlement, linkages to other economic activities, interactions with the centre, and cultural, political, and institutional patterns. "Concentration on the production of staples for export to more highly industrialized areas," he writes, "had broad implications for the Canadian economic, political and social structure. Each staple in turn left its stamp, and the shift to a new staple invariably produced periods of crises..."[38] Furthermore, "the tendency has been cumulative."[39]

Innis asked us to think about geographic space abstractly and relationally and provides a diachronic analysis of the link between uneven development and political arrangements in Canada. Each staple was characterized by a complex web of forms located in geographic space and this web changed across time. It was as if Canadian history could be represented as a series of transparencies, each representing a different matrix of economic growth and political organisation, laid on geographic space, one on top of the other, as the demands of the international political economy changed. Each staple led to different geographical configurations which were unstable across time. Boundaries—whether national or regional—were not "in the land" but tied to the pattern of staples exploitation.[40]

Innis's staples theory, nonetheless, is a dualist perspective on regional integration wherein the centre is seen to be causing underdevelopment at the periphery. This dualist interpretation also underlies the work of the hinterland school of Canadian political economy (i.e. Macpherson, Mallory, Morton, Buckley, etc.) which framed the question of regional integration in terms of the metropolitan-hinterland thesis. Most of us are familiar with this perspective on uneven development. It posits that western Canada was created as an internal colony of central Canada and held in a subordinate and dependent relationship through the mercantilist policies of the federal government, particularly, the National Policy of 1879.

Smiley has summarized the key elements of the argument in his perceptive essay on Canadian development strategies: 1) metropolitan policies confined the hinterland to the production of a small number of staples (the principal focus of this group is the wheat staple); 2) metropolitan policies required that the hinterland buy the manufactured products of the heartland; 3) the hinterland and the heartland were physically linked by transportation facilities, established and operated to the benefit of the latter; 4) capitalist development in the hinterland was carried out through institutions centred in the heartland; 5) in the international context, the interests of the hinterland were usually sacrificed to those of the heartland; 6) many critical aspects of heartland-hinterland relations were carried out through the instrumentalities of large business organisations protected by imperial authorities from foreign or hinterland competition; 7) there was a continuing pattern controlling the political authorities of the hinterland in the interests of the heartland.[41] The result was an undiversified, non-industrial, and fragile resource economy which was tied to the "boom and bust" international commodities market by the economic and political power of the centre.

There is little question of the hinterland school's profound and enduring influence on the study of Canadian regionalism and politics. Unfortunately, too much success sometimes breeds failure and, in at least one respect, this has been the legacy of the hinterland school for students of the political economy of regionalism. The hinterlanders provided an historical elaboration of the political manifestations of the wheat staple and they revealed the political and economic linkages which held this particular spatial *relation* in place. A centre-periphery model, however, has limited utility for explaining spatial patterns of uneven development, especially diachronically or across time. In the first place, it fails to explain the process of growth in the centre. Once a centre-periphery relation is established, it is assumed to be self-sustaining. The possibility that growth at the centre may be stopped or reversed by factors unrelated to the centre-periphery relationship is ignored. Second, the model assumes that the periphery has no autonomous capacity for change. The only source of economic change in the periphery comes from growth at the centre.[42] Both of the above factors have encouraged an overly rigid conception of regional definition.

These criticisms also apply to centre-periphery models writ large on a global scale such as third world dependency models. Dependency theory was initially developed by scholars studying patterns of economic development in Latin America as a critique of the modernization approach provided by mainstream economics and sociology. Modernization theory, similar to theories of regional self-balance, posits that the cause of underdevelopment can be located internally, within the structure of traditional society.[43] Dependency theory, in contrast, advances the proposition that development and underdevelopment are reciprocal processes: underdevelopment results from the domination of less by more developed societies. Each spatial unit is the effect of the other.

The term "dependency theory" actually incorporates a vast literature employing different concepts, methods and emphases, which cannot be outlined in detail here; ultimately, most are based on a theory of capital drain whereby one *spatial* unit, the centre, extracts surplus from another *spatial* unit, the periphery. This approach has been adopted recently to explain the persistent problem of underdevelopment and poverty in Atlantic Canada and, in fact, has been judged by one prominent academic in the field as the most promising avenue for future research.[44] Nevertheless, in addition to its limitations as a dualist model of economic development, there are a number of reasons why we should hesitate to borrow these models for the analyses of intranational regionalism. First, there are logical inconsistencies within the model itself, particularly with its crude application of the spatial transfer of surplus. Dependency theory ignores questions about the *use* of the surplus transferred.[45] Contrary to the assumptions of the dependency model, the region that gains value is not necessarily the one in which value is capitalized.[46] More fundamentally, there is the question of whether or not it is appropriate to equate international and intranational development processes and relationships.[47] To equate the two is to ignore that we are dealing with social divisions of territory and socially different types of territorial division.[48] Often, as a consequence, we eliminate consideration of the role of national politics, policies, and the state in the creation of uneven spatial development.

The major contribution of the early political economy to the study of regionalism, in my opinion, was not its centre-periphery model but, instead, its emphasis on the role of the state, politics, and policy in establishing particular patterns of economic development in geographic space. Vernon Fowke deserves special attention here because, arguably, he made the most significant contributions from this perspective. Like Innis, he had an explicitly relational approach to uneven development but he moved the focus away from the staple to the more pervasive process of capital formation and state economic development strategies.

Fowke explicitly rejected geographic criteria for the determination or explanation of regional development patterns.[49] Instead, he argued that "the frontier at any given point in time is whatever place and whatever economic activity gives rise to investment opportunities on a substantial scale." The "investment frontier may be geographically diffused but it nevertheless has concrete expression in the process of real capital formation."[50] Although Fowke's work concentrated on western agriculture, he diverted our attention away from the explicitly conjunctural, single-commodity, and spatially-rigid focus of other early Canadian political economists to the more general question of the spatial implications of historical patterns of capital accumulation.

Fowke, however, did not reduce uneven development to the invariable laws of capitalism as is often the case in the radical geography literature. He argued that the state played a major intervening role in the political economy of regions but his state was not simply a reflection of the demands of staple exploitation, as Innis and others after him have argued.[51] For Fowke, it was a necessarily political and somewhat vulnerable entity encumbered with the responsibility of developing a territory and designing policies to achieve this goal under conditions set internally by the prevailing system of class relations and by constraints imposed internationally. This theme also has been emphasized by Smiley in his discussion of Canada's three National Policies.[52]

In understanding the role of the state in the creation of uneven spatial development, Fowke directed our attention to economic development policies. He argued that governmental policies could be ranked according to their impact on patterns of national economic development. "When the policies are grouped according to their collective purposes," he writes, "gradations of importance can readily be distinguished. Some groups clearly relate to minor or temporary, others to fundamental and persistent governmental aims."[53] The thrust of Fowke's work was to show that the National Policy was an example of the latter group of policies which he argued entailed much more than Macdonald's pronouncements of 1878. The term included "collectively the group of policies...[including Confederation itself] designed to transform the British North American colonies into a political and economic unit."[54] Moreover, he considered it a policy of desperation dictated by the disappearance of the favoured alternatives of imperial and continental economic integration. It was an encompassing developmental strategy which structured accumulation activities within the context of historically-specific class forces and international pressures.

At the risk of reading too much into Fowke, I would suggest that there are three important themes in his work which are integral to the study of Canadian regionalism. The first is his recognition that the overall process of capital accumulation during a period, not simply the dominant staple, shapes and reshapes geography and social relations. In other words, regions are defined historically by the contingencies of capitalist development and their integration with other regions. The nation-state can only be understood in terms of the on-going demands of the accumulation process which, Fowke argued, was structured by governmental development policies.

To digress from Fowke momentarily, I should point out that his focus on accumulation is not unique in the literature on uneven spatial development. This theme has been pursued recently by radical geographers such as Harvey, Webber, Massey, and Gore.[55] What can be termed as "the capitalist accumulation approach," (which includes Fowke) begins, like dependency theory, with the assumption that uneven spatial development is not simply a product of some malfunction in the market system but is intrinsic to the capitalist mode of production. This stream of study, however, departs from the dependency perspective on two fundamental issues. It does not accept that uneven development is necessarily either dualist in nature (that is, the outcome of the domination of one spatial unit by another) or that its contours are fixed in space and time between the centre and the periphery. Similar to Innis and Marx, this school begins with the observation that capitalism has profoundly transformed the geographic landscape and that its impact has been uneven. The central question for this school, therefore, is what is it within capitalism itself which causes and reproduces uneven spatial development across time?

The capitalist accumulation stream regards space as integral to or an "active moment within the overall temporal dynamic of accumulation and social reproduction."[56] Beyond this point of agreement, there are considerable differences in approach. Broadly speaking, however, this work tends to ignore the explicitly political dimensions of regionalism and is ahistorical, economistic, and, sometimes, teleological. In a round-about way, this literature also locates the cause for underdevelopment within the region itself. For many of these writers, the fact that capitalism establishes production facilities in a particular spatial unit constitutes a necessary and sufficient cause for the devaluation of that unit and for the eventual mobility of capital.

This point draws us back to Fowke and the second important theme in his work which subsequently has been developed by Smiley—notably, his emphasis on major state developmental strategies in the creation of uneven spatial development and spatial politics. Fowke and Smiley suggest that Canadian economic history can be periodized into a series of "national policies," that is, overarching state developmental strategies formulated in response to internal political pressures and to the demands of the international political economy. Fowke regarded the period of 1825 to 1930 as the era of the first national policy. With its goals accomplished and with changes in the international order, "the federal government worked gropingly and against substantial difficulties toward the formulation of a new set of national policies."[57] He and Smiley suggest that the second national policy was the welfare state while Smiley suggests that the nationalist initiatives undertaken by the federal Liberals between 1980 and 1984 constitute a "Third National Policy."[58]

The third important theme in Fowke's work, and that of the hinterland school generally, was to demonstrate how the governmental economic development strategies, although purportedly "national" and neutral in design, necessarily contained class and spatial biases. As important, he suggested that the class origins and substantive content of regional protest movements were tied to the specific developmental strategy of the period. Fowke emphasized the material and class foundations of regionalism and, at the same time, suggested that the specific form and content of regional protest would be structured by the overarching developmental strategy of the period. There is an echo of Innis here (i.e. policies instead of staples are setting successive regional imprints on geographic space) but there is an important distinction. For Fowke, regionalism develops in relation to overarching state developmental strategies. This emphasis on policy directs our attention to the *political* creation of uneven development and makes the state a necessary focal point for regional protest.

Fowke's work gives us a critical perspective on regionalism which has been conspicuously absent from the so-called "mainstream" analyses of recent decades—notably, that the state is actively involved in *creating and sustaining* patterns of uneven development. This point also has been emphasized by Smiley in his recent analysis of the "Third National Policy." He observes that "the National Policy, whether of Macdonald or Trudeau, has had both continentalist and provincialist consequences, leading to interregional conflict and to American resistance."[59]

Conclusion

This paper has traced the use of the term "region" in Canadian political science and has argued for its retention in our conceptual armory. This is not to say that popular approaches to the spatial dimension of Canadian politics have been satisfactory. As Smiley accurately points out, they have not. It has been argued here, however, that many of the theoretical difficulties encountered in the study of Canadian regionalism can be traced back to the analytic issues of regional definition and integration. In particular, formal definitions were found wanting because of their rigidity while their accompanying theories of regional self-balance tend to ignore the explicitly political dimensions of the phenomenon.

This paper argues that the early Canadian political economy school offers an alternative approach to the regional question and the processes whereby considerations of space are interwoven into the social and political fabric of a country. This indigenous tradition of scholarship treats regionalism as a relational phenomenon. Regions have fluid boundaries which shift in conjunction with national development strategies.

The work of Fowke and, following him, Smiley, suggests that a crucial key in the study of Canadian regionalism is the recognition that the dominant economic activity at any point is defined and structured by state developmental strategies and that these strategies usually have pronounced spatial implications. So-called "National Policies" are an expression of, and a response to, underlying phases of capitalist accumulation and they imprint themselves in the geographic landscape, in the character of economic activity and in social and political conflict. Regionalism, thus, is essentially a political creation whereby the state, through its role in facilitating and directing development and capitalist accumulation, establishes, legitimizes, and enforces particular spatial contours of economic activity and following that, political conflict. While the revived political economy tradition has offered many insights into the nature and function of the state in capitalist societies, the spatial impacts of state activity have yet to, but necessarily must, be elaborated.

Notes

1   Donald Smiley, *The Federal Condition in Canada* (Toronto: McGraw-Hill Ryerson, 1987), 22-23, 156-58. Like so many political scientists of my generation, I was introduced to the study of Canadian politics through, and continue to prosper from, Professor Smiley's numerous and insightful writings. For this, I will always owe a great intellectual debt. As important, I want to thank Professor Smiley for his unfailing example of what it means to be a good teacher and a supportive colleague.

2   William Westfall, "On The Concept of Region in Canadian History and Literature," *Journal of Canadian Studies* (Summer 1980), 6.

3   David Elkins and Richard Simeon, (eds.), *Small Worlds: Provinces and Parties in Canadian Political Life* (Toronto: Methuen, 1980), vii.

4   Only 3.7% of the 2562 respondents in the 1974 national election study equated region with province. See David Elkins, "The Sense of Place," in *Ibid.*, 6.

5   See, for example, Mildred Schwartz, *Politics and Territory* (Montreal: McGill-Queens Press, 1974); Elkins and Simeon, *Small Worlds*,.

6   See, for example, Paul Phillips, *Regional Disparities*,(2nd ed. Toronto: Lorimer, 1982).

7   Ralph Matthews, *The Creation of Regional Dependency* (Toronto: University of Toronto Press, 1983), Chap. 1.

8   Garth Stevenson, "Canadian Regionalism in Continental Perspective," *Journal of Canadian Studies* (Summer 1980), 17 (emphasis mine).

9   Richard Simeon, "Regionalism and Canadian Political Institutions," in J. Meekison, (ed.), *Canadian Federalism: Myth or Reality* (3rd ed., Toronto: Methuen, 1977), 293.

10 Stevenson, "Canadian Regionalism," 16.

11 Matthews, *The Creation*, 22.

12 R. Breton, "Regionalism in Canada," in David Cameron, (ed.), *Regionalism and Supranationalism* (Montreal: Institute for Research on Public Policy, 1981), 59.

13 Matthews, *The Creation*, 19 (emphasis his).

14 Westfall, "On the Concept," 7-10; Gore suggests that administrative boundaries constitute a third way of making regional boundaries but, as Westfall, explains administrative boundaries can be subsumed under either the formal or relational perspective. Charles Gore, *Regions in Question* (London: Methuen, 1984), 9-10.

15 *Ibid.*; see also, Smiley, *The Federal Condition*, 22.

16 Westfall, "On the Concept," 7-8.

17 *Ibid.*, 8.

18 Task Force on National Unity, *A Future Together* (Hull: Supply and Services, 1979), 28.

19 Westfall, "On the Concept," 8.

20 Task Force, *A Future*, 27.

21 For example, Ontario, British Columbia, and Quebec have been designated as separate regions.

22 Alan Cairns, "The Governments and Societies of Canadian Federalism," *Canadian Journal of Political Science* (1977), 699.

23 See Harvey Lithwick, "Is Federalism Good for Regionalism," *Journal of Canadian Studies* (Summer 1980).

24 For a discussion see, Richard Simeon, "Federalism in the 1980s," in Thomas Courchene, *et. al.* (eds.), *Ottawa and the Provinces: The Distribution of Money and Power* (Toronto: Ontario Economic Council, 1985), 29-30.

25 See Janine Brodie, *The Political Economy of Canadian Regionalism* (Toronto: Harcourt, Brace, Jovanovich, 1990), Chapters 2,3.

26 Most of the recent government studies which have equated regionalism with provincialism arrive at institutional solutions to spatially-based political conflict. See, for example, The Task Force, *A Future*; or more recently, the Report of the Royal Commission on Economic Union and Development Prospects, Vol. 3. (Hull: Minister of Supply and Services, 1985).

27 For a discussion see Stuart Holland, *Capital vs the Regions* (London: Macmillan, 1976); L. G. Barrett, "Perspectives on Dependency and Underdevelopment in the Atlantic Region," *Canadian Review of Sociology and Anthropology* (August 1980), 273.

28　Thomas Courchene, "Avenues of Adjustment: The Transfer System and Regional Disparities," in M. Walker, (ed.), *Canadian Confederation at the Crossroads: The Search for a Federal-Provincial Balance* (Vancouver: Fraser Institute, 1978).

29　D. Massey, "Regionalism: Some Issues," *Capital and Class*, 6 (1978), 17.

30　For an extended discussion see Brodie, *The Political Economy of Canadian Regionalism*, Chapter 2.

31　Gore, *Regions*, 10; Westfall, "On the Concept," 8.

32　This may seem a questionable point of departure because some argue that Innis's work is not a relational approach to regional definition and integration but, instead, an example of vulgar resource determinism. Admittedly, strong currents of determinism do run through his work but they are not sufficiently deep to dismiss his potential contribution to the study of Canadian regionalism. See, Gregory Kealey, *et. al.*, "Canada's Eastern Question," *Canadian Dimension*, 13:2 (1978), 37.

33　See Harold Innis, "The Teaching of Economic History in Canada," in Mary Q. Innis, (ed.), *Essays in Canadian Economic History* (Toronto: University of Toronto Press, 1956), 85.

34　*Ibid.*, 10.

35　See Daniel Drache, "Harold Innis and Canadian Capitalist Development," *Canadian Journal of Political and Social Thought* (Winter 1982), 39; K. Marx, *Grundrisse* (London: Penguin Books, 1973), 740.

36　Carl Berger, *The Writing of Canadian History* (Toronto: Oxford University Press, 1976), 91.

37　It is important to stress here that it was not the staple itself that stimulated uneven spatial development, as the launderers' version of staples' theory suggests, but rather prices, markets and the monopoly of markets, all of which are defined historically.

38　Harold Innis, *Empire and Communications* (Toronto: University of Toronto Press, 1956), 5.

39　H. Innis, *The Fur Trade in Canada* (Toronto: University of Toronto Press, 1956), 385.

40　William Westfall, "The Ambivalent Verdict: Harold Innis and Canadian History," in W. Melody, *et. al.* (eds.), *Culture, Communications and Dependency* (New Jersey: Ablex Publishing Corporation, 1981), 48.

41　Donald Smiley, "Canada and the Quest for a National Policy," *Canadian Journal of Political Science* (1975), 43.

42　Gore, *Regions*, 191.

43　Henry Veltmeyer, "The Central Issue in Dependency Theory," *Canadian Journal of Sociology and Anthropology* (August 1980), 199.

44　Matthews, "On the Concept," 74-75.

45　Gore, *Regions*, 198.

46　Mark Webber, "Agglomeration and the Regional Question," *Antipode*, 17:2 (1982), 4.

47　Massey's objections to the use of dependency models to explain intranational uneven spatial development revolves precisely around this point. She argues that it is a fallacy to "simply transplant" models which were developed to explain the impact of monopoly capitalism *on a global scale*, "to a lower level of spatial disaggregation;" see Massey, "Regionalism."

48   *Ibid.*, 109.

49   Paul Phillips, "The Hinterland Perspective: The Political Economy of Vernon Fowke," *Canadian Journal of Social and Political Thought* (Spring 1978), 77.

50   As quoted in *Ibid.*, 71-72; From V. Fowke, *Canadian Agricultural Policy* (Toronto: University of Toronto Press, 1946).

51   Drache, for example, argues that the Canadian state is autonomous in neither a relative or absolute sense; see Drache, "Harold Innis," 56.

52   See *The Federal Condition*, Chapter 8, *passim*.

53   Vernon Fowke, "The National Policy—Old and New," *Canadian Journal of Economics and Political Science* (August 1952), 272.

54   *Ibid.*, 274; see also Smiley, *Federal Condition*.

55   D. Harvey, *Limits to Capital* (London: Basil Blackwell, 1982); Webber, "Agglomeration"; Massey, "Regionalism"; Gore, *Regions*.

56   Harvey, *Limits*, 374.

57   Fowke, "The National Policy," 278.

58   See Smiley, *The Federal Condition*, Chapter 8. I tend to view the 1980-84 period as part of the process of "groping" for a Third National Policy which has yet to be established, but may very well be continental rationalization through a free-trade agreement. For a discussion see Brodie, *Political Economy*, Chapter 7 and Janine Brodie and Jane Jenson, *Crisis, Challenge and Change: Party and Class Revisited* (Ottawa: Carleton University Press, 1988), Chapter 10.

59   Smiley, *The Federal Condition*, 178.

VIVE LE QUÉBEC LIBRE!
OR
PUTTING THE LEADER BACK IN[1]

Stephen Clarkson, University of Toronto

A shock wave swept through the group of dignitaries gathered on the terrace of Montreal's city hall on the afternoon of July 24, 1967. The occasion was the spectacular arrival of General Charles de Gaulle, the President of France, at EXPO '67, the world exposition mounted in celebration of the 100th anniversary of Canada's confederation. Having debarked from the French cruiser, *Colbert*, the day before in Québec City, de Gaulle had just been driven along the old Chemin du Roy on the St. Lawrence River's northern shoreline, through towns and villages festooned with bunting and lined with cheering crowds. By the time his triumphal cavalcade reached Montréal, an intoxicating patriotic excitement had built up. Responding to the huge crowd gathered in front of the municipal centre, de Gaulle abruptly indicated his desire to address it. Though no speech had been announced in the official programme, a microphone was already in place on the building's balcony and the general proceeded to seize both the instrument and the moment that history was offering him.

After a few sentences invoking the spirit of the liberation of France and the affection that France was starting to feel again for "the French of Canada," he raised his long arms to make his familiar "V" gesture and began to intone the kind of litany that characterizes the ceremonial declarations of French officialdom. First came "Vive Montréal!" which elicited a roar of cheering from the crowd. Then came "Vive le Québec!" which brought a louder and longer response. The general waited a moment, then detonated his bombshell: "Vive le Québec... libre!"

(Ever since the study of politics became institutionalized in universities and professionalized as a discipline operating by the norms and codes established by its guild of practitioners, the intellectual activity known as "political science" has had great difficulty dealing with the role played by the individual in politics. Although historians could legitimately write biographies of great political men, political scientists have been loath to tackle the impact of the individual leader on his—still less her—political system, its policies or its processes. The paucity of literature dealing with political leadership is a mute testimony to this reality. Recently some scholars have pointed out the seriousness of this gap in the profession's intellectual repertoire and called for the devotion of more resources to the study of leadership in a period of history where human society is increasingly vulnerable to the follies of misguided leaders.[2] This essay proposes a simple proposition—that if Charles de Gaulle hadn't made his dramatic gesture, Pierre Elliott Trudeau would not have come to power—as a contribution to the project of bringing the leader back in as a factor in the deliberations of Canadian political science.)

The consternation created by the French president's audacity in uttering the Québec separatist movement's inflammatory slogan was instantaneous. The crowd, which was liberally sprinkled with separatist "Québec libre" placards, went wild. Around the world, wire services flashed the astonishing news of this provocative intervention by the redoutable French president in the politics of his country's present ally and former colony. On the Montréal city hall terrace, Daniel Johnson, the premier of Québec, remonstrated with his guest for endorsing his opponents' slogan. At the same time, René Lévesque, the former broadcast journalist turned politician who was moving hesitantly towards embracing separatism himself, was equally dubious. "C'était un mot de trop," he remarked to a French reporter, indicating he felt the intervention premature. Still, he mused, "ça allait accélérer beaucoup de choses."[3]

"Vive le Québec libre!" did indeed accelerate many things, but not in the way de Gaulle intended or Lévesque hoped. While successful in its immediate goal of dramatizing the cause of independence for Québec, de Gaulle's famous four words failed in the longer term because of the miscalculations which had inspired it. Two decades later it is apparent that the "Vive le Québec libre!" episode was a pivotal moment in Canada-Québec-France relations and in Canadian political history but that it ultimately strengthened rather than weakened the Canadian federal state and helped stymie the thrust towards Québec's independence it was designed to encourage. Detached from the realities of French foreign policy that he had come to embody, the aging statesman promised far more with his dramatic gesture than France could deliver. Indifferent to the contradictions bedevilling Québec's independence movement, de Gaulle overestimated its capacity to exploit his offer of support. Blind to the interconnections between provincial and federal politics, he underestimated Ottawa's reaction to his provocation.[4]

De Gaulle's Grandiosities and France's Constraints

The French diplomats in the president's entourage that July 24th had their own reasons to be dismayed with their leader's behaviour. De Gaulle's foreign minister, Maurice Couve de Murville, was furious. He dreaded having to manage yet another change of direction in French foreign policy, one that would be exceedingly difficult to justify, let alone sustain. A blatantly disruptive intervention in a hisotric ally's internal affairs was hardly consistent with the spirit of France's post-war policy of decolonization in its empire and solidarity with its allies. On multilateral issues, France's relations with Canada had been harmonious. Prime Minister Lester Pearson's constructive middle-power role in the North Atlantic alliance had been appreciated as sound and helpful. As for the specific bilateral question of France's links with Québec, it was Pearson who had pressed for, and French diplomats who had initially resisted, the proposal that the Québec government open a delegation of its own in Paris with semi-diplomatic standing. In the French view, such subnational representation would set a dangerous precedent. Besides, the French government had no special relationship with the French-speaking population of Canada that merited privileged status. July 24 made it evident to Couve that such informed opinion in the Quai d'Orsay had less impact on France's foreign policy than did the historical visions dancing in the head of the French president.

It had taken de Gaulle himself a long time to warm to the French Canadians. He had written them off early in World War II as sympathisers with the Vichy regime and later saw them as francophobes under the aegis of that arch-provincialist premier, Maurice Duplessis, who suspected all things French of anti-papal and republican free masonry. It was only after the death of Duplessis and the defeat of the Union Nationale government in 1960 that the Québec government's former antipathy towards France turned into an infatuation. For Québec of the Quiet Revolution France became a potential source of cultural reinforcement and perhaps even political support against the federal power in Ottawa. This shift from hostility to supplication coincided with a significant turn in de Gaulle's own global view.

In the light of France's shrinking claims to great-power status, de Gaulle's long-held resentment of "anglo-saxon" dominance was enflamed. His withdrawal from NATO in 1966 had been a move to military autonomy from American domination of the Atlantic alliance. When Prime Minister Pearson refused to sell France uranium without strict anti-proliferation controls and failed to get Air Canada to buy Caravelles rather than Boeings, Canada became in de Gaulle's eyes little more than an American pawn, a collaborator in the attempt to keep France from attaining its rightful position as a great nuclear power. Destabilizing Canada was part of a gaullist scheme for undermining the hegemony of the United States and for rebuilding that of France.[5]

The movement towards autonomy in Québec played into de Gaulle's grandiose notion of himself as the restorer of France's historic greatness. As a young officer steeped in the triumphs and tragedies of France's history, he had bemoaned Montcalm's defeat by Wolfe in 1759 and deplored France's subsequent abandonment of its settlers on the shores of the St. Lawrence. As early as 1960 he had mentioned to André Malraux the "potentiel énorme" of the French Canadians and asked him as minister of culture to investigate its enhancement. The president's rekindled interest in Québec was fuelled further by a handful of gaullists, some of whom were descendents of the elite who had returned from la nouvelle France in 1763, after the treaty handing over the French colony to Britain had been signed, and who were now developing a passionate commitment to the rescue from "les Britanniques" of their former domain. An independent Québec could provide the base for a new "francophonie" under France's tutelage, they argued. By 1963, de Gaulle himself was talking of Québec's "indépendance" as "un état." In 1964 he was referring to French-Canadians proprietorially as "Français", toasting them in Paris at an official dinner in Prime Minister Pearson's honour as "notre peuple installé au Canada." Clearly his behaviour on July 24, 1967 was no impulsive gaffe of a senile megalomaniac; it was part of a pattern.

When the press and the left-wing opposition in France expressed shock in the days and weeks following the episode in Montréal it was because they had not understood these cues. The ageing president had not lost his grip as his opponents implied. The need for the microphone on the balcony had been foreseen by his advance men. The general had practised the delivery of his

"Vives!" aboard the *Colbert* during the voyage. For him it was a case of coming to New France to correct the historic wrong of 1763 by playing once again in his life the role of liberating hero.

Far from regretting the mischief, he appeared to be enormously pleased with his dramatic coup: "J'ai fait une bonne farce," he told one inquiring aide on the plane that returned him precipitately to Paris in response to Lester Pearson's official rebuff. "De Gaulle ne pouvait pas parler autrement," he told another, referring to himself characteristically in the third person historical.[6] At a press conference four months later he pointedly enlarged on his notions of the inevitability of Québec becoming an independent state. Recalling "the wave of patriotic liberating passion" in Montreal, he confirmed his intention that France support "her children" in "their effort of emancipation" that "will necessarily result in the advent of Québec to the rank of a sovereign State."[7]

Whether de Gaulle could actually offer support beyond rhetoric was quite another question. The answer hung on what France was actually able to offer, on how much and what kind of aid Québec could absorb and on whether the federal government had the strength internationally to contain both France's manoeuverings and Québec's ambitions. Beyond moral support and cultural exchanges what France could offer was limited by economic and political realities. France's economic base in Canada was small, and in Québec, even more marginal. French direct investment in Canada made up just 1.3 per cent of total foreign direct investment in the country. Its exports amounted to only 1.2 per cent of Canada's imports.[8] French banks had no network in Québec to provide a base for an enhanced commercial relationship substantial enough to free Québec from its one-sided dependence on the North American market. More important, Paris's major economic and political interests lay in the European community. France could not make seriously disruptive moves to encourage the independence movement in Canada without causing repercussions among the French-speaking in Belgium and Switzerland, and so imperilling its status in the Common Market which had brought prosperity to its farmers, its entrepreneurs and its workers. In short, there was no constituency in France that had a real interest in diverting resources to promoting Québec's secession from Canada. Official Paris could harass the Canadian government with petty insults—not inviting its ambassador to a state dinner for the Québec premier, sending cabinet ministers to

Québec without informing Ottawa—and treat the now burgeoning Délégation Générale du Québec in Paris as though it were a
free-standing embassy sustaining direct relations with France's
social and cultural ministries. It could use its power in the capitals
of francophone Africa to fight a covert diplomatic war against
Ottawa on Québec's behalf. Beyond these limited means, it could
do little more for Québec than Québec could do for itself. And
what Québec could do was constrained by the dilemmas inherent
in its movement towards independence.

Québec's Limited Capacity to Manoeuvre

Québec's move into the heady world of international relations
had been as precipitate as it had been unexpected. Barely mentioned in the provincial Liberal party's winning campaign platform of 1960, the establishment of quasi-diplomatic relations had
rapidly become linked to breaking out of the constraints imposed
on the province of Québec by the Canadian constitution. To
direct, control and finance the many ventures of social engineering it hurried to launch, the Lesage government had mounted
increasing pressure on Ottawa for a larger share of the country's
tax revenues and constitutional powers. At the same time
Québec's search for more constitutional room received an unexpected boost from its education minister.

When Paul Gérin-Lajoie signed an educational entente with
France in 1965 he quickly realized he had done far more than just
break out of the cultural isolation Duplessis and the Roman
Catholic church had imposed on the province. As a former student of constitutional law, the education minister knew that
treaties signed by the federal government covering areas of
provincial jurisdiction could not be implemented without the
agreement of the provinces. From this he went on to claim
Québec's right to develop its own international relations as an
"external extension of its internal rights." In effect he was claiming exclusive treaty-making powers for Québec in the social-wel-
fare, educational and cultural fields. From being a means for
modernizing Québec's culture in the industrial era, the establishment of cultural relations with France soon became a device
for gaining legitimacy on the world stage for the independent state
of Québec.

Up to a point the Liberal government in Québec was able to
proceed unhampered with its surreptitious strategy. It erected a

bureaucratic structure under the direction of Claude Morin who established a ministry of intergovernmental affairs as an embryonic foreign office to orchestrate the many aspects of Québec's expanding relations with France, francophone Africa and other countries such as the United States. It put on its statute books laws to control the behaviour of diplomatic personnel. Yet the more the Québec government leaned towards indépendantisme, the less it reflected a general consensus of the province's main social groups.

The tremendous burst of economic and social-policy energy released by the Lesage Liberals had set Québec firmly on the path of catching up to other industrial societies, particularly in building the structures of an interventionist Keynesian welfare state. But the more the government accomplished—modernizing and secularizing the educational system, nationalizing Québec's hydro-electric companies, appropriating more powers from the federal government—the less easy it was to maintain the broad class coalition that had brought the Quiet Revolution to life in the first place. With its eyes on the North American market, the growing francophone capitalist class was leery lest too much nationalism damage its markets in English-speaking Canada and the U.S.A. The working class soon became disillusioned by the new school system's failure to open up opportunities for social advancement in the North American economy. As for those parts of the middle class that had gained most in the shape of jobs in the expanded public service, their appetite for full independence had only been whetted.[9] These diverging class concerns meant that the consolidation of cultural links with France was as crucial to middle class elites who turned from the Church to France as the guardian spirit of the French-Canadian collectivity as it was irrelevant to those market-based interests—bourgeois and working-class alike—which, in the absence of serious economic ties with France, were primarily focussed on expansion through deepening their integration in the North American economy.

What further diminished Québec's capacity to exploit de Gaulle's offer of support was a crisis in political leadership. The defeat of the Liberal premier, Jean Lesage, in 1966 seemed to indicate that the Quiet Revolution's momentum had stalled. Even though his Union Nationale successor, Daniel Johnson, also turned out to be anxious and able to garner support from the Elysée Palace, his health was failing. By 1969 he was dead and his successor, Jean-Jacques Bertrand, turned out to be more concerned with pragmatic economic problems than symbolic international ventures. At the same time that leadership on the independence question was passing from the hands of elected politicians to the agitation of extremists, the separatist threat was being raised as an issue on the federal political agenda by a handful of bureaucrats in Ottawa supported by a trio of newly elected federalists from Québec. Had de Gaulle not made the prospect of separatism so palpably real for English Canada by adopting the "Vive!" slogan it is doubtful that these men would have been able to seize power and hold it for over fifteen years, least of all under the leadership of a diffident intellectual called Pierre Elliott Trudeau.

Ottawa Provoked

Concern that the Quiet Revolution was getting out of hand had been mounting in Ottawa's privy council office since 1964 when an aggressive Premier Lesage had pushed a conciliatory Prime Minister Pearson to make major concessions to Québec by ceding constitutional and fiscal powers over social programmes. Ottawa mandarins worried that a trend had been established: Lesage would demand more powers and Pearson would give in, unable to say No. When Québec signed its educational entente with France, this concern spread to Ottawa's department of external affairs.

Under the direction of the Under-Secretary of State for External Affairs, Marcel Cadieux, Canadian diplomacy moved quietly to contain Québec's threat to Canadian sovereignty. In what was really the beginning of a special, though reactive Canada-France relationship, an "accord cadre" was negotiated and signed with Paris in late 1965 retroactively placing Québec's ententes under the umbrella of a formal inter-state arrangement. Cadieux assigned his most brilliant protégé, the international legal expert, Allan Gotlieb, as staff for a political group that was to monitor and respond to what he regarded as Québec's back-door route to separation. Active in Gotlieb's group were two members of the prime minister's staff, Marc Lalonde, Pearson's policy advisor, and Lalonde's bureaucratic associate, Michael Pitfield. Chairing the committee was the Québec polemicist who had made a name for himself as the author of many biting attacks on the "counter-revolutionary separatists" both inside and outside the Québec government, the fledgling Liberal parliamentarian, Pierre Trudeau, who had been rapidly promoted by Lester Pearson, since his election in 1965, to be the prime minister's own parliamentary secretary.[10]

Having developed a political stand on Québec's position in the Canadian federation that was increasingly unpopular in Québec—that all Québec's legitimate political aspirations could be realized within the existing Canadian constitutional system—Pierre Trudeau had entered political life poorly positioned for a great public career. By spotlighting Québec's apparently imminent accession to independence, de Gaulle's "Vive!" so alarmed English-Canadian public opinion that the tough, unrepentant federalism Trudeau believed in suddenly became attractive outside Québec. Certainly the "Vive!" attack gave immediate legitimacy to Ottawa's hardliners. On the morning after de Gaulle's coup, Lalonde and Trudeau, now minister of justice, were able to prevail over the inclination to appeasement of External Affairs Minister Paul Martin and to persuade Pearson to declare de Gaulle's words "unacceptable." Trudeau was not even publicly prominent in Ottawa's first stiffening against Québec's venture in diplomacy. But when he emerged in February 1968 as the dark horse candidate for the succession to Prime Minister Pearson, federalist opinion among the country's elites and public had been so sensitized to the separatist threat that Trudeau became an overnight favourite to lead the country through the difficult years ahead. In effect, de Gaulle's personalization of Québec's aspiration to independence produced Trudeau's personalization of the federalist counterattack.

The doctrine for the Trudeau's government's strategy after he became prime minister in April 1968 had been partly spelled out in two white papers that grew out of Gotlieb's work. Published in February, 1968, they rejected Québec's claims for diplomatic independence, on the grounds that national sovereignty is indivisble in international law, and went on to lay out a scenario for increased participation by interested provincial governments both in the making of Canadian foreign policy in fields of their constitutional jurisdiction and in its implementation abroad in international organizations and conferences.[11] In essence this Trudeauvian theory legitimized provincial diplomacy at the price of coopting it in the federal foreign policy process. This defensive attempt to subsume with a Canadian label Québec's quite independent ventures with France was complemented by the broader redefinition of Canadian foreign policy that Trudeau commissioned in order to make Canadian external policy answer

Canada's internal political needs. The foreign policy review's heavy emphasis on aid to francophone Africa, bicultural representation on international organizations and making External Affairs itself fully bilingual reflected Trudeau's personal determination to use Canadian external relations to wage his internal battle against his separatist foes.

He fought that fight tenaciously for nearly two decades. Trudeau had been sent to francophone Africa early in 1967 by Pearson to reconnoitre the political terrain. With its large number of recently decolonized, economically vulnerable francophone states, Africa had turned out to be the major battlefield for the Canada-Québec-France tussle. For France, Africa provided many client states who could be manipulated to favour Québec without the Quai d'Orsay getting involved too directly. These newly minted states' urgent need for educational and cultural assistance offered many chances for Québec to develop international links within its own fields of constitutional competence. But the French Africans' desperate need for economic aid also gave Canada a means to exploit its superior financial muscle to buy their compliance with Ottawa's position against Québec's activities and France's machinations.[12]

In his 1968 election campaign Trudeau harped on the Gabon affair. Canada had cut off diplomatic relations with Gabon for directly inviting, without Ottawa's prior approval, Québec's education minister to a francophone conference. Canada, the new Liberal leader insisted, could only have one voice in international affairs. A year later, Trudeau was able to lay down detailed conditions to Premier Bertrand for Québec's participation—as part of a Canadian delegation with but one vote—in a second francophone conference in Kinshasa. By the time the Agence pour la coopération culturelle et technologique (ACCT) had been established in 1970 Ottawa's position had prevailed. While Québec could take the lead in the Canadian participation in the ACCT, the indivisibility of Canadian sovereignty was recognized by there being but one vote for Canada.

The Trudeau government's containment strategy succeeded less well with France directly than it did in francophone Africa. While France's efforts on Québec's behalf had begun to lose their explosive force by the time of de Gaulle's retirement in 1969, his successor as president, Georges Pompidou, refused to back down from de Gaulle's formal positions of support for Québec's autonomy. In 1975 Trudeau sent his closest friend and colleague,

Gérard Pelletier, to be ambassador in Paris, confirming a message he had already made clear when standing up against de Gaulle: he would maintain constant vigilance to contain Québec's activities within the bounds of Canadian sovereignty. After the occupancy of the Elysée Palace changed again, Trudeau made efforts to establish a better bilateral relationship, but poor personal chemistry doomed to failure his meetings with President Valérie Giscard d'Estaing.

In sum, the story of France-Canada-Québec relations in the 1970s was stalemate. Québec had secured a beachhead in Paris for a special relationship, but, thanks partly to an agreement Trudeau made with Québec Premier Robert Bourassa in 1971 on their respective roles abroad, its activities remained within the bounds Ottawa had striven to prescribe. Even when the Parti Québécois came to power in Québec in 1976, Premier René Lévesque's external priorities were concentrated on not rocking the boat before his referendum on sovereignty-association, particularly because investors in the United States were already made nervous by talk of separation. Canadian, French and Québec diplomats continued their petty guerrilla warfare over questions of protocol without any one team being able to prevail. What broke the stalemate was decisive change in all three political systems.

The Second Federal Counterattack

Pierre Trudeau's defeat of the PQ's referendum on sovereignty-association in May 1980 and his patriation of the Canadian constitution over the objections of Lévesque the next year coincided with a different watershed in French politics—the election of François Mitterrand, the first socialist president of the Fifth Republic. Seeing the chance to scotch the separatist threat abroad as he had done at home, Trudeau launched a diplomatic offensive aimed at persuading Mitterrand to disavow the gaullist legacy and put the separatist genie back in its bottle. The prime minister pressed the president to host a summit of the francophone nations that would exclude Québec. Mitterrand concurred, provided that Trudeau could get Québec's agreement. Trudeau was unable to deliver Lévesque's agreement. He also failed to produce the concrete contracts for actual economic collaboration that he had offered.

Put off by Ottawa's pressure tactics and its bureaucratic fights

with Québec over red carpet questions, the Mitterrand government moved only halfway towards the position Trudeau had requested. "Non-ingérence mais non-indifférence" was France's
formula for a compromise that fell short of conceding complete
victory to Trudeau. It was an Atlanticism that married an acceptance of Canada's importance as an ally in Nato with a continued
support for Québec that nevertheless kept well away from political interference.

Devastated politically by the referendum and constitution
defeats and buffeted economically by the ravages of the 1981-82
recession, Québec's adventure in provincial foreign policy was
coming to an end just as surely as were the careers of Pierre
Trudeau and René Lévesque. In fact it would take the departure
from the political scene of these two veteran combattants in 1984
and 1985 to allow a final normalization of the Canada-France-
Québec relationship.

Normalization with Mulroney

History is seldom a fair mistress. What was denied Pierre Trudeau,
who fought for sixteen years to contain and repulse the French
threat, Brian Mulroney, the new Conservative prime minister, was
able to achieve with apparent ease. Mulroney negotiated a deal
with Québec that allowed a summit of the francophone countries
to be held in 1986. The conditions were the same ones Québec
had accepted in 1970 for its activity in the ACCT: separate provincial participation in the conference, but a single vote for
Canada.[13] In return for Ottawa's recognition of its special
relationship with France, Québec was accepting the indivisibility
of Canadian sovereignty. The status quo of the 1970s had been
endorsed as the ground rules for the future.

By the time President Mitterrand came to Canada in 1987 for
an official visit concerned with platitudes and fishing limits, the
impact of de Gaulle's "Vive le Québec libre!" on the three
protagonists in this fateful triangle could be assessed. France
seems to have been the biggest loser. On the diplomatic level it
gained no significant territory for a new French-dominated francophonie, while losing face through its failed intervention in
Canadian affairs and having to accept some dilution by Canada of
France's economic and cultural dominance in francophone
Africa. France may have been marginally enriched by the more
active participation of Québec artists and intellectuals in its cul-

tural life, but its economic expansion had made no signficant gains. From 1966 to 1984 French direct investment in Canada grew only from 1.1 to 1.4 per cent of total foreign direct investment in Canada, while Canadian imports from France declined marginally from 1.1 to 1.0 percent of total Canadian imports.

Québec did little better, increasing its exports to France from 1.2 per cent of its total exports in 1966 to 1.4 per cent in 1983.[14] This lack of economic progress confined Québec's gains from its French connection to the cultural and symbolic levels. The fifty thousand young people and five thousand cadres who have visited France within the context of various exchange programmes testify to the significantly strengthened cultural connection that has been an integral part of Québec's reaffirmation of its francophone identity and its development as a "distinct society." These programmes came to life under de Gaulle's presidency, though they had been established well before he uttered his historic exclamation. But if his "Vive!" promised juridical recognition for Québec as an international actor, then history did not keep the promise he had made.

Paradoxically it was federal Canada that turned out to be the winner. De Gaulle's intervention sparked a reaction in federal politics that brought to power in Pierre Trudeau a man who had the clarity of analysis and the strength of will to contain and roll back France's threat to Canada's integrity. More positively, Trudeau's redesigned foreign policy made biculturalism so central a focus of the Canadian state's international action that Canada emerged more secure in its bilingual character—with Québec more integrated in its federal system—than it had ever been before. The main cost to Canada of its two-decade-long cold war with the spectre of gaullism bore out the original concern of France's anti-gaullist diplomats. By diverting so much energy to the containment of the French threat, the Trudeau government was not able to take on the much more fundamental problem of American dominance. By selling Canadian politicians short and by exaggerating the liberation potential of the Québécois, de Gaulle's action helped slow down rather than speed up the decline of American hegemony.

Had de Gaulle expressed his support for Québec nationalism less flamboyantly and tailored it more incrementally to Québec's capacity to absorb it, Pierre Trudeau and his hardline federalism would probably not have taken hold in Ottawa and "sovereignty-association" would not have been relegated—along with "Vive le

Québec libre!"—to the status of a historical footnote.

Notes

1   This is an expanded version of "Vive le Québec libre! Twenty Years On,"
    French Politics and Society 5 (1987).

2   Michael Keren, "Introduction," Special Issue on Visionary Political Leader-
    ship, *International Political Science Review 9* (1988), 5.

3   For this quote and a description of the atmosphere of national liberation
    surrounding de Gaulle's trip to Canada see Pierre-Louis Mallen, *Vivre le
    Québec libre: Les secrets de de Gaulle* (Paris: Plon, 1978) 172. For the texts
    of his speeches and statements see Renée Lescop, *Le pari québécois du
    général de Gaulle* (Montréal: Boréal Express, 1981). A recent French assess-
    ment of de Gaulle's voyage can be found in Jean Lacouture, *De Gaulle* Vol.
    III (Paris: Seuil, 1986) Vol. III., ch. 19, "La dette de Louis XV."

4   Apart from documented sources, material for this study came from confiden-
    tial interviews in Paris with MM. Fred Bild and Gilles Duguay at the Canadian
    Embassy; the former gaullists Maurice Couve de Murville, Xavier Deniau,
    Martial de la Fournière, Jean de Lipkowski, Pierre Maillard, and Pierre-Louis
    Mallen; Bernard Garcia, François de Laboulaye, François Leduc, and Jean-
    Marie Soutou from the Quai d'Orsay; the political scientist Alfred Grosser;
    the journalists Claude Julien, Jean Lacouture, Georges Many, and Pierre-
    Henri Menthon; the director of the budget, Michel Prada; Claude Roquet at
    the Délégation Générale du Québec, during April 1986. Closer to home I
    interviewed Allan Gotlieb, Canadian ambassador to the U.S. in Washington;
    Louise Beaudoin, André Dufour and Gérard Pelletier in Quebec; John
    English and Krystyne Griffin in Toronto in 1986 and 1987.

5   Alfred Grosser, *Affaires extérieures: La politique de la France 1944-1984*
    (Paris: Flammarion, 1984), 209-11.

6   Information gathered from confidential interviews.

7   "President Charles de Gaulle's News Conference, Nov. 27, 1967," *Atlantic
    Community Quarterly* (Winter 1967-68), 615. Emphasis added. This was the
    press conference that shocked the Jewish world by its strongly anti-Zionist
    remarks.

8   Investment and trade data in this chapter come from Statistics Canada,
    Canada's International Investment Position, various years, *Exports by
    Countries* (Series 65-006) and *Imports by Countries* (Series 65-006).

9   For a sophisticated analysis of the shifting class interests underlying the Quiet
    Revolution see William D. Coleman, *The Independence Movement in Quebec
    1945-1980* (Toronto: University of Toronto Press, 1984).

10 An example of his federalist attack on separatism can be found in Pierre
    Elliott Trudeau, "Les séparatistes: des contre-révolutionnaires," *Cité libre*,
    No. 67 (mai 1964) 2-6, translated in his *Federalism and the French Canadians*

(Toronto: Macmillan of Canada, 1968) 204-212.

11 Canada, Department of External Affairs, *Federalism and International Relations* (Ottawa, 1968) and *Federalism and International Conferences on Education* (Ottawa, 1968).

12 Canada's aid to francophone and anglophone Africa increased from $10.7 and $12.3 million in 1967 to $195.8 and $195.1 million in 1984 respectively. (Canada, Canadian International Development Agency, *Annual Review*, 1966 to 1986.)

13 Claude Morin, *L'Art de l'impossible: La diplomatie québécoise depuis 1960* (Montréal: Boréal Express, 1987) 456-59.

14 Quebec, Bureau of Statistics, *Annuaire de Québec* (1965-1985).

THE ROLE OF THE STATE IN

CANADIAN LIFE

HEALTH INSURANCE:
THE ROLLER-COASTER IN
FEDERAL-PROVINCIAL RELATIONS

Malcolm G. Taylor, York University

Within the vast panoply of federal-provincial relations that Donald Smiley has so brilliantly chronicled and analyzed throughout his distinguished career, federal health insurance policies have been among the most mercurial, ranging from proposed unilateral intervention, to resistance, to diplomatic seduction, to a shift in power and responsibility, and, most recently, to blatant intrusion in provincial policies. Although the historical events to which I will refer have been analyzed in my book, this paper will focus on the vagaries of federal health insurance policies in what may be discerned as five separate stages, each presenting different objectives and strategies.

Stage 1: The 1945 "Green Book" Proposals

On December 27, 1939, the Hon. Ian Mackenzie, Minister of Pensions and National Health, wrote to Prime Minister Mackenzie King, strongly urging that, in view of the sacrifice and effort that the war effort would demand of Canadian workers, unemployment insurance and health insurance be immediately introduced as wartime measures. Mackenzie King laid the proposals before Cabinet but both ideas were rejected, although unemployment insurance would shortly resurface.

Ian Mackenzie bided his time while expanding efforts to study health insurance. In 1941-42 Dr. J.J. Heagerty, Director of Public Health Services, worked with committees representing the Canadian Medical Association (CMA), five health professions and nine consumer groups. An Inter-Departmental Committee on Health Insurance was also established. In December 1942, the Heagerty Committee released its statistics-laden, 558-page report. The two most important parts of the Report were the cost estimates of a health insurance program and two draft health insurance Bills—one for Parliament and one for the provinces—that incorporated almost all of the Canadian Medical

Association's "principles" governing health insurance, including provincial administration by an "independent" commission. The draft provincial Bill clearly proposed the most extensive intervention into provincial law-making and autonomy in Canadian Confederation history. Moreover, disregarding the strong objections of the Royal Commission on Dominion-Provincial Relations (1940) to the grant-in-aid device, the Committee recommended that the program be subsidized by federal conditional grants-in-aid of up to 60 percent of the *estimated* costs of each of the recommended services—medical, hospital, dental, nursing, pharmaceutical, and laboratory—to be introduced in two stages. Since the estimates were crude at best, the proposed formula was clearly a trial and error method in which the federal government's errors would have become the provinces' trials.

On January 8, 1943, Mackenzie took his detailed proposal and draft legislation to Cabinet, where it was decided to refer the entire matter to the Economic Advisory Committee chaired by Deputy Finance Minister W.C.Clark. On January 20, the Clark Committee recommended that the Bill be deferred for further study. Later in the same day, Mackenzie wrote an angry letter to the Prime Minister, protesting the "stalling" by the Finance Department but, recognizing Clark's enormous influence, offering a compromise: the setting up of a Select Committee of Parliament to consider the draft legislation.

The Prime Minister agreed. A 41-member House of Commons Select Committee on Social Security was appointed, and public hearings commenced on March 16, 1943. Ian Mackenzie outlined the proposals, including the cost estimates, and submitted the two draft Bills. There then followed a host of witnesses, the most influential being those who had served on the fourteen advisory committees. Mackenzie's strategy in inviting these interest groups to consult with the Department paid off handsomely as every single group—including the Canadian Medical Association, the Canadian Hospital Council, and the Canadian Life Insurance Association—strongly supported the health insurance proposals.

After four months of hearings the Committee submitted its report, approving the general principles and endorsing the draft legislation. It also recommended a conference of Dominion and provincial representatives and that study of the legislation should be continued by a Committee of the House and by the Interdepartmental Committee.

As a result of the criticism of the financial proposals by the Finance Department and by some members of the Select Committee, on November 19, 1944, Ian Mackenzie appointed several senior officials to a Committee on Health Insurance Finance. The committee recommended increases in personal income tax and contributions from federal consolidated revenue, but the ceiling on the federal contribution of 60 per cent of the *estimated per capita* costs for each service remained. However, that was not all, for the report also recommended even greater federal government intervention in provincial day-to-day administration, namely, "...that the province appoint an officer of the Department of National Health and Welfare and an officer of the Department of Finance to the provincial Health Insurance Commission."

As astounding as the proposed degree of federal government intervention in a field of provincial jurisdiction may appear to us today, it is likely—indeed in the light of subsequent events, it is certain—that it would not have come to pass. In August, 1944, Ian Mackenzie was transferred to the new Department of Veterans' Affairs, and on becoming Minister of the newly-created Department of National Health and Welfare in 1944, Brooke Claxton abandoned the entire strategy of imposing legislation or any form of administration on the provinces.

With the end of the war in sight, planning for a federal-provincial conference to renegotiate the tax agreements signed in 1940 shifted into high gear. But more than taxation was involved as the Cabinet set up two committees, the first on Post-War Reconstruction and the other on Dominion-Provincial Relations. Mackenzie King had decided that the conference could not be held until after the election, which he called for June 11, 1945. As might have been expected from a war-weary electorate, the election was a near disaster for the Liberals who lost 53 seats but managed to hold on to a slim majority.

And so the Dominion-Provincial Conference on Post-War Reconstruction opened on August 6, 1945 to consider a vast array of what became known as the "Green Book Proposals," two of which are of concern here, those related to health and those on taxation. There were four health proposals: (1) a planning and organization grant to enable each provincial government to establish a full-time planning staff, (2) health insurance grants providing up to 60 per cent of the estimated cost of each of a broad range of health services to be introduced in two stages, (3) health grants for specified programs—public health, mental health, tuberculosis, venereal disease, etc., and (4) financial assistance for the construction of hospitals.

The taxation proposals were, in essence, an extension of the war-time tax agreements whereby the federal government would retain exclusive jurisdiction over personal and corporation income taxes and succession duties and would, in return, increase substantially the per capita grants currently being paid to the provinces.

The conference, through continuous meetings of its committees and frequent meetings of senior ministers, extended over nine months, finally collapsing, without agreement, on May 3, 1946. Although the health, social security, and other proposals had appeared seductively attractive, the price tag of the proposed tax field transfers had been too high.

The aborted proposals remind us of the tremendous imbalance in federal-provincial power relationships engendered by the war. The provinces—shorn of much of their revenues—became relatively weaker, and the federal government—with its control of the major revenue sources and its magnificent war effort—became more confident and powerful; indeed, some would even say, more arrogant. The next scenario reveals how greatly the balance shifted in only a decade.

Stage 2: The Roles Reversed

There had been, in 1948, an extraordinary change in the *dramatis personae* on the federal-provincial scene and a consequent change in direction. Gone were those two implacable enemies—Mackenzie King and George Drew—from their former positions, the former into retirement and the latter from Premier of Ontario to leader of the Progressive Conservative Opposition in Ottawa. They were succeeded by Louis St. Laurent, the Minister of Justice and a corporation lawyer, as Prime Minister, and by Leslie Frost, Provincial Treasurer, also a lawyer, as Premier of Ontario. They became good friends and a more amicable relationship between Ottawa and Queen's Park began.

The differences between Mackenzie King's and St. Laurent's views on social issues could scarcely have been greater. Although St. Laurent had served as chairman of the Cabinet Committee on Dominion-Provincial Relations that prepared the proposals on health insurance for the Conference in 1945, now, as Prime

Minister, he was strongly opposed to any government involvement in health insurance.

But events were over-taking the Prime Minister. Voluntary prepayment plans and commercial insurance were rapidly expanding their coverage, clearly demonstrating that the public wanted insurance protection against medical and hospital bills, and were willing to pay for it. But even more significant was that by 1950 government hospital insurance programs had been introduced in four provinces—Saskatchewan, British Columbia, Alberta, and Newfoundland—and all without federal subsidy. Their leaders and members of parliament constantly reminded the federal government that the time had come for the 1945 offer to be fulfilled.

In 1953 the day of reckoning was at hand; the Liberal government had to face the electorate. Still opposed to health insurance, St. Laurent devised a strategy that had three objectives: to postpone the issue as long as possible; to maintain the Liberal party's identification with health insurance; and to place the onus for further action on the provinces. Accordingly, the election platform stated, "The Liberal party is committed to support a policy of contributory health insurance to be administered by the provinces when most of the provinces are ready to join in a nation-wide scheme." As the pundits said, "That put the ball in the provinces' court."

To meet the federal government's condition, it was clear that either Quebec or Ontario must come on board. But the opposition of Premier Duplessis to health insurance was well known. That meant that the one person who would decide the fate of health insurance in Canada was now, unwittingly, Premier Leslie Frost of Ontario. Unwilling to assume the mantle, and angry that it had been thrust upon him, he decided that the responsibility must be returned to the Liberals who had been holding out the promise of health insurance since 1919.

The opportunity came in 1955 as Prime Minister St. Laurent, responding to angry criticisms about previous conferences, invited the provinces to an April meeting to set the agenda for the main federal-provincial conference in October. St. Laurent opened the conference by suggesting that only taxation agreements and unemployment insurance be discussed. Premier Frost, however, insisted on an expanded agenda which included health insurance. The two leaders battled with little hope of compromise until Paul Martin, St. Laurent's Minister of Health, threatened to resign if health insurance was not put on the table, especially since it was party policy. Mr. St. Laurent finally agreed to list the issue on the agenda under the non-commital term, "Health and Welfare Services."

The media interpreted the decision as a victory for the provinces, a typical headline shouting, "Provinces Win." But there would be two years of dogged negotiations, mainly between Ottawa and Ontario, before the legislation would be passed unanimously in both the House of Commons and the Senate in April, 1957.

Those negotiations need not concern us here. But what is significant were the conditions that the federal government attached to its financial contribution of one-half of the aggregate national cost of hospital insurance and diagnostic services. It was as if the Government, forced against its will to proceed, retaliated by making the conditions as stringent as possible. A more charitable interpretation would be that it feared the consequences of writing blank cheques without all the controls it could legitimately exercise. There were six key federal conditions: (1) the program would go into effect only when a majority of the provinces representing a majority of the Canadian people were ready to proceed. (2) Provincial hospital plans (a) should make coverage universally available (a euphemism for "compulsory") to all residents of the province; (b) include provision of specific diagnostic services; and (c) limit co-insurance or "deterrent" charges. (3) Federal payments would not include capital costs. (4) The federal contribution would not be made in respect of mental hospitals or tuberculosis sanatoria. (5) The federal contribution to each province would be (a) 25 per cent of the average per capita cost of (standard ward) hospital services in Canada as a whole, plus (b) 25 per cent of the average per capita costs in the province itself, multiplied by the number of insured persons in the province. On the surface this appeared benign since it resulted in a high cost province receiving less than 50 per cent of its expenditures and a low cost province receiving more than 50 per cent. But, in reality, it resulted in high cost (read high income) provinces receiving higher per capita payments from the national treasury than did low income provinces, an inequity that would not be rectified until 1979. Finally, a sixth condition required that no contributions were to be made towards the costs of administering the program.

With the gazetting of the order-in-council containing the regulations in February, 1958, the degree of federal control was seen to be extraordinary. Every essential requirement for the operation of the program was prescribed. The provincial government must establish a hospital planning division. It must license, inspect and supervise hospitals and maintain adequate standards; it must approve hospital budgets and the purchase of equipment; it must collect the prescribed statistics and submit the required reports; services must be available on equal terms and conditions; and, finally, the provincial government must submit all its expenditures on hospitals to federal audit. All these requirements were incorporated in Agreements which both governments must sign.

Stage Two had been characterized by a 180-degree turn in federal policy and by the determination of several provinces, led by Premier Frost, to ensure that the federal government redeemed at least part of its offer of 1945. In the mid-sixties, the pendulum was to swing back, but ostensibly in a more gentle way.

Stage 3: Political Seduction

It had been without doubt the most turbulent period in Canadian politics in a generation. Four elections in six years had produced three minority governments as the Liberals, also in minority, assumed office from the Diefenbaker government in April, 1963. The Liberals, led by Lester Pearson, were now about to take another turn with respect to health insurance, bringing their policies full circle since 1945. The commitment to Medicare had been firmly announced in both the 1962 and 1963 elections. Although in a minority position in the Commons, the Liberals could count on support for Medicare from the New Democratic Party which would give them a majority vote.

There had been three major events giving impetus to the Medicare thrust: the firm commitment of the Liberals in the 1962 and 1963 elections to introduce Medicare; the successful, though traumatic, launching by Saskatchewan of the first provincial Medicare program in July, 1962, following a 23-day doctors' strike; and the release in June, 1964, of the *Report of the Royal Commission on Health Services*, chaired by the Hon. Emmett Hall, Chief Justice of Saskatchewan, which had been appointed by Prime Minister Diefenbaker in 1961 at the request of the Canadian Medical Association. To the dismay and frustration of the CMA, the Commission rejected the policy of the CMA and the insurance industry that the role of government should be restricted to that of paying in whole or in part the premiums of social assistance recipients and low income earners to the voluntary plans and commercial insurance companies, and had strongly advocated a national Medicare program paralleling the Hospital Insurance program and similar to that of Saskatchewan. The Report was clearly a ringing endorsement of the initiatives to which the Liberal Government was committed.

With the strong urging of Walter Gordon, the only Finance Minister in Canadian history strongly to support health insurance, and the leadership of Health Minister Judy Lamarsh, the Government decided to act, inviting the provinces to a conference on July 19, 1965. The conference opened with the traditional first statement by the Prime Minister. Mr. Pearson was diplomacy incarnate. The federal government would not impose its views on the provinces. Rather, "[It] is now the responsibility of the Federal government to cooperate with the provinces in making Medicare financially possible for all Canadians. The Government accepts that responsibility."

To disabuse the provinces of any intention of federal domination, the Prime Minister said, "I am not proposing a new shared-cost program...in the case of Medicare I believe it is appropriate and possible to proceed by another route. The Federal government...will support provincial Medicare plans by means of a fiscal contribution of predetermined size." He continued: "This proposal does not require detailed agreements governing the Medicare plan. It calls only for a general Federal-Provincial *understanding* as to the nature of the health programs which will make a Federal government believe that there are four criteria on which such an understanding should be based [emphasis added]." The four "criteria" or "principles" were as follows:

> First, the scope of benefits should be, broadly speaking, all the services provided by physicians, both general practitioners and specialists. Second, the plan should be universal....it should cover all residents of a province on uniform terms and conditions. Third, I think it will be readily agreed that a Federal contribution can be made available only to a plan which is publicly administered, either directly by the provincial government or by a provincial non-profit agency. Fourth, I think it is important to recognize the mobility of Canadians; each provin-

cial plan therefore should provide full transferability of benefits when people are absent from the province or when they move their homes to another province.

There was a lacklustre response by the provincial leaders to this momentous announcement, several indicating that their actions would depend on the financial formula, Quebec indicating that it would operate its program outside any joint Fedcral-Provincial program, and Ontario commenting on it not at all. And so, with minimum debate and no outright opposition, the conference adjourned.

But three of the most influential provinces decisions were being taken to frustrate the federal government's objectives as British Columbia, Alberta, and Ontario introduced or planned programs that were based on the CMA/CHIA policies of government support for the voluntary and commercial insurance sector.

?Ominous as these provincial counteractions were, the most dissapointing and frustrating set-back was the Liberal's failure to obtain a majority in the national election that Walter Gordon had advised Pearson to call in November, 1965. The electoral results did not reflect the optimistic public opinion polls on which Gordon had based his counsel. The Liberals gained only two seats and remained a minority government, although they knew that they could still count on NDP support.

There now occurred a major, and almost fatal, change in the key actors as Mitchell Sharp (opposed to Medicare) replaced Walter Gordon in the Finance portfolio and Alan MacEachen became Minister of Health and Welfare. We need not, for our purposes here, examine the internecine warfare in Cabinet that almost scuttled the entire project—and did succeed in having the "appointed day" postponed from the symbolic date of July 1, 1967, to July 1, 1968—nor the vitriolic opposition of the medical profession and that of several provinces—especially at the Provincial Premiers Conference held in Toronto on August 1-2, 1966. So great was the expressed opposition to Medicare that one journalist summed up: "The Federal Government's proposed legislation lies torn, tattered, and politically rejected."

But, as we know, the Act was passed in the House of Commons on December 8, 1966 (missing unanimity by only two votes) and by the Senate on December 16. There was one new criterion, relating to accessibility, not included in the Prime Minister's statement to the Federal-Provincial Conference in 1965:

The plan provides for the furnishing of insured services upon uniform terms and conditions...by the payment of the cost of insured services in accordance with a tariff of authorized payments established pursuant to the provincial law...on a basis that provides for reasonable compensation for insured services rendered by medical practitioners *and that does not impede or preclude, either directly or indirectly whether by charges made to insured persons or otherwise, reasonable access to insured services by insured persons* [emphasis added].

In short, if a doctor extra-billed, the amount of the added fee should not be of such magnitude as to deny "reasonable access." However, the elastic interpretation by hundreds of doctors, mainly specialists, of "reasonable access" bedevilled the system for the the first nine years of the operation of the plan. One other provision of the Act merits noting. The federal contribution, in contrast to the Hospital Insurance formula, would be 50 per cent of the *national per capita* costs, thus equalizing the per capita payments in both high and low-income provinces.

But, given that in the Prime Minister's words, the arrangements between the two orders of government were to be based on an "understanding," and that it was not to be "a new cost-shared program" but was "to follow a new route," it is remarkable what enormous adjustments some provinces had to make to meet the "criteria." "Principles" or "criteria" may not be "conditions" but surely the difference must lie in the eyes of the beholder.

Alberta, British Columbia and Ontario were forced to abandon their subsidies of voluntary and commercial insurance and all provinces established administrative organizations to insure the entire population and meet the Act's requirements—universal coverage, reasonable compensation, portability of benefits, and reasonable access—a Herculean task under the best of conditions. The Prime Minister's proposal to "proceed by another route," based on mutual "understanding," had clearly not lived up to its advance billing. It *was* a conditional program like the others.

Stage 4: Shifting Power and Responsibility

Despite the strong public support for the hospital and medical care insurance programs, there was genuine concern on the part of both provincial and federal officials over the original financing formulas. The provinces objected to the inflexible regulations they had been required to accept in the hospital insurance agreements; they also resented the federal audit to determine shareable costs; and low income provinces objected to the hospital insurance funding formula which resulted in higher per capita payments from the federal treasury to high-income than to low-income provinces. In addition, the provinces claimed that the sharing of only two programs effectively distorted provincial priorities. Ottawa's growing concern, on the other hand, was that it had no control over its rapidly increasing, "open-ended" health budget since it was required to match the expenditures determined by provincial governments. Even the Economic Council of Canada was alarmed at the escalating costs, warning in its 1970 annual review that health and education expenditures alone would absorb the entire national product before the year 2000, if recent rates of increase continued. A fundamental restructuring of the financial supports of education and health insurance therefore seemed necessary and inevitable.

Negotiations on a new formula were introduced at the federal-provincial conference in June, 1976. Prime Minister Trudeau proposed termination of the open-ended 50-50 cost-sharing arrangements for post-secondary education and the two health programs. In their stead, the federal government offered to vacate 12.5 points of personal income tax and 1.0 per cent of corporation income "tax room," which the provinces could then occupy. This was calculated to approximate one half of the existing federal contributions. In addition, the federal government offered a cash grant equal to the other half of its 1975-76 payments for the three programs, to be escalated annually in accordance with a three-year moving average of increases in per capita GNP.

Although there were initial differences among the provinces—high income provinces wanted the total in tax transfers, and low income provinces wanted to retain the 50-50 cost-sharing—they finally presented a united front, accepting the federal proposals, but demanding that the Revenue Guarantee (which had been introduced in 1972 to compensate the provinces for the reduction in the federal basic income tax on which all provinces, save Quebec, base their income tax levies, and which was due to expire in 1977) be continued by a transfer of an additional four income tax points. After lengthy negotiations, to achieve agreement on the whole package, the federal government agreed to one additional tax point and its 1975-76 equivalent in cash, to be escalated as in the basic offer—or one-half the amount the provinces had demanded. These funds were included in the Established Programs Financing Act (EPF) package, a decision that would come to embarrass the government.

But the story did not end there. In the 1981 negotiations on renewal of the Taxation Agreements for the 1982-87 period, the federal government held firm to its decision, on which it had compromised in 1977, to end the revenue guarantee. This represented an estimated aggregate loss to the provinces of just under $5 billion over the 1982-87 period, and although the revenue guarantee funds were wholly unrelated to EPF, any decline in overall provincial revenues cannot fail to adversely affect many programs. But there was more bad news to come. EPF was to be directly attacked.

With the election of the Conservative party to office in September, 1984, the government was immediately confronted by the magnitude of the deficit and the ever-increasing debt, and in his May, 1985 and February, 1986 budgets Finance Minister Michael Wilson took steps to reduce the first and slow the rate of increase of the second. But three months later he decided that it was not enough, and in May, 1986, announced a reduction of two per cent in the growth rate of the EPF transfer payments, effective April 1, 1986. The decreases in annual payments to the provinces are projected to rise from $318 million in 1986-87 to just over $2 billion in 1990-91, or a total of $5.689 billion in the five year period.

In reviewing the effects of the EPF period the following comments can be made. All of the provinces took advantage of the vacated tax room, and although these were now provincially-levied taxes, the federal government continued to include their revenue totals in all statements of its "contributions." The immediate effect of adopting the new arrangements was to increase substantially the federal share of aggregate costs of the two programs from 46.5 per cent in 1976-77 (the last year of cost-sharing) to a high of 54.2 per cent in 1978-79, as was anticipated. From there, the federal share began to decline, reaching a low of 47.8 per cent in 1982-83. It then began to rise again and preliminary data for 1985-86 indicate a federal contribution of 50.7 per cent.

The ending of cost-sharing of the three programs meant that the provinces could henceforth allocate their funds in any way they decided. Since they are now spending 100-cent dollars on all programs, there is no longer any steering effect resulting from the federal contributions. It was clearly a major shift of power to the provinces. But it was equally a transfer of responsibility, for the provinces are now solely responsible for any expenditure increases exceeding the three-year average rates of increase in GNP. Since inflation rates in the health sector have typically exceeded increases in CPI, this places the provinces at risk, while under the EPF arrangements the federal government is effectively insulated against any excess increases. The net result is that the federal government got the handle on its health budget it so desperately wanted; indeed, with the Wilson decreases in the EPF payments, it now has achieved more than it originally negotiated in 1986—but clearly at the expense of the provinces.

Stage 5: Intervention Again: The Canada Health Act, 1984

As has been indicated, the EPF represented the largest transfer of funds, and therefore the substance of power, to the provinces in Confederation history. In contrast, the Canada Health Act— designed to end extra-billing by doctors and the imposition of hospital user fees by provincial governments—appeared to the provinces and the medical profession to be the reverse: an unwarranted, powerful, and for provincial governments politically hazardous, intrusion into a field of provincial jurisdiction. The political conflict the Act engendered rivalled that over the introduction of Medicare itself. For the federal government the legal question was whether or not extra-billing by doctors and hospital user fees violated the "reasonable access" requirements of the Medical Care Insurance Act.

Prior to the Canada Health Act, three provincial governments had confronted the organized profession on the issue of extra-billing, with mixed results. In British Columbia and Quebec extra-billing was not permitted, and in Saskatchewan it was tolerated reluctantly. So, governments in provinces where the practice was tolerated or, as in Alberta and Ontario, supported, had been dramatically forewarned of what they would likely face if the Canada Health Act were passed.

And events were moving towards that end. With the ending of income and price controls in 1978, doctors, like many others, were determined to catch up. In Ontario the proportion of physicians extra-billing increased from 13.5 per cent to 18 per cent in 1979, levelling off to about 12 per cent by 1983. In Nova Scotia approximately 53 per cent extra-billed, and in Alberta about 47 per cent. It was estimated by Health and Welfare Canada that extra-billing by doctors in Canada totalled approximately $100 million by 1983.

The increased extra-billing in 1978-79 brought public demand for an end to the practice to a fever pitch in the election of 1979, with Madame Monique Bégin, the erstwhile Health Minister, leading the attack on the provinces that permitted it. She was joined by hospital association spokesmen and health workers' union leaders who also charged that provincial governments, under the unrestrictive terms of EPF, were diverting federal health contributions to other purposes, thus underfunding both hospitals and doctors, causing the latter to opt out and extra-bill.

With the defeat of the Liberals in the elections of 1979, the new Prime Minister, Joe Clarke, appointed David Crombie as Minister of Health and Welfare; and he was immediately confronted by charges that the provinces were diverting federal health funds to non-health purposes, and that extra-billing and hospital user fees were violating the principle of the "reasonable access" clause of the Medicare Act. Mr. Crombie's response was to launch an inquiry, the Health Services Review, to assess the validity of these criticisms. The Hon. Emmett M. Hall, the chairman of the Royal Commission on Health Service in the early sixties, was named commissioner.

As research consultant to the commissioner, I was responsible primarily for ascertaining whether provincial governments were indeed diverting federal health funds, for analyzing the briefs to prepare for the questioning of witnesses in the public hearings, and for preparing drafts for other parts of the report. Without independent research staff, we relied on senior researchers at Health and Welfare Canada to analyze pre-EPF and post-EPF federal and provincial health spending. That group completed the monumental task of examining provincial public accounts, and all its data were submitted to provincial health and finance departments for verification. This was followed up by my personal interviews with federal and provincial health and finance officials. The results were indisputable: provinces were not diverting federal "health contributions" to non-health purposes. The whole misunderstanding—some would say "fiasco"—had occurred because the federal government had included the Revenue Guarantee funds as a "contribution" under EPF. The proportions of aggregate provincial governments' budgets allocated to health, before and after EPF, were identical. Revenue Guarantee funds, quite properly, had been spent on other programs. That answered question number one.

On the second major question, Commissioner Hall was adamant. "If extra-billing is permitted as a right and practised by physicians in their sole discretion, it will, over the years, destroy the program, creating in that downward path a two-tier system, incompatible with the societal level which Canadians have attained." But what if extra-billing were denied? What if government-medical association negotiations on the fee schedule broke down? The remedy, said the former Supreme Court justice, was binding arbitration. Although every witness speaking to the issue had opposed it, following the Canada Health Act, four provinces adopted the procedure.

There was to be a second official attack on extra-billing. The elections of 1980 had returned the Liberals to power. One effect of the Clark Conservatives' period in office and their return to Opposition was that they now demanded a greater role for Parliament in the upcoming 1982 negotiations on the tax agreements—clearly an assault on "executive federalism." They finally obtained agreement by the Government to the appointment of an all-party House of Commons task force to examine federal-provincial fiscal relations, including the impact of EPF.

The task force held public hearings in Ottawa and the provincial capitals and received briefs from a host of interest groups, most of which declared that the health system was underfunded, the most forceful of the critics being the Canadian Medical Association and its provincial divisions. The task force presented a comprehensive report covering the full spectrum of federal-provincial fiscal relations. On the issue of extra-billing the committee agreed with the conclusion of Commissioner Hall that the continuation of extra-billing would eventually destroy the system. But it was unable to achieve consensus on what to do about it. The majority recommended that extra-billing not be permitted and that this step be accompanied by provision for binding arbitration, if necessary, to settle fee disputes. Its second recommendation was even stronger: "Any province that does not meet fully all the accessibility criteria be ineligible for full federal financial support under EPF financing." It was a clarion call for the federal government to impose financial penalties on provinces permitting extra-billing or authorizing hospital user fees, thus paving the way for the Canada Health Act.

By 1983, hyperbolic rhetoric flooded the news media. Not since the issue of Medicare itself in the mid-1960s had there been such a torrent of editorials and letters to the editor. Monique Begin continued her campaign against extra-billing, and on July 25 issued her long-anticipated paper, *Preserving Universal Medicare*. Its main theme was that Medicare was being threatened by the "growing and spreading" direct charges to patients. It analyzed the issues and concluded, "We cannot preserve Medicare by charging the sick; we cannot preserve Medicare by judging who is poor and who is not; we can only preserve Medicare by ensuring its basic principles."

The reactions were not unexpected: unqualified condemnation by the provinces—"electioneering," "blackmail," "a poor example of federal-provincial cooperation," "will seriously damage the health care system"—and criticism by Dr. Marc Baltzan, president of the CMA: "an obvious back-door intrusion into an area of provincial jurisdiction," "financial blackmail." The health coalitions and consumer associations praised the document.

On December 12, 1983, the Canada Health Act (Bill C-3) was introduced in the House of Commons and given first reading. The reactions of provincial governments, medical associations and the various consumer groups duplicated those of early summer. Bill C-3 was given second reading on January 16, debated on January 17 and 20, and referred to committee where claims about all of its alleged virtues and horrendous consequences were repeated once again. On March 21, 1984, the committee reported. The Bill was then passed unanimously by the House of Commons and Senate and proclaimed law on April 17, its automatic sanctions to become effective July 1—and with the unexpected support of the Mulroney-led Conservatives who did not bow to pressures from several Conservative provincial governments.

Its most significant new stipulations were two: provision for the withholding from the cash payment to a province an amount equivalent to the total amount of extra-billing permitted and/or the amount of hospital user charges authorized by the province; and, if the practice of extra-billing or user charges were eliminated within three fiscal years, the total amount deducted would be paid to the province. The second provided the rules respecting binding arbitration. The provinces are not required to adopt the procedure, but if they do, the decision of the arbitration panel cannot be altered by the Government but must be approved by the legislature where, it may be assumed, the award would be intensely debated. This provision was added as a result of pressures by the CMA when it failed to block the measure altogether.

But Ottawa had once again sown the wind, and several provincial governments would reap the whirlwind, as they planned their strategies to meet the new conditions. Space does not permit an examination of the responses of individual provinces, but the negotiations with their respective medical associations in Nova Scotia, Manitoba, Saskatchewan, Ontario, and Alberta were bitter and painful. The most confrontational and dramatic was the 25-day strike by a majority of Ontario's doctors.

With the actions by the five provinces, the main objective of the Canada Health Act—the banning of extra-billing and hospital user fees—spearheaded by Mme. Monique Begin and supported by millions of Canadians who wanted what the profession-sponsored prepayment plans had educated them to expect, i.e., the *prepayment in full of all* their medical and hospital bills, had been achieved.

But the costs of rounding off the ragged edges of "universal accessibility" had been high in terms of political and social conflict and of the morale and public image of the medical profession, as the action struck at one of the major tenets of the profession's belief system. One can only hope that time, the great healer, will again work its miracles and that lowering the temperature of rhetoric on both sides will conduce to a rapid restoration of more reasonable and harmonious relationships between two interdependent groups—the profession and the public, represented by their governments.

Conclusion

This brief over-view of federal-provincial relations focussing on the health sector in Canada illustrates two major characteristics of federal systems. The first might be called the genius of federalism, in that social progress is not dependent on action by the federal government on a given issue. The collapse of the Dominion-Provincial Conference on Post-War Reconstruction in 1946 appeared to bring progress to a halt. But immediate action by Saskatchewan to introduce hospital insurance not only demonstrated that a universal program was as feasible as it was desirable, but it also created a domino effect in that within three years Alberta and British Columbia also had programs in operation. With the funds available from the introduction of national hospital insurance in 1958, Saskatchewan was able to provide the second initiative with Medicare in 1962, and four years later the federal government acted again. One cannot say that we would not have achieved national health insurance without the provincial initiatives, but there can be little doubt that they accelerated the process.

The second feature, so cogently illustrated in this review, is the power of the device of the conditional grant-in-aid in a federal system. Although five provinces, led by Ontario, forced a reluctant Prime Minister St. Laurent to honour part of the 1945 offer, it was Ottawa who called the shots on the design of the program, and compelled the other five provinces, including a resistant Quebec, to undertake the onerous financial, organizational, and administrative burdens of putting programs in place. The power is even more dramatically illustrated in the case of Medicare, as one recalls the opposition of the provinces expressed at the Premiers' Conference in Toronto in August 1966, and the major adjustments that Alberta and Ontario were compelled to make in their programs in order to conform to the federal "principle" requiring administration by a public agency. No provincial government could resist the inducements of the grant from the federal treasury to which its citizens were contributing.

But, as we have also seen, an open-ended grant also contains risks for the federal government, mainly in its lack of control over the amounts of the federal contribution in a matching formula. And each episode in the saga of health insurance in Canada has shown the lengths to which the federal government deemed it must go in limiting its expenditures. In 1945 it proposed a rigid, fail-safe, financial formula: up to 60 per cent of a federally-determined estimated per capita cost of each service. And the experience of Saskatchewan two years later showed how far apart estimates and reality can be. In 1956, recognizing that the resurgent provinces would never accept such a loaded formula, the federal government offered 50 per cent of the aggregate national costs of hospital insurance but hedged its contributions by an extraordinary range of controls which were a constant source of federal-provincial acrimony. But these proved not enough, as hospital and medical costs continued to escalate at rates considerably above the Consumer Price Index. So the federal government negotiated EPF which tied its rates of increase to the more stable base of increases in the rate of growth of GNP.

But that, of course, placed the provinces in much the same position they would have encountered under the 1945 proposed formula: solely responsible for expenditures in excess of the rate of increases in GNP. And with Finance Minister Wilson's unilateral reduction in EPF contributions ($5.689 billion, 1987-92), the provinces' burdens will inexorably increase.

The Canada Health Act constitutes a final example of the power of the federal purse for it was clearly a major intervention into the provinces' jurisdiction. It remains to be seen what the Supreme Court's determination will be when it considers the appeal of the Canadian Medical Association against the Act.

Although Donald Smiley has described the provincial governments in Canada as perhaps being more powerful than the constituent units of any other contemporary federation, it is clear from the above analysis that in the past, and especially when backed strongly by public opinion, as in the case of the Canada Health Act, the federal government has wielded enormous influence through the power of the purse. I have used the past tense in making that observation for, under the Meech Lake Accord, the ability to launch new programs in fields of provincial jurisdiction has been vastly circumscribed. It seems reasonable to say that, had Meech Lake been in place since the early 1950s, we could not have achieved provincial hospital and medical care insurance programs that have been melded into a national program. We would more likely have arrived at what Premier Leslie Frost predicted in 1955 in the absence of joint federal-provincial action: "a hodge-podge that no one would be able to disentangle...a few years more and an integrated plan will become an impossibility."

Clearly, the days are over when the federal government could, by paying half the costs, dictate all the rules. Perhaps that is a good thing. Although the two health programs enjoy enormous public support, there is no doubt about the unequal burdens now shared by the federal and provincial governments. The federal government now provides less than half the costs. The provinces are responsible for more than half the financing but, in addition, daily bear an enormous political and administrative burden in processing medical accounts, approving (or worse, disapproving) requests for hospital beds and equipment, determining the mix of acute, chronic, and nursing home beds, and annually confronting the demands of medical and nursing associations and hospital unions for increased incomes. Federal politicians complain that they are given insufficient credit for their contributions. Perhaps the distribution of credit is fairer than Ottawa is willing to acknowledge.

THE POLITICAL CULTURE OF PROBLEM-SOLVING AND PUBLIC POLICY

David V.J. Bell, York University

Two students were trading complaints in the cafeteria. "The food here is terrible," said one of them. "Yes, and they give such small portions," quipped the other.

In a similar vein, Donald Smiley makes two criticisms of the literature on Canadian political culture: first that it is wrong headed; and second that there isn't enough of it. In the Postscript to the third (and last) edition of *Canada in Question*, Donald Smiley explains that his approach rests on assumptions "contrary" to those underlying "the political culture perspective." Instead of assuming that "mass attitudes and ways of behaviour are decisive in shaping political systems," Smiley's approach suggests "that the 'roots of disunity' in Canada are more attributable to the way in which political institutions work than to mass attitudes..." Yet in the same book, Smiley argues in "Appendix A: Towards Further Investigation" that "First and in my view most crucially, we need work on the linkages between political culture and the operations of our major political institutions."[1]

These two sentiments are not necessarily contradictory. Indeed Smiley's plea for more research reflects his contention that "Canadian social scientists have not as yet come forward with conclusive evidence to demonstrate that one of these sets of [contrary] assumptions is more valid than the other."[2]

This essay does not purport to resolve the issue one way or the other. It does call into question Smiley's characterization of the political culture "perspective," and outlines a quite different conceptualization of political culture that *can* help explain "the way in which political institutions work."

The Concept of Political Culture: A Brief Historical Overview

Karl Deutsch once remarked that "You can measure a scholar's greatness by his ability to retard progress in the field." By this (or probably any other) definition, Gabriel Almond is truly a great figure in the study of political culture. Almond is generally credited with introducing the concept of political culture in his famous 1956 article in *The Journal of Politics* entitled "Comparative Political Systems."[3] The political and intellectual climate of the time had a profound effect on Almond's work. Intellectually, American social science was in the throes of what might be called a revolution of rising expectations. There was a sense of optimism, a belief that by adopting a "scientific" approach, intellectual breakthroughs could be achieved in the study of the social world to parallel the fantastic successes in physics which ushered in the atomic age. At the very least, the new social science would aim to be cross-disciplinary, cross-national, quantitative, and present-minded. Almond's work on political culture was to satisfy all four criteria. In an attempt to bring political science into closer contact with the other social sciences, he deliberately looked elsewhere for a concept that would enliven and advance the comparative study of political science. He took the concept of culture from sociologist Talcott Parsons who in turn had adopted it from anthropologists . Following Parsons, Almond defined culture as "psychological orientations to social objects." The social object in question was, of course, the political system. Having satisfied the requirement for cross-disciplinary borrowing from sociology and anthropology, Almond in his mammoth study (with Sidney Verba) *The Civic Culture* (1963) met the next two criteria for the new social science by basing the study on quantitative analysis of survey data, and by surveying individuals' orientations to their political system in five countries: U.S., Britain, Germany, Italy, and Mexico. Despite their interest in political development (presumably an historical process), Almond and Verba honored the social scientific canon of present-mindedness by relying on a single synchronic survey snapshot of each country and extrapolating from that to identify an image (presumably universally valid) of the developmental pattern.

Almond and Verba's work was also affected by the political climate within which they wrote. The Cold War was in full force.[4] The United States and the Soviet Union were at loggerheads. Each country hoped to extend its influence in the Third World, and to solidify its position in Europe. It was fashionable for academics at the time to conceptualize the conflict between West and East as a conflict between Democracy and Totalitarianism. Thus, it is not surprising that Almond and Verba focussed their study of political culture on the problem of democracy. The opening sentences of *The Civic Culture* read as follows:

> This is a study of the political culture of democracy and of the social structures and processes that sustain it. The faith of the Enlightenment in the inevitable triumph of human reason and liberty has been twice shaken in recent decades. The development of Fascism and Communism after World War I...[and] events since World War II have raised the question of the future of democracy on a world scale.[5]

Clearly, theirs was not a general approach to the study of political culture but a problem-specific approach, perhaps valid for what they conceived as their intellectual mission. The relevance of that mission to later historical times and other political settings is highly questionable, however. Yet for a variety of reasons, their approach seemed to dominate work on political culture, and became the standard model for empirical work in the field. This success was achieved despite the fact that others had begun using the concept of political culture quite differently. Both Sam Beer and Louis Hartz had worked out different and, in my view, more fruitful approaches to the study of political culture.[6]

Almond and Verba's success in capturing the high ground of the study of political culture ultimately contributed to the demise of the concept among political scientists. Their approach fell quickly into disfavour for a variety of reasons. Some argued that the conception of democracy which underlay their study was hopelessly U.S.-centric: an intellectual expression of American Imperialism. Others criticized the idealism inherent in Almond and Verba's emphasis on values and attitudes as a precondition to democratic political structures. Still others (in particular students of public policy) found very little of explanatory value in a survey of mass attitudes and values which operated on the assumption that there were no significant mass/elite differences, and that seemed to ignore the important effects of political institutions.[7]

To re-fashion and adapt the concept of political culture to make it a useful instrument for the analysis of public policy requires a number of deviations from the Almond and Verba approach. The following discussion indicates how this might be achieved.

Public Policy: Some Assumptions

To begin with, it is important to make explicit several assumptions about public policy and the policy-making process. First, in many respects policy-making is obviously governed by inertia and incrementalism: often the best predictors of budgetary allocations for the next year are budgetary allocations for this year. Second, policy can emanate from a variety of sources within the government, and can be intended to fulfill a number of often incompatible objectives. Similarly, policy is devised to serve a number of purposes, some of which co-exist simultaneously at different levels. For example, a policy may be distributive, regulatory, and symbolic at once. Third, a wide range of forces and interests bear on the process of policy foundation. These forces exist in the environment of the political system and increasingly within the political institutions themselves. They are often in conflict with one another, but affect policy outcomes nonetheless.[8] Finally, it is clear that public policies need to be justified, explained, or rationalized to various publics. Such rationalizations may, however, ignore or contradict the "true" purposes and objectives of policy, and disguise or deliberately misrepresent the pressures and interests that helped generate the policy.

Notwithstanding all of these qualifications, policy-making is generally undertaken in an effort to address or respond to a problem that is believed to exist in the environment of the political system, or within or between the political institutions themselves.[9] *The way in which the problem is conceptualized has an important bearing on the nature of the response, including the kind of policy instrument selected*. This contention lies at the heart of my discussion of the political culture of problem-posing.

Public Policy and Political Culture: Re-fashioning the Concept

The first modification required in the Almond-Verba conception of political culture is to recognize explicitly that mass political culture is neither the same as, nor in many respects for policy analysis as important as, elite political culture. More accurately, mass and elite political culture affect public policy differently. We cannot explain policy outcomes on the basis of mass-based political surveys.[10] To do so ignores both the structural forces external to the political system that help shape policy, and the effects of political institutions themselves on policy outcomes.

Second, political culture should not be forced into the false dichotomy of cause or effect. Clyde Kluckhohn once suggested that the very language of cause and effect is inappropriate for understanding the complexity and interactive effects present in social situations. It is better to speak of the "influence" of political culture on public policy than try to discuss its so-called "causal significance."[11] A useful metaphor for capturing its importance is the term "cultural lens." Political culture constitutes a cognitive and evaluative lens or filter that helps shape our perception of problems and situations.[12] It affects how we interpret the situation, what importance we give to it, and what kinds of solutions or remedies we think are appropriate. This remark applies to everyone: members of the mass public, political elites, and even academics.

Third, in giving conceptual substance to the notion of political culture, we are well-advised to relate the conceptualization to a specific "problem." However, it is unlikely that we will want to focus exclusively on the problem of democracy. Therefore Almond and Verba's measures and concepts will prove of limited use. Imitation of their research instruments is mindlessly anachronistic.

Fourth, the notion of political culture should be broadened to include metaphors, symbols, and myths. Almond and Verba's narrow focus on the psychological dimensions of political culture ignores a wealth of external, objective manifestations of political culture.

> Lacking an external, material basis, culture leads a phantom existence, without shape or categories, its presence guaranteed only by the 'indicators' which are supposed to measure something going on in people's heads. It can never be known directly, but only by its epiphenomenal traces. The fact that the psychocultural approach aspires to be systematic, even comparative, cannot hide the fact that it has produced little reliable evidence about political culture as such or a set of useful concepts for talking about it.[13]

Political life is replete with symbols that serve as a kind of cognitive shorthand for problems and issues, grievances and beliefs. The symbol conveys simultaneously a definition of the problem, a diagnosis of its causes, a prescription for its cure, and a powerful affective cue indicating how one should respond to it. Because of the capacity of symbols to condense cognitions, beliefs and feelings into a set of cued responses, manipulation of symbols is often a substitute for political action addressed to the substance of the problem. This insight underlies Murray Edelman's extensive work on the symbolic aspects of politics.

Symbols are joined together in the "primal matrix" of myths, which often

> take the form of...well rounded stories with an extensive cast of characters and many episodes...in which the facts are distorted in order that persons and events may symbolize the appropriate values and express 'truths' which are fundamental to the life of a policy.[14]

In instances where a given problem or issue is fundamentally disputed, we may expect to find rival myths with all of the attendant implications for symbol structures, rituals, and slogans.

Even more common than myths are metaphors that convey a compelling if implicit image of both situations and responses. Canadian federalism has evoked the metaphor of the family from both journalists and political cartoonist. The federal government appears as a stern if anxious parent confronted with the task of keeping in line ten jealous and sometimes rebellious siblings.

In summary, to re-fashion the concept of political culture and make it into a useful instrument for public policy analysis, we must abandon the assumption that elite political culture is congruent with mass culture; move away from simple assumptions about culture as cause (or alternatively as effect); develop problem-specific conceptualizations of political culture that relate to the public policy area under study; and broaden our conceptual horizon beyond the psychological orientation of Almond and Verba to include attention to symbols, myths, metaphors, and slogans. In other words, we must examine political discourse.

Problem Conceptualization: An Anatomy

In light of these modifications to the notion of political culture, how can we accomplish the major objective of relating our conceptualization to specific problem areas? It is helpful to distinguish five aspects of problem conceptualization.

First, the nature of the problem: how is the problem perceived and defined?[15] Moore discusses alternative conceptualizations of the "heroin problem" and indicates the public policy implications of each. Some people view heroin use as a medical problem, others as a law enforcement problem, while still others focus on the socio-economic aspects. The way in which a problem is defined will affect all other aspects of its conceptualization.

Second, diagnosis of origins or causes: what circumstances have created this problem? Is it a matter of individual responsibility, or are larger structures involved?

Third, the role of government: what should government attempt to do about the problem?[16] Does the problem demand some sort of public policy response, or is it purely a "private" matter? In recent years, the range of problems deemed to require government action has expanded dramatically. This growth in politicization has in turn generated a neo-conservative negation, particularly in the United States, where notions of "deregulation" and demands for a cutting back of governmental activity have gained popularity.[17]

Fourth, the appropriate kind of policy response: assuming that government is seen to have some responsibility to respond to a problem, what form should that response take? From the vast repertoire of public policy instruments, which ones should be selected? For example, should government provide more medical facilities for the treatment of heroin abuse, or step up law enforcement? Answers to these questions presuppose some knowledge or speculation about the likely effects of various policy initiatives. All too often, however, slogans and myths crowd out evidence and analysis.

Fifth, how can the policy be rationalized or explained?: whatever policy response is selected, some sort of public account must be given to justify its use. At this stage, sharp divergences between elite political culture and mass political culture can pose serious difficulties. If the elites conceptualize a problem quite differently than the general public, they will obviously have a hard time "selling" their policy response. Attempts to bridge this conceptual gap probably account for the widespread use of "symbolic politics," particularly in policy areas related to problems that are prominent in the public consciousness.

In order to explore the usefulness of this general framework, we will present a case study of alcohol policy in Ontario.

Alcohol Policy in Ontario

Alcohol plays a major role in Ontario society. Approximately 85 per cent of Ontario adults consume alcoholic beverages, and in 1986 they spent nearly $1.7 billion in doing so. The use of alcohol is widely accepted and deeply ingrained in our culture. Many view it as an indispensible accompaniment to various social occasions, and an essential feature of pleasurable dining. Yet the Ontario public has also at various times demonstrated great concern about such negative effects of alcohol abuse as alcoholism, public drunkenness, and drinking drivers. In short, public attitudes to alcohol are ambivalent: they include simultaneous demands for wider brand choices and less restrictive liquor laws mixed with concern about the deleterious social and health effects of alcohol abuse.[18]

From the perspective of government, alcohol has long been a controversial issue. Only decades ago the fate of Ontario governments hung largely on their views and policies regarding alcohol. While the issue is less politically volatile at present, it still touches many ministries in an important fashion. Alcohol revenues poured nearly two-thirds of a billion dollars into the provincial treasury in 1986. At the same time, vast sums went out through the Ministry of Health in the treatment of alcohol-related diseases and injuries.

In a strict sense it is misleading to speak of Ontario alcohol policy as if it were singular or uniform. Instead of a unified policy regarding alcohol, one finds a "quasi-policy"[19]: a myriad of different policies—some complementary, some overlapping, some contradictory. Despite the provincial government's efforts to coordinate policy "fields" by introducing "policy field committees" drawing together several ministries and chaired by "super ministers," alcohol-related policies emanate from ministries as diverse as Health, Parks and Recreation, and Consumer and Commercial Relations. In introducing one rather straightforward amendment to the Liquor Licence Act in 1974, Consumer and Commercial Relations Minister Allan Grossman referred to five other ministries besides his own, each of which had some interest in the changes.

The absence of a coordinated alcohol policy reflects more than bureaucratic complexity and inefficiency. To be sure, thorough coordination of the various alcohol-related activities of ministries and agencies would require a great deal of reorganization and the setting up of some new structures. Maintaining a *lack* of coordination, however, has been beneficial for the provincial government insofar as it has permitted the revenue side of the alcohol equation to be kept separate from alcohol-related expenditures.

Although many ministries have involvement in alcohol-related policy, the task of administering the major legislation concerning alcohol has been given to three semi-independent government agencies. The Liquor Licence Board of Ontario (LLBO) oversees regulations concerning "on premise" consumption, while the Liquor Control Board of Ontario (LCBO) regulates "off premise" alcohol use. (Approximately 85 per cent of alcohol sold in Ontario is consumed at home.) These two boards were set up after World War II as Ontario moved inexorably toward more liberal alcohol policies.[20]

The third alcohol-related special agency is the Addiction Research Foundation (ARF). When it was first being set up, the ARF was funded through the LCBO budget as a matter of administrative convenience.[21] This link was broken the next year when ARF was formally established.[22] By contrast, in Finland such a link has been institutionalized as a conscious choice. The predictable result is that Finnish alcohol policy really does emphasize *control*. In Ontario, on the other hand, as a result of the divorce of these two concerns, the LCBO has lost entirely its initial control orientation and has become instead a marketing body concerned primarily with increasing sales. From the perspective of government, LCBO's chief importance is its revenue-generating capabilities. This fact was formally acknowledged when ministerial responsibility for the agency was shifted in 1973 to Consumer and Commercial Relations. From the perspective of the alcohol industry, the LCBO has become a vitally important target of public relations activities. The industry has focussed considerable attention on lobbying the LCBO to shift policy in a favourable direction. Until very recently the ARF has taken a secondary or even tertiary role in policy formation, by and large eschewing direct policy intervention in favour of a passive research-only role.[23] It has thereby abandoned the field to the pro-alcohol interests, and to those few declining outside groups that speak for moderation and conservatism in alcohol policy.

The Political Culture of Alcohol Policy

As pointed out above, political culture serves as a filter or lens through which political events and activities pass before they are interpreted or acted upon. It is an important aspect of what Simeon calls the "political framework"—the constraints and opportunities defined by "the broad social and economic environment, the system of power and influence, the dominant ideas and values in society, the formal institutional structures." This framework "greatly restricts the alternatives [policy-makers] consider and the range of innovations they make."[24] Hence understanding the political culture with respect to alcohol policy is a precondition to understanding this area of public policy. How do members of the political elite perceive the problem of alcoholism? What other forms of alcohol abuse are they aware of and what importance do they assign to them? In light of perceptions of alcohol problems, what solutions do they view as appropriate? To what extent do they believe that government must play a role in helping to solve the problems created by alcohol abuse? Attitudes on this issue will of course reflect to some extent broader beliefs about the role of government in society as well as specific notions about the nature of the problem and the capacity and legitimacy of government's intervention to bring about changes. Finally, what positive benefits are attributed to alcohol and to the alcohol industry? To what extent do individuals weigh off the benefits against the costs in arriving at overall conclusions about control policy and other forms of government intervention?

A similar set of questions can be addressed to the mass public. What are the generally held beliefs about alcohol: its usefulness, the abuse of alcohol, and the role of government in responding to these abuses, in the general public? It is on the basis of these beliefs and other aspects of the common stock of knowledge about alcohol that the public will respond to changes in alcohol policy and their attendant justifications and rationalizations.

Although the beliefs and attitudes that make up the political culture of alcohol are potentially unlimited (i.e., it is conceivable that different individuals could have any number of combinations of beliefs and attitudes about the nature of alcohol problems, benefits of alcohol, the role of government intervention, etc.), in actual practice, beliefs tend to cluster into particular combinations which might be described as ideologies of alcoholism.[25] In principle it is possible to trace the development of alternative ideological outlooks, and to monitor changes in the political culture of alcohol through this process. For example, it is likely that prior to about 1950, most people subscribed to a moralistic concept of alcohol. Alcohol abuse was viewed as an indication of moral degeneration, caused by an inherent or acquired weakness in an individual's moral fibre. The appropriate response to this malady was some form of moral or spiritual regeneration achieved through religious activity. Adherents of the moralistic ideology disagreed about whether the government should allow the sale of alcohol (given its capacity to corrupt). This ideology gave little importance to government sponsored treatment centres. Indeed, the notion of treatment in hospital as opposed to a mental institution or religious organization seemed inappropriate.

In the post World War II period, a new conception of alcohol abuse known as the disease theory gained popularity.[26] This ideology fitted well the new policy of liberalization of alcohol availability, for it attributed the causes of alcoholism to some physiological condition which was unaffected by increased availability. Hence those who subscribed to the disease concept (including most notably the distillers themselves) could (and did) argue that alcohol was no more the cause of alcoholism than was sugar a cause of diabetes. By corollary, the government could increase alcohol availability with a clear conscience, and merely put aside funds for treatment of alcoholics in the same manner as they would provide for hospital facilities for tuberculosis or other kinds of diseases.

In the late 1950s and early 1960s, a number of academics, health professionals, and even policy-makers, were attracted to what became known as the "integration theory." This theory encouraged relaxation of drinking laws to remove the taboo and mysticism surrounding alcohol. Stripped of its forbidden fruit quality, alcohol would be integrated into the life patterns of "normal" drinkers, who would be taught the fundamentals of "responsible drinking." Strong social sanctions against alcohol *abuse* would lead to much more "civilized," "continental style" drinking habits.

Throughout the 1960s, a small group of researchers (comprising several ARF staff) undertook epidemiological research to learn more about the characteristics of drinking populations as a whole. Their findings challenged the basic assumptions of both disease theory and integration theory. Over the next decade, they accumulated massive cross cultural evidence indicating that:

1. no clear differences (e.g., in Socio-Economic Status) exist between heavy drinkers and alcoholics;
2. alcoholics exhibit no apparent pattern of unique susceptibility (physiological or otherwise) to alcoholism;
3. alcoholics constitute only a minority of those drinkers whose alcohol use adversely affects their physical, social, or psychological well-being;
4. a strong and direct relationship exists between the prevalence of users of hazardous amounts of alcohol, and the amount of alcohol consumed by the population as a whole.

Together, these findings pointed toward what ARF researchers called the "single distribution theory." (It was also called the "availability theory.") This new conception of the nature of alcohol problems generated a revolutionary set of policy proposals.[27] Contrary to widely held premises of both disease theory and integration theory, increasing consumption of alcohol in the population as a whole *did* entail increases in forms of alcohol abuse. The more "available" alcohol is, the more the society as a whole consumes. The higher the "model consumption" rate of the society as a whole, the larger the group of problem drinkers. Other studies began to show that consumption patterns were negatively affected by both *price and availability*. Accordingly, ARF recommended

1. changes in alcohol taxation policy to index cost of alcohol to disposable income and to equalize alcohol cost regardless of beverage type;
2. cessation of further liberalization regarding availability of alcohol; and
3. public education to increase public awareness of health implications of alcohol (similar to smoking warnings, etc.).

Since these recommendations contradicted the trend of government policy and posed a threat to the perceived interests of the alcohol lobby, they initiated a new role for ARF in the policy process, and occasioned new counter-measures by other actors in the system. Brewers and distillers both published pamphlets attacking the ARF for postulating this theory. Echoing the argument of the NRA in the United States ("Guns don't kill people, people kill people"), the distillers announced that alcohol was no more responsible for the disease of alcoholism then was sugar a "cause" of diabetes. Non ARF researchers were hired to discredit ARF findings. And so the competition between conceptions of the alcohol problem became a mini-war between the alcohol lobby and the ARF.

Summary and Discussion

On the basis of the preceding analysis, the following points emerge:

1. Ideologies of alcohol (i.e., widely held beliefs and attitudes) have tended to lag behind theories of alcohol (i.e., researchers' beliefs and attitudes) by 20 to 30 years;

2. The vast popularity of the disease ideology among the community at large reflects researchers' near consensus regarding the disease theory in the late 1940s and early 1950s;[28]

3. If a growing number of researchers became "converted" to the single distribution theory, eventually the single distribution theory may "filter down" to the mass level and supplant the disease concept in the popular culture;

4. Alcohol theories or ideologies (or "governing images") tend to dictate or prescribe appropriate policy responses;

5. Actors who have strong commitments tend to believe and cling to an ideology compatible with their interests. Thus the brewers and distillers espouse the disease concept or integration theory;

6. Until policy-makers (and a substantial body of the general public) have been convinced of the validity of the single distribution theory, recommendations based on it can (and will) be easily dismissed or discredited;

7. Alcohol ideologies cannot be considered in isolation from other aspects of the political culture. The single distribution theory recommends strong governmental policy measures that tend to have a regressive tax effect. These recommendations apparently run counter to a belief in free enterprise and a commitment to social equality.[29]

Conclusion

This paper has suggested that a reformulated conception of political culture can illuminate the study of public policy. To the extent that public policies are addressed to particular "problems," the conception of the nature of the problem, its causes, the perceived role of the government, and the most appropriate policy response are all influenced by political culture. An important methodological implication of the framework outlined in this paper is this: in examining public policy in a specific area, researchers should develop a problem-specific conceptualization of the political culture for that policy area.

This advice may appear to neglect larger questions about overall ideological orientations. While it is true that specific orientations to particular problems may all be determined by a more inclusive ideology such as conservatism, liberalism, or socialism, the relationship between the general and the problem-specific culture requires empirical research. I see no reason to assume that general ideology determines problem orientation, and therefore would counsel against attempting to force these conceptualizations into pre-cast ideological molds. We must avoid what Wolin calls "the fetish of ideological interpretation which compels us to look at (the world)...through constrictive peepholes."[30] Thus I made no effort to classify ideologically the various conceptions of the alcohol problem, but noted the obvious implications for alcohol policy of broader cultural notions about the role of government, ideas of equality, and so on.

Political culture does not exist in a vacuum. On the other hand, it does exist and it does exert an influence on behaviour, particularly at the elite level. To synthesize these two assertions requires attention to the linkages between cultural and structural variables. Economic, social, and political interests may not causally determine cultural orientations, but they certainly affect them. Rival interests seek out and defend conceptualizations of the problem that serve their needs. Government does not remain a neutral, passive arbiter of the resultant conflicts. Nor is government single-minded. Bureaucratic agencies actively develop and promote their own conceptions of problems and, where possible, link up with allies in the "environment" of the political system. Consequently, changing the dominant conception of a problem involves much more than persuasion or education, for it usually entails a significant shift in power and resources. By the same token, however, we cannot confine our attention to the structural forces that affect policy and ignore the influence of the particular cultural lens (lenses) through which the elite view policy problems.[31]

Notes

1 Donald Smiley, *Canada in Question: Federalism in the Eighties*, Third Edition (Toronto: McGraw-Hill, 1980) 304.

2 *Ibid*, 332.

3 Gabriel Almond discusses the classical roots of the concept of political culture in his essay *The Civic Culture Revisited*.

4 Lucian Pye suggests that World War II had an impact on American social science even greater than that of the Cold War.

> The time was thus ripe for a new infusion and synthesis of ideas, and World War II made it urgent to get on with the task. The compelling need to train large numbers of people to understand foreign cultures so as to plan for military governments, conduct psychological warfare, and simply to interpret what made the enemy act as he did; overnight legitimized areas studies and interdisciplinary approaches. The wartime concerns with man and society opened the doors of political science to numerous emerging and powerful concepts from neighbouring disciplines.
> Quite understandably culture was one of these, particularly since for a brief period anthropology appeared as the reigning social science.

Lucian Pye, "Culture and Political Science: Problems in the Evaluation of the Concept of Political Culture," *Social Science Quarterly* (1972)285.

5 Gabriel Almond and Sidney Verba, *The Civic Culture* (Princeton: Princeton University Press, 1963) 3.

6 Louis Hartz' work appeared in 1964 under the title *The Founding of New Societies*. This book represented a series of essays in which individual authors applied Hartz' "fragment theory" to a particular society or region. Although Hartz did not use the term *political culture*, his theory attempted to account for historical variations and continuities between new world and old world patterns of political cultural development.
Samuel Beer and Adam Ulam did explicitly discuss political culture in their 1958 book *Patterns of Government*. In their words, "...political culture involves aspects of the 'general culture of society'...[that] are especially concerned with *how* government ought to be conducted and *what* it should try to do."
Despite the intellectual force of both these works, Almond and Verba's approach came to dominate work on political culture, at least with respect to "developed" countries. Key questions from their survey (particularly those concerning "trust" and "efficacy") were incorporated into most major social

research surveys conducted in the U.S. and Canada over the next two decades.

7   Donald Smiley is quite explicit in rejecting the assumption (which he attributes to the 'political culture perspective') that "...political elites...either share the political attitudes of those they govern or are responsive to such mass attitudes that they do not share." *Canada in Question*, 332.

8   Richard Simeon makes this point very effectively: "...policy-making is not, by and large, simply a matter of problem-solving.... It is rather a matter of choice in which resources are limited and in which goals and objectives differ and cannot be weighed against each other. Hence policy-making is a matter of conflict." Richard Simeon, "Studying Public Policy," *Canadian Journal of Political Science*, IX, December, 1976, 550.

9   *Ibid*,556. "[We must try to explain] the central dimensions of policy. How, for example, do current elites define and respond to problems shaped by received wisdom and general cultural norms."

10 Note, however, that in some instances governments apparently put considerable emphasis on public opinion to the point that critical observers complain of being "governed by polls," an accusation hurled frequently at the Ontario government under the premiership of William Davis. The most important scholar of elite political culture is undoubtedly Robert Putnam, whose many works on the subject include *The Belief of Politicians*.

11 "...I would always question the advisability of using the term 'cause' in social-science theory. Too much of a unidirectional force is implied. Even too say that 'culture determines' is an inexact and elliptical way of speaking...because no concrete phenomenon is ever concretely and solely determined by culture." Clyde Kluckhohn, *Culture and Behavior* (New York: Free Press, 1962) 45. *Cf.* also this comment: "It is usually wise to think of a specified factor as *influencing* (rather than as *determining*) the outcome. There are no 'determinants' as palpable, disectable elements; there are only processes that result in determination. In discussing culture as an explanatory concept, we must always favour interactive rather than descriptive notions." *Ibid*, 34.

12 Kluckhohn conveys a similar notion with a slightly different metaphor. "Between culturized organisms and their surroundings there exists, as it were, a screen which is none the less 'real' for being inferred rather than being perceived directly by the senses. This screen is 'culture'." *Op. Cit.*, 39. Note as well Marchak's point about ideologies which she describes as "screens through which we perceive the social world." Patricia Marchak, *Ideological Perspectives on Canadian Society* (Toronto: McGraw Hill Ryerson, 1975) 1.

13 Willard Mullins, *Ideology and Political Culture* (Typescript, 1981) 7.

14 *Ibid.*, 17.

15 In an insightful analysis of the "problem" of alcohol and traffic safety, Gusfield suggests that one must introduce the notions of "ownership," "responsibility," and "political obligation" in discussing public problems. Various groups may vie for ownership of (or in some instances may attempt to "disown") a problem, assign responsibility for correcting it, and establish the extent to which government has an obligation to get involved. Joseph R. Gusfield, *The Culture of Public Problems* (Chicago: University of Chicago Press, 1981) 1-23.

16 This question assumes, of course, the belief that government can do something about the problem. As Gusfield points out, the State increasingly assumes responsibility for public problems, and "appears more often as an active agent, the owner of the problems it seeks to solve... [G]overnment officials and agencies operate to define public issues, develop and organize demands upon themselves, and control and move public attitudes and expectations..." *Ibid.*, 1-23

17 Similar notions of neo-conservatism have become firmly established in Britain under Margaret Thatcher and have affected Canada as well. The Clark government campaigned heavily on neo-conservative issues, only to lose the 1980 election. Mulroney's victory in 1984 was more ambiguous. Although several key Conservatives mentioned deregulation during the campaign, Mulroney's own commitments were unclear. Subsequently privatization and deregulation were attempted in some areas but other neo-conservative policies were abandoned in the face of surprisingly strong opposition.

18 In the 1985 provincial election campaign, Liberal Leader of the Opposition, David Peterson, attracted much press coverage for promising to loosen up liquor laws by allowing the sale of beer and wine in grocery stores and supermarkets. Despite his convincing victory he has to this date (fall 1989) failed to implement this proposal.

19 cf. Richard Simeon, "Studying Public Policy," *Canadian Journal of Political Science*, IX: 4 (December, 1976) 548-580.

20 Although a thorough study of the origins of the LCBO and LLBO remains to be undertaken, one scholar has suggested that an agency structure was chosen in order to deflect possible criticism of day-to-day alcohol policy away from politicians.
See Fred Schindler, *The Government of Ontario* (Toronto: University of Toronto Press, 1966) 72.

21 Before the first "Alcoholic Research Foundation" bill was introduced to the Legislature to permit allocation of funds directly to the Foundation, the salary of director designate David Archibald was paid through the LCBO budget. He was appointed Director of Research for the LCBO. Later the name of the organization was changed to the Addiction Research Foundation.

22 The connection between LCBO and ARF has weakened considerably. Until approximately 1973, the ARF Executive Director was regularly invited to attend the annual conference of Liquor Commissioners of Canada. Following an incident in which a social control paper he sponsored was hastily withdrawn and replaced by an industry-sponsored study, the invitations ceased. Relations between the two organizations appeared to have soured. LCBO resolutely refused, for example, to print moderation messages on its packages (as recommended by ARF), despite the fact that several other provincial boards do so. In 1978 the Chairman of LCBO refused (after considerable internal discussion) to attend the first ARF Senior Executive Seminar. However, some cooperation has taken place at lower levels between researchers in the two organizations.

23 In 1980 the ARF struck a Task Force to examine its role in policy formation and public education. The Task Force report was published under the title *Alcohol: Public Education and Social Policy* (Toronto: Addiction Research Foundation, 1981).

24 Simeon, "Studying Public Policy," 555-556.

25 cf. Robin Room, "Governing Images and the Prevention of Alcohol Problems," *Preventive Medicine*, 3: 11-23 (1974); who uses the term "governing images" in much the same manner. See also David K. Damkot and Elizabeth Meyer, "Alcohol and Social Policy: A Historical Perspective on Evolving Intervention Strategies," *Journal of Drug Issues* (Summer 1984) 479-490 and Mac Marshall, "Social Thought, Cultural Belief, and Alcohol," *Journal of Drug Issues* (Winter 1985) 63-71.

26 Disease theory's popularity reflected a general trend to "medicalize" social problems. It later permitted treatment for alcoholism to receive coverage under OHIP.

27 To the extent that these proposals urged reducing the availability of alcohol, they resembled in form the prohibitionist arguments, which arose out of the "moralistic" ideology. In "Governing Images," Room groups the epidemiological and moralist-prohibitionist arguments together under one of his three "governing images." Equating these two outlooks ignores obvious differences between them in assumptions and values.

28 This conversion resembles what Thomas Kuhn calls a "paradigm shift." Thomas Kuhn, *The Structure of Scientific Revolutions* (Chicago: University of Chicago Press, 1963). It involves a substitution of a new scientific worldview for a previous outlook. Such conversions always involve of blind (i.e. unsubstantiated) faith that the new paradigm is better (i.e. more accurate) than the old.

29 Thus in 1971 a *Toronto Star* editorial entitled "Double Standard" attacked the single distribution theory recommendations because they discriminated against the poor. Similarly two conservative Ministers of Commercial and Consumer relations made public statements disclaiming a major role for government intervention:
Allan Grossman: "...alcohol abuse is in large measure beyond the power of government and the reach of legislation."
Frank Drea: "...the use of alcohol is an individual decision and you can't legislate a person to stop drinking."

30 Sheldon Wolin, *Politics and Vision* (Boston: Little, Brown & Co., 1960) 358.

31 In "Studying Public Policy," Richard Simeon points out that the rules of decision-making are affected by "procedural values," just as policy content is affected by "substantive values," such as the ones discussed throughout this paper. A "complete" study of political culture and public policy would obviously require attention to both. It would also entail a careful assessment of what Jane Jenson calls "the universe of political discourse," a notion complementary to the conception of political culture developed in this paper.

POLITICAL COMMUNITY AND
POLITICAL TRADITIONS

POLITICAL SCIENCE, ETHNICITY AND THE CANADIAN CONSTITUTION

Alan C. Cairns, University of British Columbia

> If the need to feel worthy is a fundamental human require-
> ment, it is satisfied in considerable measure by belonging
> to groups that are in turn regarded as worthy. Like in-
> dividual self-esteem, collective self-esteem is achieved
> largely by social recognition. Everywhere...collective so-
> cial recognition is conferred by political affirmation. For
> this reason, struggles over relative group worth are readily
> transferred to the political system.
> Political affirmation confers something else that ethnic
> groups seek...ethnic identification with the polity.
>
> Donald L. Horowitz[1]

Constitutional Change and Constitutional Commentary: The Declining Relevance of Political Science?[2]

For the foreseeable future Canadians will be working out the
changed internal structure of the constitution and its modified
relation to Canadian society occasioned by the 1982 Charter. At
a minimum these tasks include the following:

1. Refining the complex relationship of the Charter to both
   federalism and parliamentary government, each of which
   has lost relative status in the constitutional order.

2. Rethinking the role of the courts, especially the Supreme
   Court, given its new responsibilities for Charter adjudication which supplement its former role as umpire of
   federalism. This requires attending to the procedures and
   criteria for appointments to the bench, and the elaboration of an indigenous jurisprudence appropriate to the
   enhanced judicial role in making significant value choices
   for the Canadian people.

3. Developing a constitutional theory of citizenship applicable to the more explicit and prominent status citizenship now enjoys. Historically, citizenship has been a thin,

almost non-existent category in Canadian constitutional analysis. This neglect is now glaringly unacceptable.

4. Modifying the language of political discourse by incorporating the language of rights that the Charter legitimizes.

5. Alleviating the tension that now exists between governments and various citizen groups over their respective roles in future processes of constitutional amendment. Governments' monopolization of the amending formula, in the manner of Meech Lake, is incompatible with the new culture of constitutional participation towards which the Charter leads.

In sum, the task is to respond to the emerging centrality, enhanced visibility, and the increasing comprehensiveness of the constitution, as the supreme law of the land, in Canadian life.

These challenges are all well known, although the nature of the answers they will receive is unclear. The latter will depend on the skills with which tomorrow's constitutional players perform, and on the nature of the ends they pursue within the leeway that the constitution provides.

The 'living' constitution of the future, however, will emerge not only from the efforts of explicit constitutional actors, but also from ongoing constitutional commentary that responds to and influences constitutional evolution. That commentary, marked as it will be by intellectual creativity, is itself unpredictable, as also is its symbiotic relationship with the actions of those who more directly work the constitution. Thus, how the relevant academic communities respond to their task of interpreting the changed constitutional order that the Charter has bequeathed to Canadians will influence future constitutional evolution. Clearly the understanding and analysis required of the academic community cannot be confined to yesterday's world of parliamentary government and federalism. The rearrangement of our constitutional structure tinges previous research foci and even the disciplinary division of labour with obsolescence. Much of our former scholarship reflects constitutional assumptions no longer valid. The impediments to relevant constitutional analysis, therefore, reside in inherited intellectual patterns sustained by the organizational structure and status system of academic life.

There are, however, some grounds for optimism that an intellectual reorientation is occurring. The new Canadian Law and Society Association, and the *Canadian Journal of Law and Society* that it publishes, help to pull understandings out of traditional disciplinary grooves. New centres for constitutional studies and the study of law and policy at Calgary and York respectively, testify both to interdisciplinarity and to an expanded conception of law and the constitution. In general, a developing interaction between law and the social sciences is evident on university campuses around the country, and in the footnoting practices of scholars. Indeed, the response of the academic community to the Charter and to the new constitutional arrangements of which it is a central component has been considerable, including changes in curricula, in research foci, and in the shedding of disciplinary parochialism.

Nevertheless, I believe that the academic/intellectual community is having some difficulty in responding to the new constitutional arrangements, and that the difficulty is especially pronounced in political science. Political science students of the constitution have built up sophisticated expertise and extensive intellectual capital around the twin concerns of parliamentary government and federalism, the primary institutional components of the Canadian constitutional order since 1867. Both have attracted sympathetic scholarly attention from political scientists.[3]

The response of political scientists to the Charter and the courts, however, is much less developed, partly because of the recency of the 1982 Constitution Act. Also, historically, constitutional law has not enjoyed the prominence for political scientists in Canada that it has had for their American counterparts. Retooling, therefore, requires overcoming what Veblen called the trained incapacity of experts to respond to new challenges for which their expertise has diminished relevance. This is not just a matter of technical knowledge, but also of basic values. The mainstream political scientists' version of the biographers' disease of identifying with their subjects is to become committed to the defence of the institutions they have long and lovingly studied. Accordingly, a successful response to the prominent role of the Charter in the post-1982 constitutional order will require a move away from past attitudes.

Impressionistically, at least, political scientists displayed limited interest in, or empathy for, the unremitting federal government support for a charter from the late sixties to the Constitution Act 1982. In general, political scientists saw the constitutional issues of the sixties and seventies in terms of a resurgent government-led provincialism that had to be given a more expansive constitutional recognition. Such assumptions clearly lay behind the pioneering introduction of the intrastate federalism thesis into Canadian constitutional discourse by Donald Smiley in his seminal 1971 article.[4] The necessity of a positive response to dualism and regionalism advocated by the Task Force on Canadian Unity in the late seventies was informed by similar assumptions.[5]

An alternative reform posture, that provincialism/regionalism should be contested and that institutional engineering should aim at drawing Canadians out of provincial frames of reference by giving them enforceable pan-Canadian rights, and thus, national lens through which they could assess the performance of provincial political systems, had only limited support among political scientists. It was, however, central to federal government objectives, via the instrumentality of a Charter of Rights, through the entire Trudeau period. Thus, in general, political scientists and federal government practitioners of constitution-making did not share a common frame of reference in the Trudeau era. That disinclination to see the significance of a charter, and the related propensity to see Canada in terms of its territorial particularisms also accounts, I suspect, for the tepid reception of the Constitution Act 1982 by most political scientists, a response summed up in the volume appropriately titled *And No One Cheered.*[6]

While there may have been little cheering at the time, from the vantage point of 1988 it is evident that the Charter has not only elicited a broad basis of general support, but has also attracted the specific support of particular groups,—women's groups with S. 28, ethnic Canadians with S. 27, official language minorities with S. 23, aboriginals with S. 25 (and S. 91-24 of the BNA Act of 1867, plus S 35 of the Constitution Act 1982, and the now obsolete S. 37 with its requirement of constitutional conferences on aboriginal matters), and of those Canadians whose interests are encompassed in the various social categories listed in S. 15 (1) and (2) with their equality rights and affirmative action possibilities. Thus the 1982 Charter has positively linked many Canadians to the constitution and given them constitutional identities they formerly lacked. On the whole, however, these groups have received limited attention from political scientists who, possibly for that reason, appear to have underestimated the political significance of their constitutional recognition.

Also revealing of the political science perspective is the relatively positive political scientists' response to the Meech Lake Accord, which contrasts markedly with the responses of historians and law professors, both of whom have been much more critical of the Accord's ambiguities, its provincializing thrusts, its concern for governments, and its repudiation of the more open process of constitution-making of 1980-82.[7] Political scientists, by contrast, appear to support a highly federalist and governmental view of Canada that accords limited significance or credibility to the numerous groups that lack automatic government sponsorship— women, aboriginals, third force Canadians, visible minorities, official language minorities, and the numerous groups that cluster under the rubric of the various categories of S. 15 of the Charter. In these circumstances, the tendency of the federal government to strengthen the legitimacy of the Accord by citing supportive political scientists is not surprising. Eight of the twelve academics who signed a brief to the Special Joint Committee that was strongly supportive of Meech Lake were political scientists. They described themselves as a group "all of whom have devoted much of their professional careers to the study of Canadian federalism."[8] Another political scientist, Kenneth McRoberts, passionately defended the Accord on the ground that if it "accomplishes nothing else, at least it will establish once and for all that Canada is a federal country."[9]

Richard Simeon suggests that lawyers "anxious to cross every t and dot every i have generally been more critical of the Accord than have political scientists," because the latter "have more faith in political forces."[10] An alternative explanation would be that lawyers are less prone to collapse the constitution into its federalism component, and, partly because of a strong cadre of feminist women lawyers, treat both the Charter and the groups that support it with greater seriousness than do political scientists.

If this somewhat impressionistic assessment of the intellectual orientations of mainstream political science commentary over the past two decades is even approximately correct, there are good reasons to fear that political scientists will lose ground as constitutional analysts in the future. In the absence of a significant intellectual reorientation they will correctly come to be viewed as too wedded to institutional arrangements, such as federalism, of diminished constitutional importance.

This concern is strengthened when the qualitative changes in the relation of the post-1982 constitution to Canadian society are further explored. These changes go far beyond the stimulation on the one hand of a rights-bearing consciousness among the citizenry, and a rearrangement of the relative powers of various institutions of government on the other. They draw constitutional discourse into new themes of ethnicity, culture, race, and identity which, apart from the French-English cleavage, have historically attracted limited attention from political science students in Canada. The expansion of constitutional language to encompass new themes requires political scientists to modify their understanding of the constitution and its role in Canadian society. Much assistance is available in the pioneering work of the sociologist Raymond Breton on the state's management of ethnicity, partly by its manipulation of the symbolic order.[11]

The following section briefly notes the recent tension between competing views of the constitution, with particular reference to ethnicity.

From the Constitution Act 1982 to Meech Lake: What is the Constitution About?

The Constitution Act 1982, mainly by the vehicle of the Charter, has made the constitution the supreme instrument of social recognition in a society whose multiplying cleavages are not so much transcended as differentially included in its clauses. The 1982 Act is honeycombed with particular recognitions—women, aboriginals, official language minorities, third force Canadians and visible minorities under multiculturalism, and the disabled and others in the equality rights section.

These varied recognitions differ in their nature, in their probable policy consequences, and in their psychological significance to the groups they encompass. Further, these constitutional categories, which have been explored elsewhere,[12] are still in flux. They are viewed as temporary constitutional stopping points, rather than as settled equilibrium arrangements by the groups whose interests they reflect.

This instability is partly due to the recency of the Charter and partly to the constitutional developments that followed its introduction. Before these newly constitutionalized social categories had adjusted to their new status, and only two years after the coming into effect of the equality rights of S. 15 in 1985, the 1987 Meech Lake Accord aggravated the uncertainties derived from the previous bout of constitutional change.

The challenge that Meech Lake offered to the Constitution Act 1982 was not trivial but, as various authors have suggested,[13] was a powerful counter-attack to reinstate the dominance of governments, and to reassert the primacy of federalism, and to do so essentially from a provincial perspective. Meech Lake addressed Canadians largely in terms of their membership in national and provincial communities, especially the latter, rather than as aborigines, visible minorities, women, rights bearers, and related constitutional categories indifferent to federalism's spatial construction of communities. Further, by its processes Meech Lake clearly defined Canadians as subjects of an elite-government-dominated constitutional order rather than as citizen participants in its unfolding.

Both the implicitly asserted primacy of federalism and the explicit domination by governments of the levers of constitutional change, along with the constitutional theory behind them, confront a counter-constitutional discourse that stresses non-federal cleavages and a citizen role in constitutional change. This counter-discourse, like the official discourse of governments, displays a crude intellectual symmetry within its own framework of assumptions. As long as constitutional change can be defined as a response to problems of federalism the primacy of governments as constitutional change agents plausibly follows. Conversely, if governments do control the working of the amending formula they will rework the issues pressing for constitutional attention to make them compatible with their concerns as governments of the federal system.

On the other hand, if the issues on the constitutional agenda pertain to women, aboriginals, ethnic Canadians, and the disabled, for example, the appropriateness of involving spokespersons from the affected groups in modifying the constitution has considerable plausibility. Again, if these groups are involved they will try to structure the constitutional debate in terms of their concerns that display remarkably less sensitivity to federalism and its governments than the latter automatically bring to the constitutional bargaining table. Thus how the constitution is defined, as an affair of governments, of citizens, or both, is relevant to the decision of who should be allowed to participate in changing it. The converse is also true. Whoever controls constitutional change will pull the working definition of the constitution in the direction of their natural preferences.

Although women, aboriginals, official language minorities, and others have been defined as outsiders—as audience—by the processes of Meech Lake, they have explicit niches in the constitution. Their constitutional status, recognitions, and rights were typically achieved against the resistance or hostility of most governments,[14] and were sought because of their distrust of governments. Further, since it is not possible in major packages of constitutional change to sever the concerns of governments from those of other actors who enjoy a constitutional presence, it is scarcely surprising that Meech Lake has unleashed a challenge to official constitutional discourse, the examination of which tells us much about the constitutional disarray in which we find ourselves.

Amongst the various critical public reactions to Meech Lake in English Canada—from frustrated northern residents, from social policy activists, from women, from basic defenders of the Charter and supporters of the national community and its government—one of the most revealing comes from Canadians outside the privileged category of the two founding peoples. These ethnic critics of Meech Lake from traditional third force groups such as Ukrainians, newly prominent visible minorities, and from the various aboriginal communities contested definitions of Canada that privileged majorities, charter peoples, and community cleavages defined by federalism.

This ethnic/aboriginal discourse not only reveals pervasive disagreement with government definitions of community structured by federalism, but also underlines the extent to which the Canadian constitution is now embroiled in the tensions of an ethnically plural society. This discourse also confirms the enhanced role of the constitution, in the way so brilliantly described by Raymond Breton,[15] as an instrument of selective social recognition, engaged in fashioning and refashioning the Canadian symbolic order and differentially allocating official status to the multiplying ethnic diversities of a heterogeneous society. In general, it confirms that the constitution is now an arena within which competing ethnic and aboriginal Canadians battle for relative status vis-à-vis each other and with the two founding peoples privileged by past history and, even now, by the contemporary constitution.

This constitutional discourse grapples with issues of community and identity that are not reducible to federalist terminology. Nevertheless, it is now anchored in the constitution in the same way as constitutional controversies over preferred forms of federalism. As Canada becomes more multicultural and multiracial and the population of British and French descent continues to decline in relative strength, the impact of ethnicity on the theory and practice of the Canadian constitution can only increase.

The British background component of the Canadian population slipped below 50% in about 1940 and soon may drop below 40%. The French background component fell below 30% in the early 60s and is now nearing the 25% mark. By 1981 the 'other'—non-British and non-French—had passed the French component and is now nearly one third of the population. By the first half of the twenty-first century the 'other' could be the largest single element of the population.[16] Thus the evolution of Canadian society confirms William H. McNeill's assertion that polyethnicity is the norm in contemporary societies.[17]

The constitutional theory of the future will have to seek an intellectual rapport with the sociology of race and ethnicity. Put differently, constitutional scholars have to try and understand the reciprocal relations between the constitution and ethnicity—how on the one hand, the Canadian constitution has responded to ethnic (and linguistic) pluralism, and how on the other ethnicity is itself shaped and given meaning by the constitution. For those political scientists who have stressed class and regionalism as the most relevant or exciting cleavages, and have seldom strayed beyond the French-English dualism in their analysis of ethnicity this reorientation will not come easily.[18] In general, social scientists are much more likely to find virtue in class conflict than in ethnic conflict, partly because, "especially in the West, ethnic affiliations have been in disrepute, for deep ideological reasons," with the consequence that the study of ethnic relations was for long a "backwater of the social sciences."[19] Similar deficiencies exist in "Western political thought," which, according to Kenneth McRae, "in general has shown little understanding or respect for the cultural diversity of mankind and has made scant allowance for it as a possible concern of government."[20] An additional impediment to the requisite intellectual reorientation is suggested by my UBC colleague Robert Jackson, who observes that the question "What have constitutions to do with ethnicity?...is not asked as often as one would expect in today's world of pervasive ethnic awareness." He finds the reasons for this unfortunate weakness in the division of labour between legal theorists and social scientists, with the former typically neglecting ethnicity, and the latter devoting limited attention to jurisprudence concerns.[21]

A political scientist, perhaps especially one with an ethnically privileged WASP background, may fail to see the relevance of a constitutional discourse that focuses neither on federalism, parliamentary government, nor even rights, but seems more concerned with status, identity, recognition, dignity, etc. The constitutional language of ethnicity wielded by ethnic elites is emotional and passionate—a Mediterranean language—rather than calculating and instrumental. Its affinities are with such concepts as shame, envy, resentment, honour, and pride.

The overriding issue is how one's ethnic group is recognized and treated relative to other groups. It is a language haunted by comparison, driven by the ubiquitous fear that one has lost, or might lose, constitutional ground relative to some other group. In an odd way it is like a court language in which the processes of constitutional change are the contemporary equivalent of a dyspeptic monarch who might unpredictably cast a jaundiced royal eye on a formerly favoured courtier.

The next section of this paper will illustrate the constitutional language of ethnicity by sampling the responses of representatives of various ethnic groups and aboriginal Canadians who feared a relative loss of status occasioned by the distinct society and linguistic duality clauses of Meech Lake. If space allowed, similar examples could easily be taken from women's groups and official language minorities who also saw Meech Lake as weakening their recently-won constitutional status.

Meech Lake, Ethnicity and the Constitution[22]

The Accord's portrayal of Canada is unacceptable to ethnic and aboriginal Canadians. To the Inuit the prominence given to French- and English-speaking Canadians, whose existence is a "fundamental characteristic of Canada," "continues to be an insult."[23] To the President of the Makivik Corporation the apparent move from multiculturalism to biculturalism is "offensive and insulting to the fact that we [Inuit] are not being recognized as being contributing members to this country." The failure to give "the Inuit and the aboriginal people...the same level of recognition we find to be stating a falsehood into the Constitution."[24]

Not surprisingly, aboriginal groups assert that historical priority, in which they ranked first, and which is the logic behind their self-descriptive label as 'First Nations,' should be the central factor in determining constitutional ranking. Indigenousness, as Horowitz notes, is "by far the most common claim to legitimacy."[25] Aboriginal advocates are particularly upset at the recognition of Quebec as a distinct society when they see that their own much greater distinctiveness with deeper historical roots that, according to one Yukon Chief, go "back to before Christ and [are] synonymous with the great flood of the world,"[26] is not recognized. John Amagoalik, Co-Chairman of the Inuit Committee on National Issues, repudiated the status of French and English as founding nations on the grounds that "My ancestors occupied this land when the Mulroneys and the Bourassas and Vander Zalms of this world were still living in caves in Europe."[27]

Aboriginal frustrations are fostered by the fact that the conceptual fuzziness that was a barrier to the constitutional recognition of aboriginal self-government was not a barrier to constitutionalizing the vague distinct society concept,[28] whose lack of definition is defended as a virtue by Premier Robert Bourassa of Quebec. Some aboriginal leaders also suspect that the raising of the barriers to province-hood in the north is partly explained as an act of discrimination against the majority native population in the Northwest Territories.[29] Further, status Indians, with their special link with the federal government, are concerned that, whenever the federal government is weakened, their own influence diminishes.[30]

The aboriginal position is effectively summed up by George Erasmus of the Assembly of First Nations with his criticism that the distinct society "perpetuates the idea of a duality in Canada, and strengthens the myth that the French and the English peoples are the foundation of Canada. It neglects the original inhabitants and distorts history. It is as if the peoples of the First Nations never existed... If anyone is more distinct, surely it is the peoples of the First Nations."[31]

For those Canadians who can claim no founding status the stress on priority of arrival as the basis for contemporary ranking is unacceptable. They seek to deny the truth in the jest that "the definition of a Canadian is an immigrant with seniority."[32] To

Liberal MPs Charles Caccia and Sergio Marchi the Accord is a voice from the past, "a rear-view mirror vision which may have been valid two generations ago,"[33] an "outdated [definition of Canada]...primarily satisfied with only depicting our people's past and our country's history."[34] "Millions of Canadians are left out who do not identify with either French or English. They have no place in the Accord, and they are outside the Constitution."[35] In Marchi's words, "not all the people of this country have been dealt the same constitutional card, nor have they been equally credited with being a dignified and contributing part of this country..."[36]

The Ukrainians cannot support a constitution "whose underlying rationale is the outdated and discredited concept of two founding nations."[37] The Canadian Institute of Minority Rights asserts the inappropriateness of giving constitutional recognition to "societal concepts dictated by 19th century realities..." in the "increasingly pluralistic and multicultural society" of Canada.[38] The brief of the National Association of Canadians of Origins in India asserts that the use of the Constitution to single out and rank Canadians is wrong in principle and divisive in practice. A preferred strategy would be for the Constitution to "regard all persons, regardless of their cultural, linguistic, racial, or political background, as Canadians, and other definitions should be discarded."[39]

The protection of S. 27 of the Charter from the interpretation clause of the Accord by S. 16 of the latter[40] does not mollify third force Canadians. They see an unacceptable distinction in the fact that S. 27 applies only to the Charter, in contrast to the Accord's requirements that "the Constitution of Canada" is to be interpreted consistent with linguistic duality and Quebec as a distinct society.[41] Accordingly, this invidious distinction that seems to weaken multiculturalism relative to linguistic dualism should be rectified by adding multiculturalism as a fundamental characteristic of Canada.[42]

For the ethnic and aboriginal minorities who feel left out by Meech Lake the latter's provisions are experienced as a sense of loss, of status deprivation, of non-recognition, of being rebuffed. For the Ukrainian Canadian Committee, "if there are groups within society that are alienated and do not feel represented by the Constitution, they will have less respect and affection for that Constitution. That is the way we feel, that we are being abandoned."[43] To the Ontario Black Coalition, the "overt recognition of English and French and the non-recognition of all the other groups, including large numbers of blacks, seems to be a denial of our existence on the part of Canada."[44]

For the NDP MP Howard McCurdy, the Accord's message "to a third of the population—the blacks, the Ukrainians, the Poles, the Italians,...and the variety of other people who compose my riding—[is] that they are not really an inherent part of the country. There is still the recognition inherent in all that has happened that there is some primacy to the two founding people. As long as that message is maintained, the country cannot be whole...it implies that those of us who are neither English nor French are not really a part... It is unacceptable to me and all others...that we should in any way be considered as second class citizens...those of us who are neither French nor English [must] be welcomed into the Constitution."[45]

For the liberal MP Charles Caccia, "a constitution must include all members of society, rather than putting some in and leaving some out... Let us not drift with the divisive notion that some are members of a founding group and some are not."[46] For Sergio Marchi, what is the Government "to say to those Canadians whose origins are neither English nor French, and who feel the isolation of being left out? I am one of those Canadians, and I do not feel, according to Section 1 (sic), that I am as constitutionally relevant as my French Canadian or English Canadian colleagues in this House of Commons, for instance. I do not accept that while they can be recognized in Section 1, I must accept to be in Section 16 at the very end of the Accord..."[47]

For Louis 'Smokey' Bruyère, President of the Native Council of Canada, the Accord "promotes a view of reality that ignores the first founding people of Canada—the aboriginal peoples. It provides a vision of the future in which aboriginal peoples cannot hope to share...it completely ignores aboriginal peoples and their place in the existing constitutional order. In that sense, it totally misstates Canada as it is. It takes us back to a myth of 120 years ago that the fundamental character of Canada is of the French and the English."[48] Spokespersons for the Nishnawbe-Aski Nation lamented that "we are the first nations of this country and we have been left out of Meech Lake. They do not want us...It is our land and resources that built your country."[49]

The purpose of the preceding few pages in this section, that may appear to be a tedious litany of repetitive emotional outbursts, is to underscore the pervasive nature of ethnic and aboriginal constitutional grievances, and to indicate the existence of an admittedly inchoate but not formless style of constitutional discourse. The following section attempts to draw out some of the salient characteristics of ethnic and aboriginal constitutional discourse in Canada.

The Nature of Ethnic Constitutional Discourse

These ethnic grievances, which could be multiplied many times over, and which with suitable modifications could be supplemented by similar protestations by women, official language minorities, and northerners, as well as by basic Charter defenders, graphically reveal the many constituencies outside of governments that now see themselves in constitutional terms. They all accept the basic proposition that the constitution is now the crucial instrument for defining one's place in Canadian society. The constitution is seen as making an official statement of who counts, and for how much, and in what ways in Canadian society.

This ethnic and aboriginal minority constitutional discourse has the following salient characteristics:

1. It is predominantly a non-official discourse. Indeed, in the Meech Lake process it is explicitly an anti-official discourse that overtly challenges the legitimacy of an elite-dominated executive federalism as the instrument of constitutional change as well as the government-sensitive outcomes to which it leads. Ethnic and aboriginal groups do not trust the elected leaders of government to deal fairly with them when the constitution is on the agenda and they are not present.

2. They are not, however, complete outsiders. They have constitutional identities. They occupy niches in the constitution, and often think of particular clauses as specifically theirs, clauses whose presence and wording in the constitution is the result of past battles successfully fought. Thus they think of themselves as legitimate constitutional actors. Their situation is not the same as status Indians who were treated as wards before receiving the vote in 1960, or gays and lesbians excluded from explicit inclusion in S. 15 of the Charter. Although their discourse is non-official, it is grounded in the constitution.

3. Their agenda is to protect or strengthen the constitutional recognition of their members. They clearly view the

constitution as a vehicle for the enhancement (and loss) of status. Indeed, their distrust of majorities and their perception that only rarely do they have the ear of government make them especially dependent on the constitution as a lever.

4. They do not view the constitution as fixed or stable, but as highly mutable. This belief is a product of the recency of the Constitution Act 1982, followed three years later in 1985 with the implementation of the S. 15 equality provisions of the Charter, in turn followed shortly after by the Meech Lake Accord. These developments coincided with a series of high profile, but ultimately unsuccessful, aboriginal constitutional conferences. The previous history of tentative constitutional recognition and rebuffs of ethnic groups and aboriginals in the 1980-82 constitutional exercise, allied with their success in extracting the protections of S. 16 of the Accord by a frantic application of pressure, undoubtedly leads them to view the process of constitutional development as whimsy moderated intermittently by ad hoc political pressure.

5. Their language is often highly emotional. It is the language of shame, pride, dignity, insult, inclusion or exclusion, humiliation or recognition. Their concerns are not narrowly instrumental. Recognition of constitutional status seems to be sought for its own sake, rather than for what tangible benefits might be expected to flow from it. Raymond Breton has described how the policy of multiculturalism evolved to quell the status anxieties of the non-British, non-French element that the language of Charter groups, two nations, and biculturalism would lead to their marginalization.[50] Meech Lake generates similar tensions with the basic difference that the ethnic and aboriginal communities are now larger, more diversified, better organized, and can wield constitutional clauses in their self-defence.

6. Ethnic and aboriginal constitutional discourse employs multiple criteria in the making of claims, unfailingly in the self-interest of the advocate, ranging from claims for special recognition based on historical priority of arrival to egalitarian denials of any form of special status as

inimical to a common citizenship.

An alternative strategy to challenging the criteria employed by ethnic rivals is to make claims in terms of criteria that might initially be thought to be more applicable to other ethnicities. Thus the Ukrainian Community Development Committee (Prairie Region) has pleaded for "a concept of founding peoples that is more elastic," and capable of including the Ukrainians as a "founding settler people in the Prairie provinces" whose forefathers settled on lands that "had hardly felt the hand of man before...[and]...were open and sparsely populated by natives."[51] A functionally similar claim is made by the Ontario Black Coalition in the statement that "Black people have been a part of Canadian history since approximately 1600. Historians have downgraded or completely ignored the facts about blacks in Canada."[52]

7. An emerging distinction that will grow more important in the light of anticipated demographic change is between visible minorities and the older, more traditional European groups outside of the French-English duality. S. 27, with its reference to the preservation and enhancement of the multicultural heritage of Canadians, is of more significance to the latter, while the former, especially those of lower status, see Canada through a multiracial rather than multicultural lens. For them, S. 15 is of more significance and their goals are less those of cultural protection than of equal treatment or positive discrimination. As their numbers grow to an anticipated 10% of the Canadian population by the turn of the century,[53] excluding aboriginals, the two groups will probably diverge in their constitutional demands. The older European groups will maintain their concern with the expressive dimension of ethnicity and cultural recognition, while the newer visible minorities will be motivated by more instrumental concerns of economic advancement and race relations issues. As Daiva Stasiulis observed, the 1981 establishment of a Race Relations Unit within the Multiculturalism Directorate was a response to "the increased proportion of non-white immigrants from Third World countries for whom the major substantive concerns—such as securing employment, and seeking protection from racial harassment, discrimination and

inequality—diverge from the cultural and linguistic priorities of European groups whose political pressures were operative during the initial development of the Multicultural policy. In addition, these 'visible minority' groups began to voice their own status anxieties over the symbolism of a multicultural Canada which was not also conceived as multiracial."[54]

8. An anomalous characteristic of the constitutional language of ethnicity is the relative absence of unofficial voices from the big battalions of the two linguistic majority communities of francophones and anglophones. As majority communities in Quebec and Canada respectively, their concerns are normally incorporated in the objectives of the governments they control. The unofficial anglophone voice comes from the English minority in Quebec and the unofficial francophone voice from French-speaking minorities outside of Quebec, neither of whom, with the possible exception of the Acadians in New Brunswick, see their provincial governments as allies.[55] This asymmetrical participation damages the quality of the debate.

9. Organizational fluidity occasionally precipitates battles over which organization is the proper representative of a constituency with a constitutional identity. Organizational competition is especially evident for aboriginals whose concerns are ill-served by the cacophony of dissimilar peoples grouped under the aboriginal rubric.[56] If Meech Lake is ratified and constitutional discussions take place on an annual basis, and there is meaningful public involvement, the state will acquire an interest in the representativeness of the various elites that claim to speak for particular communities/constituencies. Federal funding may facilitate the employment of selective inducements.

10. The constitutional language of ethnicity is still in its infancy, somewhat rudimentary and dominated by the various ethnic claimants seeking to protect or improve their constitutional recognition. The ethnic and aboriginal population from which it derives only recently attained the visibility, heterogeneity, numerical strength, organizational infrastructure, and self-confidence that

now command constitutional attention. The very labels under which the competing groups vie for status are often of recent vintage—Inuit, Dene, visible minorities, third force, and first nations. Their proliferation indicates the complexity of Canada outside of the Charter peoples, and the search for status-giving identities.

In its early stages this language suffers from two fundamental weaknesses. It is a centrifugal language more successful in capturing our separate ethnic selves than in addressing our common membership in a single polity by a contemporary theory of citizenship appropriate to our linguistic, multicultural and multiracial composition in the era of the Charter. No less demanding than the construction of the latter is the necessity of developing a composite constitutional discourse that simultaneously captures the territorial dimensions of national and provincial communities fostered by federalism and the growing racial and ethnic diversities within them. At the moment, these two languages of community and identity, one sponsored by federalism and the other largely by the Charter, appear more as rivals than as complementary versions of the same phenomena viewed from alternative perspectives.

Conclusion

Constitutions and ethnicity are locked in an inescapable interdependence. The full meaning of each depends on an intimate understanding of the other. To Lord Durham constitutional engineering was to be directed to the assimilation of the backward French-Canadian population. To the subsequent generation of statesmen escape from the French-English impasse under the Act of Union required a resort to federalism which would minimize ethnic conflict by its principle that fences make good neighbours. The other half of the Confederation agreement, however, parliamentary responsible government, confirmed the British political heritage of the colonists, captured in the preamble to the BNA Act in the phrase "a Constitution similar in Principle to that of the United Kingdom." The British cast of the constitution was reflected in parliamentary supremacy, and allegiance to the Crown, the 'Mother' country, and the Empire.

The other explicit link between ethnicity and the constitution was S.91 (24), which gave legislative authority over 'Indians, and

Lands reserved for the Indians' to the federal parliament. That grant of authority and the policies based on it gave status Indians a uniquely intimate relationship with the federal government, a suspicion of the provinces, and a political identity that separated them from other peoples of aboriginal descent who lacked explicit constitutional recognition.

Various developments in the decades that followed World War II upset the ethnic constitutional equilibrium that had functioned tolerably well for three-quarters of a century. A simple listing, which is all that space limitations allow, underlines the magnitude of the ethnic challenges even if it does little justice to their complexity: the emergence of an independence-seeking Quebec nationalism that challenged the survival of the Canadian state; the emergence of the aboriginal peoples as political actors with distinct political and constitutional demands; the emergence of the third force of white ethnics outside of the French and English founding peoples as a political constituency that resisted the second class citizen status that it feared was a byproduct of the attempt to define Canada in terms of French-English dualism; and the numerical growth and enhanced political profile of visible minorities that emerged in response to more liberal immigration requirements.

These domestic developments in ethnic demography and political demands were stimulated by various international trends. The crumbling of the great European empires destroyed the legitimacy of ideas of racial hierarchies on which they had rested and stimulated ethnic consciousness and sub-state nationalism within western states. The intellectual legacy of World War II included a renewed search for mechanisms to protect citizen rights and, with the strong backing of the United Nations, not only stimulated a rights consciousness that swept across national borders but also fostered support for entrenched judicially enforced Charters as instruments for their protection. In Canada this climate of assumptions chipped away at the principle of parliamentary supremacy at a time when, for many additional reasons, the United Kingdom was receding in importance for Canadians. For Canada the retreat of imperial Britain was accompanied by the transformation of Empire into a multi-racial and multiethnic Commonwealth. The desire of successive Canadian governments to play a leading role in the Commonwealth, partly to give Canadians a prominence in an arena in which the United States could not participate, contributed to the more open immigration policy that changed the ethnic and racial composition of Canadian society.

For many students the central challenge to the constitutional order that emerged from World War II has been the accommodation and containment of wide-spread centrifugal pressures which were strongest in, but not confined, to Quebec. The response to dualism and regionalism, which sometimes took the form of a combative pan-Canadian nationalism, is undeniably the dominant theme of recent decades. Its centrality in our collective self-analysis reflects its status as the traditional fare of a century-old federalism, and the dominance by governments of the constitutional agenda.

For political scientists who study governments the focus on federalism, dualism, regionalism, province-building, and similar subject matter appears natural, almost inevitable. Indeed, if such a disciplinary focus did not exist we would need to invent it for it clearly reflects realities that require constant analysis and attention.

However, the Canadian people, their governments, and the constitution have simultaneously been responding to the ethnic and racial transformation of the Canadian population which, as noted earlier in this paper, has markedly reduced the proportion of the population of French and British background, and politicized those of other backgrounds. These demographic facts, in conjunction with the international phenomena identified above, are the social base and intellectual currents that lie behind a succession of state responses to accommodate and incorporate the galloping ethnic and racial diversities that have emerged in the past half-century. These responses include the post-war extension of the franchise to formerly excluded groups; the pan-Canadianism that lay behind the Diefenbaker Bill of Rights; the defeated assimilationist thrust of the 1969 policy paper on Indians; the changed immigration requirements of the sixties; the 1971 policy of multiculturalism; Quebec language policies to channel immigrants into the French-speaking community; the development of human rights commissions and codes at both federal and provincial levels; and the Constitution Act 1982 with its clauses pertaining to aboriginals, to multiculturalism, and to 'race, national or ethnic origins, [and] colour...' These examples of a broad current of policy emanating from both orders of government are not issues of federalism as such, but rather of our response to who we are as a people.

Meech Lake with its distinct society and distinct identity clauses, its statement 'that the existence of French-speaking Canadians, centred in Quebec but also present elsewhere in Canada, and English-speaking Canadians, concentrated outside Quebec but also present in Quebec, constitutes a fundamental characteristic of Canada,' its immigration provisions, and its S.16 protection for aboriginal peoples and Canadians' multicultural heritage, is the most recent constitutional response to the changed composition of Canadian society. As shown earlier, third force, visible minority, and aboriginal Canadians oppose what they see as a constitutional package that reasserts the primacy of governments, of majorities, and of founding peoples. They define Meech Lake as speaking to the Canada of yesterday. They share the apprehensions of Dean John Whyte of Queen's Law Faculty that

> constitutional changes in our present age that do not strive to express the worth of cultural diversity fail to perform one of the chief roles of a Constitution—the expression of a social vision, even a utopian social vision. In Meech Lake we have let this opportunity for visioning our future fall prey to the frantic process of recapturing our past."[57]

Constitutions are always in transition. The society that they shape and that shapes them is continuously transformed by socio-economic pressures emanating from the domestic and international environments. The necessary adaptation of the constitution to these new pressures is inevitably constrained by the bias of past arrangements and the historic values embedded in them. These constraints operate in intellectual communities as well as in the mentalities and behaviours of governing elites. To an earlier generation of English-Canadian political scientists responsible parliamentary government was the revered centrepiece of the Canadian constitutional tradition. For Brady and Dawson the British heritage was central and positive, an orientation that, especially for the latter, distracted attention from the French fact in Canada and from the significance of federalism for its accommodation.

By contrast, federalism became the leading institutional focus for the next generation of political scientists. Further, as the popularity of the province-building rubric suggested, federalism lost many of the negative connotations it had acquired in the thirties' depression as a barrier to central government leadership, and as a constraint on the development of the national community. While this disciplinary orientation was an understandable response to the centrifugal pressures emanating from Quebec and elsewhere, and also to the trauma of constitutional introspection to which they led, it is the argument of this paper that students of the constitution should now recognize the diminished significance of federalism in the constitutional order, and the emerging role of the constitution, especially the Charter, in responding to ethnicities other than French and English.

The Charter is not a minor addition to the Canadian constitutional system, but a profound wrenching transformation. It elevates the constitution as a whole to a level of symbolic and practical significance far surpassing its previous status as an instrument of governance. It brings new groups into the Canadian constitutional order and gives them constitutional identities. And from the perspective of this paper it generates a vigorous constitutional discourse responsive to aboriginal Canadians, visible minorities, and white ethnics who are not linked to the communities which did battle more than two centuries ago on the Plains of Abraham.

The constitution is not the only arena within which our ethnic, aboriginal, and other diversities jostle for recognition and power. Further, it is in part a historical accident—a byproduct of the salience of the constitutional issue originally directed to concerns arising from dualism and federalism—that the constitution has become so intimately connected to those aspects of Canadians' ethnic composition that transcend French-English dualism. However, now that the constitutional connection has been made its repudiation is impossible.

"Ethnic conflict," as Donald Horowitz observes, "is, at bottom, a matter of comparison."[58] In the Canadian case the use of the constitution to allocate ethnic status greatly facilitates and stimulates comparison because its categories are so public and so heavily freighted with symbolic meaning. What was formerly implicit, and hence somewhat indeterminate and supportive of coexisting conflicting interpretations that did not confront each other, is now explicit. The constitution thus reinforces ethnic consciousness in a society whose ethnic and racial heterogeneity can only increase.

The desire for ethnic identification with and inclusion in the polity "derives...from a quite general urge to be in harmony with one's surroundings, to belong in a territory, to be comfortable and at home."[59] In Canada the constitution has become a key instrument for the attainment of these objectives. Success, however, has been only relative. Elliot Tepper is correct in his prediction that a new definition of Canada will be required for the twenty-first century. "Canada tomorrow will be more than a country with no single majority. *It will be a country where no group is a dominant plurality*...The task of politics is to keep the definition of nationality related to the actual composition of the nation. It is time now to prepare for a more pluralistic future."[60]

Notes

1. Donald L. Horowitz, *Ethnic Groups in Conflict* (Berkeley: University of California Press, 1985), 185.

2. Throughout this paper my references to political science are restricted to political science in English Canada. Their applicability to political science in the francophone Quebec community is an open question.

3. In the depression of the 30s, of course, many English Canadian scholars were highly critical of the constraints federalism placed on the central government, while more recently Quebec scholars have been critical of the constraints it put on Quebec nationalism.

4. Donald Smiley, "The Structural Problem of Canadian Federalism," *Canadian Public Administration*, 14 (Fall, 1971).

5. Canada, Task Force on Canadian Unity, *A Future Together: Observations and Recommendations* (Ottawa: Supply and Services Canada, 1979).

6. Keith Banting and Richard Simeon, eds., *And No One Cheered: Federalism, Democracy and the Constitution Act* (Toronto: Methuen, 1983).

7. See, for example, Ramsay Cook, "Alice in Meachland or the Concept of Quebec as 'A Distinct Society'," and John D. Whyte, "Submission to the Special Joint Committee of the Senate and the House of Commons on the 1987 Constitutional Accord," both in *Queen's Quarterly*, 94 (Winter, 1987), and Bryan Schwartz, *Fathoming Meech Lake* (Winnipeg: Legal Research Institute, University of Manitoba, 1987).

8. Ron Watts, *et al.*, to the Special Joint Committee on the 1987 Constitutional Accord, 22 July 1987.

9. Kenneth McRoberts, "The Case for Meech Lake," *The Canadian Forum* (December, 1987), 13. In marked contrast, the masthead of the Canadian Coalition on the Constitution, the organized focus of opposition to the Accord, which lists 68 names, about one-third of whom are academics, has

only three that I recognize as political scientists. Other political scientists who have serious reservations about the Accord are Roger Gibbins, Al Johnson, Orest Kruhlak, and the author of this article.

10. Richard Simeon, "Meech Lake and Shifting Conceptions of Canadian Federalism," *Canadian Public Policy*, 14, Supplement (1988), S-24.

11. Raymond Breton, "The Production and Allocation of Symbolic Resources: An Analysis of the Linguistic and Ethnocultural Fields in Canada," *Canadian Review of Sociology and Anthropology*, 21 (2) (1984).

12. Alan C. Cairns, "Citizens (Outsiders) and Governments (Insiders) in Constitution-Making: The Case of Meech Lake,", *Canadian Public Policy*, 14, Supplement (1988).

13. See in particular Katherine Swinton, "Competing Visions of Constitutionalism: Of Federalism and Rights," and John D. Whyte, "The 1987 Constitutional Accord and Ethnic Accommodation," both in Katherine E. Swinton and Carol J. Rogerson, eds., *Competing Constitutional Visions: The Meech Lake Accord* (Toronto: Carswell, 1988).

14. The protection of minority language education rights, of course, was the centrepiece of the federal government's constitutional goals.

15. Breton, "Production and Allocation of Symbolic Resources."

16. Elliot L. Tepper, "Demographic Change and Pluralism." Paper presented to the Conference on Canada 2000: Race Relations and Public Policy, October 30-Nov. 1, 1987, Carleton University, Ottawa,. mimeo, 6.

17. Wm. H. McNeill, *Polyethnicity and National Unity in World History* (Toronto: University of Toronto Press, 1986).

18. "Thus far the study of multiculturalism has been pursued mainly by sociologists, anthropologists, and historians. Other social scientists such as political scientists have largely ignored the area." Gilbert Scott, Director General, Multiculturalism, Department of Secretary of State, "Race Relations and Public Policy—Uncharted Course," June 8, 1987, mimeo, 3. Howard Palmer also asserts that "Political historians and political scientists in Canada have shown very little interest in ethnic relations, other than their concern with the all-pervasive question of conflict and accommodation between English and French." "Canadian Immigration and Ethnic History in the 1970s and 1980s," *Journal of Canadian Studies*, 17 (Spring, 1982), 45. There are some exceptions—the work of Freda Hawkins and Gerry Dirks on immigration and refugee policy respectively, and John Wood and Elliot Tepper on East Indians and South East Asians in Canada. See also the impressive early work by the University of British Columbia political scientist J. A. Laponce, *The Protection of Minorities* (Berkeley and Los Angeles: University of California Press, 1960). See also John Solomos, "Trends in the Political Analysis of Racism," *Political Studies*, 34 (June, 1986), 313-24, for the limited contributions of British political scientists to the analysis of racism, compared to the contributions of sociologists and anthropologists.

19. Horowitz, *Ethnic Groups in Conflict*, 13.

20. Kenneth D. McRae, "The Plural Society and the Western Political Tradition," *Canadian Journal of Political Science*, 12 (December, 1979), 685.

21. Robert H. Jackson, "Jurisprudence and Multi-Ethnic States," delivered at the International Congress of Anthropological and Ethnographic Sciences, Zagreb, Yugoslavia, 24-31 July, 1988, mimeo, 2-3.

22. Several of the quotations used in this section are also cited and discussed in Cairns, "Citizens (Outsiders) and Governments (Insiders) in Constitution-Making."

23. Zebedee Nungak (Co-Chairman, Inuit Committee on National Issues), *Minutes of Proceedings and Evidence of the Special Joint Committee of the Senate and of the House of Commons on the 1987 Constitutional Accord*, No. 3, Aug. 5, 1987, 28 (Cited hereafter as *Special Joint Committee*).

24. *Special Joint Committee*, No. 14, Aug. 27, 1987, 26.

25. Horowitz, *Ethnic Groups in Conflict*, 202.

26. Chief Hammond Dick, Senate of Canada, *Proceedings of the Senate Task Force on the Meech Lake Constitutional Accord and on the Yukon and the Northwest Territories*, No. 1, Sept. 3, Oct. 24 and Oct. 25, 1987, 96. (Cited hereafter as *Senate Task Force on...Territories*); Chief Charles K. Shawkence of the Chippewa informed the Ontario Select Committee that "we have been here at the very minimum of 10,000 years, and in the Ohio valley, at least 20,000 years." *(Ontario) Select Committee on Constitutional Reform 1987 Constitutional Accord*, Feb. 25. 1988, afternoon sitting, draft transcript, C-71. (Cited hereafter as *Ontario Select Committee*).

27. *Senate Task Force on...Territories*, No. 3, Nov. 2, 1987, 32.

28. Zebedee Nungak, *Special Joint Committee*, No. 3, Aug. 5, 1987, 30; and Ernie Daniels, Interim President, Prairie Treaty Nations' Alliance, *Debates of the Senate*, Dec. 16, 1987, 2458.

29. Hon. Stephen Kakfwi, *Ontario Select Committee*, Feb. 16, 1988, morning sitting, C-19.

30 Gregg Smith, President, Indian Association of Alberta, *Proceedings of the Senate Submissions Group on the Meech Lake Constitutional Accord*, No. 4, March 15, 16, 1988, 26. (Cited hereafter as *Senate Submissions Group*); Bill Cachagee (Chairperson Wabun Tribal Councils), *Ontario Select Committee*, March 7, 1988, C-12; Chief Gordon Peters, *Ontario Select Committee*, Feb. 17, 1988, Afternoon sitting, C-65; Harry Doxtator (President, Association of Iroquois and Allied Indians), *Ontario Select Committee*, Feb. 18, 1988, morning sitting, C-7; Chief R. K. Miskokomon (Union of Ontario Indians), *Ontario Select Committee*, Feb. 18, 1988, afternoon sitting, C-23.

31. *Special Joint Committee*, No. 9, Aug. 19, 1987, 50. See also Louis 'Smokey' Bruyère (President, The Native Council of Canada), *Debates of the Senate*, Dec. 2, 1987, 2258. See the *Report of the Task Force to the Committee of the Whole, Senate of Canada*, February, 1988, Chap. 6, for the recommendation that the Meech Lake Accord should also recognize "that the aboriginal peoples of Canada constitute distinct societies." 23. However, not all aboriginals seek recognition as distinct societies. The Legal Counsel for the Four Nations of Hobbema argued that to put the distinct society label on the Indian people would be doing an injustice, for "a distinct society connotes something domestic, something within Canadian Confederation. This does not describe adequately what we as Indian people are. We, the Four Nations of Hobbema, are nations, a people in the international usage of the word...We have our own unique culture, language, government, and political affiliations, and our own land. We are more than a distinct society, and to classify us as a distinct society would be to derogate and/or abrogate our right to self-determination." *Senate Submissions Group*. No. 5, March 18, 1988, 63. See also

Chief Gordon Peters (Chiefs of Ontario,) *Ontario Select Committee*, Feb. 17, 1988, afternoon sitting, C-72.

32. Dr. Louis Melosky (National Director, Canadian Multiculturalism Council), *House of Commons, Minutes of Proceedings and Evidence of the Standing Committee on Multiculturalism*, No. 4, Feb. 4, Feb. 26, March 4, 1986, 13.

33. Charles Caccia, *House of Commons Debates*, Sept. 30, 1987, 9508.

34. Sergio Marchi, *House of Commons Debates*, Oct. 6, 1987, 9743.

35. Charles Caccia, *House of Commons Debates*, Sept. 30, 1987, 9508.

36. Sergio Marchi, *House of Commons Debates*, Oct. 6, 1987, 9743.

37. Thor Broda (Vice-President, National Executive, Ukrainian Canadian Committee), *Special Joint Committee*, No. 7, Aug. 13, 1987, 100.

38. Arthur Heiss (Co-President, Canadian Institute on Minority Rights), *Special Joint Committee*, No. 12, Aug. 25, 1987, 22. See also the brief of the Canadian Ethnocultural Council, *Special Joint Committee*, No. 7, Aug. 13, 1987, 41-61, and of the German Canadian Congress, *Special Joint Committee*, No. 7, Aug. 13, 1987, 70-80, and Council of Christian Reformed Churches in Canada, *Special Joint Committee*, No. 8, Aug. 18, 1987, 105.

39. Tej Pal S. Thind (National Secretary, National Association of Canadians of Origins in India), *Special Joint Committee*, No. 7, Aug. 13, 1987, 82.

40. Nothing in Section 2 of the Constitution Act 1867, affects section 25 or 27 of the Canadian Charter of Rights and Freedoms, section 35 of the Constitution Act 1982, or class 24 of section 91 of the Constitution Act 1867.

41. Andrew Cardozo (Executive Director, Canadian Ethnocultural Council), *Special Joint Committee*, No. 7, Aug. 13, 1987, 52; Dieter Kiesewalter (Executive Member, German-Canadian Congress) *Special Joint Committee*, No. 7, Aug. 13, 1987, 72.

42. National Congress of Italian Canadians, *Ontario Select Committee*, Feb. 17, 1988, morning sitting, C-22; Canadian Ethnocultural Council, *Special Joint Committee*, No. 7, Aug. 13, 1987, 42. Spokespersons for virtually all ethnic groups made this demand in all the arenas available to them.

43. Thor Broda (Vice-President, National Executive, Ukrainian Canadian Committee), *Special Joint Committee*, No. 7, Aug. 13, 1987, 103.

44. Roy Williams (President, Ontario Black Coalition for Employment Equity), Senate Submissions Group, No. 3, March 4, 1988, 108.

45. Howard McCurdy, *House of Commons Debates*, Oct. 2, 1987, 9619.

46. Charles Caccia, *Debates of the Senate*, Nov. 4, 1987, 2139.

47. Sergio Marchi, *House of Commons Debates*, Oct. 6, 1987, 9743. See also the presentations of the Canadian Multilingual Press Federation in the *Ontario Select Committee*, Feb. 22, 1988, C-15—C-30 and in the *Minutes of Proceedings and Evidence of the Standing Committee on Multiculturalism*, No. 11, Dec. 7-8, 1987, 26-41.

48. Louis 'Smokey' Bruyère, *Special Joint Committee*, No. 12, Aug. 25, 1987, 95-6.

49. Deputy Grand Chief, Lindbergh Louttit (Nishnawbe-Aski Nation), *Ontario Select Committee*, March 7, 1988, C-14.

50. "Production and Allocation of Symbolic Resources," 134.

51. Ukrainian Community Development Committee, *Building the Future: Ukrainian Canadians in the 21st Century* (Edmonton: Report to the Canadian Ukrainian Committee, 1986), 5, 24.

52. Roy Williams (President, Ontario Black Coalition for Employment Equity), *Senate Submissions Group*, No. 3, March 4, 1988, 108.

53. T. John Samuel, "Immigration, Visible Minorities and the Labour Force in Canada: Vision 2000," Paper presented at the Conference on Canada 2000: Race Relations and Public Policy, October 30-November 1, 1987, Carleton University, Ottawa, mimeo, 7.

54. Daiva K. Stasiulis, "The Antinomies of Federal Multiculturalism Policy and Official Practices," paper presented at the International Symposium on Cultural Pluralism, Montreal, October 19-20, 1985, mimeo, 13. As Jean Burnet wrote in 1983, many new Canadians of non-European background "joined the Native peoples, now urbanizing, and earlier Asian and Black arrivals to constitute visible minorities far larger than Canada has been accustomed to. For them, the problems of learning English or French or maintaining ancestral languages and cultures is far outweighed by the problem of winning the right to be treated like everyone else by judges, policemen, teachers, employers, landlords, neighbours, and fellow passengers in buses and subways," Secretary of State of Canada, *Multiculturalism ...Bing Canadian* (Ottawa: Supply and Services, 1987), 14. See also Dr. Harish C. Jain, *Minutes of Proceedings and Evidence of the Standing Committee on Multiculturalism*, No. 6, May 26, 1987, 18; the evidence of Jean Gammage (Vice-President, Urban Alliance on Race Relations), *Minutes of Proceedings and Evidence of the Standing Committee on Multiculturalism*, No. 10, Dec. 7, 1987, 41-56; and John Cordice (Chairman, Research and Education Committee, Ontario Black Coalition for Employment Equity), *Minutes of Proceedings and Evidence of the Standing Committee on Multiculturalism*, No. 12, Dec. 15, 1987, 20.

55. Both official language minority communities, of course, had the strong support of the federal government during Mr. Trudeau's Prime Ministership.

56. Thus Doug Sanders notes that a "persistent problem [at first ministers' constitutional conferences on aboriginal self government] has been the grouping of Indians, non-status Indians, Metis and Inuit in one forum." "An Uncertain Path: the Aboriginal Constitutional Conferences," in Joseph M. Weiler and Robin M. Elliot, eds., *Litigating the Values of a Nation: The Canadian Charter of Rights and Freedoms* (Toronto: Carswell, 1986, 74). Note also the controversy over which organization speaks for Japanese Canadians seeking redress. See the statement of Otto Jelinek (Minister of State for Multiculturalism), *Minutes of Proceedings and Evidence of the Standing Committee on Multiculturalism*, No. 7, May 13, 1986, 11-12, and the evidence of Arthur Miki (President, National Association of Japanese Canadians), *Minutes of Proceedings and Evidence of the Standing Committee on Multiculturalism*, No. 9, May 27, 1986, 17-20.

57. John D. Whyte, "The 1987 Constitutional Accord and Ethnic Accommodation," in Swinton and Rogerson, eds., *Competing Constitutional Visions*, 268-69.

58. Horowitz, *Ethnic Groups in Conflict*, 197.

59. *Ibid.*, 186.

60. Tepper, "Demographic Change and Pluralism," 24 (italics in original).

MAKING CANADA BILINGUAL: ILLUSIONS AND DELUSIONS OF FEDERAL LANGUAGE POLICY

Kenneth McRoberts, York University.

One of the few political scientists of his generation to have roots in Western Canada, Donald Smiley has often seemed more fully aware of the complexities of the Canadian experience than have many of his Central Canada-bred colleagues. Thus, during the 1960s Smiley was one of the rare English-Canadian political scientists both to recognize and to address publicly the inherent flaws of the effort then underway in Ottawa to recast the image and reality of Canada into that of a bilingual society.

In *The Canadian Political Nationality*, published in 1967, Smiley inveighed against an emerging revisionist historiography which, by treating English-French relations as the only important theme, was producing "a gross distortion of the Canadian experience." He warned that:

> ...there are other cleavages in Canada than those dividing English-Canadians and French-Canadians, and Confederation will almost inevitably fail if extremists from both groups combine successfully to have political conflict revolve almost exclusively about relations between two cultural communities.[1]

Smiley argued that in parts of Canada the French presence was so marginal if not non-existent that many English-Canadians could only resent the federal government's attachment to a dualist vision of Canada, and the concomitant preoccupation with expanding the French presence in Canada. In the first edition of *Canada in Question*, published in 1972, he noted that "residents of that region [Western Canada] have come to feel outside the mainstream of national life by the acceptance in Ottawa and among the elites of the central heartland of an orthodox formulation of Canada and of the Canadian experience which has little relevance to western life and traditions." He went on to cite the Reports of the Royal Commission on Bilingualism and Biculturalism as the leading expression of the "emergent orthodoxy."[2] Eight years later, Smiley expressed his contention in terms that went beyond Western Canada alone, claiming that within Canada as a whole:

>...a decreasing proportion of Canadians experience duality as an important circumstance in daily life. The human implications of these demographic trends have been much neglected—on a day-to-day and a week-to-week basis most citizens have little direct contact with members of the other linguistic community.[3]

On this basis he found it quite understandable that most non-Francophones would resist the dualist vision of Canada.[4]

In effect, then, Smiley was one of the few English-Canadian scholars to recognize openly from the outset how the federal government's language program has sought to make a "national" experience out of what is manifestly a local or regional one. In present-day Canada, after three decades of concerted activity by the federal government, Smiley's diagnosis remains just as valid. Yet, there has been little readiness among English-Canadian scholars and opinion leaders to re-examine critically the underlying assumptions of federal language policy.

The assumptions guiding federal language policy were first set in the early 1960s, through the efforts of the Royal Commission on Bilingualism and Biculturalism. They were not the only available bases for a language regime. The Commission made a conscious choice: to apply to the maximum the personality principle. Thus, a particular conception of a language regime for Canada, one among several possibilities that might have been proposed by the B&B Commission, became entrenched as the *official* conception. Apparently, the choice was dictated as much by political considerations as by any appreciation of the specific patterns of language use in Canada.

The policies the Commission derived from this principle have not accorded well with the linguistic reality of Canada, as Smiley so well noted. They have aroused fierce opposition both in English Canada and in French Quebec. Typically, they have been ineffective in achieving their stated objectives. And, perhaps most importantly, they served to frustrate rather than facilitate a meaningful response to Quebec nationalism, which had been the primary stimulus to the Commission's deliberations, and the federal government's linguistic initiatives. Thus, before tracing the fate of Ottawa's linguistic reforms it is important first to examine how the Commission reached its fateful conclusions about a language regime for Canada.

The B&B Commission: Formulating a Language Policy for Canada

When, in the mid-1960s, the Royal Commission on Bilingualism and Biculturalism cast about for a language policy for Canada, it could not ignore the fact that in Canada the simultaneous presence of the two official languages was relatively limited, whether it be in the form of individual bilingualism or in the form of cohabitation by French-speakers and English-speakers within the same region. In all of the provinces but Quebec and New Brunswick the official-language minorities were small in numbers and precarious in condition. Nonetheless, in selecting a language regime for Canada the Commission resisted drawing the conclusions that might have flowed from this.

In a comparison of four other multilingual states, Belgium, Finland, South Africa and Switzerland, the Commission noted that they offered two competing principles for language regimes: the territorial principle and the personality principle (which the Commission clearly favoured). Under the territorial principle, which was most clearly embodied by the Belgian case, language rights vary from one part of the country to another; the rights available to citizens are dependent upon the region in which they reside.[5] Typically, territoriality is combined with unilingualism. Thus, different languages enjoy monopolies within different regions. Equality in the status of languages lies in the fact that each has at least some area in which it is guaranteed such a monopoly. Under the personality principle, language rights adhere to individuals, to be exercised wherever these individuals may happen to be within the country. This principle was most clearly represented by South Africa, the only one of the four to recognize individual language rights throughout its territory. (There is surely some irony that, in terms of language rights, South Africa should emerge as the most "liberal" state.)

The Commission concluded that there are two criteria which distinguish the preferred South African case from the others, where territoriality tends to be the rule: the proportion of population that can speak the official languages and the territorial concentration of the languages. By its own evidence, Canada falls far short of the South African ideal. Whereas 66% of South African Whites claimed to be bilingual, only 12% of Canadians made this claim. The offical language minorities of the South African provinces represented proportions ranging from 23% to 39%. In nine of the ten Canadian provinces, they constituted less than 14%. On this basis, Canada would have had difficulty pursuing:

> ...a policy of the South African type, where a full range of governmental and educational services is provided in both official languages in all provinces of the country. Such a thorough-going policy seems not to be required in many parts of Canada; *but more important*, our present linguistic resources are no doubt inadequate to carry it out.[6]

In effect, Canada's linguistic makeup seemed to be much closer to that of Belgium, where territorial unilingualism was the rule. Moreover, the Commission recognized that the territorial principle was not without advantages: "it has two advantages: the minority language is guaranteed priority in some areas and a large majority of the total population may be served in its own language."[7] Nonetheless, the Commission claimed that the Canadian population was too mobile for such a scheme to be realistic.[8] More importantly, the Commission insisted that "where members of the two language groups are widely scattered across the country...a principle of personality rather than territoriality is considered more appropriate."[9] On this basis, they rejected application of the territorial principle to the Canadian case, which would have led to official unilingualism for the provinces with bilingualism reserved for federal institutions:

> Such a solution would doubtless have the advantage of simplicity and would follow the tradition established in several English-speaking provinces. However, it would lead to the recognition of only the majority's rights and to oppression of the official-language minorities.[10]

By the Commission's calculations, these "official-language minorities" amounted to "about 700,000 Canadians in Quebec whose mother tongue is English and some 850,000 scattered throughout the rest of the country whose mother tongue is French."[11]

In fact, more than linguistic justice was involved. Clearly, the Commission saw these official-language minorities as important forces for Canadian political integration.[12] In its *Preliminary Report*, the Commission had emphasized the "symbolic" importance of the Francophone minorities. The bond which Quebec Francophones had formed with these minorities constituted an important force for national cohesion:

> ...If, therefore, French-speaking Quebecers should decide to dissociate themselves from the fate of the French minorities, and particularly if they should adopt this attitude because they felt English-speaking Canada was not giving the minorities a chance to live, separatist tendencies might then be that much more encouraged.[13]

Prevented by "present linguistic resources" from proposing the South African ideal, but unprepared to accept the Belgian and Swiss models of territorial unilingualism, the Commission proposed the next best thing: "we take as a guiding principle the recognition of both official languages, in law and in practice, wherever the minority is numerous enough to be viable as a group."[14]

On this basis, the Commission recommended that French and English should be formally declared the official languages of Parliament, the federal courts, the federal government and the federal administration, and that the federal government should, in consultation with the provinces, set up bilingual districts in which it would provide a range of services in both languages. (The bilingual districts were inspired by the Finnish example.) But it also had recommendations for the provincial governments. All provinces were to declare that both official languages may be used in their legislatures and were to provide "appropriate services" to their official language minorities. These services would involve minority-language schools in bilingual districts and "other appropriate areas" and "judicial and administrative services" in bilingual districts. Only three provinces (Quebec, New Brunswick, and Ontario) were to be officially bilingual and thus assume obligations which go beyond this minimum. Nonetheless, there was hope that, with time, the Francophone minorities would increase to the point that these additional obligations should apply to other provincial governments as well. As the Commission's proposals were implemented, it would have become increasingly viable for French-Canadians to reside throughout Canada:

> We can well imagine the day when the French-speaking minorities in one or more of the seven other provinces will become more numerous. What criterion should we then use to decide whether a province is to become officially bilingual: number or proportion?[15]

The Commission decided that the criterion should be 10% of the population.

In effect, the Commission rejected not only the Belgian model but also the Swiss model. There, a distinction is made between federal institutions, which serve citizens in whichever of the three official languages the citizen chooses, and the local or canton level, where a single language prevails in most instances (21 of 25 cantons). In Canada, bilingualism was to be as much a responsibility of provincial governments as of Ottawa.

By the same token, the Commission consistently assumed that where "the minority is numerous enough to be viable as a group" the two languages should be in *full equality* within a province. Thus, in the future, once the threshold of 10% is reached in a province, the minority official language should be entitled to full equality. In fact, one of the provinces slated to become officially bilingual forthwith, Ontario, had a Francophone population of only 7%. (For that matter, the English mother-tongue minority of Quebec was no more than 13%.) At these levels, the linguistic minority is still in a relatively marginal position. (In the South African example the lowest minority proportion of any province was 23%.) Under such conditions, formal equality between languages is bound to appear contrived. Yet, the Commission apparently had no interest in more flexible formulae which recognize minority language rights within the framework of preeminence for the majority language. Ultimately, of course, this is what emerged in the Commission's "model" province of Quebec, through Bill 22 and Bill 101.

In effect, the language regime then operating in Quebec and Quebec alone, full equality between the two languages, became the model to be applied to Canada as a whole. This was not the only conceivable language regime for Canada. Beyond the opposite extreme of complete territorial unilingualism, the Belgium solution, the Commission might have restricted application of the personality principle to the federal level, as in Switzerland. Or, in imposing obligations upon the provincial governments, it might have conceived schemes in which the minority language would be recognized for specific purposes while the majority language would retain preeminent status. But, if only because Quebec seemed to demonstrate so compellingly the possibility of full equality, the Commission apparently saw no need to explore such hybrids.

Constructing a New Language Regime: Ottawa and the Provinces

When, in 1967, the Commission released the recommendations outlined above, in the first volume of its Report, they were warmly received by the federal government. In fact, under Lester Pearson the government had already begun an effort to expand bilingualism within its own institutions. In 1966, Pearson had set as an objective that "it will be the normal practice for oral and written communication within the [public] service to be made in either official language at the option of the person making them, in the knowledge that they will be understood by those directly concerned."[16] And a systematic effort was under way to give federal institutions a resolutely bilingual face.

Moreover, with the arrival of Pierre Trudeau to the prime ministership, the Commission's program of expanding government services to the French-language minorities had a ready advocate. Strengthening the Francophone presence outside Quebec was central to his whole strategy for combatting Quebec nationalism and separatism. Rejecting the efforts of the Pearson administration to accommodate Quebec nationalists through devolving responsibilities to the Quebec government, Trudeau called for strengthening the bonds of Quebec Francophones with Canada as a whole. For this to happen, not only did Quebec Francophones have to see the federal government as "their" government, they had to see Canada as "their" country. They would do this, he argued, only if there were a meaningful Francophone presence outside Quebec. Then, the Quebec government could no longer claim to speak for French Canada; only the federal government could make such a claim. As Trudeau declared in 1968, once Francophone language rights across

Canada are constitutionally entrenched the French-Canadian nation will stretch from coast to coast and:

> Mr. Robarts will be speaking for French-Canadians in Ontario, Mr. Robichaud will be speaking for French-Canadians in New Brunswick, Mr. Thatcher will speak for French-Canadians in Saskatchewan, and Mr. Pearson will be speaking for all French-Canadians. Nobody will be able to say, "I need more power because I speak for the French-Canadian nation."[17]

Thus, not only did Ottawa adopt the measures recommended by the Commission, and vigorously lobby the provinces to do likewise, it added some measures of its own. The Official Languages Act of 1969 is the best-known part of the federal government's campaign to strengthen the presence of French outside Quebec. Beyond specifying that French-language and English-language services should be available in federal establishments, such as airports, the act called for the designation of bilingual districts where the full range of government services would be available in both languages. In point of fact, the districts were never created, for reasons to be discussed later. However, Ottawa proceeded with greater success on other fronts. The French-language radio and television services of Radio-Canada were very rapidly expanded. Moreover, the Secretary of State began a massive program of subsidies to organizations representing Francophone minorities. At the same time, recognizing that the greater share of direct services are provided by the provincial governments, Ottawa began to pressure actively the provincial governments to increase the provision of their services in French. In fact, Ottawa proceeded to subsidize the provinces that were willing to do so.

Yet, from the outset, Ottawa's effort to establish this new language regime has encountered very serious obstacles. Twenty years later, as we shall see, within almost all provinces the minorities are weaker than they were at the outset. This dismal result can be traced to both political and sociological forces. First, the B&B Commission's proposed language regime has encountered fierce resistance, not just in English Canada but within Quebec, which has itself abandoned its designated role as "model" for the Commission's reforms. Second, the campaign has run up against social and demographic forces which were guaranteed to frustrate, if not totally undermine, any attempt to maintain let alone strengthen the Francophone presence outside Quebec.

By seeking to implant a vision of Canada which was so at variance with the social reality most English-speaking Canadians experienced, the federal government was bound to stimulate a backlash. Some of the forms of this backlash could be readily labelled as uninformed and bigoted. In his underground best-seller, *Bilingual Today, French Tomorrow*, Lieutenant Commander J.V. Andrew offered a clearly paranoid view of federal policy: the designation of positions as requiring bilingual qualifications was no less than a plot "to hand Canada over to the French-Canadian race."[18] One might even ascribe similar ignorance and prejudice to the seventeen MPs (including a former Prime Minister, John Diefenbaker) who refused to support the Official Languages Act in 1969.

Yet, other critiques of federal policy cannot be as easily dismissed. The eminent historian Donald Creighton[19] vigorously opposed greater recognition of French outside Quebec, claiming that there was no historical basis for it. While one might try to argue that Creighton was prejudiced against the French fact, one could hardly claim that he was ill-informed about Canadian society and its history. Rather, his protest stood as a testament to an older vision of Canada which may have been rendered illegitimate in the 1960s, but continued to have a strong appeal for many Canadians of British origin. By the same token, in 1973 J.T. Thorson, former Liberal cabinet minister and President of the Exchequer Court of Canada, was moved to publish a volume entitled *Wanted: A Single Canada*. Thorson used the writings of such historians as Creighton to demonstrate the invalidity of the dualist interpretation of Canadian history. At the same time, he rejected the federal government's language policy as prescription for the future, not only decrying its expense but drawing upon statements of prominent Québécois to show that Ottawa's language reforms do not in any event respond to the discontents of Quebec Francophones. For Thorson, there was only one solid basis upon which to build Canadian unity:

A *Single Canada*, such as that which Canadians of many origins have been trying to build, in which the prime concern is for its individuals and all Canadians stand on the footing of equality with one another without any preference to the members of any component of the Canadian nation.[20]

Such sentiments were echoed by many Canadians who, of neither English nor French origin, could see no place for themselves in a country based upon two founding "charter groups."

Beyond English-Canadian opposition, the federal government's language plans were increasingly threatened by developments within Quebec. By the late 1960s, Quebec, the very "model" upon which the federal government's language strategy had been based, was no longer as supportive of official bilingualism at the provincial level. Nationalists began to campaign for the preeminence of French within Quebec. This disaffection from bilingualism, it must be borne in mind, was not triggered by a reaction to the failure of the other provinces to accord official status to French. After all, there was nothing new here: official unilingualism in the other provinces had been the established norm for many decades. Rather, the determination to accord preeminence to French was a response to changes that had been occurring within Quebec itself.[21]

Prompted by fears over the demographic position of Francophones within Quebec, nationalists began to challenge the right of immigrant parents to send their children to English-language schools. With the 1970s, especially after the publication of the Gendron Commission's report in 1974, public debate increasingly focussed upon the continued role of English as a working language in the upper levels of private corporations in Quebec. Clearly, neither problem could be adequately addressed by the Quebec state without departing from the formal equality with French which English had conventionally enjoyed within Quebec. Thus, rather than a model to be emulated by the rest of Canada, formal bilingualism became for many Quebec Francophones an obstacle to their own aspirations; it had to be abandoned once and for all.

The Royal Commission on Bilingualism and Biculturalism had fiercely resisted this conclusion. However, it could not address the desire of Quebec Francophones to be able to work in French without contradicting itself. As we have seen, the Commission had always insisted that language equality in Canada can only mean that individual Canadians have the maximum opportunity to use either English or French, as in Quebec. On this basis, it had rejected the "territorial" principle. Yet, when it came to the language of work in Quebec the Commission found itself recommending that "in the private sector in Quebec, governments and industry adopt the objective that French become the principal language of work at all levels."[22] In his dissent from the recommendation, Commissioner Frank Scott had no difficulty demonstrating the contradiction:

> It seems to me that, consciously or unconsciously, the other Commission members have departed from the principles laid down in Book I of our *Report*, where we defined "equal partnership" and rejected the territorial principle as being inappropriate for determining a language policy for Canada.[23]

Scott noted that for Ontario and New Brunswick the Commission had proposed that task forces be created to determine what measures were necessary to put French on the same basis as English as a language of work. In the case of Quebec, the Commission set out rigid guidelines for such a task force to adopt:

> So the principles differ depending on the provincial boundaries. This is a virtual acceptance of the territorial principle. My idea of "equal partnership" is that it operates in similar fashion all across Canada, "wherever the minority is numerous enough to be viable as a group."[24]

For its part, the Gendron Commission, mandated by the Union Nationale administration of Jean-Jacques Bertrand to enquire into the condition of French within Quebec, recognized forthrightly that improvement in the role of French within Quebec could only come at the expense of English's historical co-equal status. Setting as its objective that within Quebec French should be the language of communication between Francophones and non-Francophones and the language of internal communication in the work place, the Commission proceeded to recommend that French alone should be the official language of Quebec. English, and French, would have the status of a "national" language.[25]

The combined impact of these factors—the marginality of the Francophone presence in most of Canada and the opposition within both English Canada and French Quebec to formal bilingualism—perhaps can be most clearly seen in the federal government's effort to create bilingual districts. The Commission had seen the districts as the "cornerstone" of its proposed language regime.[26] Ottawa incorporated the notion in its Official Languages Act.[27] Yet, twenty years later the districts have not been created and it appears certain that they never will be. This episode tells us much about the political obstacles to any rigorous application of the personality principle in contemporary Canada

From the outset, responding to pressure from their constituents, several Liberal MPs led campaigns against the creation of bilingual districts within their constituencies.[28] Moreover, within French Quebec opposition was steadily mounting against the province's official bilingualism. Even the Quebec government opposed the creation of bilingual districts within its territory (as did Ontario).[29] Nonetheless, the federal government's Bilingual Districts Advisory Board proceeded to recommend that 37 districts be created, covering all ten provinces. In the case of Quebec and New Brunswick it proposed that whole provinces be declared bilingual districts (the B&B Commission itself had not gone that far).[30] Not surprisingly, the recommendation for Quebec generated a storm of protest, obliging the federal government to create yet another Board.

This second Board was much more aware of the sensibilities of Quebec nationalists, yet in attempting to accommodate this sensibility it arrived at conclusions which simply lacked coherence.[31] With respect to the rest of Canada, the second Board recommended 24 bilingual districts which largely paralleled the first Board's proposed districts. (British Columbia would have no district: on the basis of the 1971 census the sole district proposed by the first Board no longer qualified.) As with the first Board, all of New Brunswick was to be declared a district. In the case of Quebec, however, only parts of the province were to be so designated, for a total of five bilingual districts. At the same time, through rather convoluted reasoning the Board concluded that Montreal should *not* be a bilingual district, despite the fact that over 21% of the residents in the Montreal metropolitan census area had English as a mother tongue.[32] This particular recommendation had been the focus of strong minority opposition within the Board itself, as expressed in dissenting statements which accompanied the report. By the same token, it ensured that this second report would receive the same fate as had the first one: to be rejected by the federal government.

It would be unfair to ascribe the failure of this exercise simply to incoherence or confusion on the part of the two Boards. After all, they had been charged with finding a way to implement a policy for which there was no clear social consensus. Thus, presuming, as had the B&B Commission, that Quebec pointed the way to a language regime for the rest of Canada, the first Board sought to formalize Quebec's status as the "model" province only to discover that many Québécois resented it. In attempting to render the federal government's notion of official bilingualism acceptable to Quebec nationalists, the second Board found itself constrained to interpret its mandate differently in the case of Quebec. In the process, it demonstrated the inadequacy of formal equality between French and English as the sole formula for language reform in Canada. Protecting and strengthening French required prior status for French, not equality:

> We...believed that it would be completely contrary to the basic intent of the Official Languages Act, which is designed to establish the equal status of French and English, if we were to make recommendations that were disadvantageous to the survival of French in the province which is its essential base.[33]

For the Board, the long-term survival of French rather than English in Quebec was in question, and required protective measures. Echoing the concern of Quebec nationalists that "if the public use of English increases in Montreal, the future of French in the metropolis and the province may well be more than a theoretical question,"[34] a majority of the Board members feared that creation of a bilingual district "might well adversely affect the position of the French language in Montreal by increasing the pressure upon French."[35]

The Assimilationist Pressures on the Francophone Minorities

The effort to reinforce the Francophone presence outside Quebec was compromised by more than difficulties in orchestrating what Ottawa saw to be the appropriate governmental actions. The campaign was also compromised by the very sociological forces which had been responsible for the historical decline of the

TABLE ONE
OFFICIAL LANGUAGE MINORITIES
BY PROVINCE

	Minority mother tongue as a % of poulation		Minority language at home as a % of population
	1961^1	1981^2	1981^2
Nfld	0.7	0.5	0.3
NS	5.4	4.3	2.9
NB	35.2	33.7	31.4
PEI	7.6	4.9	3.1
Que	13.3	10.9	10.0
Ont	6.8	5.5	3.9
Man	6.6	5.1	3.1
Sask	3.9	1.6	1.1
Alta	3.2	2.8	1.3
BC	1.6	1.6	0.1

[1]*Census of Canada*, 1961, as reproduced in RCBB, Book I: *Official Languages*, Table 5B

[2]*Census of Canada*, 1981, 92-991, Table IV

minorities, and which have acquired even greater force in recent years. To a very real degree, these assimilationist pressures on the Francophone minorities are simply beyond the range of governmental action, however comprehensive and coordinated it may be.

Such measures as increasing the availability of French-language public education, expanding the range of other governmental services in French, and extending the facilities of Radio-Canada, can reduce to only a limited degree the pressures on Francophones outside Quebec, and perhaps New Brunswick, to live much, if not all, of their lives in English. Especially within urban centers the assimilationist pressures are overwhelming. First, in most urban centers the very presence of Francophones is minimal: within all major metropolitan areas outside Quebec and New Brunswick the proportion using French at home is less than two per cent, with the exception of Winnipeg (3.3%) and Windsor (3.9%).[36] Thus, among other things, the chances of intermarriage with non-Francophones are correspondingly high. By the same token, the language of work clearly is English. To the extent that opportunities to work in French persist, they tend to be at the lower ends of the occupational ladder. Thus, even if the children of Francophones can secure a complete education in French in these urban centers, chances are that they will have to work in English if they are to put their education to use. Finally, even if the facilities of Radio-Canada should be available, the English-language media will still offer far greater diversity and appeal.

Due to these pressures, assimilationist rates have been especially high in urban areas. For instance, in Saskatchewan, according to the 1971 census, the percentages of people of French-origin who used French as the language at home were 41% in farm areas and 36% in non-farm rural areas, but only 15% in Saskatoon and 9% in Regina.[37] As the Francophone populations continue to move to urban centers, so the overall rates of assimilation are bound to increase, however extensive may be governmental support for the French language. In fact, as the numbers decline the very provision of these services will become more difficult. Writing in 1978, Richard Joy predicted that by the mid-1980s the number of French-language children available for French-language schools throughout the seven provinces other than Quebec, Ontario, and New Brunswick would be only 19,000.[38]

As a result of these political and sociological forces, the dualist experience is even more marginal now than it was in the

1960s. In fact, in terms of its stated objective, strengthening the official language minorities, the campaign has been an unqualified failure. As Table I shows, over the period 1961 to 1981, in virtually all provinces the proportions of residents declaring the minority mother tongue have declined significantly. As Table I also shows, if one focusses upon the continued use of French at home, so as to control for loss or disuse of a French mother tongue, then in most provinces the Francophone presence is very marginal. By this measure, in 1981 the Francophone minorities fell to 3% or less in all provinces but Quebec, New Brunswick and Ontario. In fact, these three provinces alone accounted for 98% of all Canadians who used French at home.

To be sure, there has been an apparent increase in individual knowledge of both languages, or personal bilingualism,[40] as opposed to social dualism: the presence of both Anglophones and Francophones, on the basis of *primary* language, within the same community or province. Between 1961 and 1981 the proportion of Canadians who are English-French bilingual rose from 12% to 15%. This increase in bilingualism was strongest among Canadians whose mother tongue is English—especially those living outside Quebec. In the latter group, the number of bilinguals rose by 78% so as to constitute 5% of the group as a whole.[41] Yet, the significance of this trend is far from clear. First, one can question the meaningfulness of respondents' claims to census-takers that they have a working knowledge of another language. Second, and more importantly, one can question the extent to which, especially outside Quebec, acquired knowledge of French by Anglophones actually can lead to greater bilingual exchange. After all, as we have seen, in most parts of Canada the numbers of Francophones and thus the opportunities to use French are small and in quite rapid decline.

In short, after twenty years of intensive effort to expand dualism, the simultaneous presence of Francophones and Anglophones within Canadian society, it is weaker than ever. Moreover, by all projections the trend will become even stronger in the coming years, such that by the year 2000 no more than 3% of the population outside Quebec will be Francophone.[42] Conversely, within Quebec, Anglophones may fall to little more than 10% of the population.[43]

It is difficult to imagine how the result could have been otherwise. The essential difficulty lay not with imperfections or limitations in the strategies which were pursued but with the linguistic structure of Canadian society and the insurmountable obstacles that flow from that. Even if Ottawa had been able to create the bilingual districts, they could not in themselves have maintained, let alone increased, the size of the Francophone minorities. Nor was it simply a matter of securing fuller cooperation from the provincial governments. As we have seen, whatever the range of governmental services provided by the federal and provincial governments combined, in most parts of Canada the pressures to lead one's life in English would still have remained overwhelming.

This bleak reality was in fact mapped out more than twenty years ago by Richard Joy in his *Languages in Conflict*.[44] Carefully examining 1961 census data and comparing it with data from earlier censuses, Joy traced and analyzed the historical patterns of assimilation among French-speakers. On this basis, he demonstrated that only within parts of Quebec and in regions of New Brunswick and Ontario which border on Quebec, areas which he dubbed "the Bilingual Belt," could there continue to be the joint presence of English-speakers and French-speakers. All the rest of Canada was fated to be unilingual, whether Anglophone or Francophone.

Yet, ever since the fundamentals of language policy were first formulated by the Royal Commission on Bilingualism and Biculturalism there has been a surprising resistance to rethink them. Public discussion about language policy and language equality in Canada continues to accept without much question that they must be based upon the personality principle. By and large, at least among English-speaking Canadians, the debate has continued to be over whether official bilingualism, based on the personality principle, should be expanded to all of Canada or restricted only to part of it, namely Quebec. Few people, including scholars, have argued that language equality and linguistic justice should be conceived in an altogether different fashion, based upon the territorial principle and patterned after language regimes in other settings.

In 1979, the Pepin-Robarts Task Force on Canadian Unity did suggest that the provinces should be allowed to determine for themselves the language regime which was most appropriate for their conditions. It argued that "differences in perspective and in language policies between the federal and provincial levels of government, or among provincial governments themselves, need not be a major obstacle to Canadian unity."[45] And, contending that under federalism governments should be sovereign within their jurisdictional spheres, the Task Force recommended that the only constitutional restriction upon a province then existing, the part of Section 133 pertaining to Quebec, should be abolished.[46] But these recommendations were treated as little less than heresy by Prime Minister Trudeau and his colleagues. In the end, they served to guarantee that the report would be totally ignored by the government which commissioned it. Instead, of course, the Trudeau government persisted with its own project of constraining the provincial governments through constitutional entrenchment. With the Charter of Rights and Freedoms the Trudeau government secured a partial success, obliging provincial governments to provide minority-language education where numbers "warrant."[47]

Recent years have seen a continuing debate over the expansion of bilingualism within provincial institutions. Most recently, in Saskatchewan and then Alberta the issue has arisen as to whether the provincial laws must be published in French as well as English, whether both languages can be used in legislative debates, and whether the records of debates must be maintained in both languages. Those who maintained that the legislatures were so obligated tended to gloss over the fact that in present-day Alberta and Saskatchewan the Francophone communities constitute very marginal forces indeed. According to the 1981 census only 10,090 residents of Saskatchewan (1% of the total population) use French at home. In Alberta they number 29,550 (1.3% of the population).[48] Certainly, they are a far cry from the communities which existed in 1886 when the Northwest Territories Act was passed, and for which the linguistic provisions of the Act were included. It is not at all clear how the small Fransaskois population would make sufficient use of the French versions of provincial laws to justify the $5 million, or more, needed to translate existing laws into French.[49] After all, even the B&B Commission did not call for bilingual statutes in Alberta and Saskatchewan; it simply called upon the two provinces to allow French to be used in legislative debates.[50] Ultimately, these measures only can be justified, not in terms of a meaningful need within the provincial populations, but in terms of a particular conception of Canada as "a bilingual country," a conception based upon the personality principle.

Even in the instance of Manitoba, which became engulfed in a bitter struggle over the expansion of French-language rights, the

Francophone presence is a relatively marginal one. In 1981, on the basis of use of French at home, Francophones numbered only 31,045 or 3% of the population.[51] Even if the Pawley government had succeeded in its most ambitious of projects—making French and English official languages, expanding French-language services by not just the provincial government but municipalities and school boards as well, and entrenching language rights in the constitution—such assimilationist influences as the English-language media and the dominance of English as language of work, let alone the high frequency of social interaction with Anglophones in urban areas, would have remained as powerful as ever. In short, the future of French in Manitoba may well be a moot point. One would not know this from the political debate.

By the same token, one cannot help but be struck by the determination with which Quebec Anglophones have resisted Bill 101's requirement that French alone be used in commercial signs and outdoor advertising. Given the relatively small number of French words which must be learned to understand these messages, Anglophones are at most inconvenienced by the measure. Clearly, what they find so offensive in the measure is its symbolism: the denial of full equality between English and French within Quebec. Moreover, the reaction to Bill 178 by English-Canadians outside Quebec suggests that this attitude is widely shared. Even if bilingual signs are to be permitted inside stores, the continued prohibition of any other language than French on outside signs is found to be intolerable.

Once again, the personality principle is simply presumed to be the only just basis for a language regime in Canada. Rather than a heavily qualified application of the territorial principle used in so many other multilingual states, such as Switzerland and Belgium, Bill 101 is viewed as a violation of fundamental rights, pure and simple. Many English-Canadian attacks upon Bill 178 have extended, implicitly or explicitly, beyond regulation of outdoor advertising to the much more important aspects of Bill 101, such as restriction of access by immigrants to English-language schools or favouring French as the language of work. They too are regarded as obviously unjust.

Language Policy and Conceptions of Canadian Nationhood

This persistent commitment among English-Canadian intellectual and political elites to a language regime based on the personality principle, for federal and provincial governments alike, can best be understood in terms of its roots in a particular conception of Canadian nationhood. It is this broader ideological base which explains how the personality principle can continue to retain loyalty in the face of the widespread failure of efforts to put it into effect. Clearly, during the 1960s language policy was not developed simply in response to the demands of the Francophone minorities. After all, they had been making their claims for many decades, and to absolutely no avail. The real stimulus lay in the surge of nationalist agitation in Quebec. Canada's new language regime was formulated as the centerpiece within a much larger project: the restoration of Canadian national unity. It was part of a new pan-Canadian nationalism, designed to counter the Québécois variant.[52]

Within this "nation-saving" strategy, Quebec nationalism was to be checked by offering Quebec Francophones the promise of belonging to a much larger political community, stretching "from sea to sea." This was, in fact, the resurrection of an older version of French-Canadian nationalism, harking back to the early days of Confederation, in which a rapidly-growing French-Canadian population would expand into Western Canada and claim this new territory for *la nation canadienne*. But, of course, the earlier dream had long ago faded as the West, and the other provinces, resolutely defined themselves as English-speaking and their Francophone presence steadily declined. Thus, to restore credibility to this older pan-Canadian nationalism it was imperative that Quebec Francophones perceive real opportunities to live in French through as much of Canada as possible. Only on this basis, it was argued, would Quebec Francophones come to see Canada, rather than Quebec, as their "nation." At the same time, if they did come to see all of Canada as their nation there would be no need to accommodate the increasingly insistent demands of the Quebec government for powers and resources. Quebec would at last be firmly established as a province *comme les autres*, in part because in linguistic terms the other provinces would have become more like it.

In part, the ascendancy of this particular response to Quebec nationalism, can be traced to the rise of Pierre Elliott Trudeau to political prominence. It was his consuming aversion to Quebec nationalism which had brought him to Ottawa in the first place, and made him intent upon integrating Quebec Francophones within the Canadian political community. But, having little personal familiarity with the rest of Canada prior to becoming Justice Minister, his vision of Canada was closely shaped by his experiences in Quebec. In addition, of course, Trudeau possessed a rare level of personal bilingualism. Thus, he was a logical and powerful advocate of a language regime for Canada, modelled after the longstanding provincial regime in Quebec, that was based upon the personality principle. By the same token, given his roots in Quebec he could with some credibility promise his English-Canadian audiences that the erection of such a language regime, rather than any constitutional accommodation of the Quebec government, was the key to undermining Quebec nationalism.

Nonetheless, however well-suited Trudeau may have been to make the case for official bilingualism as the central solution to the Canadian crisis, it also was a message to which members of the English-Canadian intelligentsia (in Ontario, at least) were quite favourably disposed. It closely accorded with several of their basic assumptions. First, by promising to respond to French-Canadian discontent in terms of language rights to be held by individuals, wherever they may be in Canada, it avoided the hoary notion of collective rights which so offended English-Canadian political culture, even if it seemed so natural to Quebec Francophones.[53] Second, by being as uniform as possible throughout the country, the new language regime would respect the English-Canadian concern with the territorial integrity of Canada.[54] Language rights would be the same everywhere in Canada and, because of that, Quebec would not need any "special status." Finally, by presuming that the solution to Quebec's discontent lay with language reforms to be undertaken in English Canada, the bilingual strategy allowed English-Canadians to believe that they could, through their own efforts, resolve the Canadian crisis. And it presumed that Quebec Francophones were still very much part of the Canadian community; they simply wanted to play a fuller role within it.[55] Thus, the bilingual strategy offered the hope of a reconstituted but reunited Canada, as opposed to the various constitutional schemes, based on two nations, which Quebec nationalists were advocating. It was quite congruent with a pan-Canadian nationalism.

While the B&B Commission's notion of "equal partnership" could be rendered politically acceptable when applied to "bilingualism," by individualizing language rights through the personality principle, the Commission's twin concept of "biculturalism" was much more troublesome. This was especially so since the Commission had chosen to interpret the concept in terms that could lead quite readily to notions of "collective" rights. For the Commission, individuals could not be "bicultural" unless they were to have two personalities. Biculturalism could only refer to the presence of two distinct societies.[56] From there, it was only a short step to concluding that these two communities required separate political institutions, and that Canada should be modelled along the lines of "two nations". The Commission never took that step, especially with the death of André Laurendeau. For his part, Pierre Trudeau had long opposed the notion of official biculturalism, viewing it as a surrogate for the concept of "two nations" which he so ferociously ridiculed in the 1968 federal election.[57] Itself divided over the question of biculturalism, the B&B Commission wound up its operations in 1971.[58] And, in the same year, the federal government pronounced its commitment to "multiculturalism": a term which both reduced to language alone French-Canadian claims to collective equality and had enormous appeal for Canadians of neither English nor French descent.

In sum, Ottawa's formulation of a language regime for Canada was closely shaped by a more fundamental concern: to counter Quebec neo-nationalism and separatism. Within this "nation-saving" perspective, a language regime based on the personality principle and defining language rights in purely individual terms was the only acceptable one. However bleak their prospects for survival, let alone development, the Francophone minorities assumed a high strategical value. Accordingly, even though the historical assimilation of the minorities has proceeded unabated, despite the best efforts of the federal government and some provincial governments, the Francophone presence outside Quebec continues to have high symbolic importance. Thus, the federal government and many English-Canadians, at least in Central Canada, can insist that provincial statutes in Saskatchewan must be published in French as well as English, at very considerable expense, even though that Francophone population has become so small that it is unclear whether many individuals will actually benefit from the measure. In effect, the bilingual vision of Canada has only a loose relationship to the reality of language use in Canada; it derives its force from other considerations.

Language Policy and the Response to Quebec Nationalism

Even though it has been a patent failure in terms of its stated objectives, one might argue that the effort to strengthen the Francophone presence throughout Canada was itself of great value. If nothing else, it constituted an important message to Quebec Francophones that their language and culture are a valued and integral part of the Canadian nation. In short, it was a necessary response to the appeal of Quebec separatism. Yet, it is not even clear that the campaign served this "nation-saving" function since it is not at all clear that it responded to the concerns which had given rise to separatism in the first place. For instance, in a 1977 survey Quebec respondents were asked: "If French-speaking Canadians were treated as equals to English-speaking Canadians outside Quebec would this affect your attitude toward independence for Quebec?" A full 81% responded negatively; only 17% responded positively.[59]

If anything, the federal drive to strengthen French-language rights outside Quebec probably hindered the kinds of changes which were necessary to reconciling Quebec Francophones with the Canadian political order: reinforcement of the status of French within Quebec. It is not difficult to argue that the movement of Quebec from de facto bilingualism to formal unilingualism, in direct contradiction of Ottawa's plans, was instrumental to accommodating the concerns of Quebec indépendantistes. Through Bill 22 and Bill 101, not only was French given an official preeminence within Quebec, but the actual role of French within Quebec society was substantially strengthened.

Typically, Bill 101, passed by the Parti Québécois in 1977, is credited with (or damned for) bringing about these changes. However, it merely built upon the foundation already set through Bill 22, passed by the Liberals in 1974. It was Bill 22, not Bill 101, which established French as the only official language of Quebec. And Bill 22 established the principles that the Quebec state had a responsibility to ensure the preeminence of French within its own internal operations, to restrict access to English-language schools, and to promote transition within private enterprises to French as the language of internal communication. Bill 101 tightened some of Bill 22's provisions, making access to English-language schools dependent upon mother tongue, making francisation program compulsory for most private enterprises, and imposing French as the sole language of outdoor advertising. But the basic framework of the PQ legislation is the same as that of Bill 22.

Unalterably committed to the federal order, the Bourassa Liberals nonetheless had had to contend with mounting disaffection over the role of French within Quebec. Whatever may have been Ottawa's views, for the Bourassa Liberals it was clear that formal equality between French and English had to be abandoned. For that, of course, the Bourassa Liberals earned the undying contempt of Trudeau and his colleagues. To a 1976 Liberal Party gathering in Quebec City, Trudeau decried the "political stupidity" of Bill 22:

> One of my strongest criticisms is that Bill 22 talks about French as the only official language of Quebec. You know, if they had only said the main language, la langue nationale... You know, it would have made things easier for us...when we're saying to the rest of the country there are two official languages.[60]

Given the extent to which replacement of official bilingualism with French preeminence in Quebec has apparently served to temper the forces of Quebec separatism, there is all the more reason to question whether the federal government's conception of a language regime for Canada is the appropriate one. In all probability, Ottawa was quite correct to commit itself to formal equality of French and English within its own institutions. Doubtlessly, Quebec Francophones would be more likely to see the federal government as "their" government if not only were it to have a resolutely bilingual face but Francophones were to enjoy a proportional role within not just Parliament but the Cabinet and the public service. It can be argued that Ottawa could have been much more successful than it has been in establishing French as a working language within the public service, and that it handicapped itself in this effort by apparently rejecting on an ideological basis the French-language unit strategy. Also, it can be demonstrated that, perhaps for this reason, the increases in the

Francophone presence within the public service have involved a disproportionately small share of Francophones from Quebec, presumably the target group of these reforms.[61] Nonetheless, it can be easily argued that expansion of the French presence within the federal government's own institutions was a necessary part of any serious response to Quebec separatism, albeit of limited popular impact.[62]

It is much more difficult, however, to demonstrate that the response to Quebec separatism had to entail more than this. It is not at all certain that, in order to restore support among Quebec Francophones, the federal government had to begin offering its services in French in other parts of Canada. All that was really necessary was that it be able to serve Quebec Francophones in French, which by and large it always had been able to do. Even if one were to conclude that Ottawa did have to provide French-language services wherever they are demanded in Canada, it does not follow that the provincial governments had to do likewise. Nor is it clear that responding to Quebec separatism meant that the provincial governments had to adopt formal bilingualism within their own institutions. In short, these additional forms of bilingualism were neither fully necessary as a response to Quebec nor, as experience has shown, fully realizable. As Donald Smiley noted in 1975, the supporters of the "bilingual and bicultural" alternative need to demonstrate "a realism which dissociates dualism within the shared institutions of the government of Canada from dualism within Quebec or the other provinces".[63]

In fact, many students of language regimes have pointed to real advantages in the territorial principle. In particular, they have demonstrated that territorial unilingualism is much more effective than bilingualism in providing minority language groups with the security that they need, as well as with opportunities for growth and development. For a language group which is in an economically subordinate position, formal bilingualism, based upon individual rights, is likely to only strengthen the pressures for assimilation to the dominant group. These arguments recently have been developed with particular effectiveness by Jean Laponce. In his volume *Languages and their Territories*, Laponce argues that through providing a "security zone" territorial unilingualism has been a force for political stability in many settings.[64]

Territorial Unilingualism and Canadian Political Integration

In sum, the dream of a "truly bilingual" Canada, which mobilized a good many English Canadians intellectuals in the 1960s, has effectively died as Canadian society has continued inexorably its movement towards a "twinned unilingualism," with Francophone dominance of Quebec and Anglophone dominance of the nine other provinces broken only by "a bilingual belt" straddling Quebec's borders with Ontario and New Brunswick. Yet, the demise of this noble dream has not meant the demise of Canada. In fact, quite the opposite has occurred. Many had presumed that territorial unilingualism could only accelerate Quebec's separation. Yet, if anything, the transition of Quebec to a preeminently Francophone society has eased the discontent of Francophone nationalists and helped to reconcile them to the existing political order.

If Quebec continues to remain part of Canada it will be, as in the past, primarily because Quebec Francophones see it in their interest to align themselves with English-speaking Canada. Now, thanks to the reforms of the 1960s and 1970s, the federal political institutions which link these two entities have a strengthened Francophone presence. Even if, within the public service, Francophones from Quebec are underrepresented vis-à-vis Francophones from other provinces and still must perform much of their work in English, at least the public face of the federal government is no longer as resolutely Anglophone as it was in the past. Moreover, this political linkage of Francophone Quebec with Anglophone Canada is now supplemented by a corporate linkage as Quebec Francophone businesses have become more heavily involved in the rest of the Canadian market. At the same time, especially in terms of its economic elite, English-speaking Canada is now more clearly differentiated from Quebec thanks to the movement of Anglophone corporate offices from Montreal to Toronto. To use Laponce's term,[65] the "vital center" of English Canada no longer extends to Quebec. By the same token, the "vital center" of Quebec Francophones, Montreal, is now more clearly in their hands.

This last change is, in fact, the critical one. To a very real extent, the crisis in "Canadian unity" of the 1960s and 1970s was a "Montreal" crisis. At the center of nationalist discontents was the status of French within Quebec's metropolis, especially as a language of work and opportunity. As this question was resolved, through the efforts of the Quebec government rather than the federal government, so the Canadian crisis was resolved. In these terms, the reinforcement of French within Montreal and the rest of Quebec, was far more important than reinforcement of French in Ottawa, which has been limited, or the reinforcement of French in the rest of Canada, which has been even more limited, if it has occurred at all.

Notes

1 Donald V. Smiley, *The Canadian Political Nationality* (Toronto: Methuen, 1967), 120.

2 Donald V. Smiley, *Canada in Question: Federalism in the Seventies* (Toronto: McGraw-Hill Ryerson, 1972), 179 (emphasis in original).

3 Donald Smiley, "Reflections on Cultural Nationhood and Political Community in Canada," in R. Kenneth Carty and W. Peter Ward (eds.), *Entering the Eighties: Canada in Crisis* (Toronto: Oxford University Press, 1980), 33.

4 *Ibid.*

5 Kenneth D. McRae, "The Principle of Territoriality and the Principle of Personality in Multilingual States," *International Journal of the Sociology of Language*, 4 (1975), 35-45. See also André Donneur, "La solution territoriale au problème du multilinguisme," in Jean-Guy Savard and Richard Vigneault, (eds.), *Les Etats multilingues: problèmes et solutions* (Québec: Les Presses de l'Université Laval, 1975), 209-206.

6 Report of the Royal Commission on Bilingualism and Biculturalism, Book I: *The Official Languages* (Ottawa: Queen's Printer, 1967), 84 (emphasis added). (Henceforth, the Commission will be referred to as "RCBB.")

7 *Ibid.*, 83.

8 *Ibid.*, 84.

9 *Ibid.*, 83.

10 *Ibid.*, 86.

11 *Ibid.*, 87.

12 Kenneth D. McRae, "Bilingual Language Districts," 336.

13 RCBB, *Preliminary Report* (Ottawa: Queen's Printer, 1965), 119.

14 RCBB, *The Official Languages*,(Ottawa: Queen's Printer, 1969), 86.

15 *Ibid.*, 98.

16 RCBB, Book III: *The Work World* (Ottawa: Queen's Printer, 1969), 353.

17 Speech to Quebec Liberal Convention, January 28, 1968, reported in *Ottawa Citizen*, January 29, 1968 (as quoted in George Radwanski, *Trudeau* (Scarborough: Macmillan-NAL Publishing Ltd., 1978), 286).

18 J.V. Andrew, *Bilingual Today, French Tomorrow: Trudeau's master plan and how it can be stopped* (Richmond Hill: BMG Publishing, 1977), 11.

19 Donald Creighton, "The Myth of Biculturalism," in Creighton, *Towards the Discovery of Canada* (Toronto: Macmillan of Canada, 1972), 256-270.

20 J.T. Thorson, *Wanted: A Single Canada* (Toronto: McClelland & Stewart, 1973), 149.

21 This predominant role of conditions within Quebec itself in generating the nationalist surge was very evident to the B&B Commission when it conducted its public hearings in 1964: "The divergent preoccupations of French Quebec and the 'French minorities' of the other provinces were very evident. French-speaking Quebecers spoke insistently of their own future—they were not particularly concerned about that of the French minorities. The representatives of these minorities often appeared to be badly informed about what is happening today in Quebec, to such an extent that they are poor interpreters to their English-speaking fellow citizens of what is going on in that province."(RCBB, *Preliminary Report*, 28).

22 RCBB, *The Work World*, 559.

23 *Ibid.*, 565.

24 *Ibid.*

25 Gouvernement du Québec, Rapport de la Commission d'enquête sur la situation de la langue française et sur les droits linguistiques au Québec, Livre I: *La langue de travail* (Québec: Editeur officiel du Québec, 1972), 305.

26 RCBB, *The Official Languages*, 116.

27 For a thorough account of the notion of bilingual districts and its fate in Canada, see Kenneth D. McRae, "Bilingual Language Districts in Finland and Canada: adventures in the transplanting of an institution," *Canadian Public Policy*, IV:3 (Summer, 1978), 331-51.

28 John Gray, "French-speaking Areas Declining Outside Quebec," *The Toronto Star*, March 18, 1974.

29 *Ibid.*

30 Canada, *Recommendations of the Bilingual Districts Advisory Board*, March 1971 (Ottawa: Information Canada, 1971). The B&B Commission had designated subsets of census divisions in Quebec and New Brunswick which might be considered for bilingual district status (RCBB, *The Official Languages*, 107-110).

31 Canada, *Report of the Bilingual Districts Advisory Board*, October, 1975 (Ottawa: Information Canada, 1975). (Hereafter, it will be referred to as *Bilingual Districts Advisory Board, 1975*). This report and the previous one are analyzed in McRae, "Bilingual Language Districts."

32 This figure appears in *Bilingual Districts Advisory Board, 1975*, note 37, 105. The B&B Commission had designated both Ile-de-Montréal and Ile-Jésus as candidates for bilingual districts (RCBB, *The Official Languages*, 108).

33 *Bilingual Districts Advisory Board, 1975*, 35 (emphasis added).

34 *Ibid.*, 73.

35 *Ibid.*, 109.

36 Richard J. Joy, *Canada's Official-Language Minorities, Accent Québec* (Montreal: C.D. Howe Research Institute, 1978).

37 As cited by Joy, *Canada's Official-Language Minorities*, 10.

38 *Ibid.*, 13.

39 The only exception is British Columbia, where the Francophone proportion remained at an infinitesimal 1.6%.

40 "True" personal bilingualism is, of course, exceedingly rare: "perfect bilingualism is an ideal that is sometimes approached but almost never attained" (J.A. Laponce, *Languages and Their Territories* [Toronto: University of Toronto Press, 1987], 33).

41 Statistics Canada, *Languages in Canada* (Hull: Minister of Supply & Services, 1985).

42 Jacques Henripin, *L'immigration et le déséquilibre linguistique* (Ottawa: Main-d'oeuvre et immigration, 1974), 22.

43 Jacques Henripin, "Les anglophones pourraient ne représenter que 10.4% de la population du Québec en 2001," *le Devoir*, November 28, 1984.

44 Richard J. Joy, *Languages in Conflict* (Toronto: McClelland & Stewart, 1972)—first published by the author in Ottawa, 1967. See also Richard Arès, *Les positions éthniques, linguistiques et religieuses des canadiens français à la suite du recensement de 1971* (Montreal: les Editions Bellarmin, 1975).

45 Canada, The Task Force on Canadian Unity, *A Future Together* (Hull: Minister of Supply and Services, 1979), 48.

46 *Ibid.*, 52.

47 Minority language education is to be provided to children of a parent whose first language or language of education is the minority language (in Canada for Quebec residents), or whose sibling has been educated in the language in Canada, and who are in sufficient numbers to warrant provision of the service (*Canadian Charter of Rights and Freedoms*, Section 23). In addition, the Charter imposes official bilingualism on New Brunswick, as well as the federal government (*ibid*, Section 16).

48 Taken from *Census of Canada, 1981*, 92-911, Table IV. The much larger number of 25,000 recently cited in references to the Francophone population apparently is based upon mother tongue: in 1981, 25,320 Saskatchewan residents listed French as their mother tongue (*ibid.*). Clearly, language use at home is a much more meaningful measure of the Francophone presence.

49 The sum of the combined federal-provincial commitment to underwriting translation costs, as contained in the June 1988 agreement ("Saskatchewan to get $60 million toward French rights," *Globe & Mail*, June 16, 1988, A5). The $56 million of federal funds to be spent on strengthening French-language education in Saskatchewan might be seen as a more meaningful use of funds. But it is difficult to see how even this expenditure can arrest processes of assimilation which, on the basis of use of French at home, are virtually complete.

50 Saskatchewan's law does allow for use of French in the provincial legislature, although it does not provide for simultaneous translation.

51 *Census of Canada, 1981*, 92-911, Table IV. A total of 51,990 Manitobans listed French as their mother tongue.

52   Thus, Bill 101 is not the only instance of a language policy which is informed by nationalism. See C. Michael MacMillan, "Language Rights, Human Rights and Bill 101," *Queen's Quarterly*, 90:2 (Summer, 1983), 343-61.

53   The difference in conceptions of rights became quite evident during the B&B Commission's cross-country hearings (RCBB, *A Preliminary Report*, February 1, 1965 [Ottawa: Queen's Printer, 1965], 99).

54   See Abraham Rotstein's notion of "mapism" in "Is There an English-Canadian Nationalism?" *Journal of Canadian Studies*, 13 (Summer, 1978), 109-18.

55   Demonstration of English-Canadian proclivity for such an assessment can be seen in the representations which were made during the B&B Commission's cross-country hearings. In its *Preliminary Report* the Commission noted that English-Canadians in such cities as London, Ontario, would tend to focus upon strategies for increasing personal bilingualism in their community whereas Francophones in such places as Sherbrooke and Trois-Rivières expressed their discontents primarily in terms of the subordinate position of the French language and of Francophones within the economy and society of Quebec, making few references to the Francophone minorities. (RCBB, *A Preliminary Report*, February 1, 1965 [Ottawa: Queen's Printer, 1965], 39).

56   RCBB, *General Introduction* (Ottawa: Queen's Printer, 1967).

57   The concept was criticized in these terms in a 1965 *Cité libre* article which was signed by Trudeau's colleagues on the Comité pour une politique fonctionnelle, including Albert Breton, Marc Lalonde and Maurice Pinard, but not by Trudeau himself since he had already begun his venture into federal politics. See Le Comité pour une politique fonctionnelle, "Bizarre algèbre," *Cité libre*, XX: 82 (December, 1965), 14.

58   Douglas Verney, *Three Civilizations, Two Cultures, One State: Canada's political traditions* (Durham: Duke University Press, 1986), 325.

59   Positive responses apparently were somewhat more frequent among Quebec Francophones (as opposed to Quebec Anglophones) but remained restricted to a small minority (*Toronto Star*, May 17, 1977).

60   As quoted in *Canadian Annual Review, 1976*, 85. However, it could be argued that ultimately Trudeau did reconcile himself to a limited preeminence of French within Quebec, as with the Charter provision making access of immigrant children to Quebec English-language schools dependent upon the formal acquiescence of the Quebec Assemblée nationale.

61   The federal government does not release data on the provincial origins of its public servants. However, reanalysis of the data which Colin Campbell and George Szablowski collected for their study *The Superbureaucrats* (Toronto: Macmillan, 1979) shows that among federal "superbureaucrats" of whom one or both parents were Francophone (25% of their sample), only 39.1% were raised in Quebec. For "superbureaucrats" of whom both parents were Francophone, (18.5%) of sample, 47.1% were raised in Quebec. (As defined by mother tongue, in 1981 about 85% of Francophone Canadians were born in Quebec.) I am indebted to Professor Campbell for making this information available to me.

62   As André Donneur notes, questions of the internal operations of central institutions are bound to have much less popular impact than such issues as

the language of instruction in schools or the language of work in the private sector (Donneur, "La solution territoriale," 201).

63 Donald Smiley, *Canada in Question: Federalism in the Seventies*, Second Edition (Toronto: McGraw-Hill Ryerson, 1976), 190.

64 Laponce, *Languages and Their Territories*, 149 and 187.

65 *Ibid.*, Chapter Five.

FEDERALISM, PLURALISM, AND THE CANADIAN COMMUNITY

H.G. Thorburn, Queen's University

Over the past forty years, Canada has gone through profound changes. From a white society of mainly British and French origin, it has admitted a large variety of people from many cultures and races. Its economy has modernized and industrialized and has fallen even more deeply under American influence; so that now almost four-fifths of our exports go to the U.S.A.

The old east-west economy in which staple products moved to Britain and Europe over transcontinental railways has given way to a north-south one in which trading relations between Canada's regions and the neighbouring American states have developed, reducing national economic integration. Canadian federalism has grown more decentralized, regional rivalries have increased, especially between producers and consumers of energy, and Canada has become more internationalized in its trade and other relationships. At the same time the federal framework has remained, but has developed from a largely arms-length arrangement to one of intimate federal-provincial and inter-provincial involvement. The provinces and their people are now acutely aware of conditions in other parts of Canada, and are quick to claim for themselves any advantages they see others enjoying. There is much greater pressure on the institutions and governments than ever before to reconcile differences, and to defend the interests of cultural and economic groups. However, despite these changes the old federal institutional structure remains much as it was. True there has been a vast increase in intergovernmental relations and in staff to conduct them, creating many arrangements from first ministers' meetings down to *ad hoc* committees of civil servants of two or more governments to collaborate over specific matters. However, there has not been any permanent inter-governmental institution built to carry the freight of these burgeoning relations. The Senate remains unreformed and ineffective as a federal-provincial instrument of integration, and no other substantial institutions have been put in place. Provincial and federal policies are therefore insufficiently harmonized—a fact that has disadvantaged Canada because business organizations and foreign governments now exploit this disarray at the expense of Canadian interests. What follows is a discussion of the current condition and what might be done to improve this state of affairs.

Media-Infested Politics

The advent of television in the late 1940s was a great destabilizer of Canadian politics. It ended the isolation between regions and consequently the ignorance of one by another. The common man, through this medium, was made graphically aware of conditions and events in other parts of the country, and they became prime issues in Canadian politics. Therefore, people have come to perceive politics differently. Instead of relying on political parties with relatively known and differentiated positions, and led by relatively dull team players, now the public is exposed to a flood of lively, exciting, and constantly changing television images. Party positions have become confused and contradictory; so the salience of the parties themselves has receded. Now it is the leaders who count—and they are constantly reacting to issues in unpredictable and unexpected ways.

Politics has been converted into a kind of theatre, featuring confrontations spooned out in thirty-second clips, with a high level of emotion. Parliament is often the setting; but the scene is question period which is now made over into a bearpit of accusation and stylized insult, aimed at newspaper headlines and the ten o'clock news.

Spectacular issues are created by television reporters focussing on particular incidents, often of a human interest kind, and enlisting widespread public concern. Politicians worry that this interest represents a demand for some policy or other—and so public policy is subjected to the vagaries of television news stories, often contrived by professional advisers to bring about a calculated political outcome. The recent case of the Turkish claimants of refugee status is an example. Here theatre became an instrument to influence, or try to influence, public policy. The pictures of the unhappy Turks walking from Montreal to Ottawa, and of the little girl telling the reporter (in good French) that she wanted to stay in Montreal, had a strong emotional appeal.

Such incidents, and the apprehension that more will be contrived, affect the attitude of political leaders. They know that carefully crafted and sound policies can be 'blown away' by such incidents, and their reaction is to be cautious, to postpone decisions that might provoke them. Therefore, policy tends to be temporizing, vague, and ineffective. This is particularly true of emotional questions such as immigration policy, but it affects others as well. Recall the Prime Minister's confrontation with the aggressive lady pensioner which led to the abandonment of the de-indexation of old age pensions. While one can admire the pluck, courage, and effectiveness of the woman in question, the fact remains that public policy is now strongly influenced by calculated theatrics staged for the media—and some needed policies cannot be undertaken because of media sensitivity. The ramshackle unemployment insurance system seems safe from needed restructuring, despite the serious study devoted to it by both the MacDonald Commission and the Forget Commission.

Intergovernmental affairs too have been affected. First ministers meetings are growing increasingly frequent, and major sessions are televised. Accordingly, the biases of the medium appear there: emotion, confrontation, defence of one province's or region's interests against others, etc.

Federal-provincial relations is an area where leaders must deal with complex jurisdictional interrelations, and to do so they require time, calm, expertise, and secrecy. This is where the intrusion of the television medium is least helpful, because it compels the participants to play to the gallery, and prevents the trade-offs and bargaining ploys that so often facilitate agreement in the end. To deal with this situation, leaders have been led to collective bargaining type all-night sessions in order to reach agreements that can be announced to the horde of reporters waiting at the door. The Meech Lake Accord is a good example.

However, once agreement was announced, media activism was immediately back on track. The focus was shifted to the various interests that might conceivably be affected, and objections were elicited. As the months have passed since the agreement was finalized in the Langevin Block, the likelihood of it being ratified by all the required legislative bodies has been receding. While there are substantive aspects to the objections, there is no doubt that the ready availability of media coverage encouraged full expression of dissenting opinion. From an accord winning general support, Meech Lake became a proposal with at best a fifty-fifty chance of adoption. After the Manitoba elections the odds have lengthened substantially.

Pluralist Values

The episodic nature of media-dominated politics is further exacerbated by the development of pluralism as a public philosophy, and its passage over the U.S. border on the wings of those same media. The general emphasis on public opinion (a product of the newspaper age) as the legitimate determinant of policy gave way easily to the conviction that policy should be formulated by government interacting with interest groups. This added to the legitimacy of business interests as the major source of influence on government, especially in the area of economic policy.

This increased the complexity of political issues in the Canadian federal state as provincial governments interacted with their own interest groups and therefore asserted policies often at variance with those of other provinces, and with the federal government. It became increasingly difficult to reach pan-Canadian economic policies—a fact which became a serious disadvantage in the seventies when many developed countries were following policies of economic concertation. Canada began to notice that its manufacturing industry in particular was becoming increasingly uncompetitive—and because of competing and divided jurisdictions it was not able to do much about it.

The neo-conservatism of the eighties was a particular relief for Canadian governments. As countries were deregulating and relying more on market forces to police trade, it seemed to matter less that the policies of the provinces were at variance with each other and with the federal government. We now hear fewer complaints about Canada's failure to develop a common market between the provinces. However, the conflicting policies remain. Hope now is placed on the competitive forces of free trade to bring about better economic performance throughout the country.

This market-oriented attitude accords well with the prevailing pluralist values. Groups and governments collude to produce policies in a setting of free markets. One hears praise for competition and the market—but there is very little harmonization of policy. Planning of the economy, even in an indicative way, is quite out of the question.

Intellectual and philosophical justification for this state of affairs is supplied by designating the process "pluralist democracy," or simply "pluralism." It enjoys the popular legitimacy that inheres in democracy, and the propaganda advantage stemming from it. As a descriptive term, pluralism perceives the political process as one of bargaining between organized groups, with the government participating in this and giving its authority to the accommodation achieved. It therefore involves an "unseen hand" producing an automatic society, through continuous group interaction. The government becomes merely "an extension of the political process"—so its authority is undermined, and it generally fails to exercise leadership and pursue rigorous administration. The term "pluralist democracy" lends legitimacy to the elite accommodation process, and seems to suggest an equal participation by all groups, or even of groups representing all, whereas actually few are active participants. Pluralism masks that fact.

Pluralism is a liberal doctrine, but not necessarily a democratic one. It justifies group interaction, but does not guarantee that all can participate. Therefore it serves as a mask legitimizing rule by a small party and business elite only vaguely responsible to the electorate, and not necessarily acting in association with expert opinion.[1]

The Intermingling of State and Society

The relations between government and the society it directs and to which it is responsible have grown ever closer and more complex.[2] As the state extends its concerns and controlling arm into areas previously private to the citizens, it fragments both government and society, and produces that lack of cohesion of state institutions that we often find baffling. Government has grown so complex that it defies coordination. Its actions, however, last through regulations and legislation to bind the future. There is constant action as the state interferes with society, and the society (or groups within it) press the state for more action.

The output of governments at all three levels has proliferated, especially since World War II, and an ever greater amount of the gross national product passes through state hands, now reaching nearly half and still growing. This growth too, has occurred at all levels of government, building up loyalties and commitments to each simultaneously. The country has become both more nationalistic and more balkanized—in reality just more aware of government authority at all three levels. This has happened partly at the cost of older loyalties to family, church, and the British tradition, and has exalted new Canadian symbols—flag, nation (through the Canadian Citizenship Act), official languages, bilingualism, multiculturalism, the Charter of Rights and Freedoms. The state, at federal and provincial levels, has come to engage in benevolent social engineering as it comes actively to defend the rights of perceived disadvantaged persons and groups. By so doing, its actions become controversial, and we have seen provincial governments challenging the federal government, with struggles ensuing for the loyalty of citizens. The struggle over Quebec independence is over, but who is to say there will not be other such issues, or that that one will not re-emerge?

The state as colossus in our midst prompts citizens to claim their share and more of its proffered benefits, and to enlist it in their causes. It also leads them to try to evade the heavy burdens the state imposes—so we have tax evasion, and the underground economy. Ethnic, class, and gender groups seek state intervention in their interest to right what they see as past wrongs. So new agencies of government are created to police social relationships, and enforce new codes of conduct, thereby adding to the politicizing of society with new bureaucratic and adversarial relationships. By intervening in social affairs the state is both referee and player, and attracts the emotional reactions appropriate to these roles. Maybe it corrects injustices—but it also dramatizes differences and makes them hard to forget or forgive. As Cairns says, the state "keeps us together by separating us from one another. It fragments our civic wholeness by parcelling out our various discrete concerns to multiple separate agencies, which neither we nor the state can bring together again."[3]

At the individual or small group level there is greater reliance on the courts and quasi-judicial bodies such as human rights commissions and ombudsmen to correct perceived injustices. The Charter of Rights and Freedoms dramatizes and symbolizes this new culture of prescribed rights for the individual. Legislation and due process replace the older bonds of the organic community. *Gesellschaft* replaces *Gemeinschaft*. The assured rights are a gain, the decline of the sense of community is a loss.

The state, by such actions, parallels the actions of groups in our society, which seek to establish and defend perceived rights and any or all privileges. The result is an ossification, a new rigidity of institutions and relationships that hobbles the society in its competition with other countries.[4] When the web of regulation becomes too thick and costs too high, one sees the reaction in a reckless hacking away of the overgrowth behind such slogans as "deregulation" and "getting the state off the backs of citizens." Such acts brought on by frustration are seldom considered ones, and much necessary and valuable regulation gets jettisoned, as well-placed groups get the rules they dislike trashed, while they defend those from which they benefit. The art of government extends to calculating effective strategies to take advantage of the new complexity and the aggravation it causes. There is increasing resort to the *fait accompli* as a governing strategy, and the substance of issues is a lesser concern of policy makers than strategies of implementation. This encourages dramatic unilateralism in all players, and is grist to the mill of media dramatization and exaggeration referred to above.

Federal-Provincial Relations

When applied to federalism, the pluralist process takes the form of the first ministers' conference, which meets at least once a year to discuss and resolve outstanding issues. Below this summit is a complex web of intergovernmental consultative arrangements to deal with a myriad of specific matters.

Government authority, divided through federalism, yet compelled to work together to meet the needs of a complex modern state, operates through the improvised consultative arrangements of pluralist democracy to effect the required collaboration. This is a complex process without central direction which counts instead on the cooperation of the component governments and their leaders. Nevertheless, a large network of relationships has developed in which public servants from both levels of government have come to know and trust each other.

Professor Stefan Dupré, in his work for the MacDonald Commission, has elucidated this relationship.[5] He points out that when the major concern of the first ministers conference was the adjustment of fiscal relations between the two orders of government, relations were more harmonious and agreements were easier to secure than now, when concerns have moved on to such constitutional questions as native people's right, women's rights, etc. This is because on financial matters compromise is always available by adjusting the numbers, in the knowledge that they can later be changed, so nothing is lost forever, no matter what adjustments are made from time to time. The opposite is true in the matter of constitutional questions. Positions abandoned today are, or may be, lost forever and so agreement is very hard to reach on such matters.

Also on fiscal matters, the governments call on their financial experts—a pan-Canadian brotherhood of public servants both federal and provincial, who have come to know one another over the years, and have developed ties of trust. They share a common macroeconomic analysis and treasury mentality that facilitates the development of networks of cooperation.

However, the dominance of this "fiscal relations model" of federal-provincial relations ended with the Trudeau government's decision to resist province-building initiatives, and take a more unilateralist position in relation to the provinces. This occurred when the Department of Finance was losing its dominant position anyway, as new central agencies arose. The federal Parliament passed the Canada Health Act imposing a code of conduct on the provinces to qualify for federal medical support. This circumvented federal-provincial consultation in the very area where there was a long history of consensus-building through negotiation.

When federal-provincial relations turned to the issue of "Securing the Canadian Economic Union," agreement could not be reached, and the whole question of constitutional review led to confrontation, litigation, and the isolation of Quebec. Professor Dupré has shown how this "constitutional review model" of federal-provincial relations is not amenable to compromise and trade-offs, but is centred on abstract issues of constitutional principle; relies on the legal profession for expertise which is inherently adversarial and litigious; and focusses on the "one last play" that if reached would produce a quasi-permanent result. Not surprisingly, federal-provincial negotiations become more tension-ridden and intractable.

The advent of aggressive central agencies such as the Privy Council Office, and its offshoot the Federal-Provincial Relations Office, the ministries of state for economic and social development, and the Trudeauvian incarnation of the Treasury Board, led to the reduction of the powers of the Department of Finance, with its horizontal concerns for the whole of governmental responsibility. Federal-provincial relations shifted to intractable issues in which each government was watched over by mobilized interest groups. Small wonder that agreement became almost unattainable, and the distances between governments grew.

It must be admitted that recent federal-provincial conferences have been less acrimonious than those in the later Trudeau period, but the way the ratification of Meech Lake is dragging on and the failure of the Aboriginal rights conference suggests that the institution is still not working well; little seems to have been accomplished. Of course, if the first ministers conference is not seen to be successful, then it casts a shadow over the many other intergovernmental arrangements that have proliferated over the years. These lesser institutions, which are staffed by subordinate ministers and public servants, attract much less publicity and have generally been more successful in their areas of concern—prompting the observation that the more remote from the media-infested hyper-political atmosphere of first ministers meetings, the greater the likelihood of success and efficient, objective consideration of issues! Also, there seems to be greater harmony between official experts in substantive areas than between generalist politicians with constituencies to satisfy.

Inadequate Bridging Institutions

The post-war period has seen governments in Canada move to fill the policy space assigned to them under the Constitution, and to spill over it via shared cost programs, delegation of authority, and (rarely) re-assignment of jurisdiction. Governments, therefore, have come to interpenetrate one another, making it necessary to develop mechanisms to monitor developments and settle differences. The first ministers conference has been the summit institution to fulfill this role—the apex of the pyramid of intergovernmental committees, agencies, and so on. These arrangements have all accomplished a bridging function between the two orders of government—thereby providing the means of conducting the zero-sum game that federal-provincial relations have become. In other words, all these cooperative arrangements have no autonomy or separate identity attached to them. The persons concerned represent the federal government or one or other of the provinces—so no one is identified with an intergovernmental body or role. Rather, all are committed to the interest of their own government, for which they are the spokesmen. The functions have therefore been essentially diplomatic in the traditional sense. There has been no federal-provincial equivalent to the United Nations in international affairs.

This failure to develop a permanent institution with a life of its own has far-reaching consequences for Canada. Other federal states normally have a senate or federal council to which representatives of state governments or elected spokesmen for the people belong. Such a body takes on a separate identity, and the proceedings constitute an ongoing statement of state views within the institution of the central government. The Canadian Senate, appointed on a purely patronage basis by the Prime Minister to sit till age seventy-five, cannnot fulfill such a role. The senators represent nothing, and, to their credit, have never claimed to. Indeed the reformist step taken in the Meech Lake Accord whereby the Prime Minister will restrict his selection to a list provided by the provincial premier concerned, falls far short of what is needed to give legitimacy to senators as provincial representatives.

In default of the Senate as representative of the provinces, the task has fallen to executive federalism—to the episodic first ministers' meeting, at a time of unprecedented expansion of government roles and interpenetration of their functions. It is a tribute to all concerned that more serious difficulties have not arisen—although the Quebec-Ottawa struggle of the 1970s was bad enough. The fact is that the improvised and infrequent first ministers conference, and all the other bridging arrangements are simply not sufficient to carry the freight of modern federal-provincial relations. And because of this inadequacy and impermanence, federal-provincial relations have retained too much of an adversarial character—too much of a distant, diplomatic stance.

In some federal states, notably the Federal Republic of Germany, the political party system has played an important role in reconciling relations between the central government and the states. This is possible if the parties have clear ideological positions and programs, and if there is a high degree of coordination between the federal and state party organizations. This is the case in Germany and also in Austria; however, the Canadian situation is vastly different. Party ideology in the case of the two brokerage parties scarcely exists, and is not to be distinguished between the one and the other. The NDP too, for a socialist party, has remained remarkably non-ideological. It does have closer relations between its national and provincial sections than the two brokerage parties. However, its third party position prevents it from playing a role in reconciling federal and provincial governments.[6] The party system therefore is unable to assist in the necessary task of bridging the gap between federal and provincial governments.

A similar if lesser bridging effect can be secured by a system of national interest groups pressing concerted policies at both federal and state levels. While this obtains in Germany, Canadian groups tend to be regionalized because of the regional character of the Canadian economy, with manufacturing in central Canada and the major resource industries in the outlying regions. Also, Canada lacks peak organizations to integrate the groups by sector or industry.

There is another West German development which suggests possible adaptations for Canada: the creation of joint tasks to be shared by the two orders of government. In that country this has occurred to permit the federal government to steer the economy via special federal-state councils for financial planning. A further interlacing of functions has followed between the two levels of government, with a network of committees and other cooperative arrangements.[7] There is a single Canadian example of this development: the recognition in the Meech Lake Accord of the joint participation of the federal and Quebec governments in the immigration process. Of course, agriculture and immigration have always been shared responsibilities under the Constitution since 1867—but now Quebec appears ready to pursue an active policy in the field of immigration. It is to be hoped that this will turn out to be complementary to federal efforts, and that the Quebec minister's unfortunate intervention in the case of the Turkish refugee claimants in March 1988 will be a unique exception. Canada has still a long way to go to match west European institutional innovations.

To correct this lack of bridging mechanisms it would appear that we need to develop a new permanent institution within which federal-provincial programs can be elaborated, which has legitimacy and competence.[8] To attain the former it would have to consist of equal representation for each of the two orders of government. These representatives would have to have authority to elaborate policies with their colleagues, subject of course to endorsement by their principals. While the prime role would no doubt consist of planning for the economic development of the country, the institution could become a strong centre for developing cooperative undertakings, especially if it had a strong chairman and a competent staff of expert planners, economists, lawyers, sociologists, political scientists, etc. Such an institution could facilitate the development of a national policy by reassuring both orders of government, and offering a neutral base for the common enterprise—a kind of permanent royal commission providing expert advice and assistance.

The addition of such an intermediary institution could assist in escaping from the *ad hoc* approach to problems that our federal system has hitherto entailed. We may be able to plan cooperative federal-provincial endeavours, and avoid some of the confrontations that have so often arisen in the past. In situations where provinces speak for interests situated within their borders, and other provinces or the federal government defend others, the presence of an impartial body with professional competence could well make compromise or reconciliation possible where formerly it was unattainable, and introduce an element of flexibility and greater rationality into a heavy, slow-moving arrangement. It might, by so doing, reduce the temptation to abdicate to the competitive market as a crude and tough reconciler of differences. Then we could act rationally and deliberately, instead of responding uncertainly to invitations to undertake leaps of faith!

Notes

1   H.G. Thorburn, "Canadian Pluralist Democracy in Crisis," *Canadian Journal of Political Science*, 11(1978), 723-738.

2   Alan Cairns, "The Embedded State: State-Society Relations in Canada," in Keith Banting, ed., *State and Society: Canada in Comparative Perspective*, (Toronto: University of Toronto Press, for the Royal Commission on the Economic Union and Development Prospects for Canada, 1985), 53-86.

3   *Ibid.*, 80.

4   See Mancur Olson, *The Rise and Decline of Nations*, (New Haven: Yale University Press, 1982).

5   J. Stefan Dupré, "Reflections on the Workability of Executive Federalism," in R. Simeon, ed., *Intergovernmental Relations*, (Toronto: University of Toronto Press, for the Royal Commission on the Economic Union and Development Prospects for Canada, 1985), 1-32.

6   K. von Beyme, "West Germany: Federalism," in *International Political Science Review*, 4(1984), 382; and T.O. Hueglin, "Legitimacy, Democracy and Federalism", in H. Bakvis and W.A. Chandler, eds., *Federalism and the Role of the State*, (Toronto: University of Toronto Press, 1987), 46.

7   K. von Beyme, "West Germany: Federalism."

8   For fuller elaboration see H.G. Thorburn, *Planning and the Economy*, (Toronto: Lorimer, 1984), 210-245; and H.G. Thorburn, *Interest Groups in the Canadian Federal System* , (Toronto: University of Toronto Press, for the Royal Commission on the Economic Union and Development Prospects for Canada, 1985), 133-137.

INCORPORATING CANADA'S OTHER POLITICAL TRADITION

Douglas V. Verney, York University

I

At one time Canada had the best of both worlds. It inherited the Westminster parliamentary tradition, but without the burden of a Buckingham Palace or a House of Lords. The substance of the British political system was transferred to Canada, but not its archaic forms, except for the wording of the British North America Act.[1] Like Britain, Canada after 1867 was governed by a Cabinet responsible primarily to a House of Commons under a two-party system of alternating majorities. It was the party with the majority that ruled.

Canada also tentatively entered another political world, the world of federalism. It adopted the distribution of powers between a federal government and a number of provincial governments. At the same time, it avoided such American doctrines as republicanism, popular sovereignty, the separation of powers, checks and balances, and limited government. Of all the American principles, federalism alone was extracted, and only one part of federalism, the distribution of powers. The other part, the veto exercised within federalized institutions, could not be adopted because the veto lay with the imperial authorities. Canada enjoyed strong cabinet government both at the centre and in the provinces. What some have called "interstate federalism" and I shall call "half federalism," the distribution of powers was tempered by the conventions of a Westminster-inspired constitution, by majority rule, not a veto.

The new Dominion enjoyed more than the parliamentary tradition inherited from the United Kingdom and the federal principle inspired by the United States. Like both these countries it developed a two-party system. Canada managed to escape the violence that had marred the United States in the early 1860s and that was to engulf the United Kingdom when the Irish, like the Southerners, determined on secession. Unlike the Irish, the people of Quebec preferred to vote for MPs who belonged to the governing party. As a result, a wonderful Canadian system of double majority rule emerged. The English-speaking Canadians enjoyed majority rule in Ottawa and most of the provinces. Members of the French-speaking Roman Catholic minority were able to exercise majority rule in their province of Quebec.[2]

The remarkable polity which Canada pioneered came to be known as "parliamentary federalism." So successful was this system of government that it was copied elsewhere. Australia adopted parliamentary federalism in 1900 and India followed suit in 1950.

II

If this novel political system was so successful, why have there been increasing demands in Canada for a change?

One popular explanation is that the desire for at least a modification of the British North America Act came about because of social and economic changes in Quebec. As the province grew politically more restive in the 1960s it looked for a time as if it might become another Ireland: but fortunately Montreal did not become another Belfast. Some of the more extreme separatists appear to have compared Quebec with Algeria, where the FLN helped to drive out the French *colons*. They hoped that the FLQ would drive out *les anglais*. To judge by the sales of Pierre Valliéres' popular account of francophone history, many *Québecois* shared his view that they were treated as *nègres blancs*.[3] Certainly it was in Quebec that discontent with the BNA Act first manifested itself.

The view that Canada's political problems can all be traced to Quebec, while plausible, deserves closer scrutiny. There was a constitutional crisis in Canada it is true (with violence in 1970), but in 1975 there were also constitutional crises in Australia and India, the other two systems that were parliamentary and federal.[4] These other crises cannot be attributed to Quebec.

At the very least, then, we should study the nature of parliamentary federalism more carefully. Perhaps it was not what it seemed to be, or perhaps it changed over time.[5] The Westminster tradition of majority rule had been under pressure in all these countries as a result of demands for a more federal system in which provinces and states could play an important role. There were also strains resulting from the shift in power from the United Kingdom to the United States, so that it was Washington's example rather than Westminster's that appealed to the younger generation.

In short, we need to examine the structure of parliamentary federalism, not just Quebec's dissatisfaction.

III

I have argued elsewhere that the Canada of 1867 ought not to be described in terms of parliamentary federalism. At that time, Canada was governed as a colony from London through a form of what I have called "imperial federalism."[6] This imperial federalism provided three umpires, one for each of the branches of government. The three imperial empires (in principle) had power of veto. For the executive there was the Colonial Secretary and British Governor-General; for the legislature, Parliament at Westminster; and for the judiciary, the Judicial Committee of the Privy Council. As the empire retreated, the umpires gradually disappeared. The paternal Governor-General went first between 1878 and 1931, then the Privy Council in 1933 and 1949, and finally the Westminster Parliament in 1931, 1949, and 1982. Canada thus remained half-federal, with the distribution of powers, but without the veto. The vacuum left by the imperial umpires was filled by Ottawa, but only in part.

Quebec was merely the first province to notice what was happening. Long before the Parti Québécois became a force to be reckoned with, the Liberal government of Quebec under Jean Lesage, a former cabinet minister in Ottawa, set up an office of intergovernmental affairs. It did so in 1960, immediately after assuming power. Since then other provinces, and the Federal Government, have followed suit. The study of Canada's political traditions suggested to me that there might be a contradiction between parliamentary supremacy and federalism, the two partners in parliamentary federalism. More recently, in a paper delivered at Osgoode Hall Law School in 1987 I have asked whether, in view of the growing power of the Supreme Court of Canada, any compromise is possible between parliamentary supremacy and judicial review.[7] It is not necessary to review these arguments here.

IV

Instead, we may now take the argument a stage further. The controversy over Canadian federalism has tended to centre on the distribution of powers between the Federal Government (in Section 91 of the BNA Act) and the provincial governments in Section 92. But the distribution of powers is only half of what federalism is all about. In other words, when the umpires were withdrawn Canada was not federal, nor was it quasi-federal, to use K.C. Wheare's description. It was half-federal.

The other half of the federal principle involves the transformation of such institutions of the central government as the Senate into bodies that incorporate the federal principle. In his constitutional proposals Mr. Trudeau resisted this notion, arguing that the Westminster tradition of parliamentary government precluded having the cabinet responsible to any body other than the House of Commons. (Despite this belief he felt able to adopt as his slogan "renewed federalism".[8])

We have long recognized just how wrong were those people who in 1867 thought that the problems of Canada's new federal structure would be resolved by a Senate representing each of the main regions of the country equally. The Senate was appointed, not elected, and its role as an institution representative of the regions did not develop. Canada was to be parliamentary, but not fully federal.

And so, without a powerful Senate, and without the imperial umpires, Canada has had to wrestle with the problem of incorporating its other political tradition, federalism. Senate reform is increasingly taken seriously, even by academic political scientists. What I shall call "legislative federalism" may well become an important topic of debate in the 1990s.

V

Until recently Canadian scholars have been more interested in the executive's role in making federalism work. Over the decades, Canada has gone through a number of stages in its development towards a more federal system. The first stage was the type of executive federalism that Professor MacGregor Dawson and others described: a federalized cabinet. This I shall call, somewhat clumsily, *Federal Cabinet Executive Federalism*.

The first stage of executive federalism consisted of a federal cabinet that included men [sic] drawn from all the provinces. Dawson implied that it was the Canadian equivalent of the American Senate: executive rather than legislative federalism.[9] Dawson had no doubts as to where the responsibility of the cabinet lay. It was to the House of Commons alone. "One master is enough" he noted.[10] In Dawson's view Canada's parliamentary federalism had proved sufficiently adaptable to be able so to modify the Westminster tradition of parliamentary government as to match the American Senate by means of a federalized cabinet.[11]

Such was the theory, and for many Canadians it is assumed to have been the practice. Yet in recent years the practice seems to have fallen short of the ideal.[12] How was a Liberal Prime Minister to include in his cabinet MPs from all the provinces if a province (for example Alberta in the Trudeau era) stubbornly refused to elect a single Liberal to Parliament? And how was a Conservative Prime Minister like Joe Clark in 1979 to appoint an adequate number of Quebec ministers when Quebec still voted overwhelmingly Liberal?

Moreover, are we to assume that those MPs who were available were all of ministerial calibre? Could they seriously be compared to American Senators, those quasi-ambassadors from semi-sovereign states? Even those MPs who were of ministerial timber often had difficulty in protecting the interests of their provinces in cabinet. Here secrecy and collective responsibility were the rule. There was no veto. All that such ministers could do if they wished to register a protest was to resign. But when James Richardson of Manitoba and Jean Marchand of Quebec resigned, nothing happened. The federal juggernaut rumbled on.

Of course any federal cabinet *must* include persons from across Canada. So must the Canada Council and countless other national bodies. But they are not federal in the sense that representatives of the smaller provinces can exercise anything reasonably approaching a veto. Yet strangely enough, Dawson's notion of a Canada enjoying what I have called Federal Cabinet Executive Federalism, a federalized institution that was the Canadian counterpart of the American Senate, with its filibusters and vetoes, has not been repudiated.

VI

The second stage in the development of a more federal system has been the "Executive Federalism" associated with Donald Smiley. To distinguish it from the Dawson variety I shall call it *First Ministers' Executive Federalism*. From now on it is to Professor Smiley's federal-provincial type that I refer. In this form of executive federalism the possibility of a veto by one or more provincial premiers emerged.

First Ministers' Executive Federalism developed gradually out of a dawning recognition that mercly to distribute power between two orders of government was not enough, especially when the imperial umpires were withdrawn. These two sets of institutions, federal and provincial, had somehow to be linked together. From its beginnings in what was called "cooperative federalism" and "federal-provincial diplomacy," executive federalism developed into the full-blown televised First Ministers' Conference we know today.

Until the constitutional debates of 1981, individual First Ministers were widely thought to exercise a veto, at least by convention.[13] However, federalism depends on a legal framework, not on conventions about which governments may differ. The limitations of the First Ministers' Conference format became obvious in 1981 when agreement on the constitution was reached during a kitchen discussion in the middle of the night while the Quebec delegation was asleep. Yet it was at this point that the First Ministers' Conference was incorporated into the Constitution Act 1982 in some perverse Canadian version of one of Parkinson's laws.14 The First Ministers' role was extended by the Meech Lake Accord of 1987—just as it was becoming clear that it was legislative, not executive, federalism that needed to be incorporated into the Constitution. Let us consider for a moment some of the features of legislative federalism:

1. an impartial Speaker
2. parliamentary rules of procedure to ensure fair treatment of all parties
3. a legislative agenda agreed to in advance by all parties
4. a parliamentary secretariat serving all members impartially

5. public and leisurely debate of all issues in accordance with the norms of liberal democracy

Compare this set of arrangements with the somewhat ad hoc procedure governing First Ministers' Conferences:

1. The Prime Minister is in charge, as in a cabinet meeting.
2. There are no parliamentary rules of debate. Having been opposed all morning by a majority of premiers in the 1981 discussion of the principle of a Charter of Rights and Freedoms, the Prime Minister simply adjourned the meeting for lunch and afterwards proceeded to a clause by clause discussion of his proposal.
3. The agenda is circulated by the Prime Minister to the First Ministers.
4. However, the agenda for these Conferences is prepared by the Federal Government's own Federal-Provincial Secretariat.
5. There *are* public sessions, before the TV cameras, but these are largely for prepared statements. Real debate takes place behind closed doors and often over lunch and dinner.
6. At a First Ministers' Conference, Quebec's premier, representing over a quarter of the country's population, is neatly transformed into one of eleven equal First Ministers. Behind closed doors, pressure can be brought to bear on the odd man out.

Such brief encounters (one is tempted to call this institution Brief Encounter Executive Federalism, or BEEF) allow none of the leisurely, public, and thorough debate that takes place in a legislature. Meetings frequently end inconclusively and in acrimony, sometimes postponed until after an election. One may well ask whether this really is the best way to run a country and to deal with such important and controversial issues as constitutional reform.

It is true that the relationship between the Prime Minister of Canada and the premier of Quebec has been far more cordial than that of their two illustrious predecessors. Even so, the Meech Lake Accord of 1987 was reached only during all-night bargaining, after which the First Ministers urged the constitutional bodies involved, the House of Commons, Senate, and provincial legislatures, not to tamper with their handiwork. So delicate was the consensus that it seemed in danger of falling apart as a result of provincial elections in which a couple of the First Ministers were replaced. Clearly, this form of ad hoc executive federalism has considerable limitations, to put it mildly.

VII

If neither Federal Cabinet Executive Federalism nor First Ministers' Executive Federalism can be regarded as a permanent solution to Canada's constitutional problems, we are forced to consider the obvious alternative: legislative federalism, where all the rules of parliamentary debates are observed. While in principle legislative federalism has its attractions, it also has its defects. It is unpopular in Ontario. Here the Westminster tradition of a government responsible solely to the lower house, and majority rule governed by the old Grit principle of rep. by pop. and no nonsense about a veto, is rightly cherished.[15]

Even if we discount the views of Ontario, which would be most unwise, legislative federalism presents a number of practical problems. These will have to be attended to once debate starts in earnest over the proposed "Triple-E" Senate, one that would be Equal, Elected, and Effective.[16]

The first "E," Equality, presents a very difficult problem. How is a province like Ontario to accept equality in the Senate with all the other provinces? Having had 24 senators of its own since Confederation (out of the present 104), it is not likely to give up its share without a struggle. It is true that the present Senate is a relatively powerless body, so that the number of senators is not all that important, but its replacement is a different matter altogether.

One alternative, which proponents of equal representation in the Senate might have to consider, is to argue that the present Senate should be abolished, not reformed. In its place they could recommend a new and improved institution, one based on the existing executive federalism. At First Ministers' Conferences the Ontario premier is accustomed to being simply one of eleven equal First Ministers. He appears to accept this arrangement. In other words, the problem of equality could be resolved by recommending the creation of a new body in terms of the present arrangements for First Ministers' Executive Federalism.

The Second "E," Elected, also presents a problem. How are First Ministers who have enjoyed such a powerful role in Federal-provincial relations to be persuaded to allow themselves to be replaced or upstaged by an American-style elected Senate? Surely there is a simple answer to this question: they will not permit it.

The only way of overcoming the opposition of the First Ministers to a rival elected upper house is once again to take as the model the First Ministers' Conference, not the present Senate. In other words, the premiers themselves would have to be allowed to head provincial delegations to the new body. It could be argued that as elected MLAs their presence would in a sense fulfil the demand for an elected body.

Of course it would not be practicable for First Ministers to be in constant attendance in the new body. They might be able to be present for important occasions, for example, the final stages of a constitutional debate, but day-to-day representation would be handled by a Minister of Intergovernmental Relations and his deputies—as at the United Nations and in the European Community. In other words, it would not be feasible to attempt to impose an American-style Senate on top of the First Ministers' Conference. Rather, this conference should be transformed into a permanent legislative body with many of the characteristics of a normal parliamentary institution.

Even so, other problems remain. What would be the role of the Prime Minister? Would he be excluded from the new body? And what would be the relationship of this new institution, a House of the Provinces, with the government of the day, which traditionally has been responsible only to the House of Commons?

This leads us to the third "E" of the Triple-E Senate proposal, its Effectiveness. It is difficult to see how the new House could be effective in a system accustomed to responsible government, that is, responsibility to the lower house. Dawson expressed views held by many people today when he said "One master is enough." It is difficult to envisage Canadians taking seriously an alternative to what we may call "lower-house parliamentarism." "Lower-house parliamentarism" has long been regarded by many Canadians, including Pierre Trudeau, as the *only* form of government consistent with a parliamentary system. This is not so. In the United Kingdom itself, a unitary state, the upper house enjoyed a veto until the Parliament Act of 1911. In other parliamentary countries, for example Sweden, it was long taken for granted that government should come to terms with *two* houses of the Riksdag, one of which represented the provinces. In 1906 an anglophile Liberal prime minister boldly suggested that Sweden should adopt the British system of lower-house parliamentarism. This attracted the wrath of Swedish conservatives as being contrary to Sweden's political traditions. The Liberal government was defeated and the proposal was dropped.

Many Canadians are going to resist the notion of an effective upper house. Not only are most people, like Mr. Trudeau, imbued with what they perceive to be the Westminster tradition, but they do not appear to see the connection between the proposal for an effective upper house and the federal principle. To them, the distribution of powers, (which I have called half-federalism) is enough. Had Canadians wanted full federalism, some might say, they would have introduced it long ago. However, we may have to qualify our statement. If it turns out that Canadians in the western provinces and Quebec want full federalism, the supporters of the present system may prove to be primarily Ontarians.

There are two sets of Canadians for whom the federal principle is not paramount. One group consists of conservatives. In England the conservative tradition has been so powerful that at no time has any form of federalism for Scotland, Ireland, and Wales ever been seriously considered.[17] Similarly in English Canada, the conservative tradition has been so strong that an appointed Senate has been tolerated for over 120 years. Few political scientists have written with passion against this non-elected institution.[18] Some describe it as innocuous. They rarely indicate that it conflicts with the federal principle and sustains the "representation by population" demanded by Ontario before Confederation and supposedly modified by the creation of the Senate.

In addition to conservatives there are social democrats who have little interest in an effective upper house.[19] Many would simply like the Senate to be abolished, for experience suggests that an effective upper house tends to be an obstacle to radical reform. Consequently, if a New Democratic government ever took power in Ottawa its programme might be rejected by the upper house, as in Australia in the 1970s.

People in Ontario are likely to be particularly concerned about any new body which provides representatives from other provinces with a veto. It is the conventional wisdom in Toronto that Confederation was introduced largely to overcome the dead-lock (and the veto) that characterized government in the Province of Canada in the early 1860s. For Ontarians there would have to be emphasis on ways for overcoming the veto, for example through a joint vote of the two houses (as in Sweden between 1866 and 1970), or through a conference committee (as in the United States).

Supporters of full federalism, mindful of the capacity of the United States to survive Senate vetoes, may be tempted to argue that the veto is essential for an effective upper House of the Provinces. However we must never forget that Canada is different from the United States. For example, Canada has a disciplined party system which in the House of Commons and provincial legislatures manifests itself in predictable parliamentary voting behaviour. It is possible that Canadian representatives in the new House would behave as individuals, like American senators, but equally possible that they would emulate the Australians, where bitter partisan battles occur in both houses.

On the other hand, suppose our model is not the existing upper house in the United States or Australia but our own first ministers' conference. Here the debate does not appear to be primarily partisan. Were legislative federalism in Canada to take the novel route of being the transformation of the present execu-tive federalism into a permanent parliamentary body without the infusion of partisanship, the issue of the veto would become less intractable. The Meech Lake Accord already provides a veto for each province on a number of vital issues. It is true that observers like Eugene Forsey oppose these vetoes because they may result in stalemate.[20] On the other hand, the First Ministers who signed the Accord, the provinces that have ratified it, and a variety of observers from *The Globe and Mail* to Professor Peter Hogg think it might work.

Once again, therefore, if we think of the Triple-E proposal in terms not of a reformed Senate but of a new, improved, and transformed First Minsters Executive Federalism, it becomes less problematic.

VIII

Whether legislative federalism will be incorporated into Canada's parliamentary tradition depends very much on whether the present executive federalism, in either of its forms, is seen to be inadequate and needs to be replaced. Many Canadians, and especially Ontarians, will take a lot of convincing before they conclude that what they have been enjoying is only half-federalism, and that full federalism is preferable. They may not be upset to learn that what they have had up to now has been the distribution of powers but not the federalization of central institutions. Federal Cabinet Executive Federalism and First Ministers' Executive Federalism have yet to be perceived for what they are: stages in the development towards a more federal system, in which legislative federalism will play an important role.[21]

Indeed, many people fear that present trends are balkanizing Canada. They do not want more federalism. They still have to be persuaded that the replacement of executive federalism by legislative federalism will bring back to a single centre (Ottawa) decisions which increasingly have been made by First Ministers in eleven different capitals.

The title of this paper is "The incorporation of Canada's other political tradition." During the 1960s and 1970s, the "other" political tradition to be incorporated was of course that of French-speaking Canadians. It is arguable that this tradition has not yet been perceived (at least in English-speaking Canada outside Ottawa) as being capable of being incorporated. Be that as it may, it no longer makes sense to examine francophone Canada in isolation. The criticisms of the present system, which this paper has described as half-federal, have come from other parts of Canada as well.

Those of us who live in Ontario wonder whether the new Quebec-West axis which brought us Meech Lake and Free Trade is going to affect us adversely. Economically, of course, Ontario will remain the powerhouse of Canada. Politically, however, Ontario's dominance may be in decline. Confederation in 1867 was not intended to produce "rep. by pop." or majority rule. But in effect Confederation did give Ontario considerable clout. It is not for nothing that Toronto has been the bogeyman for so many people outside Ontario. Any reform of the Canadian political system will necessarily be in the direction of greater federalism and less emphasis on the majority rule which has allowed Ontario's MPs in the House of Commons to carry the most weight. Not surprisingly, Ontarian academics from George Grant onwards (he used to live in Ontario) have long been on the defensive with regard to the Canadian political system—and to its political economy.

Ontario's academics need to be just as concerned with their province's intellectual contribution to Canada as they are with its political economy. They have seen the ferment of ideas first in Quebec and more recently in the West (where Donald Smiley's formative years were spent). History should remember the city of Toronto not only for its interesting architecture and satisfying twentieth-century lifestyle but for its contribution to the political ideas that can inspire all Canadians. After all, the great cities from Athens onwards have been not only aesthetically pleasing but important symbols of the political vitality of Western civilization.

It would be a pity if Toronto a thousand years hence were to be viewed as a latterday Leptis Magna. That great city, it will be recalled, is admired not for its contribution to the political development of Rome but for its replication of Roman architecture. What remains of Leptis Magna are the ruins of a Roman city transplanted to Africa. As far as one can tell, its primary contribution was that of an outpost of empire. Until recently Toronto too was an outpost of empire: "Loyal She Remains."[22] Nowadays Toronto is the leading metropolis of a great and independent country about to embark on a new era in both its internal constitutional arrangements and its external economy.

It is no accident that we are witnessing today in Canada a transition from a parliamentary system of government which, though it was an imperial legacy with imperial umpires, gave Canada the best of both worlds, thanks to its North American federal features. The transition now is towards a new and equally distinctive Canadian political system, as novel a form of government as were the British and American systems in their formative years. If so, Canada may be entering the best of all possible worlds, with its legislative federalism as much an inspiration to others as parliamentary federalism was in the heyday of the Dominion.

Notes

1   The Constitution Act 1982, among other things, discarded the archaic language used in the British North America Act of 1867, except in its opening

paragraphs addressed "To the Queen's Most Excellent Majesty: Most Gracious Sovereign..."

2   On 17 April 1886 the Quebec Legislative Assembly recalled Canada's experience and passed a unanimous resolution favouring Home Rule for Ireland. J.L. Hammond, *Gladstone and the Irish Nation* (Hamden, Conn.: Archon Books, 1964 reprint), 476n.

3   Pierre Valliéres, *White Niggers of America* (Toronto: McClelland and Stewart, 1971). Now largely forgotten in English-speaking Canada, this little book was a best-seller in Quebec. It was one of the few modern books on Canada in the Delhi University Library in 1984—there were multiple copies.

4   In June 1975 Mrs. Gandhi declared an Emergency and jailed a number of MPs, including the Opposition leaders. In November 1975 the Governor General of Australia, Sir John Kerr, dismissed the Prime Minister, Gough Whitlam.

5   Arend Lijphart has drawn attention to the changes in the "Westminster" system, arguing that in its traditional form it now exists only in New Zealand. Arend Lijphart, *Democracies: Patterns of Majoritarian and Consensus Government in Twenty-one Countries* (New Haven: Yale University Press, 1984), 16-20.

6   Douglas V. Verney, *Three Civilizations, Two Cultures, One State: Canada's Political Traditions* (Durham, NC: Duke University Press, 1986), Chapter 5, "The 'Reconciliation' of Parliamentary Supremacy and Federalism."

7   Douglas V. Verney, "Parliamentary Supremacy versus Judicial Review: Is a compromise possible?" *Journal of Commonwealth and Comparative Politics*, 27, 2, 1989, 29-44.

8   Pierre Elliott Trudeau, *A Time for Action: Toward the Renewal of Canadian Federalism* (Ottawa: Ministry of Supply and Services, 1978).

9   "The Cabinet has in fact taken over the allotted role of the Senate as the protector of the rights of the provinces and it has done an incomparably better job." R. MacGregor Dawson, *The Government of Canada* (revised edition, Toronto: University of Toronto Press, 1957), 211-12.

10   Dawson, *Government of Canada*, 209.

11   "Professor McKay has rightly called attention to the fact that today many Canadians expect the Senate to have some of the prestige and glamour of the House of Lords on the one hand and some of the power and importance of the United States Senate on the other..." Dawson, *Government of Canada*, 331.

12   "...until the St. Laurent era, cabinets contained an apparently adequate intrastate element in their operation." Donald V. Smiley and Ronald L. Watts, *Intrastate Federalism in Canada* (Toronto: University of Toronto Press, 1985), 6.

13   In his white paper *The Amendment of the Constitution of Canada* (Ottawa: Information Canada, 1965), the Minister of Justice, Guy Favreau, delineated four general principles:

> The fourth general principle is that Canadian Parliament will not request an amendment directly affecting federal-provincial relationships without prior consultation and agreement with the provinces. This principle did not emerge as early as the others, but since 1907, and particularly since 1930, has gained increasing recog-

nition and acceptance. The nature and degree of provincial participation in the amending process, however, have not lent themselves to easy definition.

14   C. Northcote Parkinson noted that an institution often acquires respectability just as it becomes obsolescent. Thus the North Atlantic Treaty Alliance moved into a permanent headquarters in Paris just before the French Government withdrew from the alliance. NATO had to relocate in Brussels. See *Parkinson's Law: and other Studies in Administration* (Boston: Houghton Mifflin, 1957).

15   Before 1867 the old Province of Canada consisted of two equal sections, Canada West (later Ontario) and Canada East (Quebec). After the 1851 census indicated that Canada West had become the more populous section, the Grits (or Liberals) in Canada West argued strongly in favour of representation by population. Confederation came about after a compromise which gave English-speaking Canadians majority rule in Ontario, the Maritime Provinces and the Dominion, and francophones majority rule in Quebec. The French-speaking Canadians had expected the Senate to temper the principle of majority rule at the Federal level. This did not happen. The principle of majority rule and "rep. by pop." has continued to have many adherents in Ontario to this day.

16   The "Triple-E Senate," a proposal sponsored by the premiers of Alberta and British Columbia, was inspired by a proposal of the Canada West Foundation entitled *Regional Representation: the Canadian Partnership* (Calgary: Canada West Foundation, 1981).

17   Notably in the *Report of the Royal Commission on the Constitution* (London: HMSO, Cmnd. 5450, 1973).

18   "Senate reform...has long since ceased to be the subject of serious consideration in political science." F. A. Kunz, *The Modern Senate of Canada 1925-1963: A Re-Appraisal* (Toronto: University of Toronto Press, 1965), 367.

19   As long ago as 1935 the League for Social Reconstruction recommended the abolition of the Senate.

20   "The fact is that we now have a Constitution so rigid, so hard to amend, that it will be the devil of a job to get anything new of any consequence into it, and the devil of a job getting anything old of any consequence out of it." *The Globe and Mail* (Toronto), March 17, 1987, A7.

21   In this paper I have dealt with only one of Canada's central institutions, the Senate and its possible replacement. Other central institutions requiring investigation are the Supreme Court, a parliamentary institution which, following the Meech Lake Accord, may become fully federal, and the office of the Governor-General. This office is still thought of in parliamentary and not federal terms.

22   *Loyal She Remains* (n.a.) (Toronto: United Empire Loyalist Association, 1984). Before the second world war, public school children in Ontario studied a geography textbook which described their country's proud role in the British Empire.

The Empire extends from the farthest north to the farthest south, from farthest east to farthest west, girdling the globe with lands over which floats the Union Jack, proud symbol of power, of justice, and of freedom...Under the Union Jack live representatives of all the races of the world, from the lowest and most degraded savage to the finest types of the highest civilization.

Ontario Public School Geography (n.a.) (Toronto: W.J. Gage Nineteenth Edition, n.d.), 249.

THE SPIRIT OF MEECH LAKE

Joan Boase, University of Windsor

If Canada cannot become a political community—one community not two—it is not worth preserving.[1]

Donald Smiley

About five o'clock the morning of June 3, 1987, an "exhausted" Prime Minister Brian Mulroney emerged from an all-night session of first ministers and their advisers in the Langevin Block[2] on Parliament Hill and announced the final draft of a constitutional Accord. He presented us with a fait accompli, an agreement that he called a "seamless web" that must be accepted or rejected unaltered by the eleven governments within three years. The hasty and covert process by which consensus was reached distressed and shocked many Canadians, and it exhibited all the negative elements of executive federalism that Donald Smiley has identified and lamented.[3] Of more importance, however, is the spirit of this Accord—its underlying assumptions and its socio-political implications for the development of political community in Canada. It was declared a national reconciliation by Mulroney and an "agenda to dismember the country"[4] by Michael Bliss. It has subsequently been debated and discussed, praised and maligned, interpreted and reinterpreted, and has created schisms within Canadian political parties that have seriously strained party discipline. It is clearly not perceived as a minor constitutional adjustment. If constitutional exhaustion set in after the interminable wrangling of 1979-1982, new life has been breathed into many groups by the commissions and omissions of this Accord.

The inescapable conclusion one must reach in the aftermath of the Constitution Act 1982 and the Meech Lake Accord of 1987, is that Canadians are not very careful constitution crafters. As we continue to pile wordy document[5] on wordy document, we still cannot seem to get it quite right. Canadians in 1982, while welcoming the Charter of Rights and Freedoms, were appalled that the first ministers would proceed over the objections of Quebec and many saw this as a betrayal. This affront set the stage for the argument of desperation as a rationale and justification for the precipitate discussions at Meech Lake in April 1987 and the perception, reinforced by the Prime Minister, that to harbour reservations about the deal that emerged was to somehow be "anti-Quebec." The Accord was the fulfillment of Mulroney's 1984 election campaign pledge to find a constitutional consensus that would enable Quebec to endorse the 1982 constitution with "enthusiasm and honour"; the constitutional conference at Meech Lake was called to address the five conditions that Premier Bourassa of Quebec enunciated in 1986 so that Quebec "might take its rightful place within the federation." These conditions were:

a   the explicit recognition (in the preamble of the constitution) of Quebec as a distinct society;

b   the guarantee of increased powers in immigration;

c   the restriction of federal spending power;

d   the modification of the current form of amendment (based on seven provinces with 75 per cent of the population, establishing four regional vetoes); and

e   the participation of Quebec in the nomination of judges to the Supreme Court of Canada.[6]

This constitutional package appeared modest and reasonable but the final text that was released after the negotiations went far beyond these conditions, clearly addressing some of the concerns of other provincial premiers as well as those of Bourassa. It consisted of eight additions to the Constitution Act 1867 and several substitutions and additions to the Constitution Act 1982. This paper will discuss the additions and substitutions that specifically addressed Bourassa's conditions and their implications for the development of political community in Canada. It will proceed with three questions in mind:

1.   Will the provinces be satisfied? In the short term, yes,[6a] but in the long term, since the Accord does not adequately address either the interstate or the intrastate[7] concerns of the provincial governments and societies, satisfaction will not endure.

2.   Is the Accord likely to lead to fundamental changes in socio-political relationships in Canada? Yes—both the federal-provincial balance of power and the perception of power will undergo a significant shift towards the provinces. As Robert Campbell argues:

"The Meech Lake Accord involves a dramatic devolving of power to the provinces...the provinces will be an even more formidable check on the federal House of Commons—either via their appointees in the Senate or via a federal provincial dynamic which is more favourable to themselves."[8]

3. Will our federal system be improved? Insofar as the Accord reverses an egregious error of the Constitution Act 1982—the exclusion of Quebec—there is obvious improvement. However, the Accord could also lead to a balkanization of the Canadian provinces as each is encouraged to become more isolated from the others. Questions must also be asked about the potential effect on the spread of bilingualism in Canada implied in the constitutional recognition of Quebec as the home of French-speaking Canadians.

Immigration

Additions to section 95 Constitution Act 1867 do not appear, in the legal sense, to have greatly changed existing practice. Immigration continues to be a concurrent field with federal preeminence in provisions in regard to "...national standards and objectives relating to immigrants or aliens." Specifically, it requires that the government of Canada shall negotiate agreements regarding immigrants or aliens with any province that so requests, permitting that province to participate in the selection of persons who wish to settle within its borders. Quebec and six other provinces have already entered into agreements with the federal government regarding immigration, and Quebec is governed by the Cullen-Couture agreement.[9]

Immigration policy has long been a legitimate concern for successive Quebec governments as French-speaking immigrants to Canada have been greatly outnumbered by English-speaking immigrants and other ethnic groups. Within Quebec, a 1974 study[10] concluded that the tendency of immigrants to integrate into the English-speaking community, and a concomitant precipitous decline in the provincial birth rate would lead to a decline in the demographic position of Francophones. This resulted in what Ken McRoberts has called the "nationalist preoccupation with the immigrant population"[11] and the concerted attempts by successive governments to ensure the assimilation of immigrants into the French-speaking community. To assuage these concerns, the Trudeau government in 1978 signed the Cullen-Couture agreement giving Quebec much greater control over immigration to the province, and the Meech Lake Accord gives constitutional status to the provisions of this agreement.

As Garth Stevenson argues in his contribution to this volume, the Constitution Act 1867 anticipated provincial activity in the field of immigration. There has historically been much cooperation between Ottawa and the provinces in this field, so the Accord in many ways reflects existing practice. It does go beyond practice, however, by 1) constitutionalizing a federal-provincial agreement, thereby putting its provisions beyond an act of Parliament; the terms of this agreement have already caused some confusion abroad[12]; 2) requiring that the government of Canada withdraw its services for the reception and integration of foreign nationals who wish to settle in Quebec, accompanied by "reasonable compensation"; and 3) guaranteeing Quebec a number of immigrants within the annual Canadian total equal to its proportion of the population of Canada, with the right to exceed that figure by five per cent "for demographic reasons." The political implications of these concessions in immigration are a reduction in federal power and an enhancement (within Canada and abroad) of provincial power. It is difficult to assess the logistical and administrative difficulties that could ensue from the guarantee of a percentage of immigration to Quebec, but at a minimum, it is worth speculating on how the governments would resolve the problem if in any one year only 20,000 of an acceptable 100,000 immigrants wished to settle in Quebec. This constitutional guarantee does not go as far as Gil Remillard's request for "sole power" over immigration,[13] but it goes considerably farther than Bourassa's request for "increased powers." It can be argued that immigrants who have been recruited abroad and are received and integrated on arrival only by provincial representatives will develop a perception of provincial political community rather than national political community.

The Spending Power

Much has been said and written about the provision (106A (1) Constitution Act 1867) to permit a province to opt out of any future national shared-cost program and receive compensation provided it "...carries on a program or initiative that is compatible with national objectives."[14] This option is not new—as in the immigration provisions, it constitutionalizes existing practice. Opting out with compensation[15] has been available for many programs since the first agreement between John Diefenbaker and Paul Sauvé concerning universities in 1959,[16] but only Quebec has so far chosen it. Furthermore, in many respects we already have a "checkerboard" medicare system, since different disciplines are insured in different provinces, and some have premiums and some do not. What they all must do, however, is meet certain federal standards before they qualify for funds. The concern for this section revolves around the argument that the phrase "national objectives" is too vague a requirement and is open to various interpretations. For example, would a program that is privately administered but has the same objectives as the federal program qualify for funds? It is plausible to suggest that if this agreement had been in existence during the debate on medicare in the 1960s, the outcome would have been quite different. Ontario was very reluctant to dismantle its private insurance system for health care, and if the federal objective was simply health insurance rather than the enunciated standard of "publicly administered," then it is possible that the private system would have qualified.[17]

There are also opponents of this section who argue that it expands federal power since it explicitly recognizes the federal spending power for the first time. (Although s.106A(2) states: "Nothing in this section extends the legislative powers of the Parliament of Canada or of the legislature of the province.") This section, like much of the Accord, suffers from a lack of clarity and is vulnerable to different interpretations and speculation.

In a broader sense, however, it is possible that the thrust of the federal spending power will change. In the past, particularly with medicare, it has been used to establish programs that foster a sense of political community on a national scale rather than on a local scale. It can be plausibly argued that the less national a plan is in its scope and detail, the less it will foster this sense of national community. In 1964, Prime Minister Lester Pearson very reluctantly allowed Premier Lesage to establish the Quebec Pension Plan with federal compensation. As far as I am aware, no study has been done to determine the way Canadians perceive their pension plans, but it would be reasonable to expect that citizens outside Quebec would be more apt to identify pensions as part of a national income security plan than would citizens in Quebec.

The Supreme Court

The status of the Supreme Court of Canada has long been obscure. The Supreme Court Act, as an ordinary statute of Parliament is theoretically amendable by that body,[18] although this is not quite clear since the Constitution Act 1982. In this Act, the composition of the Court was entrenched, and requires unanimous provincial and Parliamentary agreement for change. This would appear to implicitly at least constitutionalize the Court—for surely to abolish it would be to change its composition. Nevertheless, its status has been ambiguous and in need of clarification. This the Accord does. It also gives the provincial governments the right to nominate judges to the Court.

Since the Charter of Rights and Freedoms of 1982, the role of the Court has become increasingly significant. The concern of the public and the provincial governments for the representative nature of the court has grown, yet appointments have remained the exclusive prerogative of the federal government, although consultation with the bar and government of the province usually occurs.[19]

Quebec, whose right to have three judges on the Court was implicitly recognized in the 1982 Constitution, wanted some form of participation in the selection of judges to be entrenched as well. The provinces (but, significantly, not the Yukon or the Northwest Territories) were given the right to submit lists from which the federal government must then make its selection. It can refuse, but no mechanism was established for resolving an impasse; so conceivably, a Supreme Court appointment could remain unfilled indefinitely. This is not as serious for justices from outside Quebec, for the federal government has more flexibility since there are six justices from nine provinces (although traditionally three of these are from Ontario). However, if there was no agreement on appointments from Quebec,[20] up to three appointments could remain unfilled and the legitimacy of the Court brought into question. This seems a serious oversight.

Some would argue that the new method of appointment does not stray greatly from past procedure, but provincial nominees could fundamentally alter the nature of the Court, and this procedure is clearly a reduction in the powers of the federal government. The Court must be seen to be independent and impartial, and although reform in the appointment process is clearly necessary to recognize the growing importance and visibility of the Court and legitimize its decisions, the procedure enunciated in the Accord is flawed. It is difficult to understand how provincial nomination rather than federal appointment after required consultation with some form of ratification,[21] would address the problem of suspected bias.

The Senate

Quebec enunciated no conditions in relation to the Senate, but there have been escalating demands for its reform in recent years, and its inclusion in the Accord was clearly in response to concerns expressed by the western premiers, particularly Premier Getty of Alberta and Premier Vander Zalm of British Columbia. The Accord provides that senators will be appointed in the same manner as Supreme Court justices; that is, from lists supplied by the provincial governments (and again, significantly, the Yukon and Northwest Territories were ignored, and there is no mechanism for breaking an impasse). This is intended as an interim measure, with broader Senate reform to be addressed at subsequent annual federal-provincial conferences, but there is a serious pitfall, for the Accord also stipulates that any further change to the Senate will require the unanimous approval of the provinces. One might argue that, since the Senate's powers are little-used and if it is to remain the focus of patronage appointments, it makes little difference who nominates the members (although a provincially-appointed Senate with the present Senate's broad veto powers could certainly prove to be troublesome). However, Senate reform is widely perceived to be a necessary step to make central institutions more representative of, and responsive to, the provinces and regions of Canada. The present Senate has long been accused of inadequately performing this important task. But if we are serious about achieving meaningful Senate reform, we are not likely to see it as a result of this Accord. In fact, the Accord effectively stifles Senate reform—although along with the fisheries, the eleven governments have agreed to discuss it every year.

It is difficult to understand how Premier Getty particularly, who came to Meech Lake determined to have Senate reform on the agenda, and who says that he is adamantly committed to a "Triple E" Senate (elected, equal and effective) could have signed an agreement that places such an obstacle in the path of his reform.[22]

The Amending Formula

Premier Bourassa proposed an amending formula based on a regional conception of Canada. His formula, as outlined above, would give each of four regions a veto over future constitutional amendments. The Accord, however, makes two changes to the 1982 amending formula that quite explicitly refute the concept of Canada as a regional[23] country and are clearly based on the principle of the equality of the provinces. It recognizes first, the right to compensation for a province wishing to opt out of an amendment transferring provincial power to the federal Parliament. This right was extended to all amendments; previously compensation would only be given where cultural or educational matters were involved. This stipulation addresses the concern of Quebec that it had lost its historical general veto in 1981 when René Levesque joined seven other provinces to support the Vancouver[24] amending formula rather than the Victoria formula. If there is widespread use of this section, it could lead to the "checkerboard" Canada that so concerned Pierre Trudeau, and undermine the legitimacy of the Members of Parliament from the provinces which opt out. This is a federal country, however, and the provinces clearly have the right to refuse a power transfer, but to provide compensation is to encourage opting out and a proliferation of divergent constitutional responsibilities among the provinces. A power transfer could perhaps best be addressed by requiring unanimity, although the 1982 section appears to be a reasonable compromise, since it recognizes the importance of culture and education to Quebec but does not encourage wholesale opting out. It would be interesting to speculate as to the way unemployment insurance would have developed if this section was in effect in 1940. Second, it also recognizes the equality of the provinces, by extending the requirement for unanimity to include amendments affecting the Senate, the House of Commons, the Supreme Court, the extension of existing provinces, and the establishment of new provinces.

These changes are the manifestation of the enduring Compact theory of confederation, which is seen as a pact or contract among the provinces and, in its extreme articulation, claims Ottawa is the creation of the provinces. Under the Compact theory, it is expected that the two levels of government will remain fully autonomous in their discrete jurisdictions and that the federal government will consult and obtain the consent of the provinces whenever its actions will affect them—especially in the area of constitutional change. In practical terms, the actions of the federal government are severely constrained by adherence to this theory, and in political terms, "the concept tends to stress centrifugal forces within the union, and places emphasis on strengthening the provinces rather than the central power, which would be held in close check."[25] It is not a theory that will enhance a sense of transcendent Canadian nationality.

In a discussion of what he has called the "tyranny of unanimity," Alan Cairns says that giving a veto to each government gives "the option of total selfishness without having to pay a price" and makes "the possibility of agreement conditional on the support of the most recalcitrant or demanding government."[26] The concerns expressed by the governments of the Yukon and the Northwest Territories would seem to be well-founded, as their move towards provincial status could be thwarted by any one of ten provincial premiers. It is difficult to determine a rationale for the application of the unanimity principle to the creation of new provinces (Bryan Schwartz calls this the "anti-north" provision)[27] other than a further recognition of vested government interests. The north, in five short years, has had its hopes for achieving provincial status frustrated. Prior to April 17, 1982, the federal government could have proceeded with a bi-lateral agreement to admit new provinces (as it did with the six provinces admitted after 1867), but it now must submit to the rigidities inherent in unanimity.

The Distinct Society

The new section 2 of the Constitution Act 1867 requires that the Constitution of Canada be interpreted in a manner that is consistent with the recognition that

> French-speaking Canadians, centred in Quebec but also present elsewhere in Canada and English-speaking Canadians, concentrated outside Quebec but also present in Quebec, constitutes a fundamental characteristic of Canada; and
> (b)...Quebec constitutes within Canada a distinct society.

It also affirms the role of the Parliament and the provincial legislatures to preserve this fundamental character, and the role of the legislature and the government of Quebec to preserve and promote its distinct society.

There is no consensus on what this section means—does it convey special status on Quebec or at least the legal means by which Quebec can pursue special status? It is worth noting that René Levesque said in 1968 that "Canadian federalism cannot accommodate itself to such a special status...To try at the same time for special status and for true federalism is like trying to square a circle."[28] Certainly Bourassa has interpreted this section more broadly in Quebec than have the premiers outside Quebec. He has said that Quebec got everything it wanted, although Senator Lowell Murray, chief negotiator for the federal side, said that Mulroney gave nothing away.[29] Jacques Parizeau, leader of the Parti Québécois, has said that he would use the Accord to "...grab as many powers as possible for Quebec on the road to independence."[30] The legal ramifications of this section are therefore difficult to determine, but it is certainly a much stronger recognition of Quebec's distinct status than that requested by Bourassa, which was a symbolic recognition in the preamble to the constitution.

A preamble, as a philosophical statement of principles, does not have the same force in constitutional debates as do clauses within the body of the constitution. As an entrenched section of the Act of 1867, however, the distinct society clause becomes an operative section of the constitution that must be considered to aid in the interpretation of other ambiguous or unclear sections.[31] Peter Hogg argues that the distinct society clause is basically an interpretation clause which is unlikely to have great direct legal significance,[32] but Bryan Schwartz says that "Even if the courts develop a fairly innocuous interpretation of the clause, the legislatures may not."[33] The controversy that has surrounded this section of the Accord indicates that no one—including the drafters themselves—is clear as to its meaning and implications.

Quebec's distinct society is not defined.[34] There is no doubt that although each Canadian province is unique, Quebec's difference does have a difference—a reading of the Constitution Act 1867 supports this perception and concern for the distinctive character of Quebec was basic to the decision to adopt a federal system of government. The tension between Quebec's struggles to protect and reinforce its particularities and the federal government's efforts to act as a national government has determined much of Canadian history. The Accord attempts to resolve the dilemma, but in its explicit recognition of French-speaking Canadians and English-speaking Canadians, it is more probable that it will reinforce the divisions.

There has been concern expressed about the relationship of section 2 to the Charter of Rights and Freedoms and whether it could be invoked to justify a law that derogates from the Charter. Peter Hogg states categorically that "The new s.2 does not override the Charter of Rights"[35] although he also says that s.2 could in an indirect fashion expand the power of the Parliament or a Legislature to derogate from the Charter, when used in conjunction with section 1 of the Charter. Eugene Forsey has reservations about the application of this section, and says that it is not at all clear what its significance in relation to the Charter may be.[36] Ramsay Cook goes farther and says the Accord's most damaging weakness is that the Charter "is in danger of being undermined."[37] The Accord does specifically state that s.2 does not affect sections 25 or 27 of the Charter (aboriginal rights and multicultural heritage) but makes no mention of other Charter rights.[38] It is the concern of women's groups and others that this omission implies that s.2 can be invoked to derogate from other rights in the Charter.

Without further clarification of this clause by our political elites, the courts would have to interpret it as it stands. For example, what is the significance of its insertion into the body of the constitution and what is the difference between the requirements to preserve and promote? More importantly, why was this different language employed?[39] If it was not intended to convey particular responsibilities exclusively to the government of Quebec, then why is it there? Is it valid to argue that the preservation rather than the promotion of the Canadian and provincial societies other than Quebec, may provide legal grounds for resistance by certain groups to legislation that would expand the position of the French-speaking minorities outside Quebec? Both the Official Languages Act passed by the Trudeau government in 1969 and its amendments introduced by the Mulroney government in 1988 were designed to promote rather than preserve the fundamental characteristic of bilingualism. What might be the fate of such legislation in the future if Parliament is no longer to promote this characteristic?

The answers to the many important questions here raised will depend on interpretation by the judiciary—historically an unpredictable variable. There have been suggestions that before the Accord is finally ratified, a reference should be sent to the Supreme Court to determine the meaning of this section. But should this be the responsibility of the Court? This body is expected to be independent and apolitical and it is therefore more appropriate for legislators to be responsible for clarifying political problems before they become, improperly, judicial problems. The Charter of Rights has, as Peter Russell has said, already increased the tendency to politicize the judiciary[40] and certainly decisions on the real meaning of the distinct society clause are decisions that are distinctly political. How can we ask the Supreme Court, an institution upon which there is no democratic check, to answer fundamental political questions with broad implications for evolving relationships among Canadians?

Perhaps the most significant implication of the new s.2 is its potential to affect the perception that Canadians have of themselves. The Accord officially divides us into French-speaking Canadians and English-speaking Canadians. Nowhere does the Accord recognize the rapidly-growing number of bilingual Canadians in all the provinces. If there is one fundamental characteristic of Canada that makes it distinctive and has the potential to instill a pan-Canadian sentiment, it is its bilingual nature, a Canadian condition that has been increasing since the report of the Bilingual and Bicultural Commission in the 1960s. Throughout the 1970s and 1980s, thousands of Canadians, encouraged by their governments, have discovered the "other" official language and have attempted to achieve some facility in it. This is encouragingly true even in sections of the country where bilingual cornflake boxes have caused distress. By any yardstick, we have in the last twenty years made great strides towards the goal of bilingualism, a not inconsiderable achievement, and one that perhaps takes on even more significance in the face of a free trade agreement with the United States. What will be the fate of this drive if the constitution arbitrarily divides us into English-speaking or French-speaking? I would suggest that with the increased emphasis on the two solitudes the momentum that has driven Canadians in their quest for bilingualism will be lost. With this, we could witness the final resolution of a 120-year old debate within Canada on the nature of the relationship between the two language communities. In fact, there have been two periods in our history when Canada could have become a bilingual nation. The first was the turn of the century when a previously inward-looking Quebec came to believe that its position in Canadian society could best be safeguarded by the protection of French language rights outside Quebec, and the second was the period after the Official Languages Act of 1969, when many Canadians enthusiastically supported the extension of French education and the provision of services to Francophone Canadians outside Quebec. As A.I. Silver has recently shown us,[41] between 1867 and the year 1900, within Quebec there was a gradual evolution in the perception of that province's place in the federation. Originally, French-Canadians thought of Quebec as their homeland, quite separate from the other provinces which were English. By 1900, after the trauma of the Manitoba Schools Question, the Riel Rebellion, and racial and religious incidents in the 1890s, their conception had changed and they began to believe that only by the recognition of French and Catholic rights across Canada could the federation survive. The new bilingual and bicultural theory of Canada was eloquently articulated by Henri Bourassa and he tried to pressure Laurier into imposing official bilingualism on Alberta and Saskatchewan when they were created in 1905. The troubling tension between protecting language rights outside Quebec and defending provincial autonomy was evident in this dispute, and Laurier refused.

Quebec began to retreat within itself after the several controversies of the late nineteenth and early twentieth centuries, encouraged by the teaching and writings of the Quebec nationalist Abbé Groulx. In the mid-twentieth century, under Premier Maurice Duplessis, Quebec developed a negative nationalism until the election of Jean Lesage in 1960. The Quiet Revolution under Lesage was the manifestation of an inward-looking but aggressive Quebec, determined to develop Quebec as the homeland of French-speaking Canadians—and in 1976, the tension between provincial autonomy and the protection of French language rights outside Quebec was finally resolved in favour of provincial autonomy.[42] The Official Languages Act was a response to developments in Quebec and was a deliberate decision made to promote bilingualism across Canada. The acceptance of this policy in the provinces outside Quebec was gratifying, and Canada began slowly to fulfill the dream Henri Bourassa had of it in 1900.

There has been a protracted debate over the linguistic nature of Canada—a debate between those who believe that Canadians should be able to function in French or English comfortably from coast to coast (Henri Bourassa and Pierre Trudeau) and those who believe that Quebec is a collectivity whose fundamental characteristic is its French majority, and it must remain distinct from the rest of Canada to maintain that identity (Abbé Groulx and René Levesque). Under the Meech Lake Accord, I believe the latter perception will finally prevail. Perhaps, as Lise Bissonnette has said, the dream that was shared by Henri Bourassa and Pierre Trudeau rested only on sand.[43]

Conclusion

It is time to return to the original three questions.

1. Will the provinces be satisfied?

In the short term, I would argue yes, as they have had their powers relative to the federal government enhanced, and the prospect of patronage appointments to the Senate should appease them for a while. In the long term, however, I fear that the Canadian public will endure much more constitutional wrangling. The interstate aspect of federalism has been only peripherally addressed and the intrastate aspect only obliquely and inadequately. There has been a lingering malaise in Canadian federalism, frequently identified with the lack of responsiveness of federal institutions to the needs of provincial societies. Reforms have been suggested—to the House of Commons, the Senate, the Supreme Court, the party and electoral systems, and the federal public service—to develop this responsiveness. However, the propensity of provincial governments to identify and exaggerate areas of dissension has a long history and will not likely diminish. We might call this the Canadian provincial imperative, an inexorable evolution in sociopolitical forces towards decentralization and disengagement or a centrifugal federalism.

This pressure for the enhancement of provincial power does not come only from Quebec, although it was Claude Morin who articulated the long-term Parti Québécois strategy of incrementalism—a "concession here, a concession there"[44] until there was nothing left, making political union meaningless. This may not be the conscious objective of other provincial governments, but the effect of current trends could be similar. If there is widespread use of the opting out clauses in conjunction with a devolution of federal power and visibility, diminished legitimacy of Members of Parliament, decreased enthusiasm for bilingualism, and more programs tailored by and for individual provinces, it is probable that provincial societies will be encouraged to become more inward-looking and isolated. No transcendent loyalty to Canada will develop from an agreement that places such emphasis on the provinces as individual and independent political units.

2. If adopted, will the Accord lead to fundamental changes in relationships within Canada?

I would argue that yes, in its present form it could lead to a restructuring of Canadian political society. Perhaps a majority of Canadians will welcome this restructuring as a closer reflection of their perception of the political system, but we have not really asked this fundamental question, or allowed time for its consideration. The long debate over the nature of language in Canada could finally be resolved as our move towards a uniquely Canadian bilingual country is truncated by the emphasis on Quebec as the home of French-speaking Canadians.

The other crisis of Canadian federalism—the nature of the relationship between the federal government and the provincial governments—may also finally be determined. Ken McRoberts, who argues that the Accord is of limited scope and expresses surprise that it has aroused such virulent opposition, then admits that because of the distinct society clause, "...the Accord explicitly denies an alternative vision of Canada: a national community, in which only the federal state is the legitimate expression of a national will."[45] Surely it should not surprise anyone that there has been such widespread resistance to this redefinition of Canadian political society. The perception of Canada as a nation rather than a community of communities is, not unexpectedly, a tenacious one, but the Accord, in fact, superimposes a degree of confederalization on the federal system. The principle of the equality of the provinces so assiduously pursued further legitimizes and reinforces the Compact theory of Canada first articulated by Mowatt and Mercier in the nineteenth century and more recently adopted by Lougheed and Peckford. The actual legal devolution of power in each of the separate provisions of the Accord may not be considerable, but the aggregate effect is a rewriting of political relationships in Canada. It should not surprise anyone that the original sharp criticism by a few has instilled apprehension in many and has led to demands for caution, clarification, and broader debate.

3. Will our federal system be improved?

To the extent that the Accord achieves reconciliation with Quebec as it becomes an active and willing participator, the federal system has clearly been improved. For those who identify serious problems other than the protection and enhancement of provincial rights, however, the Accord is disappointing. In fact, it greatly exacerbates one broadly recognized weakness in our system—that of executive dominance.

By ensuring that at least two federal-provincial conferences take place each year, by the language of the Accord, and by the focus on governments rather than people, we will be increasingly governed by executive federalism. Emphasis on the vested interests of governments, a by-product of executive federalism, will increase. The patriation and Charter in 1982 was not quite the "people's" package that Trudeau claimed it was, but the Accord of 1987 is clearly a government's package—or perhaps even a premiers' package.

A constitution is the fundamental link between a society and its government and should be the expression of its vision of itself as a political and social unit. Carefully drafted and nurtured, a constitution should continue to both reflect society as it perceives itself and gently mould it to become what it wishes to be. With the important exception of the Charter of Rights and Freedoms, the pursuit of such lofty aspirations has not yet been demonstrated in the "blunt and brutal compromises"[46] that have led to amendments to the Canadian constitution. Don Smiley in 1980 spoke of the compounded crisis of Canadian federalism[47] as the manifestation of the decline in Canadian nationhood and as a challenge to political community. In 1987 he optimistically suggested that "perhaps we are on the verge of new kinds of pan-Canadian mobilization."[48] Sadly, there is little evidence that the "spirit" of Meech Lake will resolve the compounded crisis or lead to the enhancement of a pan-Canadian political community.

Notes

1   Donald V. Smiley, *The Canadian Political Nationality*, (Toronto: Methuen Publications, 1967), 128.

2   The Accord was reached in two separate meetings, one at Meech Lake, April 29-30, 1987 and the second in the Langevin Block, Parliament Hill June 2-3. The outcome of the two meetings is commonly called The Meech Lake Accord, as it will be here.

3   D.V. Smiley, "An Outsider's Observations of Federal-Provincial Relations Among Consenting Adults," Richard Simeon, (ed.), *Confrontation and Collaboration—Intergovernmental Relations in Canada Today*, (Toronto: Institute of Public Administration, 1979).

4   *Globe and Mail*, May 16, 1987.

5   Undergraduate students are surprised at a comparison, in a quantitative sense, of the Canadian and U.S. constitutions. Our Constitution (without the 1987 amendments) is 82 pages in Cheffins and Johnson, *The Revised Canadian Constitution: Politics as Law*, (Toronto: McGraw-Hill Ryerson, 1986) whereas the U.S.Constitution can be reproduced in a small pamphlet of 28 pages.

6   Robert Bourassa, "The Economic Future of Quebec," speech delivered on the occasion of the 10th anniversary of *L'Actualité*, September 23, 1986.

6a   The short term proved to be even shorter than expected. Although Quebec, Parliament, and seven other provinces ratified the agreement quickly, new governments in Manitoba and New Brunswick had not ratified it it by the fall of 1989, and a new government in Newfoundland threatened to rescind its support. They cited many reservations, among them concern for the implications for the Charter, for Senate reform, for linguistic minorities and for the northern territories.

7   Under the Lesage regime in the 1960s, there were many suggestions for reform of the interstate or division of powers aspect of Canadian federalism. Toward the end of the 1970s, concern for intrastate federalism, in the sense of the need to reform central institutions to make them more representative of, and responsive to, the regions and provinces became fashionable. Intrastate federalism can be viewed in what Cairns has called its provincialist and its federalist aspects. The former would enhance the power of the provincial governments in the institutions at the centre, and the latter would enhance the influence of the federal government in the regions, at the expense of the provincial governments. The Meech Lake Accord is clearly a recognition of the provincialist aspect of intrastate federalism, particularly in its provisions for the Supreme Court and the Senate. See Alan Cairns, *From Interstate to Intrastate Federalism*, (Kingston: Queen's Institute of Intergovernmental Relations, 1979); Jennifer Smith, "Intrastate Federalism and Confederation," in Stephen Brooks (ed.), *Political Thought in Canada*, (Toronto: Irwin, 1984); D.V.Smiley and R.L.Watts, *Intrastate Federalism in Canada*, (Toronto: University of Toronto Press, 1985).

8   Robert Campbell, "Starting Over: The Reconstruction of Canada," *Journal of Canadian Studies*, 22:3 (1987), 3.

9   Cullen-Couture Agreement, February 20, 1978. Quebec was delegated the right to select candidates to settle in Quebec. Ken McRoberts says Quebec

received the fullest extent of control over immigration that would seem possible in a federal system in his *Quebec: Social Change and Political Crisis*, (3rd ed.; Toronto: McClelland and Stewart, 1988), 295.

10 McRoberts, *Quebec*, 466.

11 Ibid., 183.

12 Victor Malarek, "Quebec back door benefits wealthy," *Globe and Mail*, July 4, 1988. Hong Kong businessmen who had failed to meet the federal entry criteria were subsequently selected and approved by immigration officers from Quebec—yet they are free to move to other parts of Canada after arriving.

13 Quoted in Bryan Schwartz, *Fathoming Meech Lake*, (Winnipeg: Legal Research Institute, University of Manitoba, 1987), 132.

14 Section 106A(1), *Constitution Act*, 1867.

15 The use of the federal spending power to coerce the provinces into accepting federally-initiated programs has long been a source of serious grievance for Quebec governments. In 1960, the Lesage government proposed "an end to conditional grants and joint programs so that the central government would cease to interfere in sectors not within its jurisdiction." Daniel Latouche, *Canada and Quebec, Past and Future: An Essay*, (Toronto: University of Toronto Press, 1986), 21. The 1987 document recognizes this demand.

16 This agreement established an important precedent, even though Diefenbaker attempted to lessen its implications by referring to the importance of education in Quebec. See Latouche, *ibid.*

17 Malcolm Taylor, *Health Insurance and Canadian Health Policy: The Seven Decisions that created the Canadian Health Insurance System*, (2nd ed.; Montreal: McGill-Queen's Press), Chapter Six.

18 The Supreme Court Act has long been considered an organic Act, that is, theoretically amendable, but because of its important purpose and content, considered to be part of the constitution.

19 An elaborate system of consultation has been established. See Geoffrey Stevens, "Appointment system improved," in Paul Fox, (ed.), *Politics Canada*, (4th ed.; Toronto: McGraw-Hill Ryerson, 1987), 548-550. The possibility of ignoring the wishes of the province was sharply illustrated in 1986, however, when the Mulroney government appointed former Conservative Premier of Manitoba, Sterling Lyon, to the province's Court of Appeal, over the vehement objections of the Attorney-General of the province.

20 One must only recall the period when Pierre Trudeau was Prime Minister and René Levesque was Premier of Quebec to envision the potential impasse.

21 See Smiley and Watts, *Intrastate Federalism*, Chapter 8.

22 Getty is rationalizing this move by telling his constituents that now at least, the West cannot have Senate reform rammed down its throat by the East. Roger Gibbins, "Ottawa and the Western Provinces," unpublished paper presented at Concordia University "Beyond 1985," April 30, 1988.

23 Don Smiley suggests that: "In general, political discourse would be clarified if we ceased to use the term region." *The Federal Condition in Canada*, (Toronto: McGraw-Hill Ryerson, 1987). Janine Brodie, in this volume, argues

that spatial politics in Canada retain their importance for Canadian political study and the term regionalism should not be banished.

24   The Vancouver formula was essentially the one adopted in 1982 (7 provinces with 50% of the Canadian Population, plus Parliament). The Victoria Charter amending formula was regionally-oriented—7 provinces with 75% of the population, and any province that had ever had 25% of the population would always retain its veto.

25   Edwin Black, *Divided Loyalties*, (Montreal: McGill-Queen's, 1975), 170.

26   Alan Cairns, "The politics of Constitutional Conservatism," in K. Banting and R. Simeon (eds.), *And No One Cheered*, (Toronto: Methuen, 1983), 36.

27   Bryan Schwartz, *Fathoming Meech Lake*, 130.

28   René Levesque, *An Option for Quebec*, (Toronto: McClelland and Stewart, 1968), 110-111.

29   Sid Handelman, *Toronto Star*, May 10, 1987. Charlotte Gray, in *Saturday Night*, (November 1987), 14 makes the shocking revelation that "...Mulroney gave Murray carte blanche to negotiate away whatever federal powers were necessary to get Quebec into the constitution."

30   *Globe and Mail*, Feb. 29, 1988.

31   A constitutional adviser, in conversation, said that when the first ministers agreed to recognize Quebec's distinct society in the preamble, it was pointed out that the Constitution does not really have a preamble. Someone indicated that Section 2 of the Constitution Act 1867, had been repealed in 1893, so it was decided to make use of this long-void section. This exercise in happenstance has left us with this important and unclear clause.

32   Peter Hogg, *Meech Lake Accord Annotated*, (Toronto: Carswell, 1988), 12-13.

33   Bryan Schwartz, *Fathoming Meech Lake*, 8.

34   There has been speculation as to the nature of Quebec's distinctiveness—is it its French-speaking majority or, as some have suggested, its high level of bilingualism?

35   Peter Hogg, *Meech Lake*, 15. Robert Bourassa, however, when he introduced Bill 178 into the National Assembly in December, 1988 (invoking the 'notwithstanding clause' of the Charter to override a Supreme Court decision on minority language rights in the province), suggested that if the Accord had been in effect, he would not have needed to rely on the notwithstanding clause. Pierre DeBane, "A Shameful Strategy," *Globe and Mail*, June 29, 1989.

36   Eugene Forsey, *Globe and Mail*, September 14, 1987.

37   Ramsay Cook, *Globe and Mail*, August 31, 1987.

38   S.16 Constitutional Amendment, 1987.

39   The Supreme Court justices cannot be expected to be aware of the serendipitous nature of the circumstances of s.2. See note 31 above.

40   Peter Russell, quoted in Smiley, *Federal Condition*, 198.

41   A.I.Silver, *The French Canadian Idea of Confederation 1864-1900*, (Toronto: University of Toronto Press, 1982). For a perceptive history of Quebec, see also Susan Mann Trofimenkoff, *Action française: French Canadian Nationalism in the 1920s*, (Toronto: University of Toronto Press, 1975) and

her *Dream of Nation: A Social and Intellectual History of Quebec*(Toronto: Gage, 1983).

42 The most recent manifestation of this tension and its resolution in favour of provincial autonomy came in the spring of 1988, as Bourassa cautiously supported Saskatchewan Premier Grant Devine's right to repeal the 83-year-old Territories Act, that guaranteed the French language in Saskatchewan.

43 *Globe and Mail,* April 16, 1988.

44 Described in Ron Graham, *One-Eyed Kings: Promise and Illusion in Canadian Politics,* (Toronto: Totem Books, 1987), 66.

45 Kenneth McRoberts, *Quebec,* 400.

46 Cairns, in Banting and Simeon, 42.

47 Donald V. Smiley, *Canada in Question: Federalism in the Eighties,* (Toronto: McGraw-Hill Ryerson, 1980), Chapter 8.

48 Smiley, *Federal Condition,* 194.

THE CONSTITUTION AND THE
CHARTER OF RIGHTS

THE SUPREME COURT AND THE CHARTER: A QUESTION OF LEGITIMACY

Peter H. Russell, University of Toronto

Whatever the Canadian Charter of Rights and Freedoms may have done for the Canadian people, we know that it has become a subject of endless fascination for us scholars. Among us there is an awful lot of charter chatter in charterland. This is evident in the agenda of the present conference.

Much of this charter chatter has been concerned with the role of the judiciary in interpreting and applying the Charter, and with its implications for Canadian democracy. Canada's intellectual community was too under-developed a century or so ago to do much philosophizing about the advent of representative democracy. However, it is now carrying on a fairly sophisticated debate about the modification of democracy entailed in the judicial enforcement of rights and freedoms. What I would describe as the "moderate activism" displayed by the Supreme Court of Canada in its first few years of Charter decision-making has stimulated this debate.

The Court's moderate activism has been nicely contrived to offend both of the ideological tendencies that animate the Court's most vocal critics. Its moderation is unacceptable to those who view the Charter as a holy covenant which, in the hands of the right judicial prophets, could transform Canada into a just society. Its activism is equally unacceptable to those who lack faith in the judiciary as arbiters of our fundamental values. In this sense the prediction Don Smiley made in 1981 that "the Charter will face a legitimacy problem in at least the short term future"[1] has come to pass.

The Supreme Court's Early Activism

At the apex of our judicial system the Supreme Court of Canada has been playing a decisive role in determining how the Charter is to be treated in Canadian courts. Although the roughly 50 Charter cases the Supreme Court has now decided represent only between one and two per cent of Charter litigation, they set the tone and basic approach to be followed throughout the legal community. If these first four years of Charter interpretation by the Supreme Court reveal anything definitive about the scope of judicial power under the Charter, it is that the Court's sense of the legitimate bounds of its own power is both nuanced and evolving.

From the very beginning the Supreme Court seems to have had no doubt about its general mandate with respect to the Charter. In *Skapinker*,[2] its first Charter decision, where Justice Estey on behalf of the Court lit the Charter flame so to speak, the Court made it clear that it was prepared to take the Charter seriously, to give its terms a liberal interpretation and to strike down laws and government policies which are found to be in conflict with it. In decisions which immediately followed, various members of the Court stated their conviction that the Charter brought with it, in the words of Justice LeDain, a "new constitutional mandate for judicial review."[3] In her opinion in *Singh*, Justice Wilson referred to "a clear message," which she explained: "the recent adoption of the Charter by Parliament and nine of the ten provinces [sent] to the courts that the restrictive attitude which at times characterized their approach to the Canadian Bill of Rights ought to be re-examined."[4]

The justices did not rest this mandate on the express intentions of the politicians who brought Canada the Charter. "The Charter," wrote Justice Estey in *Skapinker*, "comes from neither level of the legislative branches of government but from the Constitution itself." The Charter, Estey suggested, must transcend the politics of its creation: "The adoptive mechanisms...lose their relevancy or shrink to mere historical curiosity value on the ultimate adoption of the instrument in the Constitution."[5] Thus, if the Charter came with a mandate for strong judicial review, it was a mandate which, in some metaphysical, Hegelian sense, came from the Canadian body politic.

The inclusion of a legislative override in the Charter lightened the weight of the mandate on the shoulders of Canadian judges. This element of the Charter expresses the unique Canadian blend of British and American constitutionalism. It may prove to be Canada's most significant contribution to the constitutional statecraft of liberal democracy. By permitting legislative review of judicial review, the override removes much of the anti-democratic sting from judicial activism.[6] Perhaps Don Smiley was not counting on its emboldening influence when he stated his belief—again in 1981—"that the Supreme Court of Canada will not adopt an activist and aggressive stance towards the Charter until those judges whose formative jurisprudential attitudes were shaped in the older traditions of Anglo-Canadian law are retired."[7]

In any event, the Supreme Court, in its first batch of Charter decisions, seemed to be setting out to prove Smiley wrong. It upheld the Charter claim in nine of the first 15 cases—a staggeringly high success rate of 60 per cent. In these cases it struck down five laws—two provincial (the section of Quebec's Charter of the French language restricting access to Quebec's English schools[8] and a section of British Columbia's Motor Vehicle Act creating an absolute liability offence with a mandatory jail term for driving while one's license was suspended[9]) and three federal (the Lord's Day Act,[10] the search provisions of the Combines Investigation Act,[11] and a section of the Narcotics Control Act reversing the onus of proof[12]). Striking down legislation was not the only mark of its activism. In these same 15 cases the Court read new and onerous procedural requirements into the refugee provisions of the Immigration Act[13]; it took a very liberal approach to the test for excluding evidence obtained in violation of an accused's Charter rights[14]; and made it clear in its approach to section 1, the Charter's reasonable limits clause, that when a law is found to violate a Charter right the onus would be on the offending government to demonstrate that its law was "justified in a free and democratic society."[15]

The Supreme Court's treatment of the Charter in this early group of cases decided between May 1984 and the beginning of 1986 sent a clear message to the lower courts and the legal profession. The Charter was not to be treated like the Canadian Bill of Rights. In Charter cases there was to be no presumption of constitutionality. Judges were not to look for easy ways of evading their judicial review mandate. Lawyers—especially in criminal cases—were encouraged to bring forward Charter claims on behalf of their clients.

But even in these early cases there were signs of caution indicating that the justices sensed some important limits to their mandate. This was evident even in the *B.C. Motor Vehicle Act* case which was widely regarded as the Supreme Court's most activist decision. Here the Court chose to ignore the reasonably clear intentions of the Charter's drafters and treat "the principles of fundamental justice" in section 7 as guaranteeing substantive as well as procedural justice. But Justice Lamer who wrote the majority opinion was sensitive to fears of what he referred to as a "judicial super-legislature."[16] He endeavoured to assuage such fears by stipulating that the constitutional requirement of substantive justice in the law would not be applied "in the realm of general public policy" but would be confined to "the basic tenets of our legal system...the inherent domain of the judiciary."[17] Further, he suggested that laws imposing absolute liability on corporations for polluting the environment might be looked upon in a very different light than similar laws affecting the liberty of human persons.

There was a similar moderation of the Court's activism in *Operation Dismantle*, the case in which it put a damper on the efforts of the "peace" movement to use the Charter to reverse the commitment of Canadian governments—under both Liberal and Conservative administrations—to the strategy of nuclear deterrence. While Chief Justice Dickson asserted that the Court would not refuse to consider a challenge to the constitutionality of government policy merely because it lay in the field of foreign policy or involved the exercise of Crown prerogative or was highly political, still he would exclude from the courts challenges which could only be resolved by adjudicating competing theories about the probable reactions of the great powers to changes in Canadian defence policy. Such theories, in the Chief Justice's view "lie in the realm of conjecture, rather than fact" and as such are not fit for adjudication by courts.[18] Justice Wilson gave a different reason for dismissing this challenge—one that may have even more significant implications for restricting the application of the Charter. She held that the right to "security of the person" in section 7—the right which Cruise Missile testing in Canada was alleged to violate—cannot be used to challenge action or inaction by government which arguably might increase the general level of risk to the lives or security of citizens, such as a failure to lower highway speed limits or a declaration of war.[19]

Putting the Brakes on the Charter Express

The Court's moderation of its activism became much more evident and systematic in the second phase of its Charter interpretation. I have taken the Court's decision in *Clarkson*,[20] its fifteenth Charter decision, as marking the end of the first phase. In

Clarkson the majority held that a murder confession must be excluded when it was given after the accused in an intoxicated condition had waived her constitutional right to counsel. In *Bilodeau*,[21] *McDonald*[22] and *Société des Acadiens*,[23] the three cases decided immediately after *Clarkson*, the Supreme Court, with only Justice Wilson dissenting, rejected claims based on constitutional language rights. Both before and after the Charter, the Court had been extremely liberal in its treatment of entrenched language rights.[24] Now the Court lowered the cost of constitutional bilingualism by finding that the right to use the official minority language in the courts did not require that court documents be issued in that language, nor that all judges hearing parties in the minority language be themselves fluent in that language. Justice Beetz explained that since language rights were "founded on political compromise...the courts should pause before they decide to act as instruments of change with respect to language rights" and "should approach them with more restraint than they would in construing legal rights."[25] The Court—or at least a plurality of its members—was now clearly putting the brakes on the Charter express.

Between early 1986 when the Court rendered its decisions in these three language rights cases and the end of January 1988 when it brought down its decision in *Morgentaler*, the Court, by my count,[26] decided 32 Charter cases. In only 8 of these was the Charter claim upheld by the Court. The Charter success rate in the Supreme Court had fallen from 60 per cent to a much more modest 25 per cent.

During this second period the Supreme Court struck down only three pieces of legislation—all in the federal domain. The most spectacular of these was, of course, the abortion law (section 251 of the Criminal Code) which was declared unconstitutional in *Morgentaler*.[27] The other two legislative victims of the Court's activism received less notice: the mandatory seven-year sentence for importing illegal drugs in the Narcotics Control Act was found to be cruel and unusual punishment,[28] and the concept of "constructive murder" in section 213 of the Criminal Code was found to be fundamentally unjust.[29]

No provincial laws were overturned for violations of the Charter. This was not for want of challenges to provincial legislation. Some important provincial measures survived Charter scrutiny—notably Alberta's and Saskatchewan's anti-strike legislation,[30] Ontario's Sunday-closing legislation,[31] and full funding of Roman Catholic separate schools.[32]

As a matter of fact, looking at all of the Supreme Court's Charter decisions up to now it can hardly be said that they have devastated provincial or territorial statute books. Only two provincial laws—the two struck down in the first period—have been rendered null and void. For that matter the Court has overturned only six federal laws, all in the area of criminal justice. More laws have, of course, been struck down by lower courts. But most of these decisions have been rendered by provincial or territorial courts and so are not binding across the country. Moreover, it should be noted that in most cases governments have not felt keenly enough about their loss to appeal the decisions, let alone use the legislative override. Aside from Quebec's entirely symbolic, blanket use of the override,[33] its only practical use has been by Saskatchewan to protect strike-breaking legislation from judicial review[34]—a measure which subsequent Supreme Court decisions would render unnecessary.

From a quantitative perspective, the Charter, thus far, has not meant that appointed judges have supplanted elected politicians (or their official advisers) as the country's principal law-makers. The Supreme Court has become a fairly active criminal law reformer. But in the setting of Canadian federalism where criminal law is under the jurisdiction of the central legislature this development does not have centralizing implications. However, section 15, the Charter's equality section and a section on which the Supreme Court has not yet rendered a major decision, could dramatically change this picture. This section has the greatest potential for imposing national standards on provincial policy-making.

Most Charter victories in this second period have involved challenges not to legislation but to police investigation techniques and to the conduct of cases in the trial courts. Although in several cases[35] the Court held that admitting evidence obtained in violation of an accused's constitutional rights would bring the administration of justice into disrepute, in other cases it began to moderate this dimension of its activism. In *Tremblay*,[36] the Court found that the accused's right to counsel had been infringed when the police administered a breathalizer test before his lawyer arrived at the police station. Nevertheless it held that the resulting evidence should not be excluded because "From the moment the accused was intercepted on the road to the moment he was asked to give his first sample of breath his behaviour was violent, vulgar, and obnoxious."[37] In *Rahey*,[38] the Court, for the first time, quashed a conviction because it deemed the delay before trial amounted to a violation of the right under section 11(b) of the Charter "to be tried within a reasonable time." In this case there was an eleven month-delay caused by adjournments initiated by the trial judge. But in *Mills*,[39] Justice Lamer could not win the support of the majority for a mammoth opinion expounding a set of national standards for assessing the reasonableness of delay in the country's trial courts.

The Court sounded what is perhaps its loudest and most questionable note of restraint in this second period of Charter decision-making in *Dolphin Delivery*.[40] Here the Court ruled, unanimously, that judge-made common law could not be directly challenged as violating the Charter when common law is being applied in private litigation. The judiciary, said Justice McIntyre, "ought to apply and develop the principles of the common law in a manner consistent with the fundamental values enshrined in the Constitution." But for the judiciary it would appear that this "ought" is to be strictly a self-imposed moral imperative. Section 32 limits the Charter's application to legislatures and governments in Canada and while Justice McIntyre was willing to concede that "in political science terms" it was correct to treat the courts "as one of the three fundamental branches of Government"—a gracious concession to those of us in political science who teach and write about the judiciary— he and his colleagues held that as the arbiter of the common law in private disputes the courts were not to be considered a part of government. This judgment greatly limits the extent to which the Charter will penetrate legal relationships within civil society.[41]

Division in the Court

The moderation of the Court's activism on the Charter has not been fashioned with the degree of consensus exhibited in its first decisions. All but two of those first 15 decisions were unanimous. In 16, or exactly half, of the next 32 decisions there were dissents. The consensual character of the Court was still fairly marked: most of the dissents were solo dissents; in no case did more than two judges dissent. Justice Wilson, who of all the justices has been the least inclined to judicial restraint, has dissented most often— ten times in all. The only other justice close to this record is Justice

McIntyre who is at the other end of the Court and has been least attracted to activism. He has dissented in six cases.

The differences within the Court are on small points and large. But it is the latter—the differences of constitutional philosophy which are most interesting. By considering them we can better understand the choices which must be made about how the Charter is to affect the way we are governed.

One way of identifying the Supreme Court's primary responsibility in these early Charter years is to dissent from a dissent. The dissent I have in mind is that of Justice McIntyre, concurred in by Justice LaForest, in the *Morgentaler* case. In the course of his opinion Justice McIntyre states "That it is not for the courts to manufacture a constitutional right out of whole cloth."[42] If this was meant as a criticism of what his colleagues in the majority were doing, it is an unfair—although not an inaccurate—complaint. For cutting more precise constitutional rights out of the vague generalities of the Charter is precisely what judges have been doing and must do. Phrases like "freedom of conscience," "freedom of expression," "freedom of association," "the right to liberty," "principles of fundamental justice," and "the right to equal benefit of the law without discrimination" are very whole pieces of cloth indeed. To change the metaphor, I think of these phrases as limp balloons which the constitution makers handed to the judiciary; the judges must now decide how much air to blow into them.

In these early years of Charter interpretation the Supreme Court's most important responsibility is to give some size and shape to the actual rights which these vague phrases are to entail. In discharging this responsibility the Court is performing a constitution-making role which is at least as significant as that performed by the politicians and civil servants who wrote the Charter. For what the Court is doing here is identifying the human activities and interests which are to be given a priority status in Canada's legal system such that the state must always justify its encroachment on them. This, I would maintain, is an inescapable responsibility thrust upon the judiciary by the original constitution-makers. We may fault the judges for how they carry out this task, but we should not fault them for the fact that they have this task to perform.

Determining more precisely which human activities are to be protected by the Charter's vague generalities from government encroachment involves moral and political philosophy as well as considerations of a somewhat narrower institutional nature. On the philosophical issues, Chief Justice Dickson has taken the lead by propounding, in several of his early opinions, a "purposive" approach.[43] By this he means that judges should endeavour to identify "the interests" each right and freedom was meant to protect. This search is not to focus on what was said at the time of adoption by the constitution-makers but is to be based on a much broader inquiry into the development of liberal democratic societies. While there is general agreement within the Supreme Court on this purposive approach, it is not an approach which will yield the same results to all who apply it. The history and philosophy of liberal democracy is not exactly an open book containing clear definitions of the activities and interests which are not be interfered with by government.

Cutting across and into this exercise in history and philosophy is a concern of a more institutional nature, a concern about the proper role of the judiciary. The wider judges interpret the interests which must be protected from government encroachment— the more air they blow into the rights and freedoms balloons—the more often the judiciary will be called upon to review government's reasons for limiting rights. Section 1 of the Charter gives Canadian judges a clear option: instead of building limitations on rights and freedoms into the definitions of constitutionally protected rights and freedoms as the American Supreme Court has done, they can give the widest, most absolutist, interpretation of rights and freedoms and then, on a case by case basis, assess the reasons for limiting them under section 1. A major implication of taking this option is that it will produce a lot more judicial review by every court in the land. Consider, for instance, "freedom of association" under section 2. If this freedom is interpreted widely enough to encompass business organizations and their essential economic activities, then virtually every regulation of business will be deemed to encroach on a constitutional right and can only be saved by government lawyers persuading judges that the regulation is a reasonable and justifiable limit under section 1. If, on the other hand, "freedom of association" is construed more narrowly to exclude the essential activities of business corporations, then the opportunities for judicial review will be substantially reduced.

Some judges, because they entertain doubts about the judiciary's capacity to deal intelligently and responsibly with the policy considerations which come into play in applying section 1, are more cautious than others about taking this option. It is here, I think, that we encounter the most important differences among the judges—and perhaps among their critics—about what it is legitimate for judges to do in charterland.

Justice McIntyre's majority opinion in the *Alberta Labour Reference* provides the most explicit recognition of the judiciary's limited capability. After many pages of reasoning about the meaning of "freedom of association" he concludes that this concept "on its face cannot support the implication of a right to strike..."[44] But then he adds that "there is as well...a sound reason grounded in social policy against any such implication." What is that reason? It is simply this: if the essential collective activities of labour unions and not just the individual's freedom to form and join unions become constitutionally entrenched rights, then the judiciary will be frequently called upon to assess government's reasons for regulating these activities. This will involve the courts in frequent section 1 inquiries into services which are so essential to public welfare as to preclude the right to strike, and whether or not the alternative of compulsory arbitration is adequate compensation for loss of the right to strike. Justice McIntyre and the three judges concurring with him believe that these questions "are of a nature peculiarly apposite to the functions of the Legislature."[45] This belief must have been fortified by the disagreement in two companion cases[46] between the two members of the Court, Chief Justice Dickson and Justice Wilson, who would entrench labour's essential collective bargaining activities. These two judges in applying the section 1 test came to quite different conclusions about the public interest in legislating the end to a strike and restricting wage increases in the federal public service. The majority would prefer to keep the judiciary out of these policy disputes.

Unlike most of my undergraduate students, all the justices on the Supreme Court are willing to build in some limits, some boundaries to what is included in the Charter's broadly phrased rights and freedoms. This is true even of Justice Wilson who of all those now serving on the Court is the least troubled by reviewing government policy under section 1. As I noted earlier, her opinion in *Singh* built an important limit into the definition of the right to security of the person under section 7. In *Edwards Books* she and the other justices participating in this decision supported the Chief Justice in holding that whatever the "right to liberty" in section 7 means, it does not extend "to an unrestrained right to transact business whenever one wishes."[47]

My reading of the Supreme Court up to now is that most of its members are not nearly so bullish about supporting the use of the Charter as an instrument of socio-economic reform as they are for using it to reform criminal justice. Chief Justice Dickson is a little more activist than a majority of his colleagues in that he believes one of the Charter's broad underlying purposes is to strengthen the position of social and economic underdogs in Canadian society. In the *Alberta Labour Reference*, he explained his support for including organized labour's collective bargaining activities within "freedom of association" by arguing that labour's collective bargaining power "has enabled those who would otherwise be vulnerable and ineffective to meet on more equal terms the power and strength of those with whom their interests interact and, perhaps conflict."[48] This, I think, would be his answer to colleagues who fear that including the essential activities of unions within the constitutionally protected freedom of association would commit them to also including the essential activities of business corporations within that freedom.

The majority of the Court is not prepared to espouse such an ideological purpose for the Charter. They would prefer to nurture an image of ideological neutrality on major issues of social and economic policy. Many of the justices are sensitive to the possibility that the Charter could be used in a socially reactionary way to overturn legislation designed to improve the lot of less powerful groups in society. The Chief Justice expressed this concern in his majority opinion in *Edwards Books* when he stated that:

> In interpreting and applying the Charter I believe that the courts must be cautious to ensure that it does not become an instrument of better situated individuals to roll back legislation which has as its object the improvement of the condition of less advantaged persons.[49]

I think that most of the justices would support this position because they are as reluctant to see the Charter used to foster economic *laissez-faire* as they are to see it used to enlarge the power of organized labour. This may be the measure of their own sense of legitimacy.

Public Opinion and The Charter

As I have indicated, in teaching undergraduate courses on the Charter, I have found that nearly all of my students support the widest possible definition of the Charter's rights and freedoms. They are not disturbed at all by the prospect of judges reviewing virtually every law under section 1. For most of them the legitimacy of the judiciary's doing this simply is not an issue. It is for me—and for Don Smiley—but not for them.

In their enthusiasm for the Charter and their happiness with judicial review my undergraduates are in tune with Canadian public opinion at this stage in our history. Recently I have been collaborating with three colleagues, Joe Fletcher, Paul Sniderman and Philip Tetlock, in carrying out a survey of Canadian attitudes to civil liberties and the Charter of Rights.[50] While we are just now in the process of analyzing our data, I can report a couple of simple findings about attitudes to the Charter. Ninety per cent of English Canadians and 70 per cent of French Canadians *say* they have heard of the Charter. A substantial majority of each group think the Charter "is a good thing for Canada." But most do not know much about what is in the Charter. The majority evince no great concern for the erosion of legislative supremacy. We asked our sample of 2000 citizens whether they thought courts or legislatures should have the final say when a law is found by the courts to be unconstitutional on the grounds that it conflicts with the Charter. Over sixty per cent favoured the courts. Interestingly, when we asked our sample of 500 elected politicians the same question, over sixty per cent of them favoured legislatures having the final say.

At present I think the public regard the courts as being ideologically neutral. Hence there is no reason to distrust them. With the public the judiciary may well have more legitimacy than elected legislators as decision-makers on the meaning and limits of rights and freedoms. This level of support for judicial review is likely to change, however, if the courts'—especially the Supreme Court's— interpretation of the Charter becomes associated in the public's mind with unpopular policy positions.

But even if this happens, American experience suggests that it may not generate a major legitimacy crisis in the body politic. Decisions of the United States Supreme Court interpreting that country's constitutional charter of rights have been highly controversial. Survey data show large majorities opposed to positions the U.S. Supreme Court has taken on the admissibility of confessions, busing, school prayers, and the death penalty.[51] While surveys show that support for the Supreme Court as an institution is not high, they also indicate it is not dangerously low. In a recent survey the Court rated below the Presidency and local government in public esteem but on a par with Congress and state government. Attempts to curtail its powers have been beaten back by liberal activists in Congress. Reagan's conservative appointments may soon remove the ideological inspiration for these efforts.[52] The Court survives as it adjusts to the currents of national politics.

In Canada our Supreme Court and the judicial branch it heads should have as much or even more capacity to survive and adjust to any political storms its Charter work may unleash. Once again we should give credit to the cunning of the override clause which affords political leaders disgruntled with judicial decisions a more civilized remedy than court-bashing or court-packing.

So, the legitimacy crisis predicted by Don Smiley may occur only among the judges themselves and their intellectual critics. But it is no less important—philosophically—for that. Questions of legitimacy can be experienced at two levels: as practical issues of political stability and as normative questions of political theory. I doubt very much whether the Supreme Court's interpretation of the Charter will in the foreseeable future produce a legitimacy crisis at the first level. But we members of the chattering classes will continue and, indeed, should continue to examine the legitimacy of the reasoning of our judges about what they deem to be fundamental to our liberal democracy and about their own role in its governance. On both scores I find the moderate activism exhibited by the Supreme Court in its first few years of Charter interpretation reasonably congenial. But I am pretty sure many of my colleagues do not. And I am absolutely sure that Don Smiley's formal retirement will not in the least inhibit him from participating robustly in the debate we will inevitably have on all of this in the future.

Notes

1   Donald V. Smiley, *The Canadian Charter of Rights and Freedoms, 1981* (Toronto: Ontario Economic Council, 1981).

2   *Law Society of Upper Canada v Skapinker* (1984), 1 S.C.R. 35.

3   *The Queen v Therens* (1985), 1 S.C.R. 63, at 639.

4   *Singh v Minister of Employment and Immigration* (1985), 1 S.C.R. 177, at 209.

5   *Skapinker*, 366.

6   See Paul C. Weiler, "Rights and Judges in a Democracy: A New Canadian Version," *University of Michigan Journal of Law*, Reform 18 (1984), 51-92.

7   Smiley, *The Canadian Charter of Rights and Freedoms*, 55.

8   *A.-G. Québec v Quebec Association of Protestant School Boards* (1984), 2 S.C.R. 66.

9   *Reference Re British Columbia Motor Vehicle Act* (1985), 2 S.C.R. 486.

10 *The Queen v Big M Drug Mart Ltd.* (1985), 1 S.C.R. 295.

11 *Hunter v Southam, Inc.* (1984), 2 S.C.R. 145.

12 *The Queen v Oakes* (1986), 1 S.C.R. 103.

13 *Singh.*

14 *Therens.*

15 *Hunter v Southam Inc.* (1984), 2 S.C.R. 145, at 169.

16 *Reference Re B.C. Motor Vehicle Act*, 497.

17 *Ibid.*, 503.

18 *Operation Dismantle v The Queen* (1985), 1 S.C.R. 441.

19 *Ibid.*, 488-9.

20 *Clarkson v The Queen* (1986), 1 S.C.R. 383.

21 *Bilodeau v A.-G. Manitoba* (1986), 1 S.C.R. 449.

22 *McDonald v City of Montreal* (1986), 1 S.C.R. 460.

23 *Société des Acadiens v Association of Parents* (1986), 1 S.C.R. 549.

24 See especially *A.-G. Quebec v Blaikie* (1979), 2 S.C.R. 1016.

25 *Société des Acadiens*, 578.

26 When several cases raising exactly the same point have been decided at the same time, I have treated them as a single case.

27 *The Queen v Morgentaler* (1988), 1 S.C.R. 30.

28 *Smith v The Queen* (1987), 1 S.C.R. 1045.

29 *The Queen v Vaillancourt* (1987), 2 S.C.R. 631.

30 *Alberta Labour Reference* (1987), 1 S.C.R. 313 and *Saskatchewan v Retail, Wholesale and Dept. Store Union* (1987), 1 S.C.R. 460.

31 *Edwards Books and Arts Ltd. v The Queen* (1986), 2 S.C.R. 713.

32 *Reference Re Bill 30, An Act to Amend the Education Act* (1987), 1 S.C.R. 1148.

33 This use of the override was found to be unconstitutional by the Quebec Court of Appeal in *Alliance des Professeurs de Montréal v A.-G. Québec*

(1985), 21 D.L.R. (4th) 354. At the time of writing the matter is before the Supreme Court of Canada.

34 See F.L. Morton, "The Political Impact of the Canadian Charter of Rights and Freedoms," *Canadian Journal of Political Science*, 20 (1987), 48-9.

35 *Collins v The Queen* (1987), 1 S.C.R. 265; *Pohoretsky v The Queen* (1987), 1 S.C.R. 945.

36 *Tremblay v The Queen* (1987), 2 S.C.R. 435.

37 *Ibid.*, 438.

38 *Rahey v The Queen* (1987), 1 S.C.R. 588.

39 *Mills v The Queen* (1986), 1 S.C.R. 863.

40 *Retail, Wholesale and Dept. Store Union, Local 580 v Dolphin Delivery* (1986), 2 S.C.R. 573.

41 For a strong critique of this decision see David Beatty, "Constitutional conceits: The coercive authority of courts," *University of Toronto Law Journal*, 37 (1987), 183-92.

42 *Morgentaler, supra*, 141.

43 See especially *Hunter v Southam* and *Big M Drug Mart*.

44 *Alberta Labour Reference*, 414.

45 *Ibid.*, 419.

46 *Public Service Alliance of Canada v The Queen* (1987), 1 S.C.R. 424 and *Saskatchewan v Retail, Wholesale and Dept. Store Union*.

47 *Edwards Books and Arts Ltd.*, 779.

48 *Alberta Labour Reference*, 366.

49 *Edwards Books and Arts Ltd.*, 779.

50 A description of this project and an early report of some key findings are presented in Paul M. Sniderman, Joseph Fletcher, Peter H. Russell, and Philip Tetlock, "Liberty, Authority and Community: Civil Liberties and the Canadian Political Culture," paper presented at the Annual Meeting of the Canadian Political Science Association, University of Windsor, June 9, 1988.

51 Donald Adamany and Joel B. Grossman, "Support for the Supreme Court as a National Policy-Maker," *Law & Policy Quarterly*, 5 (1983), 405-37.

52 See Sheldon Goldman, "Reaganizing the Judiciary," *Judicature*, 67 (1983), 68.

CANADIAN CONSTITUTIONALISM AND THE SEQUEL TO THE MEECH LAKE/LANGEVIN ACCORD

J. Stefan Dupré, University of Toronto

Donald Smiley introduced his recent book, *The Federal Condition in Canada*, by remarking that the volume is not in his mind "a Fourth Edition of *Canada in Question*." What is under discussion, he declares, "is a relatively stable system of government." In criticism of his own earlier work, Smiley avows that he "very much over-estimated the strength of Quebec nationalism and provincialist influences elsewhere in the country and very much under-estimated the capacity of the system to respond effectively to such divisive pressures."[1]

Smiley's reassuring words, written in 1986, took on a glowing appearance in the dawning light of the morning of June 3, 1987. The signatures of the eleven first ministers who subscribed to the Meech Lake/Langevin Accord seemingly testified to the responsive capacity of "the system." This constitutional system is one in which the federal government and each of the provinces operate according to the rules of cabinet-parliamentary government, rendered workable and responsible by elected representatives grouped in disciplined political parties. Policy-making is dominated by the executive, more precisely by cabinets which are staffed, organized and led by their respective first ministers. With respect to the federal aspects of this system, the pre-eminent non-judicial mechanism of adjustment is what Smiley baptized "executive federalism," crisply defined as "the relations between elected and appointed officials of the two orders of government in federal-provincial interaction."[2] At the apex of these relations are the processes of summit federalism, articulated by the first ministers who generated the Meech Lake/Langevin Accord. Intended as it is to terminate Quebec's self-imposed isolation from the constitution, the Accord seeks to extinguish the symbol of continued divisiveness with which the Quebec National Assembly's bipartisan resolution stigmatized the Constitution Act of 1982.

Read at the moment the Accord was announced, Smiley's 1986 words appeared positively prescient. The unfolding events that comprise the sequel to Meech Lake/Langevin are something else again. In this brief essay, written in honour of the friend and colleague whose reflections have shaped my own thoughts more pervasively than any Canadian political scientist since the late Alex Corry, I shall confess that these events leave me in a state of profound schizophrenia. One of my personas discerns that Canadian constitutionalism has never been more robust. What it sees in the ratification process is the operation of a constitutional structure that has fully emerged as an edifice true to the spirit of both cabinet-parliamentary government and federalism. Whatever the outcome of the ratification process, Canadian constitutionalism is healthier than ever.

My second persona detects that Canadian constitutionalism is in disarray. I was schooled by the late Carl Friedrich to believe that constitutionalism hinges upon an internalization by politicians, public servants, groups and citizens of values that are congruent with, and nurture the vitality of, the formal rules of a constitution. In the eyes of my second persona, the ratification process has been disclosing a frightening sense of constitutional *anomie*—an absence of widely shared values about the nature of cabinet-parliamentary government and federalism.

The bottom line of my schizophrenia is a simple one: I await a Fourth Edition of *Canada in Question*. Meantime, I shall summon my two personas to speak in turn.

The Meech Lake/Langevin Sequel and the Health of Constitutionalism

Although I happen to be among the political scientists who support the content of the Meech Lake/Langevin Accord, I have come to accept the futility of convincing those of my respected friends who are not of the same mind. Away with persuasion; let a thousand flowers bloom! Whether or not the Accord finds its way into the constitution, Canadian constitutionalism will not be in jeopardy. Whatever the outcome, my own appreciation of our constitutional system will have been enhanced because I, among others, was slow to grasp the full significance of the amendment procedure entrenched after the patriation of our constitution in 1982. For five years, my attention focused upon such aspects as what could be amended by the standard formula, what required unanimity, what matters were or were not subject to opting out by a dissenting province. It struck me, as it struck Keith Banting and Richard Simeon, that the basic mechanism for securing future amendments was "purely intergovernmental."[3]

If my obtuseness is to be understood if not forgiven, my excuse is that the process of adopting the Constitution Act of 1982 blinded me to the fact that I was witnessing the last hurrah of the only amending process I had experienced as a Canadian. Here the convention of "substantial provincial consent" was fulfilled once provincial premiers indicated their assent. What followed was the traditional domestic form of ratification signalled by the passage of a resolution in a single parliamentary arena—the one in Ottawa—humbly addressing the constitutional amending power held in trusteeship at Westminster.

The change whose profound significance I failed to assimilate is that the post-1982 amendment procedure requires that future change be ratified not only by Parliament in Ottawa but by the provincial legislative assemblies. The constitution is henceforth not only patriated; its amendment has become congruent with the rules of cabinet-parliamentary government at the provincial as well as the federal level.

As the sequel to Meech Lake/Langevin has already demonstrated, this change is anything but cosmetic. Constitutional amendment hinges upon the operation of eleven different parliamentary arenas with eleven different party configurations at eleven different phases of the electoral cycle. During the time period allotted for the ratification process, a cabinet whose majority is precarious may, as did Premier Pawley's Cabinet in Manitoba, lose the confidence of its House and suffer the subsequent rebuke of its electorate. Or a governing party at the end of its term, as was Premier Hatfield's in New Brunswick, may suffer a stunning electoral defeat. Such is the force of the checks inherent in cabinet-parliamentary government, eleven sets of which now come into play in the process of amending the constitution.

There is still more to be noted about the multiple checks that hedge the amendment process. As Smiley has taught us, the Canadian marriage of the cabinet-parliamentary form of government with federalism has begotten a basically confederal party system. Federal and provincial parties whose political persuasions feature a common brand name may diverge fundamentally over any given issue. The sequel to the Meech Lake/Langevin Accord applies this lesson to the amendment process with vigour. In that all three federal party caucuses supported the Accord, the legitimation of dissent in Ottawa was marginalized in the Senate and in the handful of MP's who broke party discipline. In Canada writ large, however, Premier McKenna's newly elected Liberal governing party looms as a non-trivial check to the ratification of the Accord and legitimates dissent from its terms.

The process of ratifying constitutional amendments is evidently anything but automatic. Amendment does not hinge upon the mere agreement of first ministers. The Constitution Act of 1982 did not governmentalize the amendment process. In contrast to what prevailed before 1982, the process was degovernmentalized. More precisely still, the Constitution Act of 1982 parliamentarized the amendment process. It did so in the full sense in which the term parliament has come to be synonymous with responsible government. The operation of our amendment process is therefore more correctly conveyed by the term responsible federalism than the term executive federalism.

Thus does the sequel to the Meech Lake/Langevin Accord attest to the health of Canadian constitutionalism. If constitutionalism is all about regularized restraints on government power, the Canadian constitutional edifice appears more soundly structured than ever. This much will have been established whatever the fate of the Accord. I do not take lightly perturbations that will ensue should the Accord fail the ratification process. But it remains, in such an eventuality, that the key consideration which gave the Accord its attraction will not go away. Having come as far as it did in according priority to ending Quebec's proclaimed isolation from the Constitution, the amendment process seems bound to yield a further attempt, and this in a context where its operation as an exercise in responsible federalism has become apparent, at least to those who understand the principles underlying cabinet-parliamentary government.

The Meech Lake/Langevin Sequel and the Disarray of Constitutionalism

If my first persona smiles pleasantly as it witnesses the sequel to the Meech Lake/Langevin Accord, my second wears a worried frown. To be sure, I find it easy to be a worry-wart. The study of political science, no less than that of economics, is the study of a dismal science. There was no shortage of political scientists to help me perceive the downside of the sequel to the Accord.

At the forefront of those who prepared me to perceive the worst is Alan Cairns. His two characteristically brilliant essays for the Macdonald Commission, one of them written with Cynthia Williams, spin out a chilling tale. Ours has become a "rights-seeking entitlement society"[4] manifest in the cacophony of groups pressing the claims of feminists, ethnics, Aboriginal peoples, Francophones, visible minorities, the handicapped. Their ongoing search for status has been recognized by a multiplicity of advocacy portfolios and agencies in and around cabinets, spawning a new "species of bureaucratized pluralism"[5] that further fragments what are already factious executives. The Charter has bestowed upon these groups the status of constitutional recognition. This status encourages them to challenge the legitimacy of cabinet decision-making from the outside at one and the same time as the new species of bureaucratic pluralism attempts to bend that decision-making to their wills from the inside. Whatever may be positive about this state of affairs is severely tempered by "a dramatic assimilation of the language of rights by the citizenry...which has not been accompanied by an equivalent assimilation of a rhetoric of duty, responsibility or obligation."[6]

The Meech Lake/Langevin hearings offer a goldmine of evidence to support these bleak observations. What perturbs me is not the criticisms of the substance of the Accord but the evident degree of alienation from the values that underpin the Canadian constitutional marriage of cabinet-parliamentary government and federalism. Executive federalism, even when its agenda has been formulated in the glaring light of election campaigns, is reviled as secretive and manipulative. The eleven "men" at the apex of our constitutional executives are not viewed as having either a duty or a capacity to discern the public interest. The values of parliamentary democracy and the primacy it assigns to party teams are besieged by those of pluralist democracy and the primacy it assigns to organized groups. The values of responsible government are besieged by those of representative government.

In his 1977 presidential address to the American Political Science Association, Samuel Beer offers what for Canadians is a highly instructive commentary on the American constitutional marriage between federalism and representative government.[7] Here a partnership which he calls "representational federalism" looked to voters as the pre-eminent mechanism of adjustment in federal-state matters. But with the rise of modern-day, activist governments, this partnership was transmogrified into a rampant version of the special interest state.

Paul Pross's writings on interest group politics in Canada offer a marvelously illuminating treatment of the perils and opportunities that hedge our constitutional system in the age of big government and vigorous group activity. He closes his *Group Politics and Public Policy* on a reassuring note. "There are," he writes, "institutional mechanisms inhibiting the full flowering of a Canadian special-interest state... Cabinet responsibility imposes limits on the diffusion of powers that do not occur in the congressional-presidential system. The spectre of the special-interest state does not loom as large for Canada, therefore, as it does in the United States."[8] To be sure, the pressures of sectoralization upon cabinet are intense. In the final analysis, therefore, "it is the Prime Minister and his closest associates—the ministers of Finance, Justice and External Affairs—who must establish and maintain a broad perspective and insist that policy address the general interest."[9] The same applies at the provincial level of government.

The extent to which the sequel to Meech Lake/Langevin has unveiled values so hostile to the operation of cabinet government, the role of first ministers, and the place of executive federalism is what leaves my second persona wearing its worried frown. Pross's views—which I fully share—appear hopelessly romantic. And the views of elected members of parliamentary assemblies themselves are no source of comfort. The Report of the Select Committee on Constitutional Reform of the Legislative Assembly of Ontario, tabled in June of 1988, is worth citing on this score. Blithely ignoring the fact that the post-1982 constitutional amendment procedure enhances parliamentary government by mandating ratification at the provincial level, the Report notes that "the current (i.e. Meech Lake/Langevin) exercise has been inimical to legislative competence of provincial legislatures...Representative (sic) democracy requires, however, that the status of our legislatures cannot be too jealously guarded."[10] With Sophoclean inevitability, the Committee goes on to conclude that "there will always be a need for executive federalism but this must be complemented by *legislative federalism*."[11] And of what might this new invention consist? "The Committee supports further investigation into the concept of a national committee on the constitution composed of members from the various jurisdictions."[12]

Is this not the language of representative government rather than of responsible government? Does it not suggest the constitutional values inherent in a system of the separation of powers rather than those supportive of the fusion of power inherent in the cabinet-parliamentary form? Politesse cautions me to refrain from answering with a resounding affirmative. However, in the context of the sequel to Meech Lake/Langevin, I have no difficulty adding the Select Committee's Report to the array of evidence which indicates that Canadian constitutionalism is in a state of disarray.

Conclusion

Two Stefan Duprés have written this little essay in honour of Donald Smiley. One perceives, in the sequel to the Meech Lake/Langevin Accord, a Canadian constitutionalism which more securely honours the principles of cabinet-parliamentary government and federalism. If it has done nothing else, this sequel demonstrates the significance of a post-1982 amendment procedure which requires the ratification of the provincial parliamentary assemblies as well as that of their federal counterpart. Constitutional amendments are not the exclusive preserve of executive federalism; they are truly exercises in responsible federalism.

The other Stefan Dupré sees Canadian constitutionalism in a state of disarray. The values that underpin what Smiley characterizes in *The Federal Condition* as a relatively stable system of government are besieged by values that extol pluralist rather than parliamentary democracy, representative rather than responsible government.

At this time, the two Stefan Duprés converge in only one respect: both would welcome a Fourth Edition of *Canada in Question*.

Notes

1 Donald V. Smiley, *The Federal Condition in Canada* (Toronto: McGraw-Hill Ryerson, 1987), xi.

2 Donald V. Smiley, *Canada in Question*, 3rd. ed. (Toronto: McGraw-Hill Ryerson, 1980), 91.

3 Keith Banting and Richard Simeon, "Federalism, Democracy, and the Constitution," in *And No One Cheered*, Kieth Banting and Richard Simeon, eds. (Toronto: Methuen 1983), 8.

4 Alan Cairns, "The Embedded State: State-Society Relations in Canada," in *State and Society: Canada in Comparative Perspective*, ed. by Keith Banting, Studies for the Royal Commission on the Economic Union, vol. 31, (Toronto: University of Toronto Press, 1986), 54.

5 *Ibid.*, 76

6 Alan Cairns and Cynthia Williams, "Constitutionalism, Citizenship, and Society in Canada: An Overview," in *Constitutionalism, Citizenship, and Society in Canada*, Alan Cairns and Cynthia Williams eds., Studies for the Royal Commission on the Economic Union, vol. 33, (Toronto: University of Toronto Press, 1985), 44.

7 Samuel H. Beer, "Federalism, Nationalism and Democracy in America," *American Political Science Review*, 72(1), March 1978.

8 A. Paul Pross, *Group Politics and Public Policy* (Toronto: Oxford University Press, 1986), 273.

9 *Ibid.*, 274.

10 Ontario, Select Committee on Constitutional Reform, *Report on the Constitution Amendment 1987*, Queen's Park, 1988, 5.

11 *Ibid.*, 36.

12 *Ibid.*

FEDERALISM FIGHTS THE CHARTER OF RIGHTS

Peter W. Hogg, York University

I. Centralizing Effect of Charter

National Standards

The Charter of Rights is a centralizing force in Canada.[1] This is not because it confers any additional powers on the federal parliament, because of course it does not do so. On the contrary, the Charter imposes restrictions on the powers of the federal parliament, as well as on the powers of the provincial legislatures. The centralizing effect of the Charter derives from the fact that it consists of a set of national standards for the protection of civil liberties. These standards apply throughout the country, and they apply within fields of exclusive provincial jurisdiction, as well as in fields of federal jurisdiction.[2] Some of these standards, particularly the mobility rights of s.6 and the language rights of ss.16 to 23, are avowedly directed to national unity, preventing the balkanization of Canada by facilitating personal mobility, and by attempting to make the whole of Canada a homeland for French-speaking as well as English-speaking Canadians. But all of the provisions of the Charter give to persons whose civil liberties have been abridged by either provincial or federal action the right to appeal to national norms which will be enforced by the court system, and ultimately by a national court. The result is "to set limits to the diversities of treatment by provincial governments, and thus to strengthen Canadian as against provincial identities."[3]

National Debates

Decisions interpreting the Charter of Rights will not be unifying in the sense of attracting a national consensus. The experience of the United States shows that judicial decisions on matters such as pornography, school prayers, police powers, capital punishment, and abortion can be highly controversial. At the time of writing, several politically charged issues have been decided by the Supreme Court of Canada: for example, the rights of criminal defendants, including the exclusion of reliable evidence obtained improperly by the police[4]; access to minority language education[5]; Sunday closing[6]; the right to strike[7]; the public funding of Roman Catholic schools[8]; and abortion.[9] Canadians have seemed much more disposed to accept the decisions of the Court than would be expected by an observer of the furious political debates that have followed judicial decisions under the Bill of Rights in the United States. Nevertheless, the fact remains that much Charter adjudication is inherently controversial and divisive. But the public debates that are engendered by Charter decisions are national debates on issues that transcend regional or provincial differences. Charter debates are premised on the assumption that on issues of human liberty it is appropriate to have a single, Canadian policy.[10]

Individual, Not Provincial, Rights

The same point may be expressed in a different way. For the most part, the Charter recognizes individual, not collective, rights. Individual rights are possessed by every individual in Canada, regardless of province of residence or membership of any other collectivity. Individual rights can be invoked by any individual anywhere in Canada; the rights do not vary from one province to another. Indeed, for natural-law lawyers, rights are universal, attaching to all individuals as an attribute of their humanity. For positivists, who see rights simply as creatures of law, individual rights are at least national in their scope, because the instrument of their creation (the Constitution) is national in its scope. Where guaranteed rights exist, there must be a single national rule. This is inconsistent with the diversity of treatment by regional governments that is the value at the core of federalism. It follows that, "in giving effect to the individualistic and universal rights reflected in the Charter, courts may directly or indirectly limit the opportunity for diversity and distinctiveness in our legal system."[11]

The rest of this paper will be concerned to explore the extent to which the Charter permits recognition of the federal values of diversity and distinctiveness.

II. Override Power (s.33)

Description of s.33

The most important protection for federal values in the Charter of Rights is s.33, which enables the parliament or a legislature to "override" many of the Charter rights. All that the parliament or legislature need do is to insert in a statute an express declaration that the statute is to operate notwithstanding a Charter right, and then the statute will operate free from the invalidating effect of the Charter right referred to in the declaration. This power of override does not apply to all of the Charter rights, but it does apply to freedom of religion, expression, assembly, and association (s.2), the "legal" rights (ss.7 to 14); and equality (s.15). The rights that cannot be overridden are the "democratic" rights (ss.3 to 5), the mobility rights (s.6), the language rights (ss.16 to 23), the enforcement provision (s.24), and the sexual equality clause (s.28). An override clause in a statute is operative for only five years, but it can be periodically re-enacted for successive periods of five years.

Origin of s.33

Section 33 was not in any of the versions of the Charter that preceded the federal-provincial agreement of November 5, 1981, in which all of the provinces except Quebec finally reached agreement on the adoption of a Charter of Rights. The power of override was the crucial new element that secured the agreement of those provinces (other than Quebec) that until then had been opposed to the Charter on the ground that it limited the sovereignty of their Legislatures.[12] Although the final version of the Charter accorded the power of override to the federal parliament as well as to the provincial legislatures, the federal government (with Ontario and New Brunswick) was the advocate of a Charter without any power of override. The purpose of the power was to protect the autonomy of the provincial legislatures, allowing them the freedom to derogate from the national Charter without the necessity to justify the derogation before the courts. Section 33 is therefore a radical qualification to the centralizing effect of the Charter of Rights. Most of the national norms, and the judicial review that enforces them, can be avoided by the power of override.

Use of s.33

The power of override has been used outside Quebec only once. That was by Saskatchewan to protect a back-to-work law[13] of a kind that the Saskatchewan Court of Appeal in the *Dairyworkers* case[14] had held was contrary to the guarantee of freedom of association (s.2[d]). When the Saskatchewan government enacted the override clause, it was in the process of appealing the *Dairyworkers* decision to the Supreme Court of Canada. The Supreme Court of Canada later allowed the appeal of the Saskatchewan government, vindicating the government's view that the back-to-work law did not offend the Charter.[15] Thus, the use of the power of override was shown to be unnecessary. Saskatchewan's use of the override power accordingly constitutes a very weak precedent. No other province except Quebec has ever used the power.

Quebec has used the power of override extensively — but only as a protest against the Charter of Rights, which had been imposed on the province against its will. After the enactment of the Charter, Quebec's Parti Québécois government secured the enactment of a statute entitled An Act Respecting the Constitution Act 1982[16] that added a standard-form notwithstanding clause to all Quebec statutes in force at the time of enactment. (Whether such a blanket declaration is effective is unclear: it has been upheld by Quebec's Superior Court,[17] struck down by Quebec's Court of Appeal,[18] and is now under appeal to the Supreme Court of Canada.) In addition, Quebec routinely inserted a standard-form notwithstanding clause in every Act subsequently enacted by the Quebec National Assembly. The latter practice was continued for a time by the new Liberal government of Quebec after it replaced the Parti Québécois government in December 1985. However, the practice was discontinued in March 1986 by the Liberal government.[19] By then the "Quebec round" of constitutional discussions that culminated in the Meech Lake Constitutional Accord of 1987 was in train. If there were any doubts about the purpose of Quebec's uses of the notwithstanding clause, they are settled by the fact that Quebec did not override its own Charter of Human Rights and Freedoms,[20] a document which guarantees most of the same rights as the national Charter and which is also subject to a power of override.[21] In this way, Quebec made clear that it was not in fact derogating from any civil rights: it was simply protesting the imposition of the Charter of Rights.

Conclusions on s.33

If we put to one side the special case of Quebec, we are left with only one use of the power of override, and that use—by Saskatchewan—was cautionary only and ultimately unnecessary. It is probably too soon to draw any conclusions from this remarkable history of political forbearance. In the six years that have elapsed from the adoption of the Charter on April 17, 1982 to the time of writing (June 1988), it is the federal criminal law and procedure that has suffered the heaviest blows at the hands of the Supreme Court of Canada. In important areas of provincial jurisdiction, the Court has so far shown restraint.[22] But if a matter of vital provincial policy was blocked by the Court, it seems likely that some provinces would have recourse to s.33.[23] In any event, that political option is open, and it constitutes the ultimate shield for provincial diversity in the treatment of issues that are the subject of the national norms of the Charter.

III. Limitation Clause (s.1)

Federalizing Potential of s.1

Section 1 of the Charter of Rights provides as follows:

> The Canadian Charter of Rights and Freedoms guarantees the rights and freedoms set out in it subject only to such reasonable limits prescribed by law as can be demonstrably justified in a free and democratic society.

By permitting laws to impose "reasonable limits" on rights, s.1 is a potential moderating or federalizing influence within the Charter. Section 1 will serve this function if the courts are willing to accept that provinces could design different forms of permissible derogations from Charter rights.

European "Margin of Appreciation"

Section 1 of the Charter of Rights has no counterpart in the American Bill of Rights, but it is modelled on limitation clauses that are to be found in international human rights instruments, especially the European Convention on Human Rights. The cases before the European Court of Human Rights have developed a body of jurisprudence as to the meaning of the several limitation clauses that are to be found in the Convention and that are expressed in language that is similar to s.1.

The European Court of Human Rights has used the limitation clauses in the Convention to permit different treatment of civil libertarian issues by the member states. The approach of the Court is to permit each state "une marge d'appréciation," which is usually mechanically rendered into English as "margin of appreciation," although "measure of discretion" would be a much better translation.

The idea of a margin of appreciation appears in many cases,[24] but the one most frequently cited is *Handyside v. United Kingdom* (1976).[25] The issue in *Handyside* was whether the United Kingdom's offence of obscenity violated the Convention right of freedom of expression. The case arose out of the conviction on an obscenity charge of the publisher of *The Little Red Schoolbook*, which is a sex manual for children. This book, originally written in Danish, circulated freely in Denmark and, in translation, in most of the other member states. The question for the Court was whether the suppression of the book in the United Kingdom, although clearly out of line with other democratic countries, could be justified under the applicable limitation clause (article 10[2]) of the Convention as "necessary in a democratic society...for the protection of...morals." Were English morals in need of more protection than Danish or French morals? Yes, said the Court. There was no "uniform European conception of morals"; and "State authorities are in principle in a better position than the international judge to give an opinion on the exact content of these requirements" of morals. Consequently, the limitation clause "leaves to the Contracting States a margin of appreciation."[26] The Court held that the obscenity law came within the margin of appreciation allowed to the United Kingdom by the limitation clause of the Convention.

Another more recent example is *Johnston v. Ireland* (1986).[27] The issue in that case was whether or not Ireland's absolute prohibition of divorce violated the Convention right to "respect" for "family life." The case was brought by a man and a woman who were living together as man and wife with their child. However, the *de facto* spouses were unable to marry, because the man was already married to another woman, and under Irish law could not obtain a divorce despite the longstanding irrevocable breakdown of the earlier marriage. This meant that the second family was denied the legal framework of rights and obligations regarding such matters as maintenance and support, succession to property, taxation, and rights to the matrimonial home, that under Irish law attached only to the legal relationship of marriage. The Court held that there was no failure of "respect" for family life. Without even addressing the applicable limitation clause, the Court held that, having regard to the diversity of practices in the member states, "this is an area in which the [member states] enjoy a wide margin of appreciation in determining the steps to be taken to ensure compliance with the Convention."[28] The dissenting judgment of Judge de Meyer held that the situation of the applicant was one that did require the legal recognition of divorce, and the failure of Ireland to do so could not be justified as necessary in a democratic society. But, for the majority, Ireland's unique and draconian law came within the margin of appreciation.[29]

For the European Court, therefore, different countries may legitimately enact different levels of derogation from the guaranteed rights. The margin of appreciation provides the necessary latitude. The experience of the European Court is obviously not wholly transferable to Canada. The Court's jurisdiction extends to the sovereign states of western Europe who adhere to the Convention. The jurisdiction of the Court flows from the Convention, which in turn derives its force from the consent of the member states. The Court's rulings are not directly enforceable in the member states; voluntary compliance is the means of implementation. These are important differences between the role of the European Court and the Supreme Court of Canada, which applies a binding Charter of Rights within a single state. And yet there is the important similarity that both Courts have to apply a single set of precepts to a variety of legal systems, namely, those of the European states and the Canadian provinces.

Denial of Rights

The early case-law in the Supreme Court of Canada interpreted s.1 so narrowly that there seemed little room for the introduction of federal values into the concept of reasonable limits. The first important s.1 decision was the *Quebec School Board* case (1984),[30] in which the Supreme Court of Canada had to determine the validity of the "Quebec clause" of Quebec's Charter of the French Language (Bill 101), which limited admission to English-language schools in Quebec to the children of persons who had been educated in English in Quebec. The Court held that the Quebec clause was invalid, because it was inconsistent with s.23(1)(b) (the "Canada clause") of the Charter of Rights, which guaranteed admission to minority-language schools to the children of persons who had been educated in the minority language anywhere in Canada.

Could the Quebec clause be justified under s.1? At the trial, evidence was led by the Government of Quebec to support the clause as necessary for the protection of the French language and culture. The trial judge, Deschênes C.J., accepted that the protection of the French language and culture was the purpose of Bill 101, including the Quebec clause. But he held that the exclusion from Quebec's English-language schools of the children of persons educated in English in Canada outside Quebec would make such a trivial contribution to Quebec's linguistic and cultural objectives that it could not be regarded as a reasonable limit under s.1.[31]

Deschênes C.J. also rejected the s.1 argument on an alternative, quite different ground. He said that s.1 did not contemplate the denial as opposed to the limitation of a guaranteed right, and the Quebec clause was so directly contrary to s.23(1)(b) of the Charter that it constituted the denial of the right. This was the basis of the decision upon which Deschênes C.J.'s judgment was affirmed, first by the Quebec Court of Appeal,[32] and then by the Supreme Court of Canada.[33] The Supreme Court of Canada refused to go into the linguistic and cultural objectives of Bill 101, because the Quebec clause was not a "limit" within the contemplation of s.1.

The classification of the Quebec clause as a "denial" rather than a "limit" of a guaranteed right seems to me to be an unsatisfactory way of disposing of the s.1 argument in the *Quebec School Board* case. I have criticized the reasoning elsewhere[34] and will not repeat my arguments here. For present purposes, the important point is this: the argument based on Quebec's distinctive language and culture, although rejected by Deschênes C.J. on these facts, presupposed that s.1 would allow Quebec to make unique rules for the purpose of safeguarding its distinctive language and culture. The Supreme Court of Canada avoided this argument[35] by its limit/denial distinction.

Least Drastic Means

R. v. Oakes (1986)[36] is the Supreme Court of Canada's second major decision under s.1. The federal Narcotic Control Act provided that if an accused was proved to be in possession of a narcotic, which was an offence under the Act, there was a presumption that the accused also intended to traffic in the narcotic, which was a more serious offence under the Act. This presumption cast on the accused the burden of disproving the presumed fact that he intended to traffic in the narcotic. The Court held that this "reverse onus" clause was a breach of s.11(d) of the Charter, which guarantees the presumption of innocence. The Court also held that the clause was not saved by s.1 of the Charter. The clause was accordingly held to be invalid.

In the *Oakes* case, the Court for the first time laid down the principles that govern the operation of s.1. In order to establish that a law is within the phrase "such reasonable limits prescribed by law as can be demonstrably justified in a free and democratic society," two criteria had to be satisfied. First, the law must pursue an objective that is sufficiently important to warrant overriding a Charter right. Secondly, the law must pursue that objective by means that are proportional to the objective. The proportionality test required, among other things, that the law be carefully designed to achieve the legislative objective, and that the law should impair "as little as possible" the guaranteed right.[37] The reverse onus clause in the Narcotic Control Act passed the first test: the control of drug trafficking was a sufficiently important objective. But it did not pass the second test: the law was too broad in that possession of even a small quantity of narcotics gave rise to the presumption of trafficking.

The categorical language which the Court employed in *Oakes* to delineate its function under s.1 appeared to leave little room for federal values to affect the outcome. To be sure, provinces could have different objectives. But once a general objective had been approved by the Court, the law was then to be judged by very strict standards, and in particular was to derogate from the guaranteed right as little as possible—or by the least drastic means. This approach did not appear to acknowledge a "margin of appreciation" in judging distinctive provincial laws. Of course, in reading the opinion in *Oakes*, it is important to remember that the Court was dealing with a federal statute that applied uniformly across the country. The Court did not need to face the question of whether or not different jurisdictions could derogate from the presumption of innocence in different ways in order to fight the drug trade.

The impact of s.1 on a provincial statute came before the Supreme Court of Canada in *R. v. Edwards Books and Art* (1986).[38] In that case, the Court upheld the Sunday closing requirement in Ontario's Retail Business Holidays Act. The Act prohibited retail stores from opening on Sundays. The Court held that this was a breach of s.2(a) of the Charter, which guarantees freedom of religion, but that the law could be justified under s.1.

In deciding that the Sunday closing law could be justified under s.1, the Court employed the *Oakes* test. First, the objective of the law, which was to provide a common pause day, was sufficiently important to warrant overriding a Charter right. Secondly, the law pursued that objective by means that were proportional to the objective. The latter conclusion involved the difficult part of the reasoning, because *Oakes* had insisted that the law should impair "as little as possible" the Charter right. Did the law meet that test?

The Act contained a "sabbatarian exception" for retailers who observed Saturday as the sabbath. If a retailer closed on Saturday, then the firm could open on Sunday, provided that the firm employed no more than seven people and used no more than 5,000 square feet. This exception went some distance to accommodate sabbatarians, but it did not cover the larger Saturday-observing retailers, that is, those who employed more than seven people or used more than 5,000 square feet. (Nor did the exception cover those retailers who observed Friday—or any day other than Saturday or Sunday—as their sabbath, but the Court had no evidence as to these practices and did not consider this point.) The principal issue in the case therefore resolved itself into whether or not the law had made an adequate accommodation of those who observed Saturday as their sabbath. On this point the Court fractured into three camps.

Dickson C.J., who had written the *Oakes* opinion, now softened his language considerably. With the concurrence of Chouinard and LeDain JJ., he said that the test was whether or not the law abridged the freedom of religion of Saturday observers "as little as is reasonably possible."[39] The word "reasonably" had not appeared in that phrase in the *Oakes* case. As to the precise form of the legislative limit, it was "one that was reasonable for the legislature to impose."[40] The courts were "not called upon to substitute judicial opinions for legislative ones as to the place at which to draw a precise line."[41] The exemption in the Act "represents a satisfactory effort on the part of the Legislature of Ontario to that end [the accommodation of Saturday observers] and is, accordingly, permissible."[42]

La Forest J. was even more deferential in his attitude to the province's policy choice. He would have upheld the law, even if it had contained no sabbatarian exemption. Having accepted the importance of the legislative objective to provide a common pause day, he concluded that "a legislature must be given reasonable room to manoeuvre."[43] In particular, it seemed to him that "the choice of having or not having an exemption for those who observe a day other than Sunday must remain, in essence, a legislative choice."[44]

Only Wilson J. applied the remorseless logic of "least drastic means" to insist that the law must contain a sabbatarian exception, and that the exception must extend to all Saturday-observing retailers, not just those with no more than seven employees and 5,000 square feet of space.[45] This caused her to dissent in part because one of the four defendants in the case was a retailer that closed on Saturdays, but employed more than seven employees and used more than 5,000 square feet of space. That defendant, in her view, was entitled to be acquitted.

The general thrust of *Oakes* was to set up such strict standards for s.1 justification that there was little room for different choices by different provinces. That approach is exemplified by Wilson J.'s decision in *Edwards Books*: the Sunday closing laws of the provinces would all have to include a similar unlimited sabbatarian exemption, because that was required by the least drastic means test. Under Dickson C.J.'s approach in *Edwards Books*, a variety of sabbatarian exemptions were all permissible: provided a genuine effort had been made to accommodate Saturday observers, the Court would not substitute its opinion for that of the legislature as to the precise scope of the exemption. Under La

Forest J.'s approach, the province's choice extended beyond the nature and scope of any sabbatarian exemption to the decision of whether or not to have an exemption at all. From the point of view of the present paper, which is concerned with the role of federalism in Charter interpretation, Wilson J.'s opinion leaves little room for different provincial policies regarding the design of exemptions to a Sunday closing law; Dickson C.J. does leave room for differing provincial policy preferences; and La Forest J. leaves even more room. The judgments of Dickson C.J. and La Forest J. provide the basis for a Canadian margin of appreciation.

Distinct Society Clause

The distinct society clause, which is to be added to the Constitution Act 1867 by the Meech Lake Constitutional Accord, provides a new mechanism for the introduction of a value of federalism into the operation of s.1. That clause will be discussed in the next section of this paper, as part of the discussion of the Meech Lake Constitutional Accord.

IV. Meech Lake Constitutional Accord

The Meech Lake Constitutional Accord proposes a set of amendments to the Constitution of Canada, the purpose of which is to reconcile the Government of Quebec to the Constitution Act, 1982, including the Charter of Rights.[46] The amendments proposed by the Accord are generally decentralizing in their effects. Naturally, this has attracted criticism from those who are concerned about the weakening of central authority. In assessing the Accord, however, it is important to remember the centralizing effect of the Charter of Rights of 1982, to which Quebec never gave its political assent. It seems obvious that any amendments to the Constitution that were intended to better accommodate Quebec within the Canadian federation would have to address in some fashion the centralizing influence of the Charter. Two of the six items in the Accord are directed, at least in part, to this end. They are the "distinct society" clause and the new provisions for appointments to the Supreme Court of Canada.

Distinct Society Clause

The Meech Lake Constitutional Accord proposes to add a new s.2 to the Constitution Act 1867. (The old s.2 was repealed in 1893.) The new s.2 provides in subsection (1) that "the Constitution of Canada shall be interpreted in a manner consistent with...(b) The recognition that Quebec constitutes within Canada a distinct society." Subsection (3) provides that: "The role of the legislature and Government of Quebec to preserve and promote the distinct identity of Quebec referred to in paragraph (1)(b) is affirmed." I shall hereafter describe these provisions as "the distinct society clause."

An important effect—perhaps the only effect—of the distinct society clause of the Meech Lake Constitutional Accord is to ensure that Quebec's "distinctness" is not lost sight of in Charter interpretation. By "affirming" the role of the legislature and Government of Quebec "to preserve and promote the distinct identity of Quebec," the Meech Lake Accord is attempting to shield Quebec from the centralizing effects of the Charter of Rights. It seems plain to me that such a vague affirmation could not directly override Charter rights, but the clause could and should give added weight to s.1 justificatory arguments based on the special nature of Quebec. Thus, laws that have as their purpose the security of the French language might be treated as "reasonable limits" under s.1.[47] This would not change the result in the *Quebec School Board* case, because of the Court's finding that the law was in such direct contradiction of the Charter right (s.23) that s.1 could not save it. If s.1 is not reached, there is no room for the distinct society clause to operate. But a law requiring commercial signs to be in French, if held to be a limit on freedom of expression (s.2[b]), might be able to invoke the distinct society clause in aid of s.1 justification.[48]

The distinct society clause has been much criticized, both for its vagueness and for its suggestion of special status for Quebec.[49] But, as I noted earlier, any accommodation with Quebec would have to address in some fashion the province's concern that the 1982 Charter of Rights, to which Quebec had not agreed, limited the powers of the Quebec National Assembly to preserve and promote the French language and culture.[50] As a response to this concern, the distinct society clause is far from radical. There is no direct amendment of any Charter right and no extension of the override clause (s.33) to language rights. The clock is not turned back to 1981, when the Quebec National Assembly was unconstrained by a national Charter of Rights. On the contrary, the Charter remains intact and in full force after Meech Lake, subject only to the requirement that its application take some account of an important federal value—the distinctness of Quebec.

Appointment of Judges

The Charter of Rights of 1982 constituted an important transfer of power to the courts. One of the most extraordinary features of the Constitution of Canada is that the federal government appoints the judges, not only to the Supreme Court of Canada but to all of the higher provincial courts.[51] The provinces have long claimed that they ought to be involved in the appointment of judges, at least to the Supreme Court of Canada.[52] Before the Charter of Rights this claim was based on the function of the Court as an arbiter of federal-provincial constitutional disputes. It was inappropriate, so the argument went, that the Court that serves as the "umpire of federalism" should be composed of judges selected by only one of the contending levels of government.

The umpire-of-federalism line of argument is just as powerful since the adoption of the Charter, but the Charter adds another line of argument. Now that the Court possesses increased powers to limit provincial jurisdiction (as well as federal jurisdiction) in order to protect civil liberties, the reduction in provincial legislative and executive powers ought to be accompanied by some provincial influence over the composition of the Court. Shortly after the adoption of the Charter, Peter Russell pointed out: "To be able to maintain that a transfer of power from politicians to judges entails 'no transfer of power from the provinces to the federal government' it may become necessary to give provincial governments a share of the action in the judicial appointment process."[53]

Russell's comment, made in 1983, has proved to be prescient. When in 1986 the government of Quebec initiated negotiations to enable it to give its "willing assent" to the Constitution Act 1982, one of Quebec's conditions was a provincial role in appointments to the Supreme Court of Canada. That condition was satisfied by the Meech Lake Constitutional Accord, which, when ratified by all eleven legislative bodies, will require the federal government to choose each judge of the Supreme Court of

Canada from names submitted by the government of a province.[54] The effect of this amendment will be to require that each appointment to the Court be acceptable both to the federal government and to the government of the province from which the appointment is made. Since three of the nine judges must be appointed from Quebec,[55] this provision gives the government of Quebec an important influence over the composition of the Court. By usage, Ontario also has a quota of three judges, and will be in a position to influence those appointments. The remaining three judges are usually distributed by region: two from the four western provinces and one from the four Atlantic provinces. Those appointments also have to be made from provincial lists, but the ability of the federal government to shop around among provincial lists will attenuate the role of the western and Atlantic provinces.

V. General Conclusions

The Charter of Rights does conflict with federalism, and does reduce the autonomy of the provinces. When enacting laws that impinge on guaranteed rights, the provinces must now satisfy a set of judicially-enforceable national standards that reduce the room for distinctive provincial policies. This centralizing effect of the Charter is moderated by the power of override in s.33 and by the limitation clause of s.1. The "distinct society" clause proposed by the Meech Lake Constitutional Accord is designed to ensure that an important federal value—the distinctness of Quebec—will be taken into account in s.1 justification.

What the provinces lost from the Charter, the courts gained through their enhanced power of judicial review. This new gain of power strengthened the movement for a provincial role in the appointment of judges, which had in the past been based only on an umpire-of-federalism argument. The provisions of the Meech Lake Constitutional Accord will provide that role.[56]

Notes

1   See Alan C. Cairns, "Recent Federalist Constitutional Proposals: A Review Essay," *Canadian Public Policy* (1979), 348; Peter H. Russell, "The Political Purposes of the Canadian Charter of Rights and Freedoms," *Canadian Bar Review* (1983), 30.

2   See e.g., *Mills v. The Queen* (1986) 1 S.C.R. 863, 935 per Lamer J. (no allowance for local conditions in determining "reasonable time" for trial of criminal case).

3   Cairns, "Recent Federalist Proposals," 354.

4   E.g., *R. v. Therens* (1985) 1 S.C.R. 613; *Dubois v. The Queen* (1985) 1 S.C.R. 350; *Clarkson v. The Queen* (1986) 1 S.C.R. 383; *R. v. Collins* (1987) 1 S.C.R. 165; *R. v. Manninen* (1987) 1 S.C.R. 1233.

5   *Attorney General for Quebec v. Quebec Protestant School Bds.* (1984) 2 S.C.R. 66.

6   *R. v. Big M Drug Mart* (1985) 1 S.C.R. 295; *R. v. Edwards Books and Art* (1986) 2 S.C.R. 713.

7   *Re Public Service Employees Relations Act* (1987) 1 S.C.R. 313; *Public Service Alliance of Canada (PSAC) v. Canada* (1987) 1 S.C.R. 424; *Retail, Wholesale, and Department Store Union (RWDSU) v. Saskatchewan* (1987) 1 S.C.R. 460.

8   *Re Bill 30* (1987) 1 S.C.R. 1148.

9   *R. v. Morgentaler* (1988).

10   Russell, "Political Purposes of the Charter," 41.

11   Ian G. Scott, "Thinking about the Charter," *Law Society Gazette* 21(1987), 213, 216.

12   Until November 5, 1981, eight provinces—all except Ontario and New Brunswick—were opposed to Prime Minister Trudeau's package of amendments, including the Charter of Rights. Agreement was reached with seven of the eight opposed provinces through two major concessions. The first concession was the inclusion of an override power in the Charter of Rights, as related in the text. The second concession was the substitution of the amending formula preferred by the group of eight for the one preferred by the federal government and its two provincial allies.

13   The SGEU Dispute Settlement Act, S.S. 1984-85-86, c.111, s.9.

14   *RWDSU v. Govt. of Saskatchewan* (1985), 5 W.W.R. 97, (Saskatchewan C.A.).

15   *RWDSU v. Saskatchewan* (1987) 1 S.C.R. 460.

16   S.Q. 1982, c.21.

17   *Alliance des professeurs de Montréal v. A.-G. Quebec* (1983) 5 D.L.R. (4th) 157 (Quebec S.C.).

18   (1985) 21 D.L.R. (4th) 354 (Quebec C.A.), overruling decision of superior court, previous note.

19   *The Globe and Mail,* Toronto, March 5, 1986, A8.

20   Quebec Charter of Human Rights and Freedoms, enacted in 1975 by S.Q. 1975, c.6; now R.S.Q. 1977, c.C-12.

21   *Ibid.,* s.52.

22 As of June, 1988, the major decisions upholding important provincial policies are: *R. v. Edwards Books and Art* (1986) 2 S.C.R. 713 (Sunday closing in Ont.); *Re Public Service Employees Relations Act* (1987) 1 S.C.R. 313 (restraints on public service collective bargaining in Alta.); *RWDSU v. Saskatchewan* (1987) 1 S.C.R. 460 (back-to-work law for dairyworkers in Saskatchewan); *Re Bill 30* (1987) 1 S.C.R. 1148 (public funding of Roman Catholic schools in Ont.).

23 For example, the Supreme Court of Canada has not yet ruled on school prayers, movie censorship, or restrictions on absentee landownership—three provincial policies with considerable popular support.

24 Francis G. Jacobs, "The Limitation Clauses of the European Convention on Human Rights," in Armand de Mestral et al (eds.), *The Limitation of Human Rights in Comparative Constitutional Law* (Cowansville, Que: Yvon Blais, 1986), chap. 2.

25 (1976) 1 European Human Rights Reports 737 (Eur. Ct. of Hum. Rts.).

26 *Ibid.*, paras. 48-50.

27 (1986) 9 European Human Rights Reports 203 (Eur. Ct. of Hum. Rts.).

28 *Ibid.*, para. 55.

29 The Court did hold that the illegitimacy of the child was a violation of respect for family life: para. 74.

30 *A.-G. Quebec, v. Quebec Protestant School Bds.* (1984) 2 S.C.R. 66.

31 (1982) 140 D.L.R. (3d) 33, 71-90 (Quebec S.C.).

32 (1983) 1 D.L.R. (4th) 573 (Quebec C.A.).

33 Note 30, above.

34 Peter W. Hogg, *Constitutional Law of Canada*, 2nd ed. (Toronto: Carswell Co., 1985), 682-684.

35 The argument was used, and rejected on the facts, in *A.-G. Quebec v. La Chaussure Brown's* (1986) 36 D.L.R. (4th) 374 (Quebec C.A.) (leave to appeal to the S.C.C. granted April 6, 1987), discussed in text accompanying note 48, below.

36 (1986) 1 S.C.R. 103.

37 *Ibid.*, 139.

38 (1986) 2 S.C.R. 713.

39 *Ibid.*, 772.

40 *Ibid.*, 781-782.

41 *Ibid.*, 782.

42 *Ibid.*, 782

43 *Ibid.*, 795.

44 *Ibid.*, 796.

45 *Ibid.*, 810. Beetz J. (with McIntyre J.) did not discuss s.1 at all, because in his view the Sunday closing law did not breach freedom of religion.

46 The text of the Accord and commentary on its terms are to be found in Peter W. Hogg, *Meech Lake Constitutional Accord Annotated* (Toronto: Carswell, 1988). See also Special Joint Committee of the Senate and House of Commons, *Report: The 1987 Constitutional Accord* (Canada, 1987); Bryan

Schwartz, *Fathoming Meech Lake* (Winnipeg, Man.: Legal Research Institute of U. of Manitoba, 1987); Forest R.-A. (ed.), *L'adhésion du Québec à l'Accord du Lac Meech* (Montréal: Les Éditions Thémis, 1988); Carol J. Rogerson and Katherine E. Swinton, *Competing Constitutional Visions: The Meech Lake Accord* (Toronto: Carswell, 1988).

47 A language example may not be the best in that the new s.2 also recognizes the existence of English-speaking Canadians in Quebec; it is plain, therefore, that Quebec's "distinct society" is not an exclusively French-speaking society.

48 This is possible now, of course, as is illustrated by *A.-G. Quebec v. Chaussure Brown's* (1986) 36 D.L.R. (4th) 374 (Quebec C.A.) (leave to appeal to the S.C.C. granted April 6, 1987) holding that a law requiring commercial signs to be in French was in breach of s.2(b). On s.1, Bisson J.A. for the majority held (at 398) that the objective of the law—to make French the language of commerce and business—was "sufficiently important to justify legislative action," but that the law failed the proportionality test.

49 E.g., Ramsay Cook, "Alice in Meechland or The Concept of Quebec as a Distinct Society," *Queen's Quarterly* (1987), 817.

50 See José Woehrling, "La modification constitutionnelle de 1987, la reconnaissance du Québec comme société distincte et la dualité linguistique du Canada," *Les Cahiers de Droit*, 29 (1988), 3.

51 For description of the current law, see Hogg, *Constitutional Law*, chaps. 7, 8.

52 *Ibid.*, 186-187.

53 Russell, "Political Purposes of the Charter," 43.

54 Meech Lake Constitutional Accord, schedule, clause 7, adding new ss.101A to 101E to the Constitution Act, 1867. The appointing provisions are in s.101C.

55 This requirement is now in the Supreme Court Act, R.S.C. 1970, c. S-19, s.6. The Meech Lake Constitutional Accord proposes that it be moved into the Constitution Act, 1867 as s.101B(2).

56 I am grateful to my colleagues, James C. MacPherson and Joel Bakan, who read an earlier draft of this paper, and made suggestions for its improvement.

THE MYTHS OF LEGISLATIVE AND CONSTITUTIONAL SUPREMACY[1]

Ian Greene, York University

When political scientists set out to study a country's political system, they often build their analysis on a principle which seems best to describe the fundamentals of the country's constitution. In Canada, legislative supremacy[2] generally served as that principle or paradigm until 1982. This was primarily because the leading British constitutional expert of the nineteenth century, A.V. Dicey, had described legislative supremacy as "the dominant characteristic of [British] political institutions,"[3] and the Canadian constitution was intended to embody the fundamental principles of the United Kingdom constitution. Dicey contrasted legislative supremacy with constitutional supremacy, which he claimed was the key principle of the U.S. constitution. Because Canada, in 1982, adopted the American invention of a constitutionally-entrenched bill of rights, many have assumed that the appropriate principle for describing our post-1982 constitution is constitutional supremacy.

This essay argues that neither legislative supremacy nor constitutional supremacy, as these terms were defined by Dicey, serves as a useful paradigm to guide Canadian constitutional studies. Although both are worthwhile as legal concepts which assist judges in determining which laws bind the courts, as will be explained below, they do not accurately describe (and never have) how our political system functions. It is suggested that Donald Smiley's concept of executive federalism is a more useful paradigm on which to base an analysis of the Canadian constitution.

Twenty years ago, Smiley pointed out the limited relevance of legislative supremacy for Canadian constitutional analysis. In his 1969 Presidential Address to the Canadian Political Science Association, he compared two approaches to the protection of civil liberties: litigation pursuant to a constitutionally-entrenched charter of rights, and an issue-by-issue consideration of civil liberties by the elected politicians. According to Smiley's analysis, the latter approach is likely to protect civil liberties more effectively in the long run. This is because of practical considerations such as accessibility, research capacity, cost, and the wider range of factors which legislatures and cabinets legitimately consider—but *not* theoretical reasons like the preservation of legislative supremacy. In his address, Smiley asked the rhetorical question, "Who cares about the *theory* of legislative supremacy?"[4]

Nevertheless, practical considerations aside, the theory of legislative supremacy still figures prominently in Canadian constitutional discussion, along with the alternative concept of constitutional supremacy. There are many legal scholars who have concluded that, with the constitutional changes in 1982, Canada rejected legislative supremacy and adopted constitutional supremacy. For example, according to Gerald Gall, since 1982 "the notion of parliamentary sovereignty or supremacy [has become] subservient to the constitution."[5] Morris Manning has written that "the Constitution Act 1982...has effectively made the courts the ultimate lawmaker. While it was arguable whether the courts were the appropriate body to decide controversial questions of social policy, the entrenchment of the rights and freedoms in the Charter has put the argument to rest."[6] Dale Gibson has asserted that because of the Charter, "the courts need not concern themselves with the question of legislative supremacy,"[7] and Herbert Marx has concluded that "the Court should now be free from the restraint imposed" on civil liberties interpretation by legislative supremacy.[8]

Others have taken the position that the incorporation of s.33 into the Charter has preserved the impact of legislative supremacy.[9] Section 33 allows Parliament or provincial legislatures to exempt any laws from being subjected to the sections of the Charter dealing with fundamental freedoms, legal rights or equality rights.[10]

Anne Bayefsky, for example, has argued that initially the Trudeau government hoped "to oust the doctrine of parliamentary sovereignty." However, by acceding to the demands of eight provincial premiers to include s.33 in the Charter, the federal government was unable to abolish legislative supremacy. She regrets this development because of its potential to encourage a narrow judicial interpretation of the Charter.[11] Other analysts, while agreeing with Bayefsky that legislative supremacy is still with us, are pleased with this situation. For example, Andrew Petter and Allan Hutchinson have argued that the preservation of legislative supremacy through s.33 is likely to advance the cause of social justice in Canada, because legislatures are generally more progressive than judges on social justice issues. "Social justice cannot be the gift of judges; it can only come from the sweat of our own democratic brows."[12]

The concepts of legislative supremacy and constitutional supremacy have become prominent in Canadian constitutional analysis largely as a result of the legacy of Dicey. Although Jennings, Marshall and others have drawn attention to problems with Dicey's explanation of legislative supremacy, it is the Diceyan notion which seems to have dominated the thinking of Canadian judges and lawyers right up to the present day.[13] The section below will consider how Dicey developed these ideas to contrast the British and U.S. constitutions. Next, the essay will show how the use of legislative supremacy and constitutional supremacy as descriptive and even prescriptive concepts has confused judicial interpretation of our constitution. Some of the potential problems associated with accepting constitutional supremacy as a paradigm will then be considered. Finally, an approach to constitutional analysis which is based neither on legislative supremacy nor constitutional supremacy will be suggested.

The Diceyan Approach

Dicey described legislative supremacy as having three basic attributes. First, the legislature (consisting of the combined assembly and executive) determines the powers of the three branches of government: assembly, executive, and judiciary. Second, the United Kingdom Parliament, consisting of the House of Commons, House of Lords, and the monarch, determines the powers of the other legislatures in the British empire. Third, the legislature is the supreme law-making body at any point in time; a current legislature cannot be limited by the laws of a previous one. In other words, no legislature can enact an unamendable law.

In part, Dicey described legislative supremacy as a device to be used by judges for determining how to apply the law; in other words, a rule of construction. Legislative supremacy implies that any valid enactment of a legislature must be recognized by the courts, regardless of the wisdom of the legislation. Moreover, in the event of a conflict between two valid statutes, legislative supremacy suggests that the more recent statute should be given priority, because a current legislature is superior to a prior one. Dicey recognized that the courts, as well as Parliament, were involved in creating law. This could occur either through the development of the common law, or through the interpretation of statutes which are not clear. Insofar as the courts made law, Dicey regarded them as subordinate legislative bodies, like municipal councils.[14] The "subordinate legislation" produced by the courts was legitimately subject to change by Parliament at any time, pursuant to legislative supremacy.

Unfortunately, Dicey extended his claims about legislative supremacy beyond its use as a rule of construction. In his major work, *The Law of the Constitution*, his emphasis gradually shifted from considering legislative supremacy as the basic rule of construction for common law judges, to regarding it as the basic political principle of the United Kingdom constitution. A major purpose of his analysis seems to have been to prove the superiority of the British constitution, which he claimed was based on legislative supremacy, over other constitutions, such as the French or American.

Dicey treated the American constitution as prototypical of federal constitutions. He noted that from a strictly legal perspective, in the United States sovereignty resides in the "aggregate legislature," which he defined as the combined legislative body required to amend the constitution; that is, the majority of legislators in each of the houses in three-fourths of the states, plus two-thirds of the members of Congress.[15] Significantly, however, Dicey dismissed the notion that the aggregate legislature is supreme in the U.S. in the political sense. If the aggregate legislature were truly supreme, he claimed, it would be able to act relatively quickly, and more frequently than a few times in a century, to assert its supremacy. Noting that the American aggregate legislature "has been roused to serious action but once during the course of more than a century,"[16] and that even then it took a civil war to precipitate a constitutional amendment, Dicey suggested that the aggregate legislature is usually supreme only in theory. In reality, the American constitution, as interpreted by the judiciary, is normally supreme. Therefore, in contrast with the United Kingdom, the basic constitutional principle in the U.S. is constitutional supremacy. The American constitution being exemplary of federal constitutions in general, Dicey concluded that as a rule, federal countries had constitutional supremacy.[17]

Parts of Dicey's analysis are useful, but other parts are misleading. What is worthwhile is his investigation of legislative supremacy as a rule of construction. His explication of the first and third aspects of legislative supremacy (the legislature determines the legal powers of the three branches of government, and a current legislature cannot limit a future one) remains a practical guide to judges and lawyers in countries with the tradition of parliamentary government, because it provides a standard for the judicial recognition of legally enforceable rules. (Of course, in countries no longer subject to the authority of the British parliament, Dicey's second rule of legislative supremacy—the omnipotence of the Westminster Parliament—is obsolete.)

There are three major deficiencies in Dicey's study. They are important to note because they are often overlooked by those who rely on the concepts of legislative or constitutional supremacy, as defined by Dicey, to guide their analysis of the Canadian constitution. One shortcoming is that Dicey's investigation fails to give adequate consideration to the implications of manner and form requirements.[18] This defect had a major impact on Canadian constitutional development because it explains why the Supreme Court of Canada declined to give a liberal interpretation to the Canadian Bill of Rights before 1982.

A manner and form requirement is a set of procedures followed by a legislature to create or amend laws. Unless these procedures are correctly followed, new or amended legislation will not be recognized by the courts. For example, the "reading" of a bill three times in a legislature so that it passes by a simple majority vote each time, followed by endorsement by the monarch (or representative) is a set of manner and form requirements established by tradition. A stipulation that a particularly important enactment, such as an elections act, could be amended in the future only with a two-thirds majority vote of the legislature at third reading, is another example. A further example is a statute which is intended to take legal precedence over future statutes, unless such future statutes contain within them a stipulation that they shall operate notwithstanding the former statute. An illustration of this type of manner and form requirement is arguably the Canadian Bill of Rights.[19]

Dicey's analysis leaves no room for the changing of manner and form requirements, for example through the enactment of a statutory bill of rights, because such changes would, to some extent, bind future legislatures. Most contemporary constitutional scholars, however, consider the amendment of manner and form requirements to be compatible with legislative supremacy as a rule of construction. Hogg suggests that changes to manner and form requirements should be recognized by the courts if they are not so strict that future legislatures would find it almost impossible to change them again.[20]

A second weakness in Dicey's analysis is his failure to deal straightforwardly with the fact that legislatures in the parliamentary system are usually dominated by the executive branch. This problem does not arise, of course, if legislative supremacy is treated simply as a rule of construction. However, if it is thought of as a political norm as well, then it is clear that this principle cannot be accepted as an accurate description of how our governmental system actually operates. Douglas Verney has pointed out that according to the theory of Parliamentary democracy "neither of the constituent elements of Parliament [the assembly and the executive] may completely dominate the other...Parliamentarism implies co-operation between the executive and legislative branches, neither dominating the other..."[21] Dicey seems to have assumed that this balance usually existed in reality.

W.J. Rees has explained how Parliament, the "legal" sovereign in the U.K., could be accepted as such without also being the "influential" sovereign.[22] According to Rees, the legal sovereign is the body recognized by the courts as having the authority to amend the constitution and ultimately to supervise the development of legal rules. The influential sovereign is the body that controls the behaviour of the legal sovereign. In Canada, the legislatures required to bring about a constitutional amendment can be considered the legal sovereign, but they are normally controlled by their respective executives. The "aggregate executive"[23] could therefore be considered as the usual influential sovereign, although the electorate is obviously the influential sovereign at election time.

The third critical weakness of Dicey's analysis concerns his handling of the concept of constitutional supremacy. He could have treated constitutional supremacy as merely another rule of construction applicable to countries with written constitutions. As a rule of construction, it would simply direct the courts to give the constitutional document priority over ordinary statutes. In countries with a Parliamentary tradition, if constitutional supremacy failed to resolve a question about the application of a statute, legislative supremacy could be turned to next. As such, constitutional supremacy could co-exist with legislative supremacy. Instead, Dicey gave the concept a broader application. He tended to write about it as the principle that best described the fundementals, not only of the U.S. Constitution, but of federal systems in general. According to Dicey, constitutional supremacy means that the three branches of government are considered inferior to the constitution, and that federal constitutions are practically unamendable.

There are three reasons why this Diceyan notion of constitutional supremacy is not pertinent to Canada. First, the American ideal of the separation of powers was one factor which led Dicey to the conclusion that constitutional supremacy accurately decribes the fundamentals of the U.S. political system. The notion of the separation of powers, as enunciated in the Federalist papers,[24] was inspired to some extent by Montesquieu's analysis of the British constitution of the early eighteenth century.[25] Montesquieu had argued that the preservation of liberty in the British constitution depended on what he perceived to be three independent and coordinate branches of government—the legislature, executive, and judiciary—which acted as checks on each other to prevent the abuse of power. The branches of government were never as separate as Montesquieu claimed they were, and after the period covered by Montesquieu's analysis, the principles of responsible government evolved which intertwined with the British executive and the legislature.

The American doctrine of the separation of powers has never been considered as a constitutional principle in Canada. This doctrine does much to promote the idea that the constitution is supreme. Because no branch of government can be supreme, the constitution, from which they all derive their powers, must be supreme.

The second reason concerns the fact that some consider the U.S. constitution to be a populist document which can claim to express the "will of the people." This populist status of the constitutional document lends credibility to Dicey's assertion that the constitution is superior even to the aggregate legislature—that the constitution has an authority, perhaps almost a sacredness that even the supreme amending body should be hesitant to tamper with.

In contrast, the Canadian constitution cannot claim to be a populist document. The major part of the constitution, the Constitution Act 1867 and its amendments, resulted from compromises worked out by political elites. The confederation bargain had enough general support so that most of the leading politicians of the day could risk staking their political futures on it, but it was imposed on the British North Americans in spite of obvious widespread opposition to it in Quebec and Nova Scotia. Although there were public hearings on the proposals which eventually became the Constitution Act 1982, they occurred over too short a time-span to support the claim that this newest part of the constitution is a general expression of the public will.[26] The majority of federal and provincial politicians were unwilling to submit the Constitution Act 1982 to a referendum because of the fear that it would be rejected at least in the West and in Quebec. The process leading up to the Meech Lake Accord included no public consultation. Several provincial governments refused to hold public hearings even after the Meech Lake Accord was announced, claiming that the process of constitutional change in Canada is the sole prerogative of elected politicians.

Unlike the American constitution, the current Canadian constitution could not seriously begin with the words, "We the people..." The Canadian constitution cannot be considered supreme in this way.

Third, it is probable that the 1982 amending formula for the Canadian constitution, together with the parliamentary system of government, have given Canada a more flexible amending procedure than that possessed by the Americans, or perhaps any other federal country. Dicey's characterization of the American aggregate legislature as "not...an ever-wakeful legislator, but a monarch who slumbers and sleeps [and who is therefore] a monarch who does not exist"[27] does not fit Canada's current situation.

In the U.S., thirty-eight out of fifty state legislatures must ratify constitutional amendments which are proposed by a two-thirds vote of each house of Congress, according to the usual amending procedure. This amending process is actually more complex than it first appears. Because all but one of the states have two legislative bodies, the least number of legislatures required to approve a constitutional amendment, including the two houses of Congress, is 77 out of 101.[28] In Canada, only eight out of eleven legislatures, including Ontario or Quebec, and Parliament, must approve amendments to the Charter of Rights or division of powers.[29] It is obviously less onerous to obtain the agreement of eight legislative bodies than of 77.[30] Moreover, Canada's parliamentary system of government is more conducive to relatively speedy agreements to amend the constitution than the American presidential system. Eight of the eleven Canadian premiers can agree on a constitutional amendment at a federal-provincial conference, and thanks to responsible government, the legislatures which they dominate are more likely than not to ratify the agreement. The 1983 constitutional amendment regarding native rights,[31] which was proclaimed a few months after a federal-provincial conference, attests to the control which the aggregate Canadian executive might have, in the long run, over changes to the Canadian constitution. The U.S. constitution has never been amended as speedily as this, and it is doubtful if it ever could be.

The Meech Lake Accord, for which the eleven first ministers announced their unanimous support on April 30, 1987, provides yet another example of the control which the aggregate executive can choose to exercise over the constitution. If the Meech Lake Accord had dealt only with amendments to the division of powers or even the Charter of Rights—two of the central components of the Canadian constitution—there would be no question about its eventual ratification. The support of only seven out of ten provincial legislatures would be required, so that subsequent changes of government in two or three provinces would not have the effect of potentially scuttling such an agreement.

The Accord, however, seeks to make changes to one of the few constitutional provisions which requires unanimous consent for change—the amending formula. There is now some doubt about whether the Accord will receive unanimous consent because of changes of government in New Brunswick, Manitoba, and Newfoundland, and because of reaction in these provinces to the Quebec government's language policy. However, even if the Accord fails to be implemented, it could nevertheless be considered as supporting the proposition that the aggregate executive has the potential to impact constitutional development in an important, ongoing way. It will be seldom that unanimous consent is required to amend the constitution, as in the Meech Lake example. Certainly, the aggregate executive in Canada has much greater influence over constitutional development than its counterparts in the U.S. or Australia. On the other hand, the difficulties encountered by the Accord show that the aggregate executive by no means has a free hand to change the constitution. The democratic process—as demonstrated by recent provincial elections—moderates executive dominance.

In this section, it has been argued that although Dicey's analysis of legislative supremacy is somewhat useful from a legal perspective, it fails to come to terms with the manner and form issue. Moreover, legislative supremacy has limited relevance for political analysis of the constitution, because it ignores the practice of executive dominance. Similarly, constitutional supremacy is worthwhile as a rule of construction, meaning that constitutional documents take precedence over ordinary statutes. However, Dicey's use of constitutional supremacy to describe power relations in the U.S. cannot be applied to Canada in the same way. Therefore, those who employ Dicey's usage of these concepts in the Canadian context are bound to encounter difficulties. Some of the predicaments which the Diceyan approach has helped to generate in some leading judicial decisions will be outlined in the next section.

The Fallout from the Diceyan Approach

If legislative supremacy (as modified by the manner and form school) and constitutional supremacy are treated by judges simply as rules of construction for the interpretation of statutes, then the two concepts are not only useful, but they can coexist with each other. Constitutional supremacy implies that in the event of a conflict between the written constitution and an ordinary statute, the constitution takes precedence. Legislative supremacy means (1) that judges must always apply valid statutes, whether or not they think them wise; and (2) in the event of a conflict between two valid statutes, the most recent one takes priority. In this sense, both concepts have always applied to Canada, and still do. However, difficulties arise if the manner and form issue is ignored, or if the two concepts are applied as descriptions of how the Canadian political system actually operates, or ought to operate. The Supreme Court has encountered both of these problems, and unfortunately has not handled them well. First, the Court's failure to consider the manner and form issue resulted in a confused and misguided interpretation of the Canadian Bill of Rights. Second, since 1982, the Supreme Court has sought unsuccessfully to find a balance between the political norms of legislative and constitutional supremacy—a daunting task if I am right in claiming that neither accurately describes how our political system actually operates or ought to operate.

It was the Diceyan concept of legislative supremacy that gave the Supreme Court of Canada so many difficulties in applying the Canadian Bill of Rights. In a 1985 Charter case, Mr. Justice

LeDain explained why the Supreme Court had refrained from giving the Bill of Rights the broad and liberal interpretation that the Court was starting to give to the Charter:

> ...a court cannot, in my respectful opinion, avoid bearing in mind an evident fact of Canadian judicial history, which must be squarely and frankly faced: that on the whole, with some notable exceptions, the courts have felt some uncertainty or ambivalence in the application of the Canadian Bill of Rights because it did not reflect a clear constitutional mandate to make judicial decisions having the effect of limiting or qualifying the traditional sovereignty of Parliament.[32]

LeDain continued that the Charter had given the courts "a new constitutional mandate for judicial review." In other words, the Constitution Act 1982 had effectively removed legislative supremacy as a barrier to judicial review on civil liberties grounds. He did not mention that there was no necessity for the theory of legislative supremacy to have been a barrier to the application of the Bill if the judges had been willing to look beyond Dicey and to embrace the manner and form school.

The Supreme Court's first major Canadian Bill of Rights decision, *Robertson and Rossetani v. The Queen*,[33] was one of those decisions in which the court demonstrated the "uncertainty or ambivalence" referred to by LeDain. The issue was whether the federal Lord's Day Act violated the guarantee of freedom of religion in the Bill by prohibiting activities such as bowling on "the Lord's day," and if so, whether the Court had the authority to strike down the Act. There is clear evidence that the Parliament enacting the Bill of Rights had intended it to be interpreted broadly so that statutes conflicting with it could be struck down by the courts.[34] However, the majority of the Court, in order to avoid an infraction of legislative supremacy, interpreted the Bill narrowly and upheld the Act. Mr. Justice Cartwright dissented, however, claiming that the Lord's Day Act plainly violated the Bill, and that the Bill instructed the courts to refuse to apply such legislation. He ignored the legislative supremacy issue.[35]

The only case prior to 1982 in which the Supreme Court applied the Bill so that a discriminatory statute became inoperative—the most famous of the "notable exceptions" referred to by LeDain above—was the *Drybones* decision.[36] During the seven years between *Robertson and Rossetani* and *Drybones*, the Supreme Court had been subjected to a great deal of criticism from civil libertarians who saw the court as slaves of the theory of legislative supremacy. Whether because of sensitivity to this criticism or for some other reason, the majority in the *Drybones* decision applied the Bill so as to render inoperative a section of the Indian Act which created a liquor offense which applied only to Indians. Chief Justice Cartwright, surprisingly, dissented. He admitted that he had changed his mind about his opinion in *Robertson and Rossetani*, and that he now feared the consequences of the courts accepting the role of striking down statutes. Justice Pigeon sided with Cartwright in the *Drybones* decision, and clearly invoked legislative supremacy to support his opinion:

> In the traditional British system that is our own by virtue of the B.N.A. Act, the responsibility for updating the statutes in this changing world rests exclusively upon Parliament.[37]

Within a few years, the majority on the Court came around to an approach approximating that of Cartwright and Pigeon in *Drybones*. In the *Lavell* and *Bedard* decisions of 1974,[38] the court again adopted the *Robertson and Rossetani* style of interpreting the Bill narrowly, so as to avoid declaring statutes inoperative. The issue was whether the section of the Indian Act which defines a status Indian, and which at that time treated Indian men much more favourably than Indian women, violated the Bill. The majority upheld the Indian Act, for reasons which do not seem very convincing.[39] The Court concluded that no discrimination exists if all Indian women are treated equally by the courts. Justice Pigeon claimed that the majority had adopted his own reasoning about the need to respect legislative supremacy.

So faithful was the Supreme Court to the Diceyan view of legislative supremacy that the "manner and form" approach to the interpretation of bills of rights was never mentioned. Had the Court adopted the manner and form approach, it could have given effect to the Bill without abandoning allegiance to legislative supremacy as a rule of construction. If the Bill is considered as an amendment to the manner and form in which federal bills become law, then all statutes enacted after the Bill should be considered as including an implicit instruction for the courts to review the statute for compatibility with the Bill. (Statutes enacted before 1960 should yield to the Bill of Rights because it is a more recent statute.) Should Parliament wish a particular piece of legislation to override the Bill, it could say so by utilizing the appropriate manner and form (that is, by including a "notwithstanding" clause in the legislation), and the courts would respect that decision pursuant to legislative supremacy.

Had the Supreme Court adopted the manner and form interpretation of the Bill, Canadian history might well have taken a very different course in the early 1980s. The major impetus for a constitutional Charter of Rights came from those who were disappointed with the Supreme Court's restrictive interpretation of the Bill of Rights. They saw the replacement of legislative supremacy with constitutional supremacy under an entrenched Charter of Rights as the only solution. If the Supreme Court had given effect to the Bill, the pressure for a constitutional Charter of Rights would have been considerably less, and the 1982 constitutional reforms might have taken a very different form.

The prevailing mythology, however, is that Canada operated according to the political principle of legislative supremacy before 1982, and that this necessarily precluded the enforcement of human rights legislation. The myth continues that now we have the political principle of constitutional supremacy, the courts can give effect not only to the Charter, a superior law, but they can also enforce the provisions of the various bills of rights and human rights codes which are ordinary statutes.40 In fact, the statutory bills of rights have now been raised by the Supreme Court to "quasi-constitutional" status. This new approach is demonstrated by the Supreme Court's decision in the *Singh* case.

While considering Charter arguments after the *Singh* hearing,[41] the Supreme Court requested additional submissions based on the Canadian Bill of Rights. At issue in this case was whether a foreign citizen claiming refugee status had a right to an oral hearing before deportation. Such a hearing might be found to be mandatory either pursuant to s.7 of the Charter, or s.2(e) of the Bill.[42] The Bill in fact provides a broader guarantee of a fair hearing in some situations than the Charter.[43] All six Supreme Court judges who heard this case agreed that Singh had a right to an oral hearing before he could be deported. Three based their reasoning on the Charter, while three relied on the Bill, although all six agreed that the Bill is still "in full force and effect [as] preserved by s.26 of the Charter."[44] Beetz, who relied on the Bill, stressed the importance which the Court had now decided to place on this previously devalued document:

> Thus, the Canadian Bill of Rights retains all its force and effect, together with the various provincial charters of rights. Because these *constitutional or quasi-constitutional* instruments are drafted differently, they are susceptible of producing cumulative effects for the better protection of rights and freedoms. But this beneficial result will be lost if these instruments fall into neglect.[45] [emphasis added]

In this case, for the first time since *Drybones*, the Bill contributed to the striking down of federal legislation by the Supreme Court.

The Court's change of policy in favour of giving full effect to the statutory bills of rights has had a major impact in the Court's December 1988 decision to strike down the sections of Quebec's Charter of the French Language (Bill 101) which prohibited the use of English on commercial signs. The most restrictive provisions of Bill 101 were not subject to the Canadian Charter of Rights because the Quebec legislature under the Parti Québécois had included a section 33 override clause in an amendment to the bill proclaimed in 1984. However, the Supreme Court found that these provisions ran afoul of the guarantees of freedom of expression in the Quebec Charter of Human Rights.[46]

The Supreme Court's major change of policy with regard to the enforcement of statutory bills of rights deserves an explanation. However, none has yet emerged from any of the Court's decisions. The Court has never mentioned the manner and form approach, let alone adopted it. One possible explanation is that the Court, like some of the legal scholars mentioned at the beginning of this essay, has concluded that Canada has exchanged the political norm of legislative supremacy for that of constitutional supremacy. This would seem to fit with the Court's declaration that the statutory bills of rights are "quasi-constitutional," and thus superior to other ordinary statutes. There are indications in four recent decisions that the Court may indeed be moving in this direction, although it has not yet developed a consistent position on the constitutional supremacy vs. legislative supremacy issue.

In the *B.C. Motor Vehicle Act* decision,[47] the Court discounted the notion of legislative supremacy. Lawyers representing the Attorney General for Ontario had argued that the courts should continue to defer to legislative supremacy. However, Mr. Justice Lamer disagreed in his majority decision:

> This is an argument which was heard countless times prior to the entrenchment of the Charter, but which has in truth, for better or for worse, been settled by the very coming into force of the Constitution Act 1982.[48]

As a result, Lamer assigned "minimal weight" to legislative history in Charter adjudication. He interpreted the phrase "fundamental justice" in s.7 quite differently from how the federal Minister of Justice in 1981, Jean Chretien, and his officials had suggested that it should be interpreted in testimony before the joint parliamentary committee on the constitution.

The results of the *B.C. Motor Vehicle* case, however, did not deter lawyers for the crown from continuing to use the theory of legislative supremacy to promote their interests. They have been partially successful in their endeavours. In the *Alberta Labour Reference*, the majority of the Court declared that the Charter does not protect the right to strike. Writing for the majority, Mr. Justice McIntyre explained that determining the limits of the right to strike "is a legislative function into which the courts should not intrude."[49] The legislative supremacy argument, however, did not fare as well in the *Morgentaler* case. During the hearing, "counsel for the Crown emphasized repeatedly that it is not the role of the judiciary in Canada to...second-guess difficult policy choices that confront all governments."[50] Commenting on this argument, Chief Justice Dickson explained, like Lamer had in the *B.C. Motor Vehicle* case, that the Charter has changed the role of the Canadian judiciary.

In the *Oakes* decision, the Chief Justice hinted that the Court considers that Canada has moved from a regime of legislative supremacy to one of constitutional supremacy. Dickson stated, "In Canada, we have tempered parliamentary supremacy by entrenching important rights and freedoms in the Constitution."[51] In the same vein, the Chief Justice made the following remarks in an address to the Canadian Bar Association in 1985:

> In Canada, unlike the United Kingdom, legislative supremacy is not absolute but is, rather, subordinate to constitutional supremacy. Our Constitution is written and justiciable and it is the duty of the judiciary, as guar-

dians of the Rule of Law, to ensure that it remains supreme. As the Supreme Court stated in the recent *Manitoba Reference*: "The Constitution of a country is a statement of the will of the people..."[52]

It is probable that the Chief Justice used the term "constitutional supremacy" here as a political principle, and not simply as a rule of construction. To conclude that constitutional supremacy describes the Canadian constitution in the political sense could have a number of unfortunate consequences, both for judicial interpretation and for how Canadians view their constitution.

The Myth of Constitutional Supremacy

Earlier in this essay, it was stressed that the Diceyan notion of constitutional supremacy does not fit the Canadian situation. There are other pitfalls associated with the concept which extend beyond the problems inherent in the Diceyan analysis. The above quote by the Chief Justice illustrates one of these problems: constitutional supremacy encourages the notion that the constitution actually represents the "will of the people." This is simply not the case in Canada. Thinking of the constitution as the "people's will" may draw attention away from the fact that Canada represents one of the few federal liberal democracies in which there is no provision for direct involvement of the people in constitutional change.

The general acceptance of the myth of constitutional supremacy, as a political norm, might also discourage a sense of public responsibility for refining and implementing the very broad principles of the Charter. Constitutional supremacy seems to connote that our rights are absolutely enshrined and protected in the constitution, and therefore there is no need for the public to do anything to protect civil liberties (except perhaps to lobby for the abolition of the section 33 override clause). Without a sense of public responsibility for the promotion of human rights, however, the task of interpreting and implementing civil liberties principles could be almost entirely taken over by the legal profession. As Russell has observed, "a constitutional charter of rights guarantees not rights but a particular way of making decisions about rights in which the judicial branch of government has a much more systematic and authoritative role."[53] Not only do judges play a greater role than before in making decisions about civil liberties issues, so do litigation lawyers, on whom the judges rely for discussion and analysis of the issues.

It is beyond dispute that the legal profession has an important contribution to make to the protection of civil liberties in Canada. Lawyers and judges, because of their training and experience, are in a good position to remind "the public and its elected representatives that some immediately attractive goal is in conflict with more pervasive and durable norms previously accepted by this society."[54] The difficulty for a liberal democracy imbued in the mythology of constitutional supremacy is the possibility that debates on civil liberties issues will occur almost exclusively within the domain of the legal profession. Even in the U.S., an important school of constitutional law holds that reliance on the lawyers and judges for wisdom in civil liberties issues has resulted in too many Americans ceasing to think carefully about human rights.[55]

The disadvantages of the legal profession becoming the major guardian of civil liberties, as opposed to the sharing of this responsibility with elected politicians and the public, have been analyzed extensively by Smiley, Russell, McRuer and others. Perhaps the most obvious disadvantage is that the legal process is expensive. Thus, those with higher incomes will have a privileged position in determining civil liberties outcomes.[56] Moreover, as Smiley has pointed out, the background training of lawyers is technical, not sociological or philosophic, so that they are conditioned to take into account only a narrow range of facts and values.[57]

This understandably narrow perspective of the legal profession has been demonstrated by several Supreme Court of Canada decisions which involved s.1 of the Charter, the limitations clause. A well-constructed argument that a particular right should or should not be regarded as having "reasonable limits" which can be "demonstrably justified in a free and democratic society," pursuant to s.1, should take into account a broad range of social, political and constitutional theory issues. In several cases, Supreme Court judges have related their disappointment with the quality of s.1 arguments presented by counsel.[58] Madame Justice Wilson has publicly drawn attention to the overall poor quality of s.1 arguments presented to the Supreme Court by counsel.[59] The difficulty which lawyers have had in developing strong non-legal, philosophic and policy-related positions pursuant to s.1 certainly vindicates Professor Smiley's analysis.

The protection of civil liberties in society requires more than the listing of some rights in the constitution so that judges can apply them to cases. As former Ontario Chief Justice McRuer showed in his report on civil rights, the protection of civil liberties often requires the creation of proactive programmes. He thought that such programmes were more likely to be successful if drawn up by the executive and legislative branches than by the judiciary.[60] Embracing the myth of constitutional supremacy could create the impression that the courts, more than elected politicians and individual citizens, should take responsibility for creating proactive civil liberties programmes.

A public left out of civil liberties debates because of blind faith in constitutional supremacy could well become insensitive to the importance of civil liberties. There can be no better protection for civil liberties than a public which is tolerant because its members are used to thinking seriously about human rights. It is worth repeating the well-known quotation of Learned Hand, "that in a society which evades its responsibility by thrusting upon courts the nurture of [the spirit of moderation], that spirit will in the end perish."[61]

Toward the Demythologization of Constitutional Analysis

This essay has argued that the principles of legislative supremacy and constitutional supremacy, although useful as rules of construction for judicial interpretation of statutes, have limited value as concepts for describing the Canadian political system.

The myth of constitutional supremacy is that no branch or order of government in Canada is supreme—the constitution, which represents the will of the people, and which is faithfully interpreted as such by the courts, is supreme. This kind of explanation is facile. First of all, the Canadian constitution cannot be considered as the will of the people. In fact, to think of it this way might actually discourage public responsibility for constitutional development. Moreover, our constitution, in contrast with the U.S. constitution, is not practically unamendable. The aggregate executive in Canada can feasibly play a major role in constitutional development.

The concept of legislative supremacy, used to describe our political system, is also misleading because it does not accommodate the reality of executive dominance. Although the aggregate legislature might usefully be thought of as the legal sovereign in Canada, this legal sovereign is rarely the influential sovereign. Legislatures in Canada tend to be dominated by the executive.

The idea of executive federalism, about which Donald Smiley has taught us so much, provides a useful starting-point for constitutional analysis in the post-1982 era.[62] After all, the major actors involved in the constitutional processes of 1982, 1983, and 1987 were the first ministers and their most powerful aides.

The question of who controls the constitution is an exceedingly complex one, and ultimately it would be wrong to describe any entity—a government institution, the people, or the constitution itself—as being "supreme" in any absolute sense. A more reasonable approach might be to describe Canada's political system after 1982 as one in which the legal sovereign—the aggregate legislature—is limited by a constitution (partly written and partly conventional) with four basic attributes: the rule of law, a federal distribution of powers, a charter of rights, and democratic accountability. In practice, legislatures are usually dominated by the executive. The judiciary has important responsibility for constitutional interpretation, but the aggregate executive, within the practical limits imposed by public opinion, has substantial real power to control constitutional amendment and development. Thus, the aggregate executive, having more influence than any other group, can be considered the predominant influential sovereign—but it is "influential," not "supreme." Its influence is modified by the rules of constitutional change, and the democratic process.

It is more than a curiosity that the Canadian constitution has so often been analyzed using the political concepts of legislative supremacy or constitutional supremacy as starting points, ideas better suited to the British or American constitutions respectively than to our own. The mind-sets created by these notions have influenced and are unfortunately continuing to influence how many constitutional analysts, politicians and judges view the Canadian constitution, with unhappy consequences. To regard the Canadian constitution as merely a hybrid of British and American constitutional ideas is far too simplistic. We need the courage to address our own constitutional reality, and executive federalism is a much more useful paradigm to guide our inquiries than either constitutional supremacy or legislative supremacy. It makes sense to develop an accurate portrait of how our constitution actually functions before we consider constitutional reform.

Notes

1   I would like to thank Donald Smiley, Douglas Verney, Peter Russell, Rainer Knopff, and Samuel LaSelva for their very helpful suggestions concerning an earlier draft of this paper.

2   The terms, "legislative supremacy," "parliamentary supremacy," and "parliamentary sovereignty" are often used interchangeably, and this is the application I adopt in this essay. Although some have argued persuasively that the terms are distinguishable, this has not affected the common usage. I prefer the term "legislative supremacy" because in the Canadian context, the word "parliament" tends to connote only one of eleven bodies with constitutionally-derived powers. As well, "sovereignty" has been the subject of so much theoretical debate that its meaning is apt to be less clear than the simpler term, "supremacy." Just as "parliament" refers to the combination of assembly or assemblies and executive, I use "legislature" to refer to the combined assembly or assemblies and executive in parliamentary forms of government.

3   A.V. Dicey, *Introduction to the Study of the Law of the Constitution* (6th ed., London: Macmillan, 1902), 37.

4   Donald V. Smiley, "The Case against the Canadian Charter of Human Rights," Presidential Address to the Canadian Political Science Association, *Canadian Journal of Political Science* 2 (1969), 277, 289.

5   Gerald Gall, *The Canadian Legal System* (2nd ed., Toronto: Carswell, 1983), 72.

6   Morris Manning, *Rights, Freedoms and the Courts* (Toronto: Emond-Montgomery, 1983), 4, 29.

7   Dale Gibson, "Constitutional Documents are Different," in W.S. Tarnopolsky and G.-A. Beaudoin (eds.), *The Canadian Charter of Rights and Freedoms* (Toronto: Carswell, 1982), 25, 29.

8   Herbert Marx, "Entrenchment, Limitations and Non-Obstante," in Tarnopolsky and Beaudoin (eds.), *The Canadian Charter*, 61, 71.

9   Although s. 33 has been widely touted as perpetuating legislative supremacy, it does not allow legislatures to undo judicial interpretation. It simply allows them to postpone judicial review on certain Charter grounds for five years, presumably to deal with unusual and temporary conditions (see Peter Russell, "The Political Purposes of the Canadian Charter of Rights and Freedoms," *Canadian Bar Review*, 61 (1983), 30,45). As well, s. 33 cannot be used to preclude judicial review on division of powers grounds; see Samuel LaSelva, "Only in Canada: Federalism, *Non Obstante*, and the Charter," *Dalhousie Review*, 63:3 (1983), 383.

10 Section 33 has been invoked substantively only twice. The first time was in 1986 when Saskatchewan enacted back-to-work legislation. (A subsequent decision by the Supreme Court that the Charter does not protect the right to strike made this intervention redundant. *RWDSU v. Saskatchewan*, [1987] 1 S.C.R. 460.) In December 1988, Premier Bourassa declared that his government would continue to invoke s.33 to shield Quebec's Charter of the French

Language from the Canadian Charter's guarantees of freedom of expression. Section 33 has also been used symbolically by the Quebec National Assembly during the tenure of the Parti Québécois. As a form of protest against Quebec's exclusion from the 1982 constitutional accord, a section 33 override was routinely inserted in all legislation, and all existing statutes were amended to include the override.

11 Anne Bayefsky, "Parliamentary Sovereignty and Human Rights in Canada: The Promise of the Canadian Charter of Rights and Freedoms," *Political Studies*, 31 (1983), 239, 256.

12 Andrew Petter and Allan Hutchinson, "Hitting home hard with Section 33," *Toronto Star*, May 3, 1986, B-5. Also in this vein, see Patrick Monahan, *Politics and the Constitution: The Charter, Federalism and the Supreme Court of Canada* (Toronto: Carswell, 1987).

13 Sir Ivor Jennings, *The Law and the Constitution* (London: University of London Press, 1959); and Geoffrey Marshall, *Parliamentary Supremacy and the Commonwealth* (Oxford: Clarendon Press, 1957).

14 Dicey, *The Law*, 58.

15 Ibid., 145.

16 Ibid.

17 In spite of this conclusion, the majority of the Canadian legal community continued to believe that Canada had legislative supremacy within the spheres of responsibility reserved for each legislature in Canada. See Douglas Verney, "The 'Reconciliation' of Parliamentary Supremacy and Federalism in Canada," *The Journal of Commonwealth and Comparative Politics*, 21 (1983) 22.

18 Exponents of the manner and form school include Ivor Jennings, *The Law*, 156 ff.; Geoffrey Marshall, *Parliamentary Supremacy*, 47 ff. and *Constitutional Theory* (Oxford: Clarendon Press, 1971), ch. 3; S.A. de Smith, *Constitutional and Administrative Law*, rev. by H. Street & R. Brazier (4th ed.; Markham, Ont.: Harmondsworth, 1981), 82 ff.; and H.R. Gray, "The Sovereignty of Parliament Today," *University of Toronto Law Journal* 10 (1953), 54. Opponents include H.W.R. Wade, "The Basis of Legal Sovereignty," *Cambridge Law Journal* (1955), 172; and O. Hood Phillips and Paul Jackson, *Constitutional and Administrative Law* (6th ed.; London: Sweet & Maxwell, 1978), ch. 4. Hogg contends that the manner and form approach is "the more generally accepted theory." Peter Hogg, *Constitutional Law of Canada* (2nd ed., Toronto: Carswell, 1985), 263.

19 For an analysis of the manner and form interpretation of the Bill, see W.S. Tarnopolsky, *The Canadian Bill of Rights* (2nd ed.; Toronto: McClelland and Stewart, 1975), 92 ff., and Hogg, *Constitutional Law*, 2nd ed., 643 ff.

20 Hogg, *Constitutional Law*, 2nd ed., 643 ff.

21 *The Analysis of Political Systems* (London: Routledge & Kegan Paul, 1959), 32-33.

22 W.J. Rees, "The Theory of Sovereignty Restated," in Peter Laslett (ed.), *Philosophy, Politics and Society* (Oxford: Blackwell, 1956), 56.

23 The aggregate executive can be defined as "the federal and provincial cabinets and the appointed officials who within the framework of law and custom work under their direction." This is Donald Smiley's definition of the

Canadian executive in *The Federal Condition in Canada* (Toronto: McGraw-Hill Ryerson, 1987), 83.

24   *The Federalist*, ed. Henry Cabot Lodge (New York: Putnam, 1891).

25   Montesquieu, *The Spirit of the Laws* (rev. ed.; New York: Colonial Press, 1900).

26   See Edward McWhinney, *Canada and the Constitution, 1979-1982* (Toronto: University of Toronto Press, 1982).

27   Dicey, *The Law*, 145.

28   If the unicameral legislature of Nebraska fails to approve an amendment, then 78 other legislative bodies must approve. Looked at from another perspective, if 13 bicameral legislatures are split, so that one house approves an amendment while the other rejects it, then even agreement among the other 88 legislative bodies out of 101 (including the two houses of Congress) would fail to produce a constitutional amendment. See John Agresto, *The Supreme Court and Constitutional Democracy* (Ithaca and London: Cornell University Press, 1984), 109.

29   The Senate has only a 180-day suspensive veto, which means that excluding the Senate, eight out of eleven assemblies are absolutely required for approval.

30   The uniquely Canadian opting-out provision in the amending formula may decrease the likelihood that provincial governments opposed to particular amendments will lobby vigorously against them in the other provinces. As well, the procedure for initiating constitutional amendments in Canada—a resolution of any provincial legislature or Parliament—is simpler than the American procedure, which involves a two-thirds vote of both houses of Congress.

31   *Constitutional Amendment Proclamation, 1983*.

32   *R. v. Therans et al.*, [1985] 1 S.C.R. 613, 638-39.

33   [1963] S.C.R. 651.

34   See W.H. McConnell, *Commentary on the British North America Act* (Toronto: Macmillan, 1977), 430.

35   In a similar case brought under the Charter, *Her Majesty the Queen v. Big M Drug Mart Ltd.*, [1985] 1 S.C.R. 295, the Supreme Court found that the Lord's Day Act, was a clear violation of freedom of religion.

36   *The Queen v. Drybones*, [1970] S.C.R. 282.

37   Ibid., 306.

38   *Attorney General of Canada v. Lavell*, and *Isaac v. Bedard*, [1974] S.C.R. 1349.

39   Mr. Justice Ritchie, in his majority decision, quoted Dicey's definition of equality, thus demonstrating the esteem in which the Court held Dicey's constitutional analysis.

40   In addition to the Canadian Bill of Rights, there are three other statutory bills of rights—in Saskatchewan, Alberta and Quebec. These bills define the civil liberties claims which individual citizens may make against government. There are also ten provincial Human Rights Codes and a federal human rights code which prohibit certain forms of private discrimination.

41   *Singh et al. v. Minister of Employment and Immigration*, [1985] 1 S.C.R. 177.

42 Section 7 of the Charter states: "Everyone has the right to life, liberty and security of the person and the right not to be deprived thereof except in accordance with the principles of fundamental justice." Fundamental justice implies a fair hearing. Section 2(e) of the Bill declares: "no law of Canada shall be construed or applied so as to...deprive a person of the right to a fair hearing in accordance with the principles of fundamental justice for the determination of his rights and obligations..."

43 See Hogg, *Constitutional Law*, 2nd ed., 645 ff.

44 *Singh*, opinion of Wilson J. (who based her opinion on the Charter), 185.

45 Ibid., opinion of Beetz J., 224. Another example is *Ontario Human Rights Commission and O'Malley v. Simpsons-Sears Ltd. et al.*, 2 [1985] 2 S.C.R. 536, 547. Here, McIntyre referred to the human rights codes as "not quite constitutional but certainly more than the ordinary."

46 *Ford v. Quebec (Attorney General)*, [1988] 2 S.C.R. 712.

47 *Re B.C. Motor Vehicle Act*, [1985] 2 S.C.R. 486.

48 Ibid., 497.

49 *Reference re Public Service Employee Relations Act (Alta.)*, [1987] 1 S.C.R. 313, 420.

50 *R. v. Morgentaler*, [1988] 1 S.C.R. 30, 45.

51 *R. v. Oakes*, [1986] 1 S.C.R. 103, 125.

52 Chief Justice Brian Dickson, "The Rule of Law: Judicial Independence and the Separation of Powers," Address to the Canadian Bar Association, August 21, 1985, 9; reprinted in *Provincial Judges Journal*, 9(3) (1985) 4, 6.

53 Peter H. Russell,"The effect of a Charter of Rights on the policy-making role of Canadian courts," *Canadian Public Administration*, 25 (1982), 1, 32.

54 Barry Strayer, *The Canadian Constitution and the Courts* (2nd ed., Toronto: Butterworths, 1983), 54.

55 See, for example, James B. Thayer, "The Origin and Scope of the American Doctrine of Constitutional Law," reprinted in Leonard W. Levy (ed.), *Judicial Review and the Supreme Court* (New York: Harper & Row, 1967), 43, at 63.

56 Peter Russell, "A Democratic Approach to Civil Liberties," *University of Toronto Law Journal*, 19 (1969), 109, 128 ff.

57 Smiley, "Presidential Address", 283 ff.

58 *The Law Society of Upper Canada v. Skapinker*, [1984] 1 S.C.R. 357; and *Singh*, 177. In the *B.C. Motor Vehicle* case, the Court made a point of noting that no s.1 arguments at all were presented.

59 Wilson J., Address to students at the Faculty of Law, University of Toronto, November 26 & 27, 1985.

60 Hon. J. McRuer, *Royal Commission into Civil Rights* (Toronto: Queen's Printer, 1969), IV, 1592-93. Section 24(1) of the Charter appears to enable the judiciary to order the creation of remedial programmes. An American example of this kind of programme is the court-ordered busing of school children to promote racial integration.

61 *The Spirit of Liberty and Other Writings* (New York: Vintage, 1959), 164.

62 Donald Smiley has described executive federalism as "...a system of government which is executive dominated and within which a large number of important public issues are debated and resolved through the ongoing interactions among governments..." Smiley, *The Federal Condition*, 83.

THE COURTS AS ARBITERS OF SOCIAL VALUES

J. R. Mallory, McGill University

The decision of the Supreme Court of Canada in the *Morgentaler* case appears to have aroused a great deal of political controversy. It has again brought out the question of how far the courts can or should define important community and social values, thus displacing the legislatures in authoritatively defining these matters. Is this simply a consequence of the Charter? Have the courts become the ultimate legislators of social norms? Whether we consider it good or bad, is this a sort of constitutional revolution? Donald Smiley sees the issue in these terms:

> ...the courts have been propelled into a vastly extended role in judicial review of the Constitution against a background in which Canadians have denied the reality of judicial power. According to common misunderstandings, the legislatures enact laws, executives execute laws, and courts interpret laws according to stable and neutral legal principles. According to the mythology, judges do not have power; they perform intricate functions analogous to those of, say, surgeons or airline pilots. Under the emergent circumstances, it is inevitable that this mythology will become increasingly unpersuasive despite the valiant efforts of the judges themselves to sustain it, and as the courts, not just the Supreme Court of Canada, but the courts in general, increasingly challenge the values and interests of important elements of Canadian society, some new reservoir of judicial legitimacy will have to be found.[1]

The judiciary of course is not always a prisoner of this simplified myth of the strict separation of powers. Fifteen years ago Bora Laskin read a paper to Section II of the Royal Society of Canada entitled "The Judge as Legislator and Administrator." He began by admitting that "to speak of a judge as both legislator and administrator is to breach the walls of separation of legislative, executive and judicial powers..." He notes that in seventeenth century England there was an attempt by Edward Coke to place the courts and the law above the crown and parliament, an attempt which was put to rest by the Glorious Revolution of 1688. The extrapolation of Coke's theory "by application to federalism especially in the United States and to a lesser degree in Canada, both operating but in different ways under written constitutions, gave it an authority which it never attained in England."[2]

Laskin was writing a decade before the adoption of the Charter, so that the law-making role of judges in Canada was largely in the area of jurisdictional issues between the two levels of government. It was a topic on which he himself had written extensively before his elevation to the bench, but perhaps not one that he could at that time re-open. "This field," he said, "has been tilled by political scientists as well as by lawyers and I leave it with the observation that judges no less than commentators on judicial decisions on constitutionality are keenly aware of the narrow line between the wisdom of legislation and its validity: the latter alone is for the courts."[3]

Dicey himself noted that federalism greatly enhanced the law-making or policy role of the courts. In the United Kingdom the development of common law principles through precedent "leads inevitably to the gradual formation by the courts of fixed rules for decision, which are in effect laws." But this is not inconsistent with the supremacy of Parliament, since statute law may, and often does, override the law of the judges. "Judicial legislation is, in short, subordinate legislation."[4] In federations where matters are different, the boundary-fixing role of the courts makes judicial decision the principal method of constitutional definition. "That a federal system again can flourish only among communities imbued with a legal spirit and trained to reverence the law is as certain as can be any conclusion of political speculation. Federalism substitutes litigation for legislation, and none but a law-fearing people will be inclined to regard the decision of a suit as equivalent to the enactment of a law."[5]

As one looks at federal constitutions, it seems obvious that substantial change and adjustment flow through the system as a consequence of litigious pressure. What needs to be looked at also is what assumptions about the role of the state, variously asserted by competing pressure and interest groups in litigation, appeal at a particular time to the value system then dominant in the judiciary. Like other persons in authority, judges are prone to be prisoners of the values taught in their youth.

As John Maynard Keynes pointed out over fifty years ago "the ideas of economists and political philosophers, both when they are right and when they are wrong, are more powerful than is generally understood. Indeed the world is ruled by little else." The principles of *laissez-faire* economics reached a zenith of public acceptance according to Dicey around the middle of the nineteenth century. The lawyers who, as judges, were to interpret the Canadian constitution had accepted these doctrines as axiomatic in their formative years, and, as Keynes said, "...in the field of economic and political philosophy there are not many who are influenced by new theories after they are twenty-five or thirty years of age."[6] The experience of the legal profession and the nature of the common law itself are both highly individualistic so that in the circumstances it is not unreasonable to expect that the social values articulated by the courts will reflect the prevailing values of their formative years.

In fact, that seems to have been the case. The general bias of the courts in constitutional litigation led them to interpret regulatory laws in as narrow a fashion as possible; in the case of the Canadian constitution, this could be done by finding that the legislature that had enacted the impugned legislation was exceeding its powers under the constitution.[7] It was common for constitutional writers in the 1920s and 1930s to lament that the effect of judicial interpretation had been to erode the powers of the federal government and enhance the powers of the provinces. What they did not sufficiently take into account was that these were not powers sought by the federal government, which was largely absorbed with railway expansion and western settlement. It was the provinces, in response to electoral pressure, which were seeking to expand their powers and their revenues to meet the problems of a more urban and industrial society. This legislative expansion was resisted in the courts by vested interests asserting a spurious concern for a federal jurisdiction which they were pleased to see was not being exercised. Before 1914, the provinces gained jurisdiction in this process, now called province-building, but they had to fight every inch of the way, and sometimes lost. The foundation of the decentralization of the Canadian federation had been laid, and there was set in motion a trend which now seems almost irreversible.[8]

When there is a sharp conflict in social values within the community, the judges may show an unusual zeal for articulating familiar and essential values which seem to them to be threatened by an almost revolutionary challenge. This was illustrated in the litigation over the social credit and debt adjustment legislation of the province of Alberta in the 1930s. In the first century after Confederation it was generally understood that economic growth and prosperity depended on the easy availability of credit. In a capitalist world there are winners and losers, the latter being those who lack the skill and knowledge to guess correctly what the market will do. The role of the state in all this was principally to protect the sanctity of contract. True, there were other perils besides the normal risks of the market. These were political. Governments reacting to the pressure of beleaguered debtors might be driven to repudiate their own debts and impose restrictions on the rights of creditors. This, in the orthodoxy of the time, was an illegitimate use of state power.

This conflict of values was most evident in Alberta in 1936, but Alberta was only a single Canadian province, so that its repudiation of economic orthodoxy could be contained. And contained it was, both through the use of the federal power of disallowance (widely thought to be constitutionally obsolete and incongruous) and by litigation in the courts on various constitutional grounds.

It should be remembered that all this happened within a couple of decades of the Russian Revolution, which was anathematized not so much because it had created a confused, tyrannical and totalitarian regime—which it had—but because it represented an apparently successful repudiation of liberal capitalism based on private property and the social engine of private profit. The demonstration effect was perceived to be a serious threat to the social order.

The fears it aroused amply demonstrate Keynes's evocation of the power of ideas. That social credit was equated with bolshevism shows something of the degree of panic in high places. What the Alberta government in those days really represented was something more modest. It was a somewhat bizarre culmination of agrarian discontent whose roots went back into the nineteenth century and reflected in large measure the contradictions of the agrarian frontier.

This period could be seen as one in which there was a sharp division in perceived community values. Particularly in the western provinces the political system, through provincial governments and legislatures, was now placing the plight of hard-pressed debtors and other victims of the depression ahead of the previously highly-prized value of the sanctity of contracts. Even in Ottawa the Bennett government, inspired by the New Deal in the

United States, was responding to the same pressures. However, the courts, reinforced in the case of Alberta by the aggressive use of disallowance by the Liberal government which succeeded the Conservatives in 1935, were successful in defending the old value system.

The climate of opinion was nevertheless beginning to change, as shown by the popularity of the Beveridge Report in Britain, the Marsh Report in Canada, and the reconstruction proposals generated on Keynesian lines in the Department of Finance during the war. The trend towards greater government intervention was strengthened by a number of developments. The first of these was the success and popularity (despite public weariness with wartime controls) of the rational and successful management of the economy during the war. The second was a striking decrease in litigious pressure by private interests against state regulation in principle. One can speculate on the reasons for this. During the war many top-level businessmen had been temporary bureaucrats in Ottawa. They may have discovered that ministers (not least C.D. Howe) and bureaucrats were decent fellows after all, and in the uncertain aftermath of the war stability was more important than ideology. For whatever reason, they lost their zest for litigation against all and every manifestation of government intervention in the economy.

There was another cause for the decline in constitutional litigation over the distribution of powers in the constitution. The federal and provincial governments, whose responsibilities overlapped in most of the new areas of social policy, developed a technique of joint negotiation and management—authoritatively delineated by Donald Smiley under the name of executive federalism—so that conflict management in the federal-provincial field shifted from the courts to the negotiating table. The great advantage of this development was not only that it made possible policies like medicare and pensions, but it did so in an atmosphere of stability and predictability. Litigation is a zero-sum game which is terribly costly to lose.

But this transition would have been impossible without the cooperation of the courts. The water-tight compartments of a federal system of the purely classical type which had been rivetted on the constitution by Lord Atkin's judgement in 1937,[9] was abandoned in favour of a view first propounded in *Hodge vs the Queen*[10] that each level of government might legislate on that aspect of a field of jurisdiction appropriate to its constitutional powers. The effect of this was that the Supreme Court, now free at last to be a final court of appeal on the constitution, was much more tolerant of the emergence of concurrent jurisdiction in many of the new policy fields, where in fact both levels of government had a role and a legitimate interest. Furthermore, there were a few cases in which the courts found a "national interest" under the general power in section 91 to justify federal jurisdiction in fields not contemplated by the Fathers of Confederation.[11] However, "the centralist tone of these early decisions of the emancipated Supreme Court did not have a major impact on the distribution of power in the Canadian federation."[12]

The Court was beginning to reflect some change in values, but not much. It was beginning to create a sort of common law protection of freedom of speech and association in a series of cases involving Jehovah's Witnesses in Quebec. It was easier to see these cases as infringements on freedom of conscience and religion, an issue which perhaps divided the court more on Protestant-Catholic lines than anything else. It was also displaying, as might have been expected, a judicial suspicion of administrative discretion and unfair procedure, which had been a live issue in Britain since the 1920s, and was evident in judicial review of debt adjustment legislation in the 1930s. The most notable of the Jehovah's Witnesses cases involving the issue of administrative discretion and procedural fairness was *Roncarelli vs Duplessis*.[13]

However, the Court was not ready to grasp the opportunity to assert a new set of constitutional values provided by the Diefenbaker Bill of Rights in 1960. The Bill of Rights itself was a consequence of a growing and widespread awareness of the dangers inherent in the unrestrained use of state power. The nature of the Nazi regime in Germany, and of fascist regimes elsewhere, demonstrated that regimes with apparently strong popular support could institute reigns of terror which victimized both political dissenters and groups proscribed on racial grounds. Surprisingly few people seemed either aware or concerned about these matters until the concentration camps were overrun by Allied armies at the end of the war. The consequent revulsion led to the United Nations Declaration of Human Rights in 1948, and alerted lawyers to the dangers inherent in the unrestrained power of majority governments.

No doubt the experience of the War Measures Act and the plight of taxpayers subject to the arbitrary whims of the Minister of National Revenue had much to do with the shift in opinion within the ranks of the Canadian Bar Association. In any event, opinion in Canada seemed ready for the Bill of Rights, even if the Supreme Court was not.[14] Admittedly, the Bill was flawed. It was not a constitutional amendment, but an ordinary Act of Parliament which of course did not apply to the provinces. And the courts, still strongly inhibited by their traditional deference to parliamentary supremacy, managed to interpret it as if the rights asserted in the Bill of Rights had existed and continued to exist, so that Parliament had not intended that laws inconsistent with it should be found unconstitutional. Where rights had been trampled on by administrative authorities, it was easier to fall back on such protection as was afforded by the Criminal Code rather than to rely on the vaguer concepts of the Bill of Rights. Accordingly lawyers soon learned that the Bill of Rights would seldom help their clients, and in the end few cases were successfully founded on it.[15]

The post-war period was characterized by a modification in the public perception of constitutional values—a growth of rights-consciousness combined with an enlarged sense of fairness and equality. This was manifested in a number of ways. The most obvious was the expansion of the reach of the welfare state, which through federal-provincial co-operation extended itself into pensions, universal medical and hospital care, and the acceptance by senior governments of at least minimal responsibility for the poor. This came to embrace also the emergence of human rights commissions, fair employment legislation, and the like.

Another aspect of the change was that Canada was beginning to come to terms with a population mix constantly enriched by a high level of immigration, which began to include a growing component from third world countries. In some respects John Diefenbaker was one of the first to perceive this. For most of its history Canada had been a deferential society in which positions of power and authority were confined to the two "charter groups"—the anglo Loyalists reinforced by immigration from the British Isles (first the Scots and later, and included more reluctantly, the Catholic Irish), and the French-Canadian elite. Diefenbaker's own ancestry was pretty sound on this definition—Pennsylvania "dutch" from the loyalist period and Scottish on his mother's side. But, skillful politician that he was, he was able to exploit the inferior self-image of "hyphenated Canadians." And he lived up to his beliefs. He was the first Prime Minister to include a Canadian of Ukrainian descent in his cabinet. It happened also that his vision of One Canada clashed with the surge of Quebec nationalism, but on balance he did much to legitimize the new kind of Canadian nationalism and reduce the subliminal racism of the old Toryism.

On another front the legal profession was in the process of transformation. Legal education from the earliest times had been largely in the control of the profession, at first purely through an apprenticeship system, and later, as the law schools emerged, through a system of instruction mostly confined to part-time practicing lawyers. The expansion of the university law schools after the war led to a large infusion of full-time law teachers to reinforce the handful of full-time legal scholars such as Frank Scott and Bora Laskin. Consequently the law schools themselves became for the first time centres of scholarship, exposing their students to the ferment of ideas which had hitherto found little nourishment in Canadian soil. This took time. The judges, even in the 1960s, had not been educated in this way, nor had the senior practitioners at the bar. It would be another generation before law students of the 1950s reached the bench. The generation gap in the legal profession was acute and it ranged over a wide spectrum of social values.

One of the most striking examples of this conflict of ideas was epitomized in the case of *Lady Chatterly's Lover*, a case argued before the Supreme Court by Frank Scott.[16] In 1959 Parliament, at about the same time as comparable changes were taking place in other countries, had somewhat liberalized the law on obscenity by an amendment to the Criminal Code. The case arose in Quebec, where the courts were notoriously conservative—perhaps mostly on issues that seemed to threaten the values of conservative Catholicism. The police raided three news agents, seized the book, and laid charges of obscenity under the Criminal Code. What was perhaps most offensive to the authorities was that the book had come out in cheap paperback. "Obscene" works for the enjoyment of the well-to-do elite posed little threat. Books available to the uninstructed masses and—worst of all—to young persons, was a different matter. The result was predictable. The prosecution succeeded both in the court of first instance and before the Quebec appeal court. The final test would be in the Supreme Court. There the appeal succeeded, but only just, by a majority of five to four. "Not surprisingly, perhaps" writes Frank Scott's biographer, "the decision was made along denominational lines, with four Anglicans and the one non-denominational supporting it and three Roman Catholics and one Anglican opposing." This split was to lead a Quebec newspaper to inquire rhetorically, "Y'a-t-il deux Cours suprême du Canada?"[17]

The incorporation of the Charter of Rights and Freedoms in the constitution by virtue of the Constitution Act 1982, made possible a more positive and authoritative role for the Supreme Court. The debate about the Charter was essentially between those who believed that popular or parliamentary sovereignty was the ultimate value in the political system and those who saw in judicial review an essential check on the raw power of majorities. As Peter Russell has pointed out, the Charter in the end contained a typical Canadian compromise, whereby parliament or a provincial legislature can, for a limited period, override the provisions of the Charter.[18]

The Charter is an invitation to the courts to legislate, for the general guarantees of the Charter will mean nothing unless the courts give them concrete recognition and definition in actual cases, and provide effective remedies for their enforcement. Today we are not dealing with the same judges who failed so signally to make the Bill of Rights a recognized part of the constitutional order. The judges of today are the generations taught by Frank Scott and Bora Laskin—a generation which found in law school a set of new and challenging ideas.

What has emerged is, according to Alan Cairns, a dispute about what the Canadian constitution is, what its relation is to Canadian society, and whose constitution it is. Before 1982, he says, the Canadian constitution was mainly about federalism, and federalism is mainly an affair of governments. "What seems to have happened is that the Constitution Act of 1982, and in particular the Charter, has produced an alternative vision of the Constitution."[19]

This alternative vision of the constitution will shift the focus of litigation and the way the whole system is perceived away from the traditional and sometimes sterile debates over the division of legislative power. It could be said parenthetically that something of the sort has happened in the United States since the 1930s. Cairns, who is less than happy about the Meech Lake Accord, is fully aware that the provincial governments are still among the most influential actors in the political system. These governments have no taste for the alternative vision of the constitution which alters the focus of political discourse. For that reason, the part of the Accord which gives them a key role in the naming of future

Supreme Court judges gives them an opportunity to alter the balance and focus of the Court. Accordingly the next generation of Supreme Court judges may be less willing to enhance the place of the Charter in the Canadian political system.

Meanwhile the Charter is opening up the political system to new political strategies by interest groups, particularly through the strengthened role of advocacy public interest groups, which are in many cases assisted by public funding. The political climate has already experienced a change in both rhetoric and vocabulary. Before 1945 the vocabulary of rights was still largely in terms of the essentially "negative" individual rights. Today it is more common to talk of the rights of groups—native peoples, the handicapped, linguistic groups, et al.—and the obligation, which is recognized in the Charter, for affirmative action programs to create conditions of equality, often at the expense of equality of treatment of individuals. This issue is sensitively explored by Cynthia Williams and it is bound to affect the intellectual climate in which political values are authoritatively proclaimed.[20]

What has the Supreme Court done with this new opportunity? The first five years give a partial answer, since the rights in section 15 did not come into force for three years, in order that the various legislatures be given sufficient time to sanitize old laws in conformity with the Charter.

In general, the way in which the courts handled these early cases did not so much challenge the capacity of the legislature to enact such laws as constrain the excessively wide discretionary authority of executive agencies to make regulations or of the police in relation to searches and investigative practices. An example of this group is the early case involving the Ontario board of film censors. The courts did not challenge the right of the Ontario legislature to censor films, but found that the act was too vague to justify the action of the board.[21] The courts went further in finding that the venerable Lord's Day Act was a violation of the freedom of religion in section 2(a) of the Charter.[22] The courts were also fairly bold in giving meaning to the linguistic guarantees of the Charter.[23] The most significant decisions of the early period were probably those which dealt with the issue of procedural fairness, of which the most striking is *Singh vs Minister of Employment and Immigration*.[24]

Professor Morton, however, sees in the early Charter cases a more significant loss of power by the provinces than by the federal government. He points out that the federal laws impugned tended to be old laws, like the Lord's Day Act and the Customs Tariff Act, while provincial laws overturned represented "major policy initiatives of current majority governments. These two trends support the 'anti-democrat' criticism that is sometimes levelled at the Charter, and the prediction that the Charter would erode the legislative autonomy of the provinces more than the federal government."[25]

I will return to this point later. In more general terms, are the courts allowing themselves to be pushed into what in effect constitutes legislating in the sticky field of moral values on which there is no consensus? Professor Russell, looking back on the first three years of the Charter, concluded "Canadian judges seem no more anxious than politicians in reforming the abortion law."[26] This, of course, was before the Supreme Court had dealt with *Morgentaler*. There the Court, adhering essentially to procedural grounds, threw out Section 251 of the Criminal Code, and passed the problem back to the politicians. Parliament could pass legislation, but the legislation would have to be revised to conform to the Charter. In Chief Justice Dickson's words, "Section 251 of the Criminal Code infringes the right to security of the person of many pregnant women. The procedures and administrative structures established in the section to provide for therapeutic abortions do not comply with the principles of fundamental justice. Section 7 of the Charter is infringed and that infringement cannot be saved under Section 1."[27] There is a fine line between upholding constitutional norms and boldly legislating in fields where the politicians are too wary to tread. Evidence that the Supreme Court perceives this is demonstrated in a caution uttered by Mr. Justice Le Dain in a case in 1987:

> The rights for which constitutional protection is sought— the modern rights to bargain collectively and to strike, involving correlative duties or obligations resting on an employer—are not fundamental rights or freedoms. They are the creation of legislation, involving a balance of competing interests in a field which has been recognized by the courts as requiring a specialized expertise. It is surprising that in an area in which this Court has affirmed a principle of judicial restraint in the review of administrative action we should be considering the substitution of our judgment for that of the legislature by constitutionalizing in general and abstract terms rights which

the legislature has found it necessary to define and qualify in various ways according to the particular field of labour relations involved. The resulting necessity of applying Section 1 of the Charter to a review of particular legislation in this field demonstrates in my respectful opinion the extent to which the Court becomes involved in a review of legislative policy for which it is really not fitted.[28]

While prudent judicial restraint may leave policy to the legislators and thus under a federal system open the way to a variety of laws representing different kinds of social consensus in different jurisdictions, there is another way in which the courts may play a predominant role in setting national community values (what Alan Cairns calls the nationalization of values) so that "the citizens of a fragmented society may achieve an integrating collective sense of themselves from their common possession of rights and the availability of a common language of political discourse."[29] The way in which the courts assert these common values is essentially a conservative one, for the courts continue to be a generation behind the development of public opinion. As Sir Edward Fry put it:

> It has often seemed to me that the army of those who work for righteousness is divided into two corps: those who strive to maintain and to protect the precious results of the past life of the race—the spoils of the ages; and those who skirmish in front and help to lead on to new victories; and I think that neither body should think lightly of the other, though too often in fact they are apt to despise one another.[30]

The function of the law, he went on to say, was along with the universities and other custodians of the values of society to preserve and protect. The function of the politicians and the legislators was by trial and error to evolve new policies which might involve new values.

The role of the courts is to protect established and deeply felt values. Until nearly a century ago these values seemed to focus on the values of property and contract which appeared to be the basis of a commercial civilization. Since the end of the first world war—and even more after the second—the courts have come to focus on the procedural values of the rule of law as a basic norm of community values. As the Chief Justice put it in *Morgentaler vs the Queen*:

> Although no doubt it is still fair to say that the courts are not the appropriate forum for articulating complex and controversial programmes of public policy, Canadian courts are charged with the crucial obligation of ensuring that the legislative initiatives pursued by our Parliament and legislatures conform to the democratic values expressed in the Canadian Charter of Rights and Freedoms.[31]

There is thus a clear functional distinction between the role of the courts and the role of legislatures. The latter are free to articulate and impose what they conceive to be community standards, which under our federal constitution, may differ from province to province. The Charter has added only one set of values, one that is clearly desirable, that all legislatures respect as a value common to all Canada procedural fairness as a basic element in legislation. But values are deeply felt, and frequently in conflict. Sometimes the conflict is pretty much on regional or provincial lines, sometimes it involves the difference between the values of an urban upper middle-class and more religiously fundamentalist and conservative *Main Street*. The courts are almost inevitably involved in such conflicts, and the fine line between judicial preservation of essential political values and the imposition of divisive moral values is hard to define. The *Morgentaler* case, which essentially imposed the Charter value of procedural fairness, has been widely perceived as challenging a great moral issue. This necessarily poses a threat to the moral authority of the Supreme Court, and to the constitutional values contained in the Charter.

We have all observed how the "moral majority" in the United States is seeking through the Reagan presidency to colour the political values of the American courts through the calculated appointment of members of the judiciary. One of the possible consequences of the Meech Lake Accord is the extent to which it may impair the ability of the government of Canada to sustain a Supreme Court of high quality which has the intellectual and political authority to perform the "nationalizing" role so fondly attributed to it by Alan Cairns. But in the end we should recog-

nize that the courts cannot escape from the role of custodian of
values. The question is—what values?

Notes

1   D.V. Smiley, *The Federal Condition in Canada* (Toronto: McGraw-HIll
    Ryerson, 1987), 56-7.

2   Bora Laskin, "The Judge as Legislator and Administrator." *Transactions of
    the Royal Society of Canada*, Fourth Series, XI(1973), 185.

3   Ibid., 190.

4   A.V. Dicey, *Introduction to the Study of the Law of the Constitution*, tenth
    edition, (London: 1961), 60.

5   Ibid., 179.

6   J.M. Keynes, *The General Theory of Employment, Interest and Money* (Lon-
    don: 1936), 383.

7   Cf. my *Social Credit and the Federal Power in Canada* (Toronto: 1954).

8   "Contrary to all predictions, post World War II Canadian politics has not
    displayed an irreversible trend to centralization, nor the manifestations of
    capitalist contradiction in polarized class politics, creative or otherwise. In-
    stead, the provinces, aided by secular trends which have enhanced the prac-
    tical significance of their constitutionally-based authority, and by the
    deliberate improvement of their own bureaucratic power and capacity, have
    given a new salience to the politics of federalism and territorially based
    diversities it encompasses, reflects and fosters." Alan Cairns, "The Govern-
    ments and Societies of Canadian Federalism," *Canadian Journal of Political
    Science*, X(1977), 720.

9   Eg., in *Attorney-General of British Columbia vs Attorney-General of Canada*
    (1937) A.C. 377.

10 (1883) 9 ACas. 117 (P.C.)

11 Eg., in *Johannesson vs West St. Paul* (1952) 1. S.C.R. 292.

12 Peter H. Russell, *The Judiciary in Canada* (Toronto: 1987), 342.

13 (1959) S.C.R. 121.

14 The best account of the origin and operation of the Bill of Rights is Walter
    Surma Tarnopolsky, *The Canadian Bill of Rights*, second revised edition,
    (Toronto: 1975).

15 One of the few successful cases was *The Queen vs Drybones* (1970) S.C.R.
    272, which overturned an old and discriminatory section of the Indian Act.

16 *Brodie, Dansky and Rubin vs the Queen*, 1962.

17 Sandra Djwa, *The Politics of the Imagination: A Life of Frank Scott* (Toronto:
    McClelland and Stewart, 1987) 347.

18 Peter H. Russell, "The Effects of a Charter of Rights on the Policy-Making Role of Canadian Courts," *Canadian Public Administration*, XXV:2, 32.

19 Canada. *Debates of the Senate*, February 10, 1988, 2739. Cairns was appearing before the Senate in Committee of the Whole to consider the Meech Lake Accord.

20 Cynthia Williams, "The Changing Nature of Citizen Rights" in Alan Cairns and Cynthia Williams, *Constitutionalism, Citizenship and Society in Canada* (Toronto: 1985), 99.

21 *The Ontario Film and Video Appreciation Society and the Ontario Board of Censors* (1983) 147 D.L.R. (3rd) 58. The appellants won the battle but lost the war, since the Ontario legislature amended the Theatres Act.

22 *R. vs Big M. Drug Mart et al* (1983) 5 D.L.R. (4th.) 121.

23 Eg., in *A.G. Que. vs Quebec Association of Protestant School Boards* (1984) 10 D.L.R. (4th) 321.

24 (1985) 17 D.L.R. (4th) 422.

25 F.L. Morton and David M. Poulton, *Judicial Nullification of Statutes under the Charter*, 1982-1986. Research Study 23. Research Unit for Socio-Legal Studies, Faculty of Social Studies, University of Calgary. November, 1986, 26.

26 Peter H. Russell, "The First Three Years in Charterland," *Canadian Public Administration*, XXVIII(1983), 381.

27 *Morgentaler vs the Queen, Leading Decisions of the Supreme Court of Canada*, the Research Unit for Socio-Legal Studies, University of Calgary. January 28, 1988, 7.

28 *Re Public Service Employee Relations Act* (Alta), Ibid., April 1987, 2.

29 Alan C. Cairns, "The Canadian Constitutional Experiment: Constitution, Community and Identity," Killam Lecture, Dalhousie University, November 23, 1983, 51-52.

30 Agnes Fry, *A Memoir of the Right Honourable Sir Edward Fry*, G.C.B. (London: 1921), 51.

31 *Morgentaler vs. the Queen*, 1.

IDEOLOGY AND THE CHARTER

David P. Shugarman, York University

Introduction

In three recent decisions the Supreme Court of Canada has
declared that certain essential activities of trade unions, namely,
collective bargaining and striking, are not protected as fundamental freedoms or rights conveyed in the revised Canadian
Constitution's Charter of Rights.[1] These decisions were rendered
4-2 with vigorous dissent from Chief Justice Dickson and Madame
Justice Wilson. In two subsequent unanimous decisions the Court
has determined that while lawful picketing *is* an activity protected
under the Charter it is an activity the right to which is subordinate
to other more pressing claims and thus subject to considerable
restriction.[2]

The Charter stipulates (in section 3) that Canadians have the
constitutional right to participate in the determination of how
they are to be governed by legislative bodies. These decisions tell
Canadian workers they have no equivalent right with respect to
how they are to be governed in the workplace. In response to such
decisions one can hold (a) that they represent confirmation of the
much remarked on conservatism of the Canadian judiciary, and/or
(b) that they reflect built-in anti-worker ideological biases located
in the Charter, and/or (c) that they demonstrate the inappropriateness of relying on appeals to rights, and ultimately to the
courts, to advance democratic social and economic interests when
the proper agency or forum should be the legislature. My own
view which I expand on in this paper is that while there is much
truth to (a), (b) and (c) are generally misleading. This is not to
deny that if consistently followed such judgments will represent
dangerous precedents militating against the translation of the
Charter's rhetoric of egalitarian, democratic rights into reality.
But there is no inevitability in this. Rather, there are good reasons
to expect that courts in the future will recognize that these
decisions are a carry-over from our first constitutional regime and
reflect ideological dispositions which are at odds with the
ideological orientations of the Charter.

Before taking up the issue of the competing ideological orientations some preliminary clarification of terminology may be help-

ful.

In some quarters the suggestion that courts and "the law" are expressive of political and ideological concerns is regarded as evidence for a demur in respect of their legitimacy. But this charge only makes sense if by political one means partisan behaviour in regard to one's party or the interests of one's family, friends, associates, and oneself; and if by ideological one is referring to something pejorative in the sense of either irrational commitment to false or mystifying ideas which function as supports for particular interests, or as purposeful deception in support of such interests. I mean to imply none of the above. By politics (and its adjectival form, political) I have in mind action which involves dialogue and persuasion in a process of collective decision-making oriented to the interests of a community of citizens. By ideology (and its adjectival form, ideological) I mean the more or less coherent beliefs, social assumptions and commitments that inform anyone's approach to making social relations explicable, relations between people and government acceptable, and social action meaningful. Wherever we encounter diametrically conflicting opinions, alternative perspectives, differing interpretations, competing assertions of the priority of some interests or rights over others we enter the world of ideological disputation over political concerns. It is not *whether* one has an ideology that is at issue but rather what *particular* ideology and ideological dispositions one has in relation to others, eg., egalitarian or elitist, democratic or authoritarian, universalist or racist, socialist or capitalist, and how they are defended, i.e., logically, and with concern for evidence, or through faith, exclamation, repetition and/or force.

With terminological matters out of the way we can now turn to the ideology of our first constitutional regime.

Pre-Charter Traditions

Canada's original constitution, as evidenced by the British North America Act of 1867 and the conventions of Westminster, reflected British imperialist and Old Whig ideological orientations with the notable exception of federalism as a new twist to the principles of parliamentary sovereignty (a twist that immediately rendered those principles contradictory). Save for references to the use of the English and French languages and the protection of the interest of denominational minorities in educational matters, the Act was primarily concerned with stipulating the legislative rights of governments in the federal and provincial sphere. The ideological context and orientation of the Act was decidedly undemocratic.[3] Two examples will suffice: "None" of the Act's framers "believed in male suffrage without a property qualification,"[4] and it would be a half-century before women attained the right to vote in federal elections.

It has been suggested that our pre-Charter constitutional tradition owed a great deal to the political sensibilities of Edmund Burke.[5] While probably true that is hardly flattering. Burke was a quintessential Old Whig: an anti-democrat who defended inherited privileges, the "real rights" of the English upper class, massive concentrations of wealth, the "laws of commerce," and prejudice, all against "the swinish multitude." He did not think democracy even merited being called a legitimate form of government, he equated it with tyranny.[6] Burke, moreover, anticipated by two hundred years the anxieties of those who have expressed doubts about the wisdom of expanding rights. His warning was direct and clearly politically tendentious: "The more the objects of ambition are multiplied and become democratic, just in that proportion the rich are endangered."[7]

To this account of Old Whig anti-democratic dispositions it is necessary to add the British *rule of law* as it was understood at the time, for this was the guiding principle which together with the doctrine of parliamentary supremacy made up what Dicey called "the law of the constitution." For Dicey the role of judges in the determination of individual rights went to the heart of his beloved constitution: "the English constitution," which Dicey referred to as a polity, is "the fruit of contests carried on in the courts on behalf of the rights of individuals. Our constitution...is a judge-made constitution [with] all the features, good and bad of judge-made law."[8] For Dicey the rule of law meant English common law and he specifically contrasted common law jurisprudence with that of written constitutions on the basis that the one represented an inductive, case by case process while the other was deductive, derived from general principles: the rule of law "pervaded" the English constitution because its general principles "are with us the result of judicial decisions," "the consequence of the rights of individuals as defined and enforced by the courts," whereas the rights of individuals in foreign countries result from "a constitutional code" or from "the general principles of the constitution."[9] Dicey was proud of the fact that one would find "in the English constitution an absence of those declarations or definitions of rights so dear to foreign constitutionalists." The principles of the English constitution were "maxims established by judicial legislation;" and he referred to legislative acts as essentially decisions reached by "the High Court of Parliament."[10] This notion of constitutional law went hand in hand with parliamentary sovereignty which Dicey referred to as "the despotism of king in parliament."[11]

Dicey's rule of law also contained the important principle of *legal equality*, which meant "the universal subjection of all classes to one law administered by the ordinary courts."[12] But for Dicey and Dicey's interpreters this principle had a very peculiar meaning. It did not mean that everyone's rights were to be substantially equal, nor that everyone could expect equal benefit or equal protection from the law but rather that everyone was subject to the same *order* of law in the sense of its administration by judges sharing the same traditions and abiding by the same rules of decorum and legal deliberation that characterized common law proceedings. It could and did mean that all classes were to be subject to laws which reflected Old Whig ideological dispositions administered by an independent and impartial judiciary which could be expected to share those dispositions.

Dicey's common law rule of law (hereinafter abbreviated as CLRL) was characterized by a concern for order and deference to authority, in the first instance the order and authority of judges, in the second the order and authority of parliament. The authority of parliament *vis-à-vis* the crown was established long before England became a democracy. Both the theory and practice of parliamentary sovereignty were developed in a pre-democratic era. At the time Dicey wrote Great Britain, like Canada, was still not a democracy. It was a sexist, class-riven, class dominated society. There is nothing intrinsically democratic about either the CLRL or parliamentary sovereignty. And there was nothing in the combination of the two which required challenge to the legitimacy of discriminatory practices. The Judicial Committee of the Privy Council's review of a provincial government's racist legislation affecting voting rights is a case in point: "The policy or impolicy of such an enactment as that which excludes a particular race from the franchise is not a topic which their lordships are entitled to consider."[13]

Indeed Dicey's *legal equality* principle did not prevent the Supreme Court of Canada from legitimizing highly discriminatory legislation of a sexist and racist nature.[14] But perhaps the best (i.e., the worst) example of pre-Charter thinking, particularly since there are strong parallels between it and the recent union cases, is the case of *Dupond v. Montreal*.[15]

In 1978 the Court, in a 6-3 decision, held that a Montreal by-law and ordinance passed in 1969 preventing assemblies, parades or gatherings of all kinds for thirty days were not unconstitutional. The Court not only found that the by-law and ordinance were within provincial jurisdiction because they were "not punitive but essentially preventive [of] conditions conducive to breaches of the peace and detrimental to the administration of justice," they were also not denials of fundamental freedoms. They were not at odds with such freedoms because, according to the majority judgment, there were no such freedoms "so enshrined in the constitution as to be above the reach of competent legislation."[16] In a series of six propositions, most of which consist of no more than a few sentences, Justice Beetz declared:

Freedoms of speech, of assembly and association, of the press and of religion are distinct and independent of the faculty of holding assemblies, parades, gatherings, demonstrations or processions on the public domain...*Demonstrations are not a form of speech but of collective action. They are of the nature of a display of force rather than that of an appeal to reason*; their inarticulateness prevents them from becoming part of language and from reaching the level of discourse.[17]

As to what the tradition of the common law might offer in the way of support for public meetings, Judge Beetz, having earlier noted that as against the recent use of "loose language" concerning rights and freedoms "couched in general terms," "the English at least have no written constitution and so they may divide their law logically," declared: "The right to hold public meetings on a highway or in a park is unknown to English law. Far from being the object of a right...it may constitute a trespass...[and] may also amount to a nuisance...Being unknown to English law, the right [is not] part of the Canadian constitution."[18]

In dissent Chief Justice Laskin noted that the rationale behind the bylaw—*any* and *all* gatherings were outlawed out of a desire to forestall the violent or the likely violent represented "the invocation of a doctrine which should alarm free citizens."[19]

Nevertheless, the bylaw and ordinance which ironically were passed "to safeguard the free exercise of civil liberties" and prevent "violations of order, peace, and public safety" were upheld.

The Democratic Charter

1. The Canadian Charter of Rights and Freedoms guarantees the rights and freedoms set out in it subject only to such reasonable limits prescribed by law as can be demonstrably justified in a free and democratic society.

Section 1 of the Charter (above) is in effect a *general* constitutional right granted to governments to pass legislation which may require reasonable limits on the other rights and freedoms *only* insofar as the legislation "can be demonstrably justified in a free and democratic society." From the outset the Charter calls for a major break with the common law-legislative supremacy ideological tradition.

The Court's expanded role is to defend the Charter rights and freedoms of "every individual," "everyone," "every permanent resident," "a party or witness in any proceedings," "any person," "any member of the public in Canada," "anyone," "citizens," "equally male and female persons," "every citizen," "persons," "the English and French linguistic minority," "aboriginal peoples of Canada," and, with respect to official language provisions, "any member of the public in New Brunswick."[20] As guardians of the Charter the judicial role is to nullify executive or legislative acts which are in breach of any Charter rights unless a section 1 defense of the infringement is found convincing.

Assuming that as one of the conditions of democratic practice is the diffusion of power, not its concentration, Donald Smiley has suggested that federalism is a buttress of democracy because it provides checks on the unfettered expansion of governmental authority. His recent assessment of Canadian federalism, particularly where he contends that "federalism can make significant contributions to sustaining democratic values", is important on its own terms.[21] But it can also be usefully drawn on to draw attention to a similar potential of the Charter.

Smiley notes that there are some circumstances when federalism displays characteristics which can undermine democratic values. In this regard he makes mention of federalism's complexity as a form of government, which tends to favour those who have the wherewithal to find their way through the complexity. He also draws attention to the related point that the complexity of the decision-making process, involving as it does various actors, now claiming, now disclaiming jurisdiction, has the effect of deflecting attention away from those responsible for public policy.

Despite these drawbacks Smiley makes three points linking federalism to democracy. First, the division of functions and political resources between federal and provincial orders of government "is an obstruction to either set of officeholders abusing its powers...federalism [then, is] a peculiarly effective device against the concentration and abuse of state power." Second, Smiley, citing approvingly the views of my co-editor and Dicey, notes that federalism is a system that both nurtures and is nurtured by a liberal polity, and one in which there is such widespread respect for law that *litigation* is often substituted for *legislation*: "Federalism then, provides both incentives and institutional procedures by which the actions of government can be challenged as to their legal validity..." Third, the plural nature of governing units means that at times "public preferences are more responsively translated into public policy in a federation than in a unitary state."[22]

Now with the exception of the last point we can substitute the Charter for federalism in Smiley's discussion of democratic values because virtually identical claims can be made. The Charter too is meant "as an obstruction to either set of officeholders abusing its powers"; and of course only in reasonably stable communities respectful of freedom and law will we find systemically litigious restraints on the legal abilities of government, a key ingredient in constitutionalism. Furthermore, the Charter can be expected to contribute to a greater awareness of and respect for civil liberties on the part of governing elites and the general public; in turn, greater respect for civil liberties will no doubt contribute to heightened respect for the Charter and moves to improve its utility and its provisions. When we come to Smiley's third point the parallel between federalism and the Charter collapses: the Charter should not function as an instrument of public policy in the hands of judicial bodies concerned to respond to public preferences. Nevertheless, it should enable the judiciary to be responsive to those seeking redress of grievances against governments. In the pre-Charter era grievances took the form, "my interests and rights have been abused by the wrong government," it being understood that there was nevertheless a right government (level) which could legally commit the abuses. A system that encourages grievances against governmental abuse, *per se*, to be aired and justly dealt with by an independent and impartial judiciary commited to a democratic ideology is a system in touch with democratic values. Federalism, it is worth remembering, was designed to meet the linguistic and cultural concerns of French Canada together with the interests of the enfranchised class and sex and their political and economic elites in existing colonial units. Federalism's origins were undemocratic; it too grew out of an ideological environment which favoured executive dominance and strong governments. Its contribution to democracy is the unintended consequence of political compromise, judicial intervention and provincial development. The Charter on the other hand evolved within a context of Canadian democracy and was designed to reflect and promote democratic concerns. In this sense the Charter should be seen as not only complementing but supplementing federalism's role in a democratic society.

Now one view of a concentration on fundamental rights—and by extension, the wisdom of providing a judicial review function to safeguard such rights—is that they are to be used as limits on what can be accomplished through the democratic process. This assumes that rights are somehow *prior* to and to some extent independent of and even antagonistic to democracy. This view is not inconsistent with the common law understanding and development of rights and theoretically owes a good deal to the natural rights theories of Hobbes and Locke.

However, as the democratic theorist Robert Dahl has recently argued, there is a very different way of understanding fundamental rights which "is more consistent with democracy."[23] From this perspective fundamental rights comprise "all the rights *necessary* to the democratic process." Since in this view the right to self-government is one of the key fundamental rights, "then citizens are also entitled to all the rights that are necessary...to govern themselves—that is, all the rights essential to the democratic process."[24] And Dahl argues that when addressing issues of self-government and democratic rights it is indefensible to exclude the workplace and economic enterprises.

Dahl's discussion of rights as democratic rights rather than as rights against democratic government is all the more interesting since it permits us to appreciate some of the differences between the evolution of the concept of rights in the U.S. and Canada. His alternative conception of rights is more germane to the Canadian experience than to the American.

Both the United States and Canada (now) can be described as countries with constitutionally derived rights and rules. However, the American emphasis on rights took place amidst a slave-owning society in a pre-democratic era. America's influential elites were concerned with avoiding duplication of the despotic form of government they had revolted against. Their understanding of rights was again largely infused with Lockean notions of inalienable property rights *prior* to and *against* government. None of these experiences is akin to the Canadian experience. A crucial difference is that we have a structure of constitutionally derived rights and rules infused with the experiences of, and designed to serve, democracy.

What Dahl points out is that when fundamental rights are seen as integral to democracy then a commitment to their interpretation and protection would be an expected element of the political culture and it would also be no contradiction to authorize some people—such as jurists—to have special responsibilities in this regard.[25] In a similar vein Philip Green claims that inasmuch as the preservation of citizen's rights, especially minority rights, and political equality are necessary for democracy then "the institution of judicial review to protect those rights and that equality is not antidemocratic but is the essence of democracy."[26] What Dahl and Green have to say with respect to the role of rights *vis a vis* democracy is not only persuasive it also helps to place the democratic purpose of our Charter and judicial review in the proper perspective.

This is a perspective enunciated by Chief Justice Dickson on behalf of the Court several years ago. In respect of the Charter, said Dickson, "The court must be guided by the values and principles essential to a free and democratic society."[27] These values and principles include *inter alia*, "commitment to social justice and equality," and "social and political institutions which enhance the participation of individuals and groups in society."[28] The time when members of the judiciary might find Old Whig values of traditional class privileges, customary rights, sexism, and elitism amenable and applicable in settling constitutional questions was to be no more.

Pre-Charter Thinking vs. the Charter

The contention that the Charter of Rights "ushers in a new era in the protection of fundamental freedoms" such that the Canadian judiciary is no longer bound by common law jurisprudence because "its applicability to the Charter is undermined by the different nature of the Constitutional documents" would seem to be a contention with which everyone whether pro or con the entrenchment of rights in our revised constitution could agree, all the more so since it issues from no less an authority than the Chief Justice of the Supreme Court of Canada.[29] And yet Chief Justice Dickson's contention was delivered as part and parcel of his dissenting opinion, supported only by Judge Wilson, in the judgments of the *Alberta Labour Reference*, *P.S.A.C. v. Canada* and the *Dairy Workers*; and it was virtually ignored by the entire Court in the British Columbia and Newfoundland courthouses picketing cases.

While over a range of other issues the Court may have struck a "tone of judicial creativity and boldness" in its embrace of the Charter, when it comes to the protection of worker's rights it has yet to enter a new era.[30]

The pre-Charter mentality of *Dupond v. Montreal* is still present in the way the Court disposed of union appeals in these cases. The majority decision in the *Alberta Labour Reference* dealing with the question of collective bargaining and strikes as fundamental freedoms (i.e., the freedom of association) was, in the manner of Judge Beetz's decision earlier, set out in declaratory fashion in a few short paragraphs.[31] Labour matters, the Court said, were the "creation of legislation," involved "competing interests" and constituted a specialized field of law, and so were not suitable for review by the courts. Like Beetz, Judge Le Dain held that constitutionalizing a matter which involved "general and abstract terms" would be inappropriate, for it was too complex for judges to address.[32] Judge McIntyre presented an elaborate argument in concurring with the judgment of Le Dain, Beetz and La Forest. But the thrust of his remarks owed a great deal to common law jurisprudence and dispositions: labour law had been a matter of legislative regulation in the past; the legalization of strikes and collective bargaining were of "relatively recent vintage"; there was no specific mention of these rights in the Charter; only individual rights were protected by the Charter—and strike action had no individual equivalent; "labour matters frequently involve...political, social and economic questions." For all these considerations, according to McIntyre, the courts should not interfere with "the field of legislation."[33]

Here again the emphasis was on the tradition of deciding issues over individual rights (collective ones were viewed as too new, too complex to be adequately dealt with), deference to the traditional legislative capacities of governments, and a concern that courts not deal with *political* and *economic* questions that arise in the course of labour disputes. For the purposes of this paper a close analysis of McIntyre's arguments is not appropriate. What does need emphasis is that McIntyre singled out the collective action of workers as an *exceptional* activity that did not merit Charter protection for the reasons mentioned. He rejected explicitly (Le Dain had done so implicitly) the contention that the *political* aspects of union action were a necessary ingredient and integral feature of modern democracy, a contention that was at the centre of the dissenting opinion of Dickson and Wilson.

That unions are *sui generis* collective entities can hardly serve as a bar to their Charter protection. After all, *governments* are *collective entities* with enormous constitutional rights: just as no individual can go on strike without colleagues, so no individual can pass legislation without her colleagues. Indeed in Canada no individual can be a registered political party campaigning for election; yet these activities are defensible as fundamental rights according to Charter interpretation. But when Old Whig perspectives are brought to bear on labour activities there is in the background concern over threats of conspiracy, of breach of contracts, threats to the stable economic order, and to political priorities.

It may be thought that I have overemphasized the ideologically negative disposition towards collective action by workers in the judgments of the majority in these cases. But when one turns to the Court's decision on the picketing of law courts there should be little question of the claim. Since the reasons given by Chief Justice Dickson for a unanimous Court in the B.C. case were used by the Court to unanimously dispose of the Newfoundland case I will direct attention to the former.

On November 1, 1983 the British Columbia Government Employees Union, on a legal strike, picketed courthouses all over the Province. When the Chief Justice of the B.C. Supreme Court arrived at the Vancouver Courthouse in the morning and saw the pickets he almost immediately issued an *ex parte* injunction ordering the picketing to cease. The union then went through various levels of the court system in order to have the injunction set aside. At issue for the union was its fundamental right to lawfully picket, as implied by the freedom of expression provision in section 2 of the Charter. At issue for the Court according to the Chief Justice was "the fundamental right of every Canadian citizen to have unimpeded access to the courts and the authority of the courts to protect that constitutional right." Where these two concerns intersected was on the question whether or not there was a right of the Union and its members to urge members of the public not to enter a courthouse. The Court answered in a firm no. Picketing a local factory was one thing, picketing the halls of justice (inside or outside) was an act of criminal contempt. According to the Court picketing was lawful and a protected freedom but picketing courthouses was unlawful and so the freedom was properly subject to restriction by the injunction.

The Court thus decided that judges could use their own initiative in defending Charter rights *and* in taking action to protect them. What the Court managed to do in this case may have put the development of Charter jurisprudence back a decade or more.

It is important to reflect again on the role of the courts in addressing constitutional questions. Aside from the traditional role of granting advisory opinions at the request of government— a role only granted to the highest courts provincially and federally—the activity of a constitutional court consists of settling disputes among contending parties appealing to and granted standing before the court. With respect to questions of redress and enforcement of protected rights sec. 24 of the Charter makes it perfectly clear that the initiation of legal proceedings is the responsibility of "anyone whose rights or freedoms, as guaranteed..., have been infringed or denied." In such instances *that* person "may apply to a court of competent jurisdiction to obtain such remedy as the court considers appropriate and just in the circumstances." The court has no duty to run interference for governments in their attempts to finesse or otherwise limit these rights. Nor is the court either traditionally, or under any Charter provision, authorized to act as a surrogate for governments with respect to the latter's executive or legislative capacity. There is, moreover, no clause, section or provision set out in either the Constitution Act of 1867 or the Constitution Act of 1982 which authorizes a court to *initiate* the constitutional adjudication process.

In pronouncing on the proper role of the judiciary *vis a vis* the application of the Charter to issues before the Court, the Supreme Court in its judgment in the *Dolphin Delivery* case said: "An order of the Court...cannot be equated with government action for the purposes of Charter application..."[34] The courts have a "duty" to

> act as neutral arbiters, not as contending parties involved in a dispute. To regard a court order as an element of governmental intervention necessary to invoke the Charter would [unduly] widen the scope of the Charter's application to virtually all litigation.[35]

And with respect to who is to be held responsible for Charter violations *or* for constitutional overrides of entrenched rights under sec. 1 the Court held that the Charter "specifies" they are "the legislative, executive, and administrative branches of government."[36] In short, the *Dolphin Delivery* judgment emphasized that the Charter only comes into play when an alleged infringement of a guaranteed right can be linked to governmental action conveyed by statute. However, when confronted with a legal strike and picketing by provincial employees the Supreme Court ignored its own strictures and the reasoning it set out in the *Dolphin Delivery* case. It proceeded to perform lateral arabesques through the Charter and reached back to the CLRL to deny unions their rights to collective action and freedom of expression.

The Court treated a judicial injunction as equivalent to a legislative act: it defended the use of a judge's initiative to limit freedom of expression by applying section 1 criteria. In holding that the Chief Justice of the B.C. Supreme Court "had the legal and constitutional right" to order legal picketing to cease the Court elevated common law principles—the law of contempt flowing from a judge's inherent and residual powers to act on his own (*ex mero motu*) to safeguard the administration of justice—to a place alongside the Charter. By drawing on these notions derived from the CLRL the judgment generated a *new* fundamental right—the right of unimpeded access to courts of law—and a *new means* of protecting Charter provisions.

In the *B.C.G.E.U.* and *N.A.P.E.* cases the Court has come dangerously close to endorsing, and perhaps entrenching, the role of judges as surrogates for government initiative. It also clearly involved itself in labour matters affecting socio-economic and political policy. The Court has achieved this *not* through recourse to any of the *specified* rights or freedoms in the Charter but rather by turning to judge-made rules governing alleged threats to the sanctity of law courts and a general concern to protect the rights of all Canadians—by restricting the rights of workers. Clearly with judgments such as these the Court is in danger of confounding the roles of rule-maker, prosecutor, judge, jury and police officer.

But just as remarkable as all this was the Court's attitude to workers and the practice of picketing. Rather than treat picketing as one of the basic features of democracy consistent with the right to participate in decisions affecting one's working life and seeing the protection of such activity as very much in the public interest, views which both the Chief Justice and Madame Justice Wilson expressed in the earlier collective bargaining cases, in the B.C. and Newfoundland cases the Court focused on the significance of a picket line less as a form of expression than as a "form of coercion," passing over the fact that a court order threatening imprisonment has much greater powers of influence as a form of coercion.[38] The Supreme Court treated a non-violent, lawful action as if it created a state of emergency with the courts under siege and all Canadians at risk of disastrous consequences.

Yet the evidence presented before the Court contained not a single hint of violence, not a single instance of a person actually having his way to court barred. So the Court had to focus on the importance of *preventing potential* disruptions and allegedly *inevitable* disasters in the name of protecting everyone's rights. This kind of logic is strikingly similar to that used by the Montreal city council in passing the bylaw and ordinance that figured in *Dupond v. Montreal*. And by treating picketing as a form of coercion constituting an obstruction to free movement rather than as a form of expression and participation in self-government the Court has returned to the sentiments of the *Dupond* case where collective action was deemed a display of force rather than an appeal to reason.

In addition, the Court also harkened back to another facet of the old regime. When it came to dealing with the effectiveness of picketing and with the fact that many citizens in Canada do honour picket lines the Court adopted and applied as part of its reasons for judgment a dismissive and insulting characterization of the capacities of trade union members and supporters. The Court endorsed the views of a judge of the High Court of Ontario to the effect that unionists who honour each other's picket lines are comparable to the followers of a fundamentalist sect, they are "all true believers." And the Chief Justice made repeated references to the allegation that honouring a picket line is a matter of automatic response by people "Pavlovian" in nature.[38] Given this depiction of hundreds of thousands of Canadian workers as having the sensibilities and reasoning capacities of programmed, salivating dogs, one would be hard put to find the Court displaying either a neutral or positive disposition to their democratic rights or to their appeal on this basis. Shades of Burke's swinish multitude!

Conclusion

Since in this series of Charter cases the Court has handed down verdicts clearly at odds with rights to engage in non-violent collective action, rights fundamental to a democratic society, it may be thought that the Charter's implications are undemocratic. This is the wrong conclusion to draw from troubling judgments.

If the majority party elected to a representative assembly seriously misconstrued its mandate from the electorate and pursued policies antagonistic to the interests of the general public we would say that the party was acting undemocratically. But it would be a mistake to conclude that the representative assembly as such stood for undemocratic values, or that the idea of representative democracy was fallacious, or that all parties would necessarily do the same. Similarly the problem with the decisions that flow out of the *Alberta Labour Reference* and the two anti-picketing cases from B.C. and Newfoundland is not that there is something inherently undemocratic in judicial review, the Charter, or the idea of entrenching rights against state infringement. Rather it may just be the fault of a particular judiciary at a particular moment in history misconstruing its new mandate under a revamped constitutional system.

The proposition that the integrity of the Charter can be defended through recourse to a version of the rule of law deeply imbedded in common law practices figured centrally in the logic of the Court in the *B.C.G.E.U.* case. That is a logic difficult to credit since the Charter came into existence largely to correct the serious deficiencies in that tradition.

Judges in the past as well as those who currently occupy senior positions on the bench have been accustomed to abide by a tradition of jurisprudence whose doctrines are inimical to our new constitutional regime, a type of constitutionalism which is founded on coercion-limiting principles characterized by a panoply of rights necessary in a democratic society.

Nevertheless, it is to be expected that as Canadians and Canadian lawyers become more familiar with the legitimacy of the Charter and more sensitive to the notion of rights fundamental to democracy future judicial authorities will put behind them the decidedly undemocratic tradition of our earlier constitutional regime. Despite the close ties existing between the legal profession and the world of business the prospect of large numbers of young lawyers developing expertise on civil liberties and earning their incomes defending and advocating democratic liberties (rather than devoting their lives to corporate mergers, tax avoidance schemes and real estate transactions) should be greeted with cheers. There will be more incentive for lawyers to move beyond the narrow confines of the corporate sector to concern themselves with the needs and aspirations of a democratic political community.

The optimistic tenor of these remarks should not be understood as a Pollyanna-like account of the significance of the Charter for wide-scale social change. By no means is optimism over the Charter an argument for leaving the struggle for democratic rights to self-government up to lawyers and judges. Smiley's reminder of federalism's drawbacks in relation to democratic goals is apposite in the case of litigating rights: the legal route is complex and expensive; and it can deflect attention away from the politicians responsible for committing wrongs. But it is simplistic to assume that the building of a democratic political community is an either/or proposition: either the legislature or the court, either the law or the streets, either elections or industrial action, either the legislature or the extra parliamentary route—these are all false dichotomies when it comes to mobilizing support and participating in the effort to develop and equally share in a justly ordered, free society.

Canada's new constitution provides us with a useful stepping stone along that path. The majority of our judicial elite have been reluctant to take that path. They have been wary of following the full implications and priorities of fusing equality, freedom and democracy. In this respect they are in conformity with our economic and political elites. When judicial review trips us up it is not because of the progressive, democratic rule of law the Charter promises, rather it is the result of the conservative, undemocratic rule of law and *its* social implications and priorities that recalcitrant judges are more inclined to uphold.

In the meantime a good deal of the Charter's promise remains as rhetoric. But as E. P. Thompson put it, the "rhetoric and rules of society are something a great deal more than sham." While they may at times camouflage the "realities of power," they also "curb that power and check its intrusions," and may very well lead to "a radical critique" of unjust social practices.[39]

Ideological disputation over rights and rival interpretations of the meaning and applicability of the Charter will continue. That is in the nature of politics. But I do not want to leave the impression that choosing among conflicting ideological conceptions is a matter of fate, faith, self-interest, tossing a coin or having a mystical experience. Some beliefs are more rationally based and defended than others. Not even an ideological commitment to equality commits one to the belief that all ideologies are equal.

Notes

1   All three decisions were released concurrently by the Court on April 9, 1987. The reports I am drawing on are *Reference Re Public Service Employee Relations Act, Labour Relations Act and Police Officers Collective Bargaining Act* (1987) 38 D.L.R. (4th) 161 (hereafter referred to as *Alberta Labour Reference*); *Public Service Alliance of Canada et al. v. the Queen in Right of Canada et al.* (1987) 38 D.L.R. (4th), 249 (shortened hereafter to *P.S.A.C. v. Canada*); *Retail, Wholesale and Department Store Union v. Saskatchewan* [1987] 1 S.C.R. 460 (shortened to *Dairy Workers*).

2   *British Columbia Government Employees Union v. British Columbia (Attorney General) and Canada (Attorney General)* [1988] 2 S.C.R. 214 (shortened to *B.C.G.E.U. v. B.C.*); *Newfoundland Association of Public Employees v. Her Majesty's Attorney General for Newfoundland and William Chafe* [1988] 2 S.C.R. 204 (shortened to *Newfoundland v. N.A.P.E.*). Both judgments were rendered on October 20, 1988.

3   Smiley puts it succinctly: The "Act of 1867 was an instrument of governments alone which embodied almost no hint of democracy or popular sovereignty." *The Federal Condition in Canada* (Toronto: McGraw-Hill Ryerson, 1987), 39.

4   *Ibid.*

5   See Peter Russell, "The Political Role of the Supreme Court of Canada in its First Century," *Canadian Bar Review* 53 (1975), 576, 592; also R.I. Cheffins and P.A. Johnson, *The Revised Canadian Constitution: Politics as Law*

(Toronto: McGraw-Hill Ryerson, 1986), 151.

6   All of these odious views are set out in Burke's *Reflections on the Revolution in France* (Middlesex: Penguin Books, 1969). The reference to "the swinish multitude" is at 173.

7   *Ibid.*, 292.

8   A.V. Dicey, *Introduction to the Law of the Constitution* (London: Macmillan, 10th edition, 1960), 196.

9   *Ibid.*, 195,203. As these remarks of Dicey should make clear, neither the language of rights nor the fundamental importance of rights adjudication is an American or Charter intrusion into "our" constitutional traditions.

10 *Ibid.*, 197.

11 *Ibid.*, 145.

12 *Ibid.*, 193.

13 *Cunningham v. Tomey Homma* (1903) as cited in R.A. Olmsted (ed.), *Judicial Committee Decisions Relating to the British North America Act, 1867*, vol. 1, 484. The reference is from Richard Van Loon and Michael Whittington, *The Canadian Political System* (Toronto: McGraw-Hill Ryerson, 3rd editon, revised, 1984), 223.

14 See the *Bliss* case [1979] 1 S.C.R. 183 and the *Lavell and Bédard* case [1974] S.C.R. 1349.

15 *Attorney General of Canada and Dupond v. Montreal* [1978] 2 S.C.R. 770.

16 *Ibid.*, 797.

17 *Ibid.*, emphasis added.

18 *Ibid.*, 798.

19 *Ibid.*, 780-781.

20 This is a compilation of the subjects of rights referred to in various sections of the Charter. It is to be noted that the subjects are designated singular, plural and linguistic and have the logical attributes of universal and particular statements.

21 *The Federal Condition in Canada.*

22 *Ibid.*, 16-18.

23 Robert Dahl, *A Preface to Economic Democracy* (Berkeley: University of California Press, 1985).

24 *Ibid.*, 25-26.

25 *Ibid.*, 30-31.

26 P. Green, *Retrieving Democracy: In Search of Civic Equality* (Totowa, N.J.: Rowman and Allanheld, 1985), 216.

27 *R. v. Oakes* [1986] 1 S.C.R. 103, at 136.

28 *Ibid.*

29 *Alberta Labour Reference*, 176.

30 On the Court's creativity and boldness with respect to giving Charter provisions a very liberal, expansive reading in *other* areas prior to the labour cases, see F. L. Morton, "The Political Impact of the Canadian Charter of Rights and Freedoms," *Canadian Journal of Political Science* 20 (1987), 31-55. The phrase cited is at 35.

31 Arguments on behalf of the majority rejecting union claims were set out in the *Alberta Labour Reference* at 239 and consistently referred to as the reasons for judgment in the two other cases, *P.S.A.C. v. Canada* and the *Dairy Workers*.

32 *Alberta Labour Reference*, 240.

33 *Ibid.*, 215-238. An excellent and more extensive commentary on these cases from a perspective sympathetic to the rights of unions is in Leo Panitch and Donald Swartz, *The Assault on Trade Union Freedoms: From Consent to Coercion* (Toronto: Garamond Press, revised edition, 1988).

34 *R.W.D.S.U. v. Dolphin Delivery Ltd.* [1986] 2 S.C.R. 573, at 574.

35 *Dolphin Delivery* at 600.

36 *Ibid.*, at 598.

37 One might well ask which form of coercion is preferable: one carried on peacefully which relies on persuasion, or one which is issued as a command threatening the use of police and confinement?

38 In *B.C.G.E.U.* [1988] 2 S.C.R. 214, at 227, 231 and 232; in *N.A.P.E.* [1988] 2 S.C.R. 204, at 212.

39 E. P. Thompson, *Whigs and Hunters: The Origins of the Black Act* (New York: Pantheon Books, 1975), 265. Also in this connection and with respect to the analysis of constitutionalizing rights more generally see Tom Campbell, David Goldberg, Sheila McLean and Tom Mullen (eds.), *Human Rights: From Rhetoric to Reality* (Oxford: Basil Blackwell, 1986).

RIGHTS IN A
'FREE AND DEMOCRATIC SOCIETY':
ABORTION

Reg Whitaker, York University

It has often been argued that the transition to rights-based liberalism as the dominant discourse of North American politics signals a decline in the role of responsible and representative democratic institutions and the concomitant rise of democratically irresponsible or non-accountable institutions (the judiciary and bureaucracy).[1] I am not entirely persuaded of the causal relation here. Or, to restate the matter carefully, the causal links do not perhaps all run in one direction.

Certainly it is self-evident that a dominant rights-based liberal discourse is tied logically to the leading role of the courts in defining the boundaries of rights and defining many of the public policy implications of these rights. Clearly the legislative majority is to this extent constrained in its scope by the limits imposed by the courts. This much is obvious. What is less obvious is the tangled relation between the claims of liberty and equality and the institutional forms in which these claims have been embodied. Much of the change in the political culture which has accompanied and stimulated the ascendancy of rights-based liberalism (and was associated with the Charter) closely related to equality claims on the part of groups which felt precisely that the "representative" institutions of parliamentary democracy were in practice *unrepresentative* and thus inequitable in their policy output. They could of course have posed their claims in a form which sought only to further democratize or make more responsible the representative institutions. This is a partial strategy of many groups, but it has rarely been more than a partial strategy, which has usually been overshadowed by the increasing reliance upon the language of rights-based liberalism.

To marginal or minority groups, the representation offered by parliamentary institutions has seemed dubious, if not in some cases downright misleading. As members of a minority group, individuals may of course share certain common public policy interests with members of other groups (class or regional interests for example). To the extent this is the case they may co-operate on common political projects through, say, voting for a particular party which seeks to represent these interests or attempting to make their common views known to legislators during the course of the policy process (Model One). Model One activities offer support to parliamentary democracy. Yet to the extent that they have strong interests in what specifically or narrowly defines them as a minority, they will be drawn almost inevitably to see parliamentary democracy as offering less of an opportunity than a threat. Lacking effective representation and thus power in the parliamentary majority, the minority will feel vulnerable even when the majority chooses not to exercise its capacity to limit or override what the minority perceives as its fundamental interests, qua minority, since there is no guarantee that the majority will not exercise its power with less sensitivity at some future date.[2]

A possible alternative strategy for such a minority is to seek out a coalition of other minorities to maximize their potential representation within parliament and widen their scope for influencing the majority (Model Two). This has inherent limitations, however, as the case of Jesse Jackson's "Rainbow Coalition" in the U.S. presidential nomination contest in 1984 demonstrates. Minorities must bargain and compromise their fundamental interests as part of the coalition process—which may alienate some minority members. Second, the perceived interests of some minorities may be set in conflict with those of others and highlighted by the coalition process: the conflict between Blacks and Jews over the Jackson candidacy in 1984 (and in the hate-filled atmosphere of the 1988 New York Democratic primary) is a sad example of this. Finally, minority coalition building may, by its concentration on minority symbols and minority interests, alienate the majority which does not share particular minority-distinguishing characteristics such as ethnicity or colour but might otherwise have found much in common with the minority coalition on economic and political issues. The white working class and the white poor did not flock to the Rainbow Coalition, and redistributive or more egalitarian economic policies were in effect lost in the process of making Democratic party policy, because of the divisions between those who favoured them.

In 1988 Jackson made a much more sustained and impressive drive for the party nomination in part because he dropped the symbol of the Rainbow Coalition and concentrated on advancing left-wing economic policies which potentially unite substantial numbers of majority and minority working class and poor voters

(In other words, the Jackson campaign in 1988 conforms more closely to Model One rather than Model Two). Ironically, Model One attracted higher levels of support and participation from Jackson's core minority constituency of blacks than was the case for Model Two in 1984, while it also succeeded in increasing levels of white support and participation. Yet this relative political success rests upon the underplaying of specific minority interests—although the symbolic value of minority participation in a relatively successful (or at least highly visible) political project should not be underestimated.

To the extent that specific minority interests cannot ultimately be met by Model One or Model Two, those interests must in effect look to non-democratic institutions to underwrite the equality rights which the democratic majority can never be trusted to guarantee. Beyond the limitations of minority political action, there is another fundamental reason why legal recognition of rights is preferable to democratic legislation. Legislation and public policy change; there is no permanence in them. With the legal recognition of rights there is at least the promise of durability. When we speak of matters as deeply important as equality rights, the evanescence of politics must seem to vulnerable minorities a stormy sea indeed, especially when their own political role is so marginal.

The case of the majority which has turned to rights-based liberalism is somewhat different. Women constitute a slight majority of the population. Gender-related equality issues have been among the most prominent in recent years. While these issues have certainly not been absent from politics, they have also been strongly focussed on the courts. Why should a majority choose a non-democratic over a democratic institution as their preferred route? A statistical majority they may be, yet women of course are also divided by almost every non-gender cleavage which runs through society. Nor is there anything approaching a consensus even on gender-related issues, which can rarely be separated entirely from non-gender-related issues. Yet these considerations merely beg a more fundamental point. Democratic legislatures and democratic legislation historically failed not only to respond to, or often to recognize, women's equality claims. Worse, the fundamental dignity of the female person—"life, liberty and security of the person"—was only weakly recognized in practice. Democratic institutions failed to deliver on the peculiarly democratic value: equality. There was a reason for this.

Female equality claims are claims based on women's differences from men. To the extent that men and women are the same, there is no requirement for special equality rights. That they have been posed as strongly as they have is obvious proof of the opposite. The democratic electoral and legislative systems experience considerable difficulty in handling this problem because there is no strong social basis for resolving it either by majority or by consensus. If the social basis existed, politics would be efficient but perhaps superfluous. Paradoxically, democratic processes cope most effectively with the politics of equality when social equality already exists. Failing this, external intervention is necessary and, in the event, this is provided by the courts applying the test of legal equality rights.

Although the Charter's equality rights apply narrowly to the relations between state and citizen, much of the thrust of feminism is directed toward social, as well as political, inequality. Questions relating to sexuality, reproduction, the structure of the family, and gender-based roles, are primary to feminism and each relate only tangentially to the state, as such. Central elements of "patriarchy" lie outside politics—at least as traditionally defined—and are anchored instead firmly within civil society, even in the cultural and psychological roots of civil society. To the extent that feminism is invoking the state to redress the imbalance of civil society, then feminist politics may be categorized as an aspect of the "embedding" of the state.[3] Obviously, there are many elements of feminism and especially of the equality claims made by feminists that are associated with the obliteration of the distinction between the political and the personal, and thus with the extension of "political" criteria into previously private areas. But this need not, and in certain crucial cases, emphatically does not, entail a statist form of discourse.

Feminism's distance from statism is nowhere more striking than in the pro-choice argument regarding abortion, an argument given partial and qualified sanction by the Supreme Court decision in the Morgentaler case. The pro-choice case is certainly one of rights-based liberalism but it in no way implies an extension of state jurisdiction to enforce rights. On the contrary, the pro-choice argument has identified the existing extension of state authority into the private/personal realm of the woman's reproductive system as the problem to be attacked. At root the pro-choice argument rests on the proposition that the woman alone is the competent agent to make the moral choices regarding the continuation or termination of a pregnancy. Legal prohibitions, standards and regulations imposed by legislatures upon abortions, and the application of criminal sanctions are all rejected as unjustifiable state intrusions into the "life, liberty and security of the [female] person." The minimal demand made upon the state by the pro-choice argument is that where universal access to publicly-funded medical services is available, it be guaranteed equally for abortion services.

The opposing pro-life argument takes an openly statist stance. The initial pro-life argument was strongly couched in conservative communitarian terms: the right of the woman to make free individual moral choices in reproductive matters was denied, or subordinated, to the higher good of the community embodied in its privileged set of moral standards.

This constituted a classic formulation of the conservative-communitarian proposition that the community Good takes priority over individual "goods." Moreover, in their strong belief that abortion (that is, any abortion, under any circumstances) is murder, pro-lifers advocate the maximum use of the coercive arm of the state to enforce their conception of the Good upon those who would practice abortion. Apparently in some desperation at their failure to impress this conservative-communitarian argument upon the community, pro-lifers have more recently reverted to a species of rights-based liberalism which emphasizes the putative right of the foetus as a trump—a claim which is being advanced by various claimants before the courts.[4] I believe that they are standing on very weak ground here: it is hard to see how, within a dominant liberal discourse, the right of the unborn (potential) person can trump the right of the mature moral agent. The main point I would like to make, however, does not rest on the eventual outcome of this struggle over rights.

What is fascinating in the abortion conflict is what it demonstrates about the limited capacity of democratic institutions to handle questions of fundamental ethics. In the aftermath of the Supreme Court decision, Parliament is reluctantly compelled to develop public policy which seeks to balance (in an inevitably arbitrary manner) the right of the mother to choose with the right of viable life. This will take the form of setting a period of pregnancy prior to which abortions are acceptable. The terrain of compromise upon which Parliament may manoeuvre has thus been delimited by the courts, after the fundamental question of rights has already been adjudicated*. Ironically, it is the courts which have forced Parliament even to consider the question; it is notorious that both the Conservative and Liberal parties have avoided all initiative on the issue. The brief and unpleasant experience of Premier Vander Zalm's eccentric initiative in British Columbia will do nothing to encourage other provincial politicians to play with this particular fire.

It is likely that the original liberalized abortion law of the late 1960s was only possible because the bitter battle lines had not yet been drawn clearly and the limited but very loud mobilizations of zealots had not yet taken shape. Once the militantly mobilized minorities had taken aim at the target, the issue was transformed into one which democratic legislatures were incompetent, as well as unwilling, to manage. Although there were clear indications that the majority of voters leaned much closer to the pro-choice argument (the unbroken string of jury acquittals of Dr Morgentaler; the evidence of opinion polls over a number of years[5]), this offered no courage to legislators who recognized that the intensity of the views of the minorities was not reflected in the opinions of the (silent) majority and that these passionate minorities threatened a kind of double veto over the actions of nervous politicians. Only the external intervention of the courts could break this policy logjam.

It is doubtful that a more direct form of democratic legitimacy, unmediated by representative institutions, could have been applied to a resolution of this issue. No referendum or plebiscite could have been shaped to comprehend the complexity of the ethical and constitutional issues with which the justices of the Supreme Court grappled. Worse, there is no reason to believe that the losing side would have accepted a democratic decision as legitimate since both sides view the matter as one of fundamental right, not policy preference. The pro-life people could no more accept a majority decision to "murder babies" than the pro-choice people could accept a majority decision to render a woman a means rather than an end in herself. Democracy as a decision-

---

*   Despite the compromise, the pro-life argument, in either its communitarian or its rights-based form, has in effect been negated. Indeed, it was negated even under the old law. The equation of abortion to murder – the fundamental moral core of of the pro-life movement – is rejected either under the old law or on the terrain of acceptable public policy within the parameters of the Morgentaler decision.

making mechanism fails on all counts in the case of an issue like this.

Yet even if it fails as a decision-making mechanism, democracy cannot be read out of the picture. Democracy, properly understood, remains a standard—even for the courts. I believe that the limited and qualified sanction given the pro-choice argument by the majority decisions in the Morgentaler case actually reflects democratic assumptions about the nature of citizenship. The justices concurring in the majority were agreed that the limitation of the "life, liberty and security of the person" (s.7) inherent in the abortion law and its procedures constituted a violation of women's status as moral agents possessing a "degree of autonomy in making decisions of fundamental personal importance." Indeed, Madame Justice Wilson spoke of the "theory underlining the Charter, namely that the state will respect choices made by individuals and, to the greatest extent possible, will avoid subordinating these choices to any one conception of the good life." These arguments are not purely liberal, however, but are premised upon an interpretation of the centrality to the constitution of the "free and democratic" nature of Canadian society.[6] Life, liberty and security of the person are crucial to the dignity of democratic citizenship:

> The Charter is predicated on a particular conception of the place of the individual in society. An individual is not a totally independent entity disconnected from the society in which he or she lives. Neither, however, is the individual a mere cog in an impersonal machine in which his or her values, goals and aspirations are subordinated to those of the collectivity. The individual is a bit of both. The Charter reflects this reality by leaving a wide range of activities and decisions open to legitimate government control while at the same time placing limits on the proper scope of that control. Thus, the rights guaranteed in the Charter erect around each individual, metaphorically speaking, an invisible fence over which the state will not be allowed to trespass. The role of the courts is to map out, piece by piece, the parameters of the fence. [Wilson J.]

The link between this notion of individual autonomy and democracy is that only those individuals who enjoy the dignity of autonomous decision-making power in matters of "fundamental personal importance" can stand as free and equal citizens of a democratic society. As Mr Chief Justice Dickson explained:

> ...at the most basic, physical and emotional level, every pregnant woman is told by [the offending abortion section] that she cannot submit to a generally safe medical procedure that might be of clear benefit to her unless she meets criteria entirely unrelated to her own priorities and aspirations. Not only does the removal of decision making power threaten women in a physical sense; the indecision of knowing whether an abortion will be granted inflicts emotional stress...Forcing a woman, by threat of criminal sanction, to carry a foetus to term unless she meets certain criteria unrelated to her own principles and aspirations, is a profound interference with a woman's body and thus a violation of the security of the person.

More light may be cast upon this point by Mr Chief Justice Dickson's discussion in the earlier case of *The Queen v. Oakes* of the place of the words "free and democratic" in s.1 of the Charter:

> Inclusion of these words as the final standard of justification for limits on rights and freedoms refers the Court to the very purpose for which the Charter was originally entrenched in the Constitution: Canadian society is to be free and democratic. The Court must be guided by the values and principles essential to a free and democratic society which I believe embody, to name but a few, respect for the inherent dignity of the human person, commitment to social justice and equality, accommodation of a wide variety of beliefs, respect for cultural and group identity, and faith in social and political institutions which enhance the participation of individuals and groups in society. The underlying values and principles of a free and democratic society are the genesis for the rights and freedoms guaranteed by the Charter and the ultimate standard against which a limit on a right or freedom must be shown, despite its effect, to be reasonable and demonstrably justified.

In other words, liberal freedom is intimately connected to the democratic nature of the political order. To put matters somewhat differently, genuine democracy is not possible without free men and women, secure in their persons and possessing inherent dignity, who may participate in democratic institutions as equals. These might of course be no more than empty words when set against social and economic realities. Yet this kind of radical criticism somehow misses the point. The words are not meant to describe reality so much as to pose a theoretical standard by which reality may be measured and judged. Or in Chief Justice Dickson's words: "the ultimate standard against which a limit on a right or freedom must be shown, despite its effect, to be reasonably and demonstrably justified."

The sovereignty of the law in a liberal democratic society is thus a concept which should encompass both the liberal and the democratic elements of the political order. Despite the sometimes compelling evidence presented by radical and Marxist critics of constitutionalism that the law is in effect an instrument of liberalism at the expense of democracy, the relationship is not so easily characterized in mutually exclusive terms. In practice, of course, in court decisions over matters which cut to the core of the capitalist economy—such as issues of trade union rights—liberalism may be twisted to the benefit of capital alone while the benefits of freedom of association are denied to labour.[7] Yet the latter instance primarily represents a contradiction within liberal discourse, since the right being claimed on behalf of unions is one anchored firmly, if expansively, within the structure of liberal freedoms which emerged with market society. As C.B. Macpherson has shown, political democracy grew out of the contradictions of liberal market assumptions.[8]

The theoretical difficulties of separating liberalism and democracy are illustrated by the shortcomings of those theorists—like Hayek or Nozick—who have seriously attempted to construct liberal philosophies that ignore the claims of democracy. In these cases, we are left with little more than rationalizations of legal barricades to protect economic privilege. Liberal-democratic theory is richer despite, or perhaps because of, its contradictions.

The nub of the Marxist critique of liberalism lies in the way in which capitalist society permits the separation of the economic from the political.[9] This latter observation (with which I am in complete agreement) is equally true with or without a dominant rights-based liberal discourse. For example, the British doctrine of parliamentary supremacy is founded just as firmly upon the separation of the economic and the political as North American rights-based variants. This point does not, however, obviate attention to the political—as Marxists have increasingly come to realize in recent years. Attention to the economic at the expense of the political does nothing to solve the political problems of democracy, particularly contradictions that are not primarily economic in nature, however intertwined they may be with economics. Contradictions of gender, race, and other distinctive group characteristics fall into this latter category.

It is my argument then that we must stay with the political to follow through some of the democratic implications of rights-based liberal discourse.

To recapitulate and return to the abortion issue: pre-Charter Canada was a relatively elitist parliamentary democracy in which elite domination was under increasing siege from democratic and egalitarian pressures. Electoral and parliamentary institutions showed limited capacity to respond to these pressures and some evidence of inability to cope.[10] The Charter and the jurisprudence beginning to grow up around it do not replace representative institutions, but they set a framework within which the claims of freedom and equality can be assessed. In the cases where claims conflict, criteria for reasonable balance or compromise may be adduced against the background of this framework. Elected institutions are still the forum within which the actual compromises must be struck and administrative mechanisms sketched out.

In the Morgentaler case, the clear direction given Parliament to legislate a time limit within which decisions to terminate a pregnancy will be at the sole discretion of the woman offers a model of this kind of judicious compromise. Although this aspect of the decision does not please the strong pro-choice advocates, a defence which is essentially grounded in the pro-choice argument may be advanced, granted that any time limit must be arbitrary and that Parliament will be seen to be leaning toward one side or the other when an actual limit is set. Nevertheless, the important point is that before the time limit is reached, a pregnant woman must be treated as a mature and autonomous moral agent. She may seek medical advice, but the moral decision to terminate or continue the pregnancy must be hers alone in the last instance. If within the framework of a reasonable time period, she is able to effectively exercise this choice—that is to say, abortion services are universally accessible and are equitably funded under existing medicare programmes—the restraint upon free choice which would come into effect after the time limit has passed does not constitute an unreasonable interference with a woman's freedom.

As the Supreme Court has indicated, at some point the foetus becomes a viable (as opposed to potential) human being. Just as obviously, one cannot escape consideration of the rights which are attached to viable life. Again, any legislated time must be arbitrary, but what is important is that on the one side the right of the woman to free choice is recognized and protected, while on the other the right of viable human life is balanced against the former right.

As Madame Justice Wilson explained:

> A developmental view of the foetus, on the other hand, supports a permissive approach to abortion in the early stages of pregnancy and a restrictive approach in the later stages. In the early stages the woman's autonomy would be absolute; her decision, reached in consultation with her physician, not to carry the foetus to term would be conclusive. The state would have no business inquiring into her reasons. Her reasons for having an abortion would, however, be the proper subject of inquiry at the later stages of pregnancy when the state's compelling interest in the protection of the foetus would justify it in prescribing conditions. The precise point in the development of the foetus at which the state's interest in its protection becomes "compelling" I leave to the informed judgment of the legislature which is in a position to receive guidance on the subject from all the relevant disciplines.

Perhaps the abortion issue will ironically furnish a model of how the courts and the legislatures can effectively interact in the name of both liberalism and democracy. As painful as the travail of participants in this most sensitive and delicate of controversies has been, from the point of view of liberal democratic theory it has the advantage of constituting a "hard case": others will be easier.

Once parliament decides on the precise balance, the remaining contention will probably be civil disobedience and possible acts of violence on the part of the only real losers in the process— the diehard pro-lifers who believe that all abortion is murder and that public complicity in abortion constitutes a form of evil. However vehement their passion, the pro-lifers were, I suggest, doomed to be losers from the start. Their quarrel is really with the dominant discourse of liberal democracy. Either in its conservative-communitarian form or in its more ambiguous rights-based form, the pro-life argument could only prevail by denial of the free moral agency of women. This in turn denies the basis of citizenship in a free and democratic society. [11]

The "inflation" of human rights claims is indeed a problem for contemporary liberal democracy. [12] As Burke long ago pointed out, the political metaphysician is of little assistance in the practical task of actualising rights in concrete form, and may indeed be a positive hindrance given the untidy compromises which politics usually necessitate. As Smiley has written, "the inflation of rights has the net effect of making conflict more uncompromising and less susceptible to solutions which are compromises among powerful values and interests." [13] Yet the "hard case" of abortion presents a more nuanced view of the problem. The Morgentaler decision suggests that it is possible to judiciously distinguish between competing rights claims when set against the context of Charter jurisprudence and a philosophical interpretation of the requirements of a "free and democratic" society. The normal majoritarian procedures of parliamentary democracy having failed to develop coherent compromises, it was judicial intervention which "kick-started" the legislative process into action, within the parameters of a compromise as effective as any likely to be found. This in turn rests squarely upon a rights-based political discourse.

Charles Taylor's "participatory society"—counterposed as it is to a "rights society"—is a dream or an ideal of a Canada which never was and which never will be, short of a profound structural transformation in the underlying political economy. The actually existing counter to the rights society is not participatory at all but resembles more the narrow, elitist and covertly (sometimes even overtly) antidemocratic politics which predated the rise of the rights model. Even in a populist guise, legislative majoritarianism which overrides the fundamental dignity of minorities—or, in the case of women, a statistical majority—is not democratic at all since it denies access to full participatory citizenship to some. In one sense this is merely a familiar paradox of representative democracy: majority rule can maintain its legitimacy only when it is self-limiting. If the majority can remove or limit the equality rights of minorities it loses its claim to being a true majority: that is, a majority in the formation of which all elements of the society have freely and equally participated.

Entrenched constitutional protection for rights is thus an important, perhaps crucial, element in the mix of law and politics appropriate to an effective liberal democracy. It is by no means the only such element, however. The introduction of the Charter has not displaced politics of either the electoral or legislative variety, any more than the Bill of Rights has displaced or completely judicialized politics in the United States over the past two centuries. It is helping to redefine politics, but the point here surely is that the same forces in Canadian society which helped to give rise to the Charter and the new emphasis on equality rights would have sought to redefine existing politics in any event. Nor has the Charter displaced politics at the mass level. Despite the fears of some observers that political demobilization at the grass roots level would result from the judicialization of politics, the interested parties in the abortion issue have clearly not lowered the intensity of their political activity as a result of judicial intervention. Perhaps the invention of the term "rights society" is simply too reckless an extrapolation of a single element—albeit an important element—to the level of global analysis.

There can be no doubt that the dominant discourse of Canadian politics has shifted over the past three decades toward a greater emphasis upon rights-based liberal arguments. A shift in emphasis should not be mistaken for a transformation in the nature of the society. Perhaps the new emphasis upon rights is best understood against the backdrop of another long change which has been in slow process in the Canadian political culture for decades: the democratization of political institutions and practices. The old mechanisms of elite accommodation have been growing more attenuated with time, not just in politics but in many areas of Canadian life. One of the primary reasons for the shift toward the language of rights is that the old "democratic" institutions were simply not democratic enough. One of the primary effects of the new rights-based liberal discourse may well be to infuse greater democratic purpose into institutions which have been too elitist and too exclusivist.

Rights discourse no doubt has a certain tendency to fragment the politics of social movements. A preoccupation with advancing the claims of one's own group through the complicated legal and/or legislative process may well induce a tendency to downplay solidarity with others. This may of course be a trend which is much more pronounced at the moment when the Charter is, in effect, finding its feet in the political and legal process.[14] Moreover, the

Charter itself was only recently in the process of definition—a process which does not appear to have yet halted. Under such circumstances, a pronounced emphasis upon establishing rights as they pertain directly to particular minority groups is scarcely surprising.

The democratic implication of rights language is tied to liberalism in one other way. There are two different concepts of rights which exist side by side in the Canadian tradition. The earlier, and historically stronger, concept is that of collective rights. In the BNA Act of 1867 there was mention of the collective rights of "the Queen's Protestant and Roman Catholic Subjects" with regard to education. During the period leading up to the 1980 Quebec referendum on sovereignty-association the air was rife with claims of the "right to national self-determination." In the present constitutional context there is much discussion of the recognition of the collective rights of the native peoples. And, of course, there is the proposed recognition of Quebec as a "distinct society" under the Meech Lake Accord. The newer, and historically weaker, concept is the liberal idea of individual rights, as exemplified in the Charter.

The problem posed by collective rights is that rights claims can only be made on behalf of designated bearers of those rights. Collective rights are borne by collective bodies. In the case of denominational educational rights, for instance, the Catholic church holds a privileged position due to its influence over publicly-funded separate schools in many provinces. In the case of Meech Lake, it is the government of Quebec which obviously gains in power and prestige from the "distinct society" clause. (Whether the society, distinct or otherwise, of Quebec will make comparable gains remains a moot point.)

The strongest case for collective rights is that mounted by the native peoples on behalf of constitutional recognition of aboriginal self-government. Native peoples have never been clearly inside the Canadian political community and in crucial ways have always been at least partially outside the definition of that community (treaties are a formal symbol of this status). However strong their claims, a problem remains: if collective aboriginal rights are entrenched, it is the native or band governments which will perforce be recognized as the holders of these rights. The problem of individuals or groups within native societies that are not fully recognized by the native governments (for instance the claims to status by native women who have

married white men embodied in the Lavell and Bédard cases[15])
will not be magically whisked away by the wand of collective rights.

In general, it is the nature of collective rights that they must
be vested in some corporate or collective body. The difficulty is
that these corporate bodies are then embedded in the constitutional and political fabric. This may well be a prescription for
conservatism. The failure of the former Parti Québécois
government's attempt to break the stranglehold of religion on
Quebec education by organizing school boards on lingustic rather
than sectarian lines is an example of the dead hand of the constitutional past weighing on the present.

For reasons which have entirely escaped my understanding,
the political Left in both Quebec and English Canada has shown
considerable sympathy for the concept of collective rights and has
often denigrated the idea of individual rights as reactionary. On
the contrary, collective rights reinforce the failing structures of
elite accommodation and may be the enemy of progress. It is
surely no accident that it is women's groups which have been in
the forefront of opposition to Meech Lake: feminists are right to
be at least suspicious of how the "distinct society" clause may be
used by the Quebec state to trump women's rights. Whether this
will actually happen is of course a matter of speculation, but
generalized anxiety is a poor basis upon which to build the consent
upon which constitutions are supposed to rest.

Individual rights suffer less from this debilitating baggage.
Such rights are borne by people, not by institutions or governments. More fluidity is imparted to the political process when the
discourse turns on individual rights. How things fall out will be
affected more by the active elements of the society than by
sclerotic establishments embedded in the structures of the state.
This need not rule out the recognition of groups as politically
relevant. The Trudeau legacy in language rights offers a kind of
synthesis between the individual and collective concepts: individuals may freely choose to avail themselves of official protections for either of two entrenched lingusitic communities. Let us
call this concept one of group, rather than collective, rights. This
approach does not deny the sociological fact of the organization
of society into groups that may well be of dominant significance
in the development of the individuals' sense of identity. In the
case of language, the Constitution recognizes the sociological and
historical priority of the English- and French-speaking com-

munities. But it does not entail or require any collective body as corporate rights-bearer.

There are distinct elements of group rights in the Charter, beyond the language clauses. Section 15 (Equality Rights) for instance begins with the statement that "every individual is equal before and under the law...," but then goes on to specify no less than nine distinct group identities that must not in particular constitute grounds for discrimination in the equal protection and equal benefit of the law. These are: "race, national or ethnic origin, colour, religion, sex, age or mental or physical disability." Of these, only religion might be taken to constitute a voluntary association; all the others are involuntary associations which might in certain circumstances adversely affect an individual's status given certain prejudices that may prevail in society.

15(2) then goes on to indicate that the above "does not preclude any law, program or activity that has as its object the amelioration of conditions of disadvantaged individuals or groups including those that are disadvantaged because of race, national or ethnic origin, colour, religion, sex, age or mental or physical disability." This latter, or affirmative action, subsection does not identify particular groups as disadvantaged but instead identifies only the general situation of disadvantage and protects affirmative action programmes that have as their object the amelioration of conditions of disadvantage. Evidence of disadvantage would presumably have to be adduced in particular cases. Given the sociological and economic realities of present-day Canada, women should have little difficulty in demonstrating a situation of disadvantage. For instance, affirmative action programs in hiring by public institutions would be acceptable even to the extent that they might involve preference for female over male candidates (otherwise a form of discrimination in itself). If we permit ourselves a moment of optimism, we might envisage a future in which women could no longer claim the protection of 15(2) because the factual grounds of disadvantage had disappeared (true equality prevailed). Thus a degree of flexibility is built into the concept of group rights.

An alternative Section 15 that was based on collective, rather than group, rights would identify particular groups as disadvantaged, would necessarily entail recognition of particular collective or corporate bodies as bearers of these rights, and would be extremely rigid and inflexible in the face of changing sociological circumstances. Such a Section 15 would look somewhat similar to Section 93 of the BNA Act on denominational educational rights, or to Section 1 of the Meech Lake Accord establishing the role of the government of Quebec in preserving and promoting Quebec's distinct society. Such a Section 15 would be a very imprudent piece of constitutional writing.

To the extent that the Charter is grounded upon the recognition of individual and group rights it may be a very flexible instrument for extending democratic equality. Further erosion of this base in the direction of collective rights, as Meech Lake suggests and as some groups and individuals have demanded, would be retrograde and, in my view, fraught with conservative threats to the democratic principle. Once again, liberalism has its advantages for democracy.

In conclusion, the warnings of such critics of rights-based liberalism as Smiley, Taylor, Sandel and others have been salutary in pointing out the potential pitfalls along the path of this political tradition. But the hard case of the abortion controversy suggests that these warnings have sometimes been overdrawn and may not be grounded quite as firmly as they seem at first glance. Above all, the abortion issue casts light upon a surprising subterranean relationship between liberalism and democracy. Parliamentary institutions, despite their legitimating cloak of majority rule, require liberalism not so much to make them freer as to make them more genuinely democratic.

Postscript

Since the Morgentaler decision, two further Supreme Court judgements relevant to the abortion controversy have been brought bown. One was a non-desision in which the Court dodged a claim on behalf of the rights of the fetus on the grounds that there was, after Morgentaler, no abortion law to be contested. The second, and more significant, decision was made quickly at an emergency sitting to hear an appeal by a Quebec woman, Chantal Daigle, against a Quebec court ruling upholding her former lover's injunction blocking her from undergoing an abortion. The Court upheld Daigle, but during the hearing it was revealed that she had already defied the injunction by having an abortion in the United States.

Two points relevant to our argument emerge from the Daigle case. First, it is evident that whatever the ultimate resolution of the question of fetal rights, a woman's autonomy cannot be infringed by the putative rights of the father to force her to act, in effect, as an instrument of his will. This amplifies the liberal-democratic principle of the majority decision in Morgentaler. Second, in practical, as opposed to theoretical, terms, the question of the legality or illegality of abortion is, and always has been, moot: women will have abortions, as they have always had abortions, under any legal regime. The relevant question is under what conditions and what terms abortions take place. The pro-life argument, insofar as it claims relevance to public policy, thus labours under a cloud of unreality, and must retreat to a more rarified level of moral abstraction.

Notes

1   Among others, see Donald Smiley, *The Canadian Charter of Rights and Freedoms, 1981* (Toronto: Ontario Economic Council, 1981) and "The Charter, citizenship and political conflict in Canada" (unpublished paper, 1986); Michael J. Sandel, "The political theory of the procedural republic," in Allan C. Hutchinson and Patrick Monahan (eds.), *The Rule of Law: Ideal or Ideology* (Toronto: Carswell, 1987), 85-96; Charles Taylor, "Alternative Futures: Legitimacy, Identity and Alienation in Late Twentieth-Century Canada," in Alan Cairns and Cynthia Williams (eds.), *Constitutionalism, Citizenship and Society in Canada* (Toronto: University of Toronto Press, 1985), 183-230; J.R. Mallory, "The continuing evolution of Canadian constitutionalism," in Cairns and Williams, contrasts an older constitutional tradition of bargaining and compromise in a plural community with a newer rights-regime based "on the ultimate and overwhelming authority of strict legality...a law-oriented rather than a politically oriented society" (93).

2   The recent case of the Saskatchewan government and its legislation regarding the linguistic rights of the Francophone minority offers a textbook case of this problem. Whether or not the assurances of good intentions on the part of the Devine cabinet are sincere, the Francophone minority was bound to reject these unsecured assurances in an appeal beyond the provincial legislature.

3   Alan Cairns, "The embedded state: state-society relations in Canada," in Keith Banting (ed.), *State and Society: Canada in Comparative Perspective* (Toronto:University of Toronto Press, 1986), 53-86.

4   The conservative philosopher George Grant has rather strangely articulated the rights-based liberal argument against abortion: Sheila and George Grant, "Abortion and rights: the value of political freedom," in E. Fairweather and I. Gentles (eds.), *The Right to Birth* (Toronto:Anglican Book Centre, 1976); and George Grant, *English-Speaking Justice* (Toronto: Anansi, 1985). Taxed with philosophical incongruity in an interview, Grant replied that "modern

bourgeois Canadians...take the language of liberalism as the only moral language they've got. Therefore one has to use it in speaking about such matters. One has to be ironic, in the classical sense." In Larry Schmidt, (ed.), *George Grant in Process: Essays and Conversations* (Toronto: Anansi, 1978), 18. William Mathie offers a critically sympathetic, if rather murky, commentary on Grant's argument in "Reason, revelation and liberal justice: on George Grant's analysis of *Roe v. Wade*," *Canadian Journal of Political Science*, 19 (1986), 443-66.

5   A Gallup poll released as recently as April 1988 indicates that 69% of Canadians agree that a decision on abortion should rest with a woman and her doctor; only 25.6% disagree: "Abortion poll reports 69% favour choice," *The Globe and Mail*, April 14, 1988.

6   See the decisions in *The Queen v. Big M Drug Mart Ltd* (1985) and *The Queen v. David Edwin Oakes* (1986).

7   See the devastating analysis of the courts' reasoning on the issue of the right to strike in Leo Panitch and Donald Swartz, *From Consent to Coercion: the Assault on Trade Union Freedoms* (2nd ed.; Toronto:Garamond, 1988).

8   C.B. Macpherson, *The Real World of Democracy* (Toronto: The Canadian Broadcasting Corporation, 1965).

9   Ellen Wood, "The Separation of the Economic and the Political," *New Left Review*, 127 (1981).

10 At least this is the conclusion of the fashionable "ungovernability" and "overload" theses which spread in Western political science in the 1970s.

11 For a vividly chilling vision of the illiberal, repressive, and authoritarian state necessary to fulfill the antifeminist agenda of moral majoritarian pro-lifers see Margaret Atwood's 1985 novel *The Handmaid's Tale* (Toronto: McClelland and Stewart).

12 Thomas C. Pocklington, "Against Inflating Human Rights," *The Windsor Year Book of Access to Justice*, 2 (1982).

13 Donald V. Smiley, "The Charter, Citizenship."

14 F.L. Morton, "The political impact of the Canadian Charter of Rights and Freedoms," *Canadian Journal of Political Science*, 20 (1987), 31-56. We should not, of course, forget that the Americans have had a bill of rights for two centuries, while Canadians have been grappling with the implications of the Charter for only half a decade, and with the equality rights provisions for less than that.

15 *Attorney General of Canada v. Lavell and Bédard*, in Peter Russell (ed.), *Leading Constitutional Decisions* (3rd ed.; Ottawa: Carleton University Press, 1982), 421-38.

MASS COMMUNICATION AND POLITICS

'GOING PUBLIC':
MASS COMMUNICATIONS & EXECUTIVE FEDERALISM

Edwin R. Black, Queen's University

The lifeblood of a political community runs through its communications. The quality of the group's life depends on the accessibility, content, and particular structures of its dominant information systems. Federations such as Canada depend critically on a multiplicity of communication systems, nearly all of which are perceived to suffer from circulatory imperfections. Despite a large literature on the Canadian federation, important questions concerning political communication[1] have been overlooked. A beginning on the subject can be made with a consideration of executive federalism.

Donald V. Smiley authoritatively identified and defined executive federalism as: "the relations between elected and appointed officials of the two orders of government in federal-provincial interactions."[2] The framework of discourse created by such interactions is today the foundation of a strong and vigorous political community, the most visible part of which involves the country's major political leaders. Smiley argued in 1967 that if Canada could not become a political community—one community and not two—then it would not be worth preserving. In such campaigning against the Deux Nations theory, Smiley ignored the evidence of his own observations. Admittedly, the intergovernmental relations community was, and is, a small one and not what either Smiley or those yearning after a single Canadian 'nation' seemed to be seeking. It is, however, a most important one and one that has as its foundation a number of other political communities, at least nine in number.[3]

During the two postwar decades very little intergovernmental business was conducted in public or even in such a way that the mass media were aware of it. Continuously growing networks of inter-official relationships were created, which in turn stimulated even more business. These networks grew rapidly, extending from the early profession-based groups to encompass almost every bureaucrat who ever dealt with another government. The 1960s began with a jumble of 'cooperative federalism' arrangements that terribly confused what parliamentary accountability there was in the system. Smiley has shown how political executives had to begin disentangling and reordering network activities within their own governments in order to gain some control over important spending and policy decisions.

This centralization of all the policy-relevant communications within individual governments was a necessary prelude to development of a full-blown 'executive federalism.' The restructuring resulted in a substantial chunk of intergovernmental business being moved out of the bureaucratic levels and up to the potentially more visible levels of the politician. Despite this, both the mass media and their audiences have been left unaware of most of the horse-trading going on between and among governments in this country. Whether deliberately or not, the public has consequently been excluded from much of the political system's most important communication arenas. The result is reinforcement rather than diminution of either the arcane or the elitist character of our polity.

Six developments in the past two decades need to be noted:

1 Changes in the ideological consensus respecting the proper role of governments in Canada;

2 Overt increases in the use of symbolism in our political discourse. As Alan Cairns has shown, the 1982 Charter has added new and developing vocabularies as well as more vocal interest groups to the national arena;

3 The growing perception of the first ministers conferences as a form of domestic political 'summitry';

4 The replacement of the railways by broadcasting as Canada's central nervous system; and

5 The major shift from verbal to visual media in our political communications, together with

6 A mass media marriage of the idea of 'open covenants openly arrived at' to notions of political legitimacy.

Only a few of these points require elaboration.

Changing Ideologies

Not a lot must be said about changes in the climate of opinions about the proper role of the state in society today. In Canada at least, the late 1940s and 1950s saw a fairly widespread consensus on the topic. It seems now to have vanished. Instead we have a widening gap between political leaders and the general public and between the demands that voters put on elected politicians and what may loosely be called the mass media orthodoxy on the role of the state. At this basic level in our system, the communication channels are carrying anything but clear and consistent messages.

Governments and observers of government need to realize that our country's political news is shaped at its most fundamental level by the visual production values that were developed fifty years ago in order to transform ex-waitresses and sodajerks into credible movie stars. When broadcasting became radio-with-pictures the infant TV industry rushed to hire the only sound-and-picture specialists around. Hollywood's production values became those of television entertainment and the same values now totally dominate television news departments.

Political Summitry

This gives rise to a basic problem which is seldom appreciated outside the TV studio. Of all social activity, the practice of politics is at once the most verbal and the least pictorial. Visual representation of its essence is impossible. Shots of a political conference tell you nothing and cannot possibly compete on the little screen with the appeal of pictures of beauty contests, winning goals, or tanks blasting the homes of helpless refugees. Nonetheless, television news producers have to make some kind of feeble bricks out of this straw, if only because government regulators say so. Solutions to this problem are many, partial, and all very unsatisfying. One of the responses in this country was to borrow the *ersatz* glamour from the international scene and to treat the first ministers conferences as a form of domestic 'summitry.'

Still to come to everybody's flickering black box is a television producer with the wit to caricature the Meech Lake agreement as a Canadian Runnymede, one that produced a Magna Carta for the barons of federal politics. Divided loyalties and regional chieftains might well justify some representation of executive federalism as a semi-democratic form of feudalism. Whatever the image in the centre, political activists in the peripheries will continue to promote the equality of both provinces and premiers as a useful counter-balance to Ottawa's modified majoritarianism.

Verbal to Visual Shift

The mass media have always exaggerated personality, and, as our modern equivalent of the parish pump gossips of another age, so they should. Anyone who thinks image politics is a recent invention has never heard or read the slogan "The Old Man, The Old Flag, and The Old Policy" with which the Tories fought the Liberals' proposal of 'Unrestricted Reciprocity' in the 1891 election campaign. The politics of personality is something we have always had. So too with 'disinformation' campaigns. Richard Needham is useful in reminding us that back in the 'good old days' of the mass media—if they ever existed—when print was king, newspapers used to "go to great pains to give honest, accurate accounts of the lies told by politicians."[4] The moaning about the lack of a 'national' newspaper comes from elites that are print-focused and centrally-oriented—not from literate, provincially-oriented general populations. Few newspapers have lost much circulation because they didn't carry enough news of the capital. They did lose subscribers, though, during the 1950s and 1960s when they failed to keep up with the great shift from words to pictures. Politicians who ignored their TV image had the same problem.

All the mass media are essentially art forms which have the power of imposing their own working assumptions, as Harold Innis pointed out. Few people realize the incredible influence that the institutional or vocational ideologies in these industries exert on their products. Nowhere is it more evident than in the mass entertainment industries, including the press.

Journalists must live with a contradictory orientation in their occupational mores. To authenticate their information reports, they are driven to seek out and quote authorities. In the political arena, however, the restless search for novelty puts better journalists into constant opposition to the society's first-order authorities, an antagonism they justify by quoting second-order authorities such as interest group leaders and opposition politicians. What damage this does to the clarity of our political communications can only be wondered about. The effect may well be close to an observation made by Eric Nicol: "Confederation has been like a mail-order bra: intended to contain and uplift, it has instead drawn attention to the cleavage."[5]

Legitimacy and Going Public

Woodrow Wilson did not get very far in promoting the practice of 'open covenants openly arrived at.' Ever since the parliamentary hearings of 1981-82, the Canadian mass media have done rather better. The local version of the notion is that, to be considered legitimate, all First Ministers' Conferences must be open to the public and press; otherwise, both the negotiators and their agreements are highly suspect. It should be mentioned—if only because nobody has done so thus far—that the promotion of this idea by press commentators seems to be remarkably self-serving.

In contrast to the regular run of First Ministers' Conferences, two important features distinguish those held on the constitution during the 1980s: private negotiations-by-exhaustion at critical points, and the creation of new pressure groups. The dangers of relying on exhausted premiers to draft sound constitutional principles during all-night sessions were easy to see. Less easy, though, would be trying to judge how such behaviour was represented in the constitutional symbolism entering into the political communication stream. All-night sessions have not been the only private aspects of the FMCs. The 1980s have seen an ever-increasing use of longer and longer private lunches and dinners to hammer out the difficult issues which politicians refused to expose to the public. Various public interests and interest groups, angry at previous exclusions from decision-making processes, were able to use the Charter, Aboriginal, and Meech Lake experiences to seize meaningful roles in the constitutional game. The 1987-88 attempts to make Pierre Trudeau's constitutional arrangements more acceptable to Quebecers were particularly noteworthy for the way in which these special interest groups demonstrated the power of their newly-won voices in the system. They took almost every possible opportunity, as Alan Cairns has pointed out, "to denounce government domination of the constitutional amending process as illegitimate." As a result, the status of federalism as a constitutional organizing principle was significantly weakened, and "government control of the amending process, once considered natural, now appears as an arrogant elitism."[6]

A democrat might ask why Canadians should ever have accepted government domination and control of the amendment process. Various explanations related to the low level of populism in central Canadian politics are plausible. It is more likely, however, that the virtual invisibility of the previous constitutional processes to most of the population—all those who were not part of the intergovernmental network—let the process remain unchallenged. Even now, some years after the 1982 Act, the larger part of even the attentive publics remain totally unaware of the first use made of the 1982 amendment provisions. What their knowledge or participation would have added to that first amendment might be debated, but only academics would see merit in doing so.

If conferences resulted in governmental elites making private agreements that nobody knew about, we would have much to complain about. However, this is not the case. The first line of accountability is not to television program producers but to the legislatures. Usually it is in the legislatures that conference agreements are first given a publicly-meaningful form. Despite this, the uncertainty of our politicians in matters of political communication causes repeated embarrassment as the press gallery insists that whatever the conference it should 'go public' for most, if not all, of its waking hours. Were they to do so, the usual result would probably be 'empty covenants openly arrived at.'[7] As, in most cases, any government representative at an intergovernmental conference can object to 'going public,' factors bearing on the decision bear some consideration. They are many, too many for easy discussion here, so a list must suffice. From the perspective of a single government they would include: whether or not a general election or a by-election is being held in the near future; the political sensitivity of the conference topic; mode of each cabinet's operation—departmental, collegial or institutionalized; the delegate's relative mastery of the topic; and the competitive implications for rival ministers and ministries at home (effects will vary here according to the nature of each government and its working cabinet system).

Consideration must be given to how well heads of government and other participants know and trust each other, and how well they are plugged into the generalist and specialist communication networks. Variations in the experience levels of key personnel are also relevant. Taking conferences into the public sphere is all about large-scale consciousness-raising; for politicians, for administrative elites, for pressure groups, and not least, for the voting public. Finally, from a communications perspective one might wonder just how much consideration is ever given to the problem of establishing the general context within which the public will come to understand or misunderstand an important issue.

Channels of Misinformation

To follow the course of intergovernmental conference discussions, one must discriminate clearly between the different interpretations given to the same agenda item. This is not the same as saying that any one problem has varying regional manifestations and priorities or that they require different approaches or solutions, although that is seldom acknowledged or perhaps even recognized by observers in the press and elsewhere.

The non-participants in First Ministers' Conferences are always prone to consider agenda items and the premiers' responses to them in terms of the observers' own Ottawa-centred, regional, or other political biases. Sometimes these biases are those of the inward-looking Ottawa Press Gallery, or of Toronto and Westmount. As Hugh MacLennan's character said, "The trouble with this whole country is that it's divided up into little puddles with big fish in each one of them." At other times, the vision is larger, like that of Nova Scotia's Sam Slick: "Provincialism and nationality are different degrees of the same thing, and both take their rise in the same feeling."[8]

Most conference participants, however, do see and understand differences in regional problems and priorities. What they frequently miss is that the same words do not carry the same political meaning around the table, let alone across the country. This problem in political communication has always been with us in Canada, and probably in most federations. As is well-known, jurisdictions are divided not simply because of administrative efficiencies but in order to accommodate the system to particularist priorities and solutions.

There is yet another reason. Particular concepts are understood differently not simply over time but across cultures and subcultures. Education is a good example. This is basically a problem in political communication and it is with us still. It becomes particularly acute when intergovernmental discourse revolves around politically trendy phrases such as high tech, health care, and universal access, or the heavily value-laden language of 'rights': the right to work, to life, and to property. It is too much to expect many people in Ontario, for example, to know that when the premiers of Newfoundland or British Columbia say something about 'universal access to medical care' they may well have in mind the difficulties and costs of providing physical access for people on the Labrador coast or in the Queen Charlottes.

> Many times what appears to be the same problem gives rise to quite diverse responses because the participants in public debate often choose to deal with different questions and frequently disagree fundamentally about what constitutes the right question. At heart, the questions and answers are usually inspired by different images of what Confederation is all about, or ought to be. The resulting confusion is enormous and it produces public argumentation of such complexity that few laymen can comprehend it.[9]

It is hardly surprising that communication between political beings is so difficult. Consider that in the human sphere so much of what each of us feels most deeply cannot help but seem to be mere trivia and a monumental bore to almost everybody else.[10] Politics, particularly in this country, is too complicated to be explained on television with eighteen-second quotations, a bar graph, two icons, and a bit of tape from the library. It all gets reduced to personalities, to a question of which *prima donna* will beat the others in their joint efforts to plunder the public purse or to sell the state lock, stock, and oil barrel to the highest foreign bidder.

It is not to be wondered, then, that the public and its commentators usually end up by dismissing many intergovernmental conferences as just another shadow game played by and for lawyer-politicians. It is a large failure in political understanding and its communication, and a failure that conceals the larger issues which are often at stake; important questions about who will get and keep what share of the public purse and public power.

Too often Canadian political communications seem to get hung up on a busy signal. Whenever they do get through, the static is so fierce that it distorts all the messages. The illness not often being recognized, there are few prescriptions for the troubles that beset the public's awareness and understanding of federal processes. Some feasible responses include: firstly, annual, public hearings by legislative committees to review issues coming up in FMCs, as this might improve the local context of meaning; secondly, moving FMCs away from the country's capital would change some of the media effects. Not only would the meeting and its issues get much more attention in the host region, but the news coverage would generally pass out of the hands of the Ottawa press gallery and into those of the best local reporters. The regional or local press is unlikely to be any more ignorant about the issues and in all likelihood would be better placed to report the problem within a meaningful context even if it were only a regional one. The two linguistic press cultures might also find the differences between their respective perceptions reduced, although one should not hope for too much. Thirdly, assigning an officer in each government to think about the mass media effects of each aspect of a conference might be salutary. What kind of pictures will result from this open, or that closed session? Apart from the choice verbal snippets, what 'visuals' can be provided? What will be the pictorial clichés used and can they be improved on by planning? Finally, discussion has proceeded as if every conference were open or closed, and as though governments did not try to manipulate the mass media. This obviously is not the case. In light of the relative clumsiness of most participants in managing the press, closed sessions of conferences might devote more discussion and frankness to questions of 'leaks' and 'leakiness.'

Whatever our complaints about intergovernmental conferences, we would do well to remember with John W. Dafoe that they have brought us "peace with friction for a century." Will Canada be as fortunate in the next century? The answer lies primarily in the shape of general communication systems: how local, provincial, Canadian, elitist, or even political will they be? The problem is one for the near to medium-term future, not the immediate present. The politically attentive elites are not deprived of information. As Michael Valpy has pointed out: "Canada is the only country in the world where you can buy a book on federal-provincial relations at the airport."[11]

The immediate problem, as has been often remarked, lies in the swamping of the country's popular channels by a foreign culture. The absorption and substitution of foreign institutional and general political values has proceeded rapidly—ever since television captured John F. Kennedy, the American presidency, and U.S. politics for starring roles in a never-ending soap opera. The bigger American stage sparks the envy of almost every ambitious Canadian journalist. They frequently follow and know American politics better than their own. A search for domestic parallels to foreign political sensation is the first order of the day whether the newsroom is in Toronto, Vancouver, or Montreal. The more a Canadian process or institution can be made to resemble an American, the better chance it has of surviving the news director's cuts. The greatest risk of not making it into the public prints is run by uniquely Canadian processes or communications, those without obvious U.S. counterparts. A Canadian premier is far more important than American state governors. The federalism of Madison and Jay is now highly centralized and has nothing to match First Ministers' Conferences and other intergovernmental meetings as the major public system of political conciliation and compromise. These, it might be argued, are among the most ignored or misunderstood of Canadian processes in the country's mass media.

Canadian news reporters and producers exhibit a near-colonial reverence for the red, white, and blue production codes espoused by network vice-presidents in New York and Los Angeles. Despite a warning from Marshall McLuhan more than thirty years ago, most of the players on the intergovernmental stages have paid little heed to the transforming effects. McLuhan warned: "The new media are not ways of relating us to the old 'real' world: they are the real world and they reshape what remains of the old world at will."[12] Scholars too have left almost totally unexplored questions about the ways in which mass media professional, craft, and vocational ideologies have shaped our federalism and our system of political communication. The new reality for federalist politics in Canada can be simply stated: so far as the voters are concerned, if it's not on TV, it doesn't exist.

Canada may well be destined to have a vigorous mass media completely devoid of domestic political intelligence. Where people consistently pay more attention to the communications of foreigners than to their neighbours, they soon lose all sense of community.

Notes

1 Political communications refers here both to the relevant institutions—intergovernmental networks and the mass media—and to its specialized vocabulary and grammar.

2   Donald V. Smiley, *Canada in Question: Federalism in the Eighties*, 3rd ed. (Toronto: McGraw-Hill Ryerson, 1980), 91.

3   One for each of nine provinces. Whether a significant political communications network operates in Ontario is debatable. Certainly there is less evidence of provincial identification among its citizens than is the case in any other province.

4   R. J. Needham, *A Friend in Needham* (Toronto: Macmillan, 1969), 44.

5   Eric Nicol, *100 Years of What?* (Toronto: Ryerson, 1966), 44.

6   Alan C. Cairns, "Ottawa, the Provinces, and Meech Lake" (a paper delivered at a University of Calgary conference Nov. 19, 1987).

7   This quirk in our political discourse sounds like a witch-doctor's painkiller for Meech Lake.

8   From Hugh MacLennan, *Two Solitudes* (New York: Duel, Sloan and Pearce, 1945), 28, and T. C. Haliburton, *Sam Slick The Clockmaker* (London: G. Routledge, 1904), 271.

9   From Edwin R. Black, *Divided Loyalties* (Montreal: McGill-Queen's University Press, 1975), 2.

10 Alden Nowlan, *Various Persons Named Kevin O'Brien*, (Toronto: Clark, Irwin, 1973), 32.

11 *The Globe and Mail*, August 8, 1981.

12 Marshall McLuhan, *CounterTSALB* (Toronto: McClelland and Stewart, 1954).

BROADCASTING IN THE FEDERATION: NATIONAL POWER, DIVIDED PURPOSE

D. E. Smith, University of Saskatchewan

Part One: Broadcasting and Federalism

In his latest book, *The Federal Condition in Canada*, Don Smiley urges his readers to look at federalism with new eyes: to see how federalism in government shapes and is shaped by other aspects of human organization.[1] In obedience to that injunction this paper will examine the contribution of broadcasting, a federally confirmed power regulated by a quasi-autonomous agency, to the definition of provincial identity. Since this analysis will be confined largely to one province, there is a need perhaps to justify so parochial a focus. First, information available in Saskatchewan on broadcasting is limited solely to that province with no comparable material on the subject elsewhere; not for the first time sources dictate research. Second, since it is the intent of the study to examine both the public and private sector, the scope of a larger enterprise which took a multi-provincial approach would be impractical for a single paper. Finally, there is analytical utility in adopting a case-study approach of this federal activity as it affects a single province. More than most topics in Canadian politics, the discussion of broadcasting is enveloped in a vocabulary of nationalism that disguises both the local and provincial dimensions of the undertaking. To the extent that broadcasting in the units of the federal system is acknowledged, recognition is invariably couched in a centrist language that speaks of regional sensitivity. This paper will argue, however, that broadcasting's development has been the product not only of direction from the centre but of societal influences manifested from within the province. Moreover, the public and private worlds of Canadian broadcasting represent more than rival commitments to broadcasting as a trust or as an industry; at the base of that duality lies a conflict of national sentiments whose origins can most clearly be examined at the level of the province.

While there are distinctive features about Saskatchewan as they touch this field of activity—geographic isolation from centres of large population in other jurisdictions being among the most significant—the organizational and theoretical implications of this activity for federalism are not particularistic. But if broadcasting sheds light on the operation of Canadian federalism, what contribution do the traditional concepts of federalism offer in return? How applicable to broadcasting are such elements of the federal vocabulary as hierarchy, orders of independence, centralization, and decentralization? Or, again, what is the contribution of such common notions in federal literature as bargaining, reciprocity or redundancy? If these fail as explanatory devices, then what criteria are to be used to evaluate broadcasting, or is the student left with theoretically neutral measures such as effectiveness, acceptance or, even, survival? These are basic yet vast questions which no single paper can answer. That they occur is testimony to the provocative writing of Don Smiley. If the academic prizes, as is sometimes said, go to the individuals who think up the *new* questions, then Don Smiley is the winner.[2] Throughout his many investigations of federalism, he has challenged his readers to re-think accepted truths and, ultimately, to ask of the institutions or processes they study: why does or ought federalism to matter?

Applied to broadcasting, does the fact that it is a matter of federal jurisdiction, or that for more than fifty years there has been a national system in the form of the Canadian Broadcasting Corporation (CBC), responsible to Parliament or to an agency of central government, have any implication for Canadian federalism? Presumably, the answer is yes, since in a jurisdictional conflict between federal and provincial governments, the former has the authority of the courts to defend its claim. Again, the CBC possesses terms of reference which impose a uniformity in broadcasting that affects all provinces. Notwithstanding the grey areas of educational and cable broadcasting, these self-evident propositions, if left unexamined, convey a picture of centralism that is true but incomplete; for as much as broadcasting has contributed to building the Canadian nation, it has as well affirmed and even strengthened provincial consciousness. Evolution of this latter strand, however, has been both slow and hesitant. Before 1932 broadcasting was conceived as local or on occasion regional in impact, while after that date and due to a coalition of forces, particularly the activity of the Canadian Radio League, it became a national endeavour that assigned a reduced role to local stations. Again, in the 1960s and in response to state policies implemented in turn by a federal regulatory body, the balance of broadcasting shifted toward promoting provincial along with national and local objectives. In a paper which takes federalism as its primary concern, it is worthy of comment that these adjustments occurred in the absence of both provincial government consultation and intergovernmental conflict. Despite its importance for the provinces, provincial governments have by and large excluded themselves from the field.

As a scientific phenomenon broadcasting knows no political boundaries and in the first decade of its infancy policy-makers were equally dismissive of geography. Only gradually but with the inexorable imperative of territorial federalism did public policy in broadcasting take geography as its appropriate unit. In response to the growth in complexity of communications, institutions and practices developed to order the new technology and these in turn helped mould the society. By itself this recursive relationship of institutions and society constitutes a determinative influence on provincial definition. Equally important for the units of the federal system, though of different origin, has been an allocation of values since the 1960s that promotes a new set of national objectives in the form of official bilingualism. The effect in Saskatchewan has been to depreciate local French programming in favour of provincial and national concerns.

Taken together, adjustments in broadcasting practices have had the effect of fostering provincialism, a development some might deem as inevitable in the larger context of federal-provincial relations that have produced strong, more aggressive provinces. Whether or not the more general evolution of Canadian federalism explains the particular development evident in the subject of this paper, the implications of the change for societal federalism have attracted little comment. There are two reasons for the silence: both have to do with attributions of bias in the literature on broadcasting.

A decade ago, in his study *Canadian Broadcasting History Resources in English: Critical Mass or Mess?*, John Twomey wrote that:

> The large number of official reports flowing from government initiated inquiries into broadcasting, (e.g., Royal Commissions, parliamentary broadcasting committees, the Special Senate Committee on Mass Media, and the CRTC) dominate the literature of broadcasting in Canada. As a consequence, published materials on broadcasting tend to be concerned primarily with legislation,

administration, and regulation. They tend to neglect programming content and its social and cultural role in Canadian life, and largely omit the very considerable role of private broadcasting in favour of detailed information on the Canadian Broadcasting Corporation.[3]

More recent history offers no reason to revise this observation. The public world of broadcasting still overshadows the private, while within the public the emphasis on structure and control occurs at the expense of attention to delivery of service. In their *Report of the Task Force on Broadcasting Policy* (1986), Caplan and Sauvageau devote only five-and-a-half pages to provincial broadcasting and another seven to regional television.[4] In light of both the size of the CBC and its extensive mandate, there may be good reason for this concentration but it nonetheless underlines the selectivity of the dominant literature.

Centralism is a second theme that runs throughout the literature which, as noted above, is mostly devoted to the CBC. The examples are legion and there is no reason to repeat them except to illustrate the continued health of their subject. In 1935, Alan Plaunt, then a leading spokesman for the Canadian Radio League, stressed that "a national chain of high power stations covering the whole settled area of Canada...would be...as important to the continued existence of Canada as a nation as transcontinental railways to its inception."[5] That analogy has been repeated in nearly every public statement made by the CBC, but its popularity and cultural implications have only recently been explored by Maurice Charland in an article he entitles "Technological Nationalism."[6] The view of broadcasting as a crucial component of Canada's defensive nationalism remains current; witness the entry written by Frank Peers on "Broadcasting— Radio and Television" in *The Canadian Encyclopedia*, where in a chronology of public broadcasting its private counterpart receives but passing mention. No slight is intended by these comments on the accomplishment of Alan Plaunt or the scholarship of Frank Peers; on the contrary both constitute impressive achievements. Instead, it is the perpetual repetition of the national and public interest in broadcasting to the near exclusion of the provincial and private that deserves notice. For this view, formed and fixed a half century ago, has assumed a constancy in the interpretation of broadcasting policy which at the provincial level misrepresents a reality of adjustment and change. For instance, broadcasting in

Saskatchewan has passed through three stages, each distinguished by a different mixture of concern for local, national, or provincial factors. It is to a discussion of these factors that the paper turns in Part Two.

Part Two: Broadcasting in Saskatchewan
Local Dominance

Except for the licensing of receiver sets, the origins of broadcasting in Saskatchewan, as elsewhere in Canada, predate federal or indeed any government regulation. Because of the nature of the medium, radio broadcasting was in the beginning intensely local with the result that the medium reflected the immediate society it served. Since radio appeared in Saskatchewan in 1922 but national radio, symbolized by the building of CBC's 50-kw transmitter at Watrous, did not arrive until 1939, broadcasting had nearly two decades during which to become identified with local needs and interests. Most histories of radio say that in the early years its chief function was to entertain; that is true, up to a point. But radio did more than that even when it entertained.

Nowhere in Canada was so large a population scattered over so wide an area as in Saskatchewan where, according to the 1931 census, 80 per cent of the population was classified as rural. The farmer and his family, isolated by a combination of bad roads and bad climate, remained stock figures of Saskatchewan life for another quarter century. A supporter sending T. C. Douglas thirty dollars to help pay for CCF radio broadcasts in 1948 noted their popularity: "You see we haven't much else to do as we can't get anywhere on account of the storm and we haven't had a mail since the first of March."[7] Radio bridged the rural-urban divide in a province where as late as 1948 only one in six rural homes received a daily newspaper and where during the Depression and drought rail service was cut because there were less crops to transport—resulting in an end to daily newspaper delivery to entire localities.[8] In the 1930s the economy was added to geography and climate as an isolating factor, one which compounded the job of politicians who sought to reach the scattered electorate. J.G. Gardiner, for instance, discovered that his legislative initiatives meant nothing to those cut off on solitary farmsteads: "Since we had no radio, many important facts escaped us, for we were too tired usually to read, and in fact could not afford to subscribe to newspapers."[9]

To those who could afford a set, radio acted as a powerful bond to the provincial capital in the south, where CKCK was established in 1922, and to Saskatoon close to the province's centre, where CFQC opened in 1923. During the years of prosperity before the collapse of 1929 the growth in radio ownership, like the growth in motor vehicle ownership, placed Saskatchewan well above the Canadian average. The automobile physically overcame distance, while radio made a psychological bridge. The implications for public policy of the first innovation took the form of a need for improved roads, which was a provincial responsibility; the implications of radio for public policy occurred more slowly but eventually appeared in the form of a federal responsibility.[10]

In the cities where the stations were located the impact of local radio was as great as in the country. It revealed the talent that existed in the community, while offering it an opportunity to perform: "In a city like Regina, with only 28,000 or maybe 30,000 people, there wasn't much else to do. There was no live theatre, no symphony. There were no jobs of any kind in the arts... A great many people in Western Canada went into radio because they were inclined toward the arts."[11] In the period before the Second World War when most radio was "live," because recording equipment was poor and tape had yet to be invented, every city had a reservoir of music and dramatic talent. It was the era of big dance bands and little theatres. Because many early stations were owned by newspapers (*The Leader-Post*, a Sifton paper, owned CKCK), they were discouraged from competing with the newspapers for advertising (CKCK went commercial only in 1929). To fill air time, stations used local talent. Even where a newspaper did not own a station, the same practice prevailed. In an intriguing account ("An Historical and Analytical Study of the Origin, Development and Impact of the Dramatic Programs Produced for the English Language Networks of the Canadian Broadcasting Corporation"), Roger Lee Jackson quotes "Canadian radio pioneer," Neil LeRoy, on his experience working for the James Richardson station, CKRC, in Winnipeg:

> Richardson didn't maintain the station to make money, but mostly as a public relations and goodwill gesture on behalf of James Richardson. I had the peculiar ex-

perience while working for him of being told that I wasn't to go out after advertising and drain it away from the local newspapers. We were out to create goodwill.[12]

Jackson credits private stations, and CKRC in particular, for introducing early dramatic series—a distinctive art form at which Canadians were to excel through the CBC on an international level. The route was via the early private stations, the western network of the Canadian Radio Broadcasting Commission (CRBC), established in 1932, and the tutelage of individuals like Horace Stovin, who gravitated to the CRBC from amateur theatre.[13] Radio was responsible for discovering talent locally and offering the best of that talent a national stage. Paradoxically, the needs of agriculture made this transition possible.

By the mid-1920s James Richardson had recognized the potential of radio in keeping farmers and elevator agents abreast of daily changes in grain prices on the Winnipeg Grain Exchange. He established a centrally located station at Yorkton (CJGX) in 1927 and the following year secured links with stations at Saskatoon and Winnipeg. Thus was born the first western network which, when not broadcasting grain prices, devoted its time to theatrical and musical offerings originating at different prairie locations. Richardson initially had been prevented from using the prairies' most powerful station, CKY, owned by Manitoba Government Telephones since 1923 and thus Canada's first publicly owned commercial radio station; CKY had not wanted to be identified by its many Pool listeners with the private grain trade. In the 1920s there was no government monopoly of the handling of wheat, as today, and the battle between those who advocated cooperative marketing and those who favoured private traders was hotly contested across the West.[14]

Radio had been present in 1924 at the epochal debate in Saskatoon between "the apostle of cooperation," Aaron Sapiro, and the Secretary of the Winnipeg Grain Exchange, Robert Magill. In *Agrarian Socialism*, Seymour Martin Lipset attributes to Sapiro a determinative influence in helping politicize Saskatchewan's farmers. The 1924 debate marked the enthusiastic beginning of that transition. CKCK transmitted the speeches over land lines to Regina, in the process securing for its owner's paper what *The Morning Leader* called "a journalistic coup," from "whence they were sent through the ether to the whole North American continent." In anticipation of hearing the arguments, "meetings were held in Regina and at various country points to 'listen-in' to the...debate. A large number of members of the Saskatchewan Legislative Assembly heard the protagonists through a special set with a loud speaker installed in the legislative room at the parliament buildings."[15] The idea of gathering around the radio set, "of establishing Listening Posts all over the province," was to have a long life in Saskatchewan but it began in the 1920s when, according to information provided by the Pool, there were, in 1928, 12,492 receiving sets at 407 elevator points.[16]

The Pool had good reason to be certain of its facts, for in 1928 it seriously discussed a proposal to create "a farmer-owned station" to combat what it saw as propaganda "undermining cooperative consciousness" from stations controlled by the private grain trade. The cooperators envisioned a commercial station with one transmitter at Watrous to cover "the cultivated area of the Province" and two studios (at Regina and Saskatoon). Difficulty in securing a clear frequency in this period before an international agreement on frequencies had been concluded delayed action on the proposal in the last year before the economic collapse.[17] Partly in light of that failure, the following year the United Farmers of Canada (Saskatchewan Section) plumped before the Aird Commission for radio as "a public enterprise...[and] Federal Government control...administered in cooperation with the provinces."[18] Although in its recommendations the Commission echoed the organized farmers' proposal, it is not possible to evaluate the influence of this one organization on the first inquiry into Canadian broadcasting for, as Frank Peers has noted, the briefs from its western Canadian hearings have been lost. At Saskatoon it was already evident, however, that at least one of the Commissioners, Dr. Augustin Frigon (who later became general manager of the CBC), was unsympathetic to the concern expressed by local station representatives, that national radio "must of necessity treat the Dominion as one vast field." In response, he asked if it was "right to encourage sectionalism."[19]

Too much should not be read into this brief exchange, although it is worth noting as early as 1929 the contrasting value placed on local broadcasting and the apprehension by some lest national programming enforce standardization without regard to regional differences. The Aird Commission acknowledged localism by recommending the appointment of provincial directors, a proposal to which both CRBC (1932) and the CBC (1936) made obeisance but did little to implement. National broadcasting with a regional face remained forty years in the future. In the meantime, the federal government set about instituting Canada's distinctive national broadcasting system: less public than Aird had proposed, less private than existing local stations wanted. By the time the CBC was created, there were seven publicly owned stations with over fifty private affiliates organized into an eastern and a western network. None of the public stations was located in Saskatchewan, with the result that broadcasting priorities did not alter significantly in the province for another decade, except for the affiliation of some private stations who now carried a portion of the national programmes.

With one exception—broadcasting in French—the historical record says nothing of minority programmes on local stations. In light of later private and public experience with French broadcasting in Saskatchewan, however, the exception is important. In 1927 L'Association Catholique Franco-Canadienne wrote (in English) to stations in the province's four major centres requesting "one hour every month a French programme or lecture." The fate of the ACFC proposal remains undocumented, although the two histories that discuss the work of the CRBC indicate an unappreciative response from English-speaking listeners in Saskatchewan to any French programming over the network. Ultimately, the province's French community had to create their own stations to satisfy the need for programmes.[20]

Regional and National Dominance

National broadcasting arrived in Saskatchewan with the construction of a 50-kw transmitter bearing the callsign CBK at Watrous in 1939. CBK and CBA (erected at Sackville, New Brunswick, the same year) were the third and fourth high-powered transmitters on the network (the first two were at Toronto and Montreal, the CBC having inherited from CRBC a high-powered station at Vancouver). They were also the last to be constructed for nine years, at which time transmitters were opened at Carmen, Manitoba and Lacombe, Alberta. This sequence of construction meant that for nearly a decade there was only one CBC station on the prairies; it also meant that until the CBC purchased the Manitoba Government Telephone station, CKY, in Winnipeg in 1948, there were no public broadcasting facilities in the region. The small studio at the base of the Watrous tower was seldom used, so that CBC programmes originating in the region emanated from the affiliated stations. In 1938, for example, when the Department of Extension at the University of Saskatchewan organized some of the Corporation's earliest farm broadcasts, they were carried over a prairie network of private stations.[21] Only a decade-and-a-half after the advent of national broadcasting, did the CBC open studios in Regina; in the interval the province existed very much as a satellite of the Winnipeg and Toronto production centres.

In retrospect, the decision to locate the transmitter on the salt flats at Watrous, forty miles east of Saskatoon and in the centre of the settled area of the province, outweighed any disadvantages caused by the delay in building studios. The contrast provided by CBC policy in Alberta demonstrated the unanticipated influence of administrative and technical decisions on social and cultural development. E. A. Weir, former Commercial Manager of the CBC, reflected on the unhappy consequence of this policy in his history of the organization:

[The] new 50-kw transmitter...at Lacombe, Alberta, which [the CBC] hoped would cover both Calgary and Edmonton...covered neither, and even its rural coverage was limited...In November, 1951, I made a voluntary report on this Albertan situation...and said:
'The Alberta situation...is fraught with real danger to nationalized radio... The daily farm broadcast is almost the one tenuous thread that ties the CBC to Alberta... The situation there is steadily deteriorating and actually constitutes a menace to the CBC and nationalization.'
It was the prolonged continuation of this situation for another ten years that made it imperative for the CBC to establish a television station in Edmonton in 1961. The neglect of Alberta for so long produced a distorted image of the CBC in that province, and this evoked public prejudices in many areas that are now exceedingly difficult to eradicate... The CBC finally, in October of 1964, opened two new 50-kw radio stations—one in Calgary, the other at Edmonton. But these appeared sixteen years late.[22]

Paradoxically, the Saskatchewan signal of the CBC proved as reliable for Alberta listeners as did the one originating in their own province. At 540 Kcs, CBK occupied the most effective frequency on the radio band, giving the transmitter a range extending from the Arctic Circle to deep into the United States and from the foothills of the Rockies to Winnipeg: "A longer radius," said one engineer, "than any other known place in the world."[23] The station's locational advantages were complemented in the early years by minimal interference (compared to today) from electrical machinery in the home and community and by the popularity of large, floor-model radios (conversely, the advent of mantle radios to take advantage of stronger signals from private stations further cut reception of CBC's Alberta signal). M. J. Coldwell, a long-time member of the Parliamentary Committee on Radio Broadcasting, echoed popular usage when he referred to CBK as "the big station," a designation that continued even when transmitters were erected in neighbouring prairie provinces, for CBK remained the only station in Canada which covered a whole province.[24]

For the first fifteen years of its life, however, CBK assumed its greatest importance as a regional signal, a role that conformed to CBC plans, said A. Davidson Dunton, General Manager of the Corporation in 1951: "We try not to deal too much in provincial terms but rather in regional terms."[25] In the prairie region, other imperatives than policy encouraged this perspective and among them, the complexities of broadcasting technology ranked high. Encompassing over 750,000 square miles, the prairies were unique in the national system in spanning more than one time zone, a feature made more complicated in the summer "by the unequal distribution of daylight saving time throughout the Prairie provinces." The result, testified the Prairie Regional Representative before the Massey Commission in 1949, was that "we are very conscious of time in Winnipeg because...in our studios, we operate one station both for CBK on mountain time and another station for CBW on central time."[26] That feat was accomplished through delayed broadcasts which were all done on discs before 1948; the introduction of tape made the process cheaper and less cumbersome but did not eliminate its need.[27]

Transcription allowed network programmes to be heard in Saskatchewan, but programmes especially designed for the province's listeners had a different set of problems to overcome. First, until after the war, CBC management had almost no idea who in Saskatchewan listened to their programmes. While licence fees continued to be required until 1953, they did not provide this information and in any case fees were not collected for some years in "the dried out areas of Saskatchewan."[28] The need for a market analysis became pressing once CBC stations opened in Manitoba and Alberta in 1948; market is the appropriate word since income from commercials in 1948-49 constituted over 29 per cent of Corporation revenue. Because Saskatchewan's population was still predominantly rural and the telephone had yet to become universal, the survey used a mail questionnaire. The results surprised, and pleased, the Corporation: CBK dominated noon listening habits when farmers and townspeople returned home for lunch ("the percentage who eat 'downtown' in Saskatchewan is infinitesimal"); almost no one in the province listened to American stations; and no private station in the province approached CBK's coverage, a fact explained in part by the transmitter's great range and power in an era when farms had yet to be electrified and two thirds of all radios were battery operated.[29]

Saskatchewan's ethnic heterogeneity presented another problem. The proportion of the province's population which is Anglo-Saxon in origin has always been the smallest of any province in Canada, while the French-speaking population has been the smallest of the three prairie provinces. Yet the CBC's mandate called for broadcasting policies which recognized both linguistic communities. After 1940, the Corporation sought to meet this obligation through joint programming in Canada's two major languages. In 1943, the General Manager of the CBC, Dr. James S. Thomson, who was then on leave from his post as president of the University of Saskatchewan, explained the operation of this policy to the Parliamentary Committee:

> The Witness: ...these programs consist, so far as entertainment is concerned, of discs on which are recorded the French programs from the French network. Then we have also a French announcer, and he is something more than an announcer. He is a member of the staff who has to translate the English news into French... The main difficulty that arises, of course, in handling programs of that kind is the fact that station CBK is also on our English network. Consequently, you have to take out from the English network certain elements and put in the French programs... I have made a calculation that somewhere between 7 per cent and 10 per cent of the programs going over CBK are in the French language.[30]

Some members of the Committee advocated extending the experiment to other languages and involving the private stations in providing the service to local ethnic communities. Nothing came of these suggestions and examination of the experiment from the perspective of French-speaking Saskatchewan residents indicates the reason: "la part faite au français est si maigre et...si mal placée...qu'ils sont dégoutés"; "les programmes en français ont été parcimonieusement mesurés"; and "le vie est loin d'être agréable pour les annonceurs de langue française à Watrous. Les gens sont étroits et le montrent souvent."[31] Dissatisfaction on the part of French-speaking residents of the province and opposition from the non-French majority ended this experiment. Of the latter group, however, at least one correspondent complained that he was "sick and tired of domination by a clique of Scots Presbyterians."[32] Nonetheless, this combined reaction did not kill Corporation commitment to help the French. Significantly, assistance came from outside the region, from Radio-Canada, who encouraged the Fransaskois to establish their own stations— two in fact, because of the bimodal concentration of French populations in the north and in the south: "Radio-Canada nous envoya deux de ses meilleurs employés en janvier 1944, pour en étudier avec nous les possibilités de réussite."[33] This encouragement, plus a later Massey Commission recommendation to use "French language stations in Western Canada as outlets for national French programmes, by transcription or by some other means," led in 1952 to the creation through province-wide subscription of CFNS (Saskatoon) and CFRG (Gravelbourg).[34] The CBC paid these stations a rental fee as compensation for broadcasting time used for French National Network programmes, a practice that continued until these stations closed in 1972 and Radio-Canada took over broadcasting responsibilities in French in the province.

In view of the truncated institutions on which Saskatchewan's Francophones have traditionally had to depend, the contribution of CFNS and CFRG in preserving their precarious community deserves investigation as a subject of societal federalism. As is evident from the unusually complete records of both stations, housed in the Saskatchewan Archives, the theme of survival which the first president of Radio-Gravelbourg detected in the station's call letters—"Civis! Façonne! Rayonne! Garde!"—underlay their every act.[35] To achieve that goal the stations had looked beyond their immediate cultural community to the provincial government who reciprocated the attention by using these broadcasting facilities to reach the Métis population among whom the CCF sought to promote the development of cooperatives.36

In the period before the establishment of CBC studios in Saskatchewan, the provincial government depended on the private stations if it wished to use radio. An attempt to avoid that recourse, by purchasing the license of CHAB (Moose Jaw) and making it a crown corporation, had been effectively denied by the federal government in 1946 on the grounds that neither other governments nor their agents should hold licences.[37] Saskatchewan's motivation stemmed from its displeasure at monopoly control of the province's media by the Siftons and from its desire to introduce legislative debate broadcasts on its own station—a first in Canada but an idea borrowed from New Zealand. The broadcasts proved extremely popular—according to T. C. Douglas they ranked next in appeal to "very popular programs such as Charlie McCarthy"—and for the same reason radio always proved popular in Saskatchewan: dispersed population, extreme climate, and frequently impassable roads.[38] In this particular instance, as more generally, radio was "almost the only way of maintaining regular contact with the society of which [isolated individuals] form a part."[39]

Until the mid-1950s the private stations still defined the provincial society. But prevented by CBC regulations from forming national networks, the private stations contributed little toward building a sense of national community. That contribution lay with the CBC and, as the prairie briefs to the Massey Commission made abundantly clear, the CBC had achieved an astounding success in this regard. The tone of the accolades is captured by the University Women's Club of Regina, who judged CBC's *Wednesday Night* series to have "done more than any other agency in Canada to equalize the cultural balance."[40] Others spoke equally warmly of *Citizens' Forum* and *National Farm Forum*. If there was any fault to find it lay in the charge that CBC drained artists (actors, writers, musicians, producers, and directors) out of the region and "to the East." It was to check this tendency that many briefs echoed the plea of the Saskatchewan Arts Board that CBC open studios in the province which would "make a contribution comparable to that which is being done so well by the CBC at the national level."[41] Radio's potential, the briefs implied, made possible a multiple identity for Canadians—provincial, regional, and national. The President of the Arts Council of Manitoba claimed that after the CBC took over CKY in Winnipeg, "the number of live programmes dropped."[42] Whether that accusation was true would require more investigation than is possible here; what is clear in light of Roger Lee Jackson's research on CBC's dramatic programmes is that the themes and intended audience had changed between the 1930s and the 1950s. In twenty years the national component of broadcasting from Winnipeg had been eclipsed by a new regional preoccupation. The reason for the change in perspective lay in the rise of Toronto as English-Canada's cultural centre.

A long excerpt from an article on CBC Winnipeg producer, Gus Kristjanson, from the prairie edition of the *CBC Times*, underlines the nature of the change that had occurred by 1959:

> What was needed was a forceful resurgence of supporting talent from a region which had already given so many famous names to Canadian drama. New writers were needed; new actors were needed; but as well a "basic idea"—a plan that would give meaning and purpose to the weekly drama shows—was needed...
>
> The "idea": to present to Canada a dramatic radio picture of the Canadian prairies, past and present. And before long it began to work. Canadian prairie themes, in scripts by prairie authors, began filtering onto Gus's desk and were soon presented on the air. Often at [Gus Kristjanson's] own suggestion radio adaptations of Canadian prairie novels were written. Historical plays, short-story adaptations, and plays with modern prairie settings soon became the hallmark of *Prairie Playhouse*.
>
> The writings of such prairie authors as Frederick Philip Grove, Gabrielle Roy, Sinclair Ross, and Edward McCourt have been introduced to the listening audience...
>
> And the blossom of the old "basic idea" is finally bearing fruit. A series of articles now being planned in a western newspaper was inspired by an original *Prairie Playhouse* production; the great revival of interest in Grove's novels had its beginnings in *Prairie Playhouse* presentations; and more recently travelling researchers, preparing material on various aspects of prairie history, have been interviewing local radio writers who have researched the same field for *Prairie Playhouse* scripts.[43]

When national broadcasting began in the 1930s the cultural core of English Canada was still British. The nationalist sentiment of the Canadian Radio League and of the CBC that it helped found ended that colonial attachment, as did the experience of the Second World War. But in the realm of broadcasting, the expression of English-Canadian nationalism gravitated toward the centre of the country. Left behind were regional facilities and a tradition that expected use to be made of them. Yet, by the late 1950s, as that began to happen anew, provincial facilities appeared which checked further development in this direction. At the same time, a more potent challenge to radio broadcasting itself arose in the form of television.

From its inception television's influence was to centralize. Unlike radio which had begun locally but become national, television began at the centre and never abandoned its original perspective. This was as true of the private stations as of the CBC, for unlike radio a national network of private television stations was allowed to form in 1971. Notwithstanding the production of some local and regional programmes, financial, administrative and technical imperatives exerted a strong centralist pull on the new medium.

Requiring a larger staff and a greater investment of capital to produce programmes, there have always been fewer television than radio stations. With a signal range much shorter than that of radio, viewers more than fifty miles from the U.S. border were captives of local station programming until the advent of cable. Early radio listeners had a choice of stations and therefore of programmes; television was a monopoly medium whose programmes were designed to please a single audience. Immediate concerns were eclipsed by national and even international considerations; in Canada, as in the United States and Europe, this meant propagating the values of the heartland which in turn echoed those of the urban culture of the western world. Radio's adaptability and range allowed it to reflect the diversity of province, region and country; television's immobility discouraged such discrimination. Radio's early development had been significantly influenced by Canada's rural society—local stations using local talent broadcasting to local listeners; television's development in post-war, urbanizing Canada remained essentially a metropolitan phenomenon.[44]

The microwave network, which brought live television direct from Toronto, reached Saskatchewan in 1957, while CBC production facilities opened in the province in 1980. Between these dates regional television declined and local programming proved negligible.

Adaptation to Provincial Broadcasting

Despite or perhaps because of television's perspective, regionalism in all broadcasting became less evident. In Saskatchewan the shift to provincial concerns was made possible with the inauguration of CBC radio broadcasting in Regina in 1954, the same year the province's first television station (CKCK) began transmissions. But in addition to new facilities that could now be used to direct programmes province-wide, there was within the CBC a disposition to see the province, and not the prairie region, as the working unit for broadcasting. That revision of operational definition stemmed from a combination of cultural, technological, and policy changes.

In its Submission to the Canadian Radio-Television and Telecommunications Commission in Support of Applications for Renewal of Network Licenses, the CBC in 1978 reviewed Canada's recent history and congratulated itself on "play[ing] a fundamental role in giving expression" to two Quiet Revolutions: one in Quebec and another in English-speaking Canada in response to "the assertion of the pluralism of the regional and cultural identities of the country."[45] In this context, the term regional is ambiguous, if not fluid, since the CBC used it on different occasions to designate sections of a province, a single province or more than one province. In the case of Saskatchewan, however, it seemed clear that CBC usage implied a contraction of territory, from the old prairie region with headquarters in Winnipeg to the province of Saskatchewan proper. And while the Corporation might talk abstractly of this development as a necessary step if Saskatchewan residents were to know themselves and Canadians to know Saskatchewan, there were eminently practical reasons for the new perspective.

Most important was CBC's own policy decision to give full service to all Canadians. For instance, the Accelerated Coverage Plan was intended to "take CBC Radio service into all communities of 500 population or larger."[46] A decade earlier, in testimony before the Standing Committee on Broadcasting, Films and Assistance to the Arts, J.P. Gilmore (Vice President, Planning), described what he called the Frontier Coverage Package.[47] Using low-power repeater transmitters, service would be extended to smaller communities. The LPRT would "be programmed either from a network connection, if we can get the network up that far, or from television recordings." In the case of Saskatchewan, the Committee was told that meant starting "the development channel" at Regina and establishing a station at Saskatoon "from which will be developed satellite stations." Once completed, it became a matter of "filling in the gaps." The size of the territory under consideration and the fact that the CBC officials were thinking in the first instance of television programming dictated a province-by-province approach to the delivery of service. The demands of television coverage in Saskatchewan created a single production base which had a direct influence on later CBC radio broadcasting. The CBC Submission in 1978 spoke of the advantages of "sub-regional programming" which allowed for different programmes "to serve urban and rural audiences." In Saskatchewan separate programmes were not feasible but "branch-plant radio" was possible so that the Regina, Saskatoon, and Lac La Ronge studios might be joined into a single programme, creating what one director has called "a provincial sound."[48] Significantly, this unity was achieved only because of the single transmitter at Watrous, constructed for regional coverage of the prairies in 1939. For reasons already suggested, Alberta, with the same population distribution between north and south as Saskatchewan, developed a different public broadcasting pattern centred around two CBC stations, in Calgary and Edmonton.

The evolution of broadcasting in the French language in Saskatchewan has followed the model established by its English counterpart. In the late 1960s, CFNS (Saskatoon) sought to extend its coverage to French communities north of Prince Albert. This was only possible with the use of LPRTs and these could only be acquired if the CBC agreed to provide financial assistance or to operate the transmitter itself.[49] At the same time the desire of Radio-Canada to establish a full-time presence in the province as part of its national network, and the desire of the private French stations to escape a precarious financial condition, appeared capable of being met through the projected new broadcasting centre for the CBC in Regina. In 1972 Radio-Canada assumed control of the former private station and soon afterwards

French broadcasting in the province was centred at Regina. Since then Radio-Canada Saskatchewan has begun to duplicate the "provincial sound" of CBC Saskatchewan.

In private broadcasting, too, regional radio has declined, though the scale of the contraction is less evident than in the public sphere because the regions of private radio never extended beyond the province's boundaries. Nonetheless the blanket coverage of stations like CKCK in the south and CFQC in the north is less evident today than thirty or even twenty years ago. A combination of disparate factors explain this development: television along with newspapers compete for the national advertiser's dollar while new radio stations in the smaller cities and towns—in 1984 there were 23 radio stations in the province compared to seven in 1948—secure the local advertiser's investment; at the same time changes in listening habits and especially the targeting of a younger audience with their ubiquitous transistors have encouraged the older and larger stations to tailor their programmes to a prime audience far more of whom are residents of the larger urban centres than in earlier times.[50] Regional radio no longer competes with or is a substitute for public broadcasting. Public broadcasting serves the province, private broadcasting the localities.

Part Three: Conclusion

Broadcasting began as a private enterprise in communities across the country, a fact that a succession of parliamentary committees were tirelessly reminded of by the Canadian Association of Broadcasters; the association cited this as evidence for its claim that private broadcasters were by tradition locally sensitive, responsive, and popular. Broadcasting became a public enterprise because of the national objectives assigned to the CRBC and later the CBC. The dichotomy between public and private has marked debate on broadcasting in Canada longer than any other issue. Prevented from establishing networks and assigned stations of limited power, private radio broadcasting never embraced a whole province. Conversely, to fulfill its mandate, public broadcasting looked beyond the province to develop regional stations, a choice influenced only in part by considerations of technology and finance. Notwithstanding the opinion of the JCPC in the Radio Case, supporters of public broadcasting remained alive to provincial (and especially Quebec) sensitivity in the matter and sought to avoid tendentious conflict with the province. Public broadcasting quickly became synonymous with the values of nation-building. The critics of private broadcasting, which was identified with commercialism, said that it had a tendency if left unregulated to gravitate in ownership and operation toward the markets of central Canada.

Deciding whether or not that last fear was realistic would require more research into the history of private broadcasting than has yet been undertaken. From the perspective of this brief survey it does appear that federalism as an organizing principle never had more than slight relevance for the conduct of private broadcasting. In the public realm, the country's federal structure in time acted as an effective counterweight to pressures for centralization; more than that, public broadcasting played a role in defining the units of the federal system.

A year before CBC radio studios opened in Regina, Lewis H. Thomas commented that while in prairie communities there "is a strong sense of community identity...there has not been a comparable sense of historical consciousness on the provincial level."[51] He attributed this slow evolution to Saskatchewan's immense size and scattered population distributed over three distinct topographies: short-grass country, parkland, and Shield. Thirty years later and despite improvements in transportation, broadcasting remains one of the few forces for integrating the settled south and the larger, less inhabited north. Notwithstanding its being a federal undertaking, broadcasting continues to influence the province's definition of itself.

Broadcasting is only one subject in the understudied area of societal federalism, but even so, partial analysis underlines a truth long suspected: needs are defined, interests are served, and provincialism is mobilized by a multitude of forces other than governments.

Notes

1   Donald Smiley, *The Federal Condition in Canada* (Toronto: McGraw-Hill Ryerson, 1987), 4.

2   Richard Rose, "The Constitution: Are We Studying Devolution or Break Up?" in Dennis Kavanagh and Richard Rose, eds., *New Trends in British Politics: Issues for Research* (London: Sage Publications, 1977), 45.

3   Canadian Broadcasting History Research Project, Ryerson Polytechnical Institute (Toronto, March 1978), 8.

4   See, however, Ronald G. Keast, "The Role of the Provinces in Public Broadcasting" (Study prepared for the Task Force on Broadcasting Policy, January 1986).

5   Alan Plaunt, "Memorandum on Canadian Broadcasting Reorganization," Dec. 1935, University of British Columbia Library, Plaunt Papers, Box 17, quoted in Frank W. Peers, *The Politics of Canadian Broadcasting 1920-1951* (Toronto: University of Toronto Press, 1969), 169.

6   Maurice Charland, "Technological Nationalism,"*Canadian Journal of Political and Social Theory*, X(1-2, 1986), 196-220.

7   Saskatchewan Archives Board (hereafter SAB), Papers of T. C. Douglas (File 701), Radio Fund, C. J. Boyle to Douglas, 10 March 1948.

8   SAB, Douglas Papers (File 757), "A Study of Radio Listening Habits in the Province of Saskatchewan," August 1948 (Toronto: Canadian Facts, Ltd., for the Canadian Broadcasting Corporation), unpaginated; Bill McNeil and Morris Wolfe, *Signing On: The Birth of Radio in Canada* (Toronto: Doubleday Canada Ltd., 1982), 125 (interview, Andy McDermott).

9   SAB, Papers of the Rt. Hon. J. G. Gardiner, Ellen (Mrs. V.) Hadley to Gardiner, 9 April 1956, 25189-92.

10 G. T. Bloomfield, " 'I Can See a Car In That Crop': Motorization in Saskatchewan, 1906-1934," *Saskatchewan History*, XXXVII (1, Winter 1984), 3-24. Author's note: "This work forms part of the research effort for the *Historical Atlas of Canada*, Volume III, edited by Professor Don Kerr, University of Toronto."

11 McNeil and Wolfe, *Signing On*, 132 (interview, Art Creighton).

12 Roger Lee Jackson, PhD dissertation (Wayne State University, 1966), 47

13 *Ibid.*, 34.

14 See, E. Austin Weir, *The Struggle for National Broadcasting in Canada* (Toronto: McClelland and Stewart, 1965), 86-88.

15 *Morning Leader* (Regina), 22 February 1924, 2.

16 SAB, Douglas Papers (File 701), Radio Fund, Douglas form letter to "telephone controls," 23 February 1948; SAB, United Farmers of Canada (Saskatchewan Section) (File 228), Radio: General, 1928-37, Report of Radio Conference, April 3, 1928, 3-4.

17 *Ibid.*

18 SAB, United Farmers of Canada (Saskatchewan Section) (File 231), Radio: Royal Commission on Radio Broadcasting, 1929, Statement to Mr. Chairman and Commissioners.

19 *Ibid.*, Statements by the Saskatoon Radio Club, and by stations CFQC and CJHS.

20 SAB, Radio-Prairie-Nord-Limitée (File 149(a)), Radio: 1927-32, correspondence with J. E. Moirier, General Secretary, ACFC, April/May 1927. See,

too, Peers, *Canadian Broadcasting*, 128-30 and Weir, *Struggle for Broadcasting*, 149-52.

21 Canada, House of Commons, Special Committee on Radio Broadcasting (1939), 316 (hereafter cited as *PCB*).

22 Weir, *Struggle for Broadcasting*, p247-48; see, too, *PCB* (1961), 605-07.

23 *PCB* (1946), 421-22 (testimony of Col. B. de F. Bayly, consultant engineer).

24 *PCB* (1943), 88.

25 *PCB* (1951), 17.

26 Royal Commission on National Development in the Arts, Letters and Sciences (hereafter cited as Massey Commission), hearings, "Canadian Broadcasting Corporation, Report on Prairie Region Programme Activity," 13. Brief 112, Session 34 (Hearings). See, too, *PCB* (1946), 33 (A. Davidson Dunton).

27 For a description of the procedure, see *CBC Times* (Prairie Edition), 26 October 1956, 1, 8.

28 *PCB* (1939), 232.

29 SAB, Douglas Papers (File 757), "A Study of Radio Listening Habits...August 1948," unpaginated.

30 *PCB* (1943), 85-90 at 85.

31 SAB, Radio-Prairie-Nord-Limitée (File 45), Correspondence Lessard, G., unsigned to Lessard,4 September 1945; (File 154), Radio-Prince Albert, "Mgr. Réginald Duprat, Evêque de Prince Albert et al. au Bureau des gouverneurs de la Société Radio-Canada," 27 March 1944; and (File 149(b)) Radio, 1932-48, "Notes, prises au cours d'un entrevu avec monsieur Gilbert Lessard, de CBK Watrous, à Prud'homme le 25/8/42."

32 *PCB* (1939), 265.

33 SAB, Radio-Prairie-Nord-Limitée, (File 88(a)), Mémoires, 1947-65, Dr. Maurice Demay (président, pour la Société Radio-Prairie-Nord Limitée) to Gouverneurs de Radio-Canada, 2 January 1951.

34 Massey Commission, *Report* (Ottawa: King's Printer, 1951), 297.

35 SAB, Douglas Papers (File 811a (32)), "Présentation du Poste CFRG aux Canadiens français de la Saskatchewan."

36 *Ibid.*, (File 811c), Radio-Television, memo T. C. Douglas to B. N. Arnason, Deputy Minister of Cooperatives, 18 September 1953.

37 Peers, *Canadian Broadcasting*, 376.

38 SAB, Douglas Papers (File 820a), Broadcasts from the Legislature, T. C. Douglas to Lloyd Stinson, MLA (Manitoba), 11 February 1952.

39 *Ibid.*, (File 267), Massey Commission, Submission of Saskatchewan Arts Board to Royal Commission on National Development in Arts, Letters and Sciences, October 1949, 8.

40 Brief 412, Session 61 (Hearings).

41 SAB, Douglas Papers (File 267), Massey Commission, Brief to Royal Commission, Submission of Saskatchewan Arts Board, October 1949, 9.

42 Brief 28, Session 33 (Hearings). See, too, evidence of H. G. Turner, member of Alberta Music Board: "When the CBC came into being ... more centralization took place," Brief 10, Session 43 (Hearings).

43 *CBC Times*, XII (27, July 5-11, 1959)

44 See, Jackson, dissertation 1966 (see note 12), 149-52 and 164-65.

45 *The CBC: A Perspective* (Toronto: Canadian Broadcasting Corporation/Société Radio-Canada, May 1978), 36.

46 *Ibid.*, 111.

47 Minutes of Proceedings and Evidence, November 17, 1966, 131-01.

48 Interview, Bill Cameron, programme director, CBC (Saskatoon), March, 1988.

49 SAB, CFNS Papers (File 46c), correspondance—R. Marcotte, "French Radio Network in Western Canada," C. H. Russell (Assistant Director of Acc't Studies CBC), March 25, 1968. See, too, SAB, Radio-Gravelbourg Limitée (File 15), directeur et executif, "Comité du Rayonnement des Reseaux Français, réunion avec des représentatives le CFRC et CFNS," August 12, 1968.

50 Canada, *Report of the Task Force on Broadcasting Policy* (Ottawa: Ministry of Supply and Services, 1986), chap. 16.

51 SAB, Saskatchewan Golden Jubilee Committee (File I.15.2), Address to Alberta Historical Society, October 27, 1953, 1-2.

FEDERALISM AND COMMUNICATION POLICY:
COMMUNICATIONS AND CONFEDERATION REVISITED

Frederick J. Fletcher, York University
Martha Fletcher, Government of Ontario[*]

This paper attempts to respond to Don Smiley's call for attention to "how federalism shapes and has been shaped by other aspects of human organization"[1] by examining the relationship between the federal system and the communication system. The focus here is on the influence of federalism on the evolution of broadcasting and telecommunications in Canada. In addition to considering jurisdictional and developmental factors in the evolution of broadcasting and telecommunications, we have tried to increase our understanding of the significance of jurisdiction for policy by imagining how the system might have evolved had jurisdiction been allocated differently. This exercise in examining the counterfactual is necessarily speculative but has the virtue of making us aware that jurisdictional patterns influence and are influenced by political forces and are not the "givens" that we often assume.[2]

Because the community-building functions of communications systems have been generally recognized, regulation of their operation and development has been of significant concern to the federal government and most provinces since the 1930s. Their concern is understandable in an electronic age in which "communications links are as vital to the Canadian union as railways were in the past."[3] At a conference entitled "Federalism and the Quest for Political Community," it seems appropriate to focus some attention on the relationship between federalism and the development of the communications infrastructure that is so vital to the social networks that must underpin any form of community. In this paper, which is in many ways a second look at the issues raised in our 1979 study, "Communications and Confederation,"[4] we examine the influence of federalism on the develop-

---

[*] The views expressed in this paper are those of the authors, and not necessarily those of the Government of Ontario.

ment of Canada's communications system, as well as some of the options for change in the federal system that have emerged from the intensive federal-provincial discussions of the past two decades. The case is particularly interesting because it illustrates the conflicts between nation-building and province-building that have been central in the history of Canadian federalism.

As in 1979, we have chosen to treat broadcasting and telecommunications as a single policy field. The convergence that we noted then has become even more pronounced now, as an ever increasing percentage of signals—radio, television, data—are distributed by the same technologies and by companies with common ownership.[5] This convergence was recognized institutionally in 1976 when telecommunications regulation was added to the responsibilities of the broadcast regulator and the CRTC became the Canadian Radio-television and Telecommunications Commission. In technological terms, broadcasting and telecommunications policy are inextricably intertwined. In addition, the issues raised by them increasingly revolve around the same conflicts between nation-building and province-building and between economic and social priorities. In terms of federalism, however, they illustrate rather different processes. Broadcasting has developed almost entirely under federal jurisdiction, a fact that has led to repeated calls for greater regional sensitivity through intrastate mechanisms, even before anyone knew what to call them. The development of telecommunications, on the other hand, illustrates the effectiveness of *de facto* concurrency and, in an era of rapid and complex technological change, the need for innovative mechanisms of interstate federalism.[6]

In our analysis, we examine not only the division of powers and the mechanisms of intergovernmental relations in this policy field, but also the ways in which the relevant institutions of the federal government have dealt with regional issues. We take seriously the analytical distinction between federalism and regionalism and look at both interstate and intrastate elements in the current system and in proposals for reform. We argue that in this policy field especially, provincial pressures, though often couched in jurisdictional terms, may in fact be seeking "a greater degree of regional sensitivity, whether through consultation with provincial governments or in the internal operations of the national government."[7]

The major institutional actors in this policy field are the CRTC for both broadcasting and telecommunications, the

Canadian Broadcasting Corporation (CBC), the federal Department of Communications and its provincial counterparts, and a variety of industry groups, representing a very wide range of interests. Although the individual provincial governments have not displayed much internal conflict over key issues in the field, the three federal institutions have often been at odds and there have been competing priorities that divided the provinces. In the private sector, the stakeholders are often deeply divided, with continuing tensions between broadcasters and cable companies and between the telephone companies, consumers, and would-be competitors.

Broadcasting

The development of the broadcasting system was fundamentally shaped by the allocation of almost exclusive jurisdiction to the federal government in the *Radio Case* of 1932. Although the Aird Commission had in 1929 recommended that programming be a provincial responsibility, the 1932 decision provided the basis for the federal government to pursue policies based on the principle of nation-building. As Jean McNulty has put it, the federal government has argued for the past 50 years that "it is necessary for national cohesion that all people in the nation can receive the same information, especially about public affairs."[8] This rationale has been employed to justify limiting provincial involvement in broadcasting, giving high priority to extension of national broadcasting services to all parts of the country in both official languages, and promoting Canadian content through regulation and subsidy, as well as extending federal jurisdiction over new broadcasting technologies as they emerged.

The Radio Reference grew out of Quebec's attempts to establish a government-owned radio station. When federal officials refused to provide a licence, though Manitoba had been operating a provincially-owned station since 1923, Quebec claimed jurisdiction. Premier Taschereau argued that provincial control was necessary to ensure that programmes were suited to the mentality and taste of Quebeckers while federal officials argued that provincial control would threaten free speech.[9] The federal government referred the jurisdictional question to the Supreme Court in February 1931 and in June the Court ruled in a three to two vote that jurisdiction was properly federal. The majority apparently accepted the arguments of the federal government, supported by the Canadian Radio League, that broadcasting was inherently inter-provincial and that it was central to "the national life and interest,"[10] but rested its decision on Section 92 (10) (a) of the British North America Act, that awarded the federal government jurisdiction over telegraphs and other works and undertakings connecting provinces. Mr. Justice Smith recognized the social uses of radio and, though voting with the majority, commented on its importance to the provinces.[11] The issue was clearly not cut-and-dried and Quebec, supported by Ontario, appealed to the Judicial Committee of the Privy Council, which had a long history of favouring provincial jurisdiction. However, the Committee ruled in favour of Ottawa, stating that federal jurisdiction rested primarily on the Peace, Order, and Good Government clause, as well as on Ottawa's responsibility for enforcing the International Radio Convention of 1927.[12] Despite these rulings, the issue refused to die. The very real concerns of the provinces and technological change kept it alive.

While television broadcasting was logically viewed as an extension of radio, the case of cable television was not as clear cut. Although cable television systems usually operate within a single province and have the potential to offer services with no broadcasting component, the federal government has consistently refused to share jurisdiction with the provinces. Exclusive federal jurisdiction was confirmed by the Supreme Court in 1977 when it ruled that the cable systems were part of a single broadcasting system.[13] The CRTC maintains control over non-broadcast cable undertakings by requiring that cable systems obtain a licence to carry broadcast signals and then regulating the services they can carry. (The technologically odd requirement that cable systems not lease their household connections from the telephone companies but own them was a simple expedient both to weaken any possible provincial claim for jurisdiction and to prevent provincially-owned telephone companies from expanding into television programming services without CRTC authorization.) The provincial argument was that the "wired city" services that could be offered by cable had no broadcasting component and, in particular, that these services could be used to further important provincial social and economic goals, especially in conjunction with provincially-owned telephone systems. Although there are still jurisdictional grey areas, the provinces appear to have given up the struggle for jurisdiction over cable, for the time being at least, though certain cable undertakings are currently operating in B.C. and Saskatchewan without federal licences.

In broadcasting, federal officials have defended their jurisdiction primarily on nation-building grounds, expressing suspicion regarding the motives of Quebec and other provinces wishing to develop broadcasting systems. Concern was expressed regarding the possible partisan use of provincial broadcasters, though this proved easy enough to deal with when provincial educational broadcasts were licenced in the 1970s. Paradoxically, the federal regulators were happy to leave local broadcasting to the private sector while promoting national unity through a focus on extension of CBC network services in both official languages throughout the country, at least from 1932 until 1961. The paradox, of course, is that the private broadcasters contributed very little to the project of countering the north-south pull that was the very *raison d'être* of the CBC, though many of them have provided important local and regional content. In 1961, of course, the federal regulator licensed the first private network, CTV. Others were to follow and the dominant role in the broadcasting system gradually moved from public sector to the private.

The federal rationale that national unity requires a single system with private broadcasters providing local and regional services under the coordinating wing of the CBC has long since evaporated. National service is now provided by a number of television networks and cable-delivered services and, even in radio, the CBC's excellent networks are supplemented by All-News Radio and a growing number of special purpose networks and syndication services. The single system is dead and the risk that an Aberhart or a Duplessis will establish a provincially-owned service for partisan purposes now seems remote. In any case, Aberhart had ready access to the airwaves via CFCN[14] and it seems reasonable to assume that Duplessis could have gained similar access using a private station had he wished to. Quebec government programmes were carried on private stations in the 1930s. Federal attempts to limit the political speech of provincial premiers through regulation would have been difficult, even with exclusive jurisdiction.

When we examine the effects exclusive federal jurisdiction has had on the development of our broadcasting system, the benefits seem fairly clear. It would have taken much longer than it did to establish a national broadcaster and provincial public broadcasting[15] would have been limited and confined in large part to the wealthier provinces. This would have given American broadcasters an even greater hold on Canadian audiences. Exclusive provincial jurisdiction would almost certainly have produced a U.S.-dominated system in most provinces. The strong national focus provided an important counter-balance to the predominantly local focus of the press and the private stations. The CBC itself provided a centre for the cultural development of the country that would almost certainly have been much weaker with exclusive provincial jurisdiction.

On the other hand, federal jurisdiction prevented the emergence of effective provincial public broadcasting in most provinces until fairly recently. The limited funding available from licence fees and from the federal treasury forced the CBC to concede much of local broadcasting to the private sector. The division of labour between public and private broadcasters limited the exchange of regional perspectives and, especially after the advent of television, there emerged a significant degree of regional alienation from the broadcasting system. This resulted largely from a lack of regional production by the CBC, except in a few areas, and regulatory policies that often responded poorly to regional desires. The provinces might well have provided more effective regional and local services, though the probability is that the poorer provinces would have suffered even more inferior service than under federal jurisdiction. An effective national cooperative system on the German model[16] might have emerged but it seems likely that it would have come slowly and with major gaps. However, innovations, like community access broadcasting, might have come more quickly.

The struggle for provincial public broadcasting is instructive. In the years after 1932, the federal government frustrated the efforts of several provinces—Quebec, Alberta, and Saskatchewan—to establish public broadcasting for educational purposes and finally enunciated a clear policy in 1946. In answer to a question in the House of Commons on May 3 of that year, the responsible Minister, C.D. Howe, stated:

> The government has decided that, since broadcasting is the sole responsibility of the dominion government, broadcasting licences shall not be issued to other governments or corporations owned by other governments.[17]

He went on to announce that the Manitoba government would be required to sell its two stations, which was subsequently done. The governments most anxious to get into broadcasting were obvious dissidents: Social Credit in Alberta, CCF in Saskatchewan, Union Nationale in Quebec. The partisan aspect of the issue reinforced the "turf war" element of the jurisdictional dispute, especially when the federal government was accused from time to time of employing the CBC to promote its policies, as in the Conscription Crisis of 1942 and later events in Quebec.[18]

Educational broadcasting developed in some provinces through the purchase of broadcast time on existing stations, but in the 1960s several provinces began to press the federal government on the issue. In 1969, Quebec revived an unimplemented 1945 statute establishing the legislative basis for Radio-Quebec and Ontario and Alberta sought broadcasting licences. Ontario had applied to the Board of Broadcast Governors for a television licence in 1966 but was turned down, with the Board citing the 1946 policy. Finally in 1969, the provinces and Ottawa agreed on a definition of educational broadcasting. After unsuccessfully floating the idea of a federal educational broadcasting organization, the federal government issued an order-in-council (PC1972-1569) directing the CRTC to issue licences for educational broadcasting to arms-length provincial agencies.[19] The process of establishing provincial public broadcasting had taken more than 25 years.

The experience of Quebec illustrates the potential of regionally-focussed broadcasting. It seems clear that the existence of a distinctive French service has contributed substantially to community-building in Quebec. Though formally controlled by Ottawa, the French radio and television networks, especially the latter, were major contributors to the development of a strong, distinctive, and politically significant popular culture in Quebec.[20] The attempts to control "separatists" in Radio Canada probably contributed to the growth of Quebec nationalism through the 1960s and 1970s. This concern reflected a recognition of the province-building role that the French service had played in Quebec and may have been responsible for the federal government's determination to include in the 1968 Broadcasting Act the requirement that the CBC promote Canadian national unity and identity.[21] Although the case is unique in its cultural and linguistic dimensions, it does illustrate the cultural benefits and, from a federal government perspective, the political risks of regional services.

It seems equally clear that the lack of regionally-oriented public broadcasting in other provinces impeded the achievement of legitimate province-building goals. Provincial demands for a share of authority over communications reflected not only the jurisdictional turf wars usually noted but also specific concerns regarding community-building within each province. For most provinces, the desire to integrate electronic communication with development planning was central, though cultural goals were also cited. This concern involved rural development in general and more particular concerns for industry relocation and preservation of the family farm. It was hoped that the provision of broadcasting and related telecommunications services to remote areas would encourage new development and provide an incentive for younger people to stay. The jurisdictional claims reflected not only the desire of the provinces to integrate communications concerns with other matters under provincial authority but also the conviction that the provincial governments were closer—and, therefore, more responsive—to the communities requiring new services.[22] For the most part, provincial officials were seeking the capacity to offer services that would necessarily be public, since their aims were often to resist market forces. The contribution of private broadcasting to the realization of these goals was, therefore, likely to be limited.

Not surprisingly, histories of Canadian broadcasting have reflected the nation-building themes of much Canadian historical writing and tended to assume that exclusive federal jurisdiction was both necessary and desirable.[23] Its benefits are rarely debated and its costs usually ignored. Commenting on the Aird Commission recommendation for provincial control of programming, Ross Eaman argues that "the result would probably have been a collection of more or less independent provincial broadcasting operations, rather than a system capable of stimulating greater national consciousness and unity."[24] Even the Commission's recommendation that the Board of Directors for the proposed Canadian Radio Broadcasting Company have provincial representation has generally been viewed as unworkable.[25]

If nation-building is the main criterion of success for the national broadcasting system, however, regional alienation from the national system is a serious problem. On the basis of its public hearings and submissions, the Task Force on Broadcasting Policy concluded that

> There is a widespread feeling that our broadcasting system, like so many other Canadian institutions, reflects reality largely as it is understood in Toronto and Montreal... The number of Canadians who feel alienated from one of the country's key instruments for enhancing national awareness is disturbingly large...[26]

In discussions during the 1970s, the British Columbia government argued that the CBC was less relevant to its citizens than the United States Public Broadcasting System and that the "Toronto-dominated and Ottawa-regulated system seriously limited production by west coast artists, writers, and producers about west coast culture."[27] Our reading of recent survey data is that support for the CBC—and appreciation for the national forum for public debate that its news and public affairs shows provide—is widespread, but fragile. More regional content—and a greater sensitivity to regional concerns—would contribute to the maintenance of the national political community. Competition between federal and provincial public broadcasters might have produced a healthy concern for regional needs and tastes. Some form of shared jurisdiction might have produced a better balance between nation-building and province-building in broadcasting.

The last few years have produced a modest but increasingly effective provincial public broadcasting system. Ronald Keast sums up the current situation as follows:

> Every province in Canada is now involved, to a greater or lesser extent, in what may be called public broadcasting, or, perhaps better, public communications. The provinces are spending, currently, well over $100 million per year on this activity and this is increasing rapidly. They all see this communications activity as important for their own cultural, social, political and economic development.[28]

Rather than competing with the CBC and private broadcasters, these operations have, for the most part, offered distinctive materials and services, educational in a broad sense. Noting the increasing role in the Canadian broadcasting system of the private sector, Eaman observes: "Only the emergence of provincial networks such as TVOntario has stemmed the increasing domination of Canadian television by private interests."[29] TVO and its counterparts offer a variety of services for formal and adult education but, most important, perhaps, provide the special interest programming that is possible for a public system that does not, like the CBC, have to serve a diverse, national audience. This increasingly important contribution might well have come earlier had the federal government not refused to provide a jurisdictional space within which it could develop.

Telecommunications

The history of federal-provincial interaction over telecommunications policy is rather different, but not unrelated, as will be seen. Jurisdiction is a patchwork. For various reasons, the federal government has exclusive jurisdiction over the largest telephone companies (accounting for 70 per cent of subscribers), including Bell Canada, which dominates in Ontario and Quebec, and B.C. Telephone. The majority of telephone companies fall under provincial authority and many of them are owned by provincial governments. Interprovincial interconnection is handled by Telecom Canada, a jointly-owned operation that is essentially unregulated. Its decisions require unanimity, giving the provinces greater influence than they would otherwise possess. Beginning in the early 1970s, the federal government sought provincial agreement to establish national priorities in this rapidly changing, economically and socially important field. For the past 15 years, the two levels of government have participated in seven ministerial conferences and innumerable intergovernmental task forces, bilateral negotiations, etc., a process that Richard Schultz recently dubbed "all talk no action."[30] The provinces have resisted federal leadership in this area, mainly because the various governments could not reconcile competing priorities, but partly because the federal government refused to concede a share of jurisdiction over cable television in return.

The fundamental intergovernmental issues in the field have changed little over the past two decades, though some new wrinkles have been introduced by technological change. In general terms, the conflict has been between a public utility approach to telecommunications services, stressing social objectives such as maintaining viable rural communities, and a market perspective, emphasizing the benefits of competition and user pay. The focus of this political conflict in recent years has been over the degree of competition in the provision of long distance telecommunication services that should be permitted. The current system involves substantial cross-subsidization, not only from urban to rural subscribers, but also from the richer to the poorer provinces. This cross-subsidization not only helps to encourage the viability of rural communities, an issue of considerable importance to the prairie provinces, it also makes telephone service available to a wider range of the population (98 per cent in Canada compared to 92 per cent in the United States, for example)[31]. On the other hand, the federal government has become increasingly concerned that relatively high long distance rates will encourage Canadian users to bypass the domestic system via the United States and, more generally, that high telecommunications rates will reduce the international competitiveness of Canadian industries. The bypass issue has obvious implications for the preservation of the Canadian community as well as for the economy, if it promotes north-south transactions at the expense of east-west ones.

The federal government has argued that the decentralized nature of the telecommunications system impedes national objectives because it fails to recognize the national dimension of the system. Most provinces have resisted greater national coordination, not primarily for jurisdictional reasons, but because the federal government's substantive priorities—more competition, lower long distance rates—conflicted with strongly held provincial priorities. The provinces that stood to gain from these policies, such as Ontario and Quebec, either remained neutral or opposed enhanced federal jurisdiction on principle.

After fifteen years of effort, intergovernmental negotiations have failed to produce an agreed-upon sharing of jurisdiction. After waiting in the wings for several years hoping for a negotiated solution, industry interests have gradually increased pressure for a more open system. CNCP gained permission from the CRTC to interconnect its telecommunications services with those of the telephone companies under federal jurisdiction in 1983. In 1985, it took court action to gain access to the telephone networks under provincial jurisdiction. It won its case against Alberta Government Telephone and is likely to win in a judgement expected soon from the Supreme Court of Canada. That judgement may award exclusive jurisdiction over telecommunications to the federal government, causing a great deal of federal-provincial conflict in the process.[32] Most of the actors in the process believe that the issues are too complex for legal solutions. Nevertheless, international pressures make some sort of accommodation imperative.

What difference has federalism made to the development of the telecommunications system in Canada? It seems likely that the predominantly provincial jurisdiction provided much more cross-subsidization and much more rapid extension of services to rural and remote areas than would have occurred under exclusive federal jurisdiction. For example, Saskatchewan undertook to establish its provincially-owned telephone system only because Bell Canada refused to do so on economic grounds. Indeed, in recent years, the federal government has taken a much more market-driven approach than have most provincial governments, regardless of partisan stripe. More recently, however, the regulatory structure has slowed down the process of adjusting to technological change and has created a degree of *immobilisme* in the policy field. In general, the Canadian response to changes in the international telecommunications system "has been fundamentally shaped by sub-national policy and regulatory actions" and left fragmented.[33] However, as Lorimer and McNulty argue, muddling through may have its benefits: "Developing a national policy means that one must produce a set of objectives and rules that are equally suitable to all regions of the country. This is difficult to achieve in a society as widely scattered and diverse as Canada's."[34] Shared jurisdiction does at least force negotiations, but the costs in terms of competitiveness and lost opportunities for technological innovation may become too high to bear.

Options

Despite changes of government and of technology, the central problem remains how to balance the competing claims of the federal and provincial governments, as well as non-governmental groups, for influence over the development of the complex and rapidly changing communications technologies. As we wrote in 1979:

> The obvious need for territorial pluralism to permit the provinces to deal with their differing problems and legitimate goals is in conflict with the equally clear need

for interregional communication, the projection of national perspectives, and central coordination of costly technological development.[35]

The most likely option at that time appeared to be some form of shared jurisdiction.

In the broadcast sector, the provinces, with the exception of Quebec, appear to have given up hope of achieving influence through interstate mechanisms. The House of Commons Committee on Culture and Communications noted that in its hearings on broadcasting policy, no-one had suggested that jurisdiction be divided between the federal and provincial governments.[36] The most recent discussions, generated by the *Report of the Task Force on Broadcasting*, revolve around greater openness by the CRTC to provincial broadcasting initiatives and mechanisms designed to achieve greater regional sensitivity in federal institutions. There is some hope that bilateral negotiations may lead to effective cooperation, as a result of a "memorandum of understanding" between Quebec and Ottawa (13 February 1986) that establishes mechanisms for cooperation in the development of the French-language television system. Federal participation in the development of *La chaine française*, the French language service of TVOntario, also suggests a new attitude towards intergovernmental cooperation. Manitoba has concluded a number of bilateral agreements with Ottawa in the general area of communications and development. However, the recommendation of the Caplan-Sauvageau report that the new Broadcasting Act require consultation with the provinces on both the awarding of broadcast licences within the province and on broad questions of broadcast policy was rejected by the House of Commons Committee. The Committee asserted that the provinces have ample opportunity to make their views known to the CRTC and to Parliament through the public hearing process, like any other intervenor.[37] The view that the provincial governments should be treated as just another interested party in federal regulatory proceedings is, at the very least, debatable.

The Task Force made a strong case for regularized consultation with the provinces, arguing that "broadcasting raises too many questions in too many different areas for the federal government to ignore the concerns of the provinces."[38] The Task Force called for a partnership in broadcasting and telecommunications, and urged that Quebec's special status be recognized. It made the point that Quebec, as the only government in Canada representing a French-speaking majority, has a moral responsibility to provide leadership in French-language broadcasting. These recommendations are more in the nature of exhortations, however, since they involved no discussion of mechanisms of consultation, and on the evidence to date are unlikely to have much influence in Ottawa.

More likely to have some impact are the Task Force recommendations for greater freedom for provincial broadcasting. Remarking that "the cultural, social, and educational development of a region can best be reflected by people who live and work there and this is a legitimate and increasingly important role for public broadcasting at the provincial level,"[39] the Task Force recommended that the CRTC continue to licence provincial broadcasters but leave to the provincial agencies involved the balance between educational and general broadcasting. The House of Commons Committee concurred but the reaction of the CRTC remains to be seen. Certainly, many provinces seem ready to move in this area. The expansion of provincial public broadcasting will almost certainly require mechanisms to alleviate legitimate federal concerns regarding partisan use and coordination of the overall system. Ronald Keast put the case as follows:

> Because the provinces are given some freedom and opportunity to develop and express their regional education and culture, indeed to express regional sovereignties, does not mean necessarily that national sovereignty or culture is diminished. In fact, the opposite is more likely. A strengthening of the regions can strengthen the whole, given that national energies and resources are not diminished. Certainly, if there is a threat to national cultural, political or economic sovereignty, it does not come from the provinces. It comes from outside.[40]

The best way to strengthen all forms of Canadian expression may well be to recognize legitimate provincial interests while preserving national licencing and insisting upon the arms-length requirement now in place.

The Task Force and the Committee recommended changes to provide more effective regional representation on the CRTC. Both took the view that the part-time commissioners, whose theoretical role had been to represent regional perspectives, had been ineffective. The Committee rejected the Task Force recommendation of a "public advocate" in each region and instead recommended the creation of regional vice-chairmen assigned permanently to each region of the country and mandated to work closely with regional groups. The regional vice-chairmen would sit with two other commissioners on each application in the region and would participate in the determination of overall policy.[41] The Task Force also recommended that the current practice of having decisions on French language services made by the francophone commissioners be continued.

With respect to the CBC, the Task Force and the Committee both recommended that the CBC Board of Directors be appointed with due concern for its representativeness, with regional representation placed on the same footing as representation of women, minorities, and the official language groups. In addition, the Task Force proposed an elaborate reorganization of the CBC to bring about more regional programming, for the regions and for the national networks.

While these forms of "centralized intrastate federalism" might well be beneficial, there is reason to doubt that representation by itself, without accountability, will produce much difference in behaviour. It may be suggested that it is the electoral calculus that makes provincial governments responsive to regional concerns. However, the Federal Economic Development Commissioner model in regional economic development, with a senior federal official resident in the region and in regular communication with provincial officials, *might* help to produce more regionally responsive policy-making at the CRTC. That would appear to depend both upon the openness of the agency to regional concerns and the extent to which the provincial governments actively pursue the role of advocate for regional and interprovincial concerns before the Commission. This model would probably make little difference to currently active provinces.

In the telecommunications field, the focus remains on trying to develop mechanisms for sharing jurisdiction. Though their hand is now being forced by the AGT case, initiated by CNCP for economic reasons, the federal and provincial governments (as well as those municipal governments active in the area) continue to assert that a negotiated settlement is to be preferred. Last April, the ministers responsible for communication in the eleven governments—and the territories—released a six-point agreement that included the following points:

1. Canadians must continue to have universal access to basic telephone services at affordable prices.

2. Policies must maintain the international competitiveness of the Canadian telecommunications sector and the industries it serves.

3. Policies must ensure that all Canadians benefit from the introduction of new technology.

4. A Canadian telecommunications policy must reinforce the goal of fair and balanced regional development, and respond to the interests of all concerned governments.

5. Telecommunications policies should be established by governments and not by regulatory bodies or the courts.[42]

While this sounds promising on the surface, it reflects very little advance from joint communiques of the late 1970s. Although the interests of both levels of government are recognized, there is no indication of agreement on priorities or mechanisms for sharing jurisdiction. One possible solution is a procedural one, involving a system of joint boards, regulating both intraprovincial and interprovincial activities. In addition, it would be desirable for some form of provincial participation, with federal paramountcy, in the regulation of interprovincial activities (and thus of national policies). Joint regulation, first proposed more than a decade ago, holds the potential to provide sufficient recognition of the national dimension while avoiding the remoteness from local and regional needs of exclusive federal jurisdiction. As Richard Schultz has put it, the system must be "one that permits respect for the concerns of all parties, provides for expeditious decision-making and for authoritative binding resolution of any conflicts that may emerge between the two regulatory tiers."[43] Whatever the mechanism for establishing national priorities, it seems clear that some means must exist to ensure that all regulators operate according to the agreed objectives.

In 1988, *in camera* discussions were dealing with a set of proposals similar to these prescriptions, with a Council of Ministers for general policy consultation; provincial regulation of rates, services and, most important, interconnection to the public telephone network; and a joint board to regulate interprovincial telecommunications.[44] The proposal leaves the largest telephone systems under federal regulation, however, and leaves those provinces without representation on the national board. The role of the CRTC remains ambiguous. This checkerboard solution is not much of an improvement on the present muddle but it does suggest that the governments continue to grope towards effective solutions. There is an abundance of regulatory reform proposals to choose from, including various forms of regulatory cooperation (such as joint hearings and studies) and the creation of joint agencies (by delegation or constitutional amendment).

For both telecommunications and broadcasting, alterations in the pattern of jurisdiction would almost certainly have had significant implications for the evolution of the Canadian communications system. The most obvious benefit of considering such implications is the identification of the costs and benefits of the pattern that did prevail. In the broadcasting case, the system failed to deal sensitively with provincial and regional needs, despite regional membership on the CRTC and the public hearing process. Among the results were regional alienation and problems of integrating communications elements effectively into provincial development programmes. The convergence of the various communications technologies has made this increasingly important. In addition, the reluctance of the federal government to permit provincial public broadcasting impeded the development of cultural production and educational innovation in several provinces. The most important lesson from the telecommunications case is that shared jurisdiction creates problems in the development of national priorities, problems with measurable economic costs, in the absence of effective mechanisms for resolution of federal-provincial conflicts. While business interests are inclined to see these conflicts as simply "turf wars,"[45] the conflicts are in fact about fundamental issues of social and economic development. Exclusive federal jurisdiction would almost certainly have subordinated the interests of the smaller provinces and of rural and remote communities to those of large corporations.

Conclusions

In this paper, we sought to answer two basic questions: How has the structure of federalism in Canada shaped the development of our communications system? What mechanisms of federal-provincial relations would allow us to develop the communications system most suited to our quest for political community? It seems clear that the edifice of exclusive federal jurisdiction erected by the federal government in pursuit of nation-building has limited the contribution of public broadcasting in Canada to local and regional development. Since culture tends to be local and regional, this limitation might be said to have hindered cultural development and created a paradox in which the system did considerably less to counter the north-south pull with an east-west pull than it might have otherwise. Exclusive provincial jurisdiction, on the other hand, would almost certainly have led to a U.S.-dominated broadcasting system in most provinces. The lack of effective federal regulation of telecommunications, in seven provinces, has led to piecemeal development that promoted province-building and, it appears, more socially conscious policies than would have emerged from exclusive federal jurisdiction, at the expense of clear national policies that would have fostered competition and economic growth. In short, this review has suggested that jurisdictional sharing and *de facto* concurrency deserve further consideration as mechanisms for promoting community development. Interstate negotiations have had only modest success and intrastate solutions have not been seriously tried. Some elements of intrastate federalism might be helpful but they raise questions of accountability at the administrative and regulatory level.

Notes

1   Donald V. Smiley, *The Federal Condition in Canada* (Toronto: McGraw-Hill Ryerson, 1987), 4.

2   In this short paper, we cannot examine these issues in much detail, but we hope to demonstrate that other jurisdictional regimes than those which did emerge could have had benefits as well as costs. For further discussion of jurisdiction and policy, see Frederick J. Fletcher and Donald C. Wallace, "Federal-Provincial Relations and the Making of Public Policy in Canada: A Review of Case Studies," in Richard Simeon (ed.), *Division of Powers and Public Policy* (Toronto: University of Toronto Press, 1985), 125-206.

3   Kenneth Norrie, Richard Simeon and Mark Krasnick, *Federalism and the Economic Union in Canada* (Toronto: University of Toronto Press, 1986), 313.

4   Martha Fletcher and Frederick J. Fletcher, "Communications and Confederation: Jurisdiction and Beyond," in R. B. Byers and Robert Reford

(eds.) *Canada Challenged: The Viability of Confederation* (Toronto: Canadian Institute of International Affairs, 1979), 158-187.

5   Many examples could be offered: (1) data is delivered via radio and television sub-carriers; (2) broadcast programming and data increasingly use satellites, as well as private microwave and telephone lines; (3) cable companies are moving into cellular radio and Bell Canada may be permitted to own cable companies; (4) Bell Canada subsidiaries are developing a proposal to offer television movies over their lines; (5) cable companies are offering some data transmission services in the form of non-programming services, such as airline schedules, stock market quotations, etc., to the general public.

6   For a discussion of intrastate federalism, see Smiley, *The Federal Condition*, 86.

7   Norrie, *Federalism*, 53.

8   Jean McNulty, "Technology and Nation-Building in Canadian Broadcasting," in Rowland Lorimer and Donald Wilson (eds.), *Communication Canada: Issues in Broadcasting and New Technologies* (Toronto: Kagan & Woo, 1988), 188.

9   Frank W. Peers, *The Politics of Canadian Broadcasting 1920-1951* (Toronto: University of Toronto Press, 1969), 69-70.

10   *Ibid.*, 71.

11   *Reference re Regulation and Control of Radio Communication* 1931 *SCR*, 541 at 572 and 576.

12   Peers, *Politics of Canadian Broadcasting*, 71-2.

13   For a discussion of this line of cases, see Fletcher and Fletcher, "Communications and Confederation," 161-6.

14   The Calgary station carried Aberhart's religious broadcasts. See Peers, *Politics of Canadian Broadcasting*, 243.

15   We have chosen the more inclusive term "provincial public broadcasting," rather than educational broadcasting, to emphasize the social role such provincial systems could play. This is in line with the actual practice of provincial systems, which have interpreted the definition of educational broadcasting broadly as a mandate to provide an alternative to commercial broadcasting.

16   In West Germany, the states have exclusive jurisdiction over broadcasting and provide national service through pooled programming. See Fletcher and Fletcher, "Communications and Confederation," 181-3.

17   Peers, *Politics of Canadian Broadcasting*, 376.

18   *Ibid.*, 328-31 and 373.

19   Ronald G. Keast, *The Role of the Provinces in Public Broadcasting* (Study Prepared for the Task Force on Broadcasting Policy, January 1986), 10-13, 41-42.

20   Frank W. Peers, *The Public Eye: Television and the Politics of Canadian Broadcasting 1952-1968* (Toronto: University of Toronto Press, 1979), 53.

21   *Ibid.*, 390.

22   For a discussion of these issues, see Keast, *Role of the Provinces*, viii, 26-7, 30-32 and *passim*. A close examination of these matters will be found in *The 1980s: A Decade of Diversity*, Report of the Committee on Extension of

Service to Northern and Remote Communities, Real Therrien, Chair (Ottawa: Supply and Services, 1980).

23 See, for example, E. Austin Weir, *The Struggle for Canadian Broadcasting* (Toronto: McClelland & Stewart, 1965) and Peers, *Politics of Canadian Broadcasting* and *The Public Eye*.

24 Ross A. Eaman, *The Media Society: Basic Issues and Controversies* (Toronto: Butterworths, 1987), 128.

25 See, for example, Peers, *Politics of Canadian Broadcasting*, 49.

26 *Report of the Task Force on Broadcasting Policy* (Ottawa: Ministry of Supply and Services Canada, 1986), 696.

27 Keast, *Role of the Provinces*, 16.

28 *Ibid*, viii.

29 Eaman, *The Media Society*, 137.

30 Richard J. Schultz, "All Talk No Action: The Telecommunications Dossier," in Peter M. Leslie (ed.), *Canada: The State of the Federation 1986* (Kingston, Ont.: The Institute of Intergovernmental Relations, Queen's University, 1986), 129-150. The movement towards jurisdictional sharing in the late 1970s has been viewed as a function of the low political standing of the federal government during that period. It can be argued that when Pierre Trudeau was returned to power in 1980 he viewed the election as a mandate to protect federal jurisdiction. See Roy Romanow, John White and Howard Leeson. *Canada... Notwithstanding: The Making of the Constitution, 1976-82* (Toronto: Carswell-Methuen, 1984), 30-32, 78-79.

31 Schultz, "All Talk," 138.

32 For a brief discussion of the issues surrounding the case, see Richard Schultz, "Forward to the Past: The Canadian Approach to Telecommunications Regulatory Reform," Paper prepared for the University of Vermont-McGill University Conference "Managing Global Telecommunications Policies: North American Perspectives", (Burlington, Vermont, June 1988), 19-20.

33 Schultz, "Forward," 10.

34 Rowland Lorimer and Jean McNulty, *Mass Communication in Canada* (Toronto: McClelland & Stewart, 1987), 207.

35 Fletcher and Fletcher, "Communications and Confederation," 160-1.

36 House of Commons, *Recommendations for a New Broadcasting Act*, Minutes of Proceedings and Evidence of the Standing Committee on Communications and Culture, Sixth Report, (May 4, 1987), 15.

37 *Ibid.*, 67 and 83.

38 Task Force on Broadcasting, 15.

39 *Ibid*, 341.

40 Keast, *Role of the Provinces*, 158-9.

41 Task Force on Broadcasting, 88-89.

42 Department of Communications, *A Policy Framework for Telecommunications in Canada* (July 1987), 4.

43 Richard Schultz, "The Case for Meaningful Two-Tier Regulation in Canadian Telecommunications." Notes for a Presentation to Telecon 87, (Montreal, September 16, 1987), 5.

44 *Ibid.*, 5-6.

45 David G. Vice, President of Northern Telecom Limited, commented in a speech entitled "Winning in the Global Marketplace," delivered at the opening of the Norstar Manufacturing Facility, Calgary (March 22, 1988), 13: "There's a global competitive war raging and we're fighting internal turf wars." Quoted in Schultz, "Forward," 10.

DONALD SMILEY AND THE

STUDY OF FEDERALISM

WE ARE ALL SMILEY'S PEOPLE: SOME OBSERVATIONS ON DONALD SMILEY AND THE STUDY OF FEDERALISM

Richard Simeon, Queen's University

Introduction

Every student of Canadian federalism is one of Smiley's people. His work epitomizes the chief strengths—and a few of the weaknesses—of Canadian political science. Many of us see in him the model of how to conduct the scholarly enterprise, infusing empirical analysis with a deep moral sense and with an engagement with the fundamental political issues of the day. There is no important issue in Canadian federalism which has escaped his attention, and no important theoretical interpretation which he has not sympathetically explored. To re-read successive editions of *Canada in Question* (1972, 1976, 1980) and his other works is to follow the twists and turns of an extraordinary period in Canadian federalism. In this essay, as a third generation student of his, I will offer some personal observations on his contributions to understanding the "federal condition."

I begin by noting some of the qualities of Smiley's work which relate not to scholarly or theoretical debates, but to the moral sensibility which pervades his work. First, I know of no scholar so open to new ideas, or so frank and whole-hearted in his acknowledgement of the contribution of others to his thinking about federalism. In the various prefaces to *Canada in Question* he generously accepts his intellectual debts to his predecessors, his contemporaries, and younger scholars. The message he sends—and in this age of specialization and competition it is a crucial one—is that our scholarship is a collective enterprise, building on past efforts and probing for new insights.

Second, few scholars are as ready to admit error or as sympathetic to and curious about new approaches. Few are as open about publicly wrestling with alternative assessments or explanations, or as ready to set aside ideas or interpretations when the evidence no longer seems to support them. His openness to new interpretations is matched by his sensitivity to changes in the wider society; he continually seeks to embrace and understand new social movements, not to ignore, exclude or rail against them. There is, as a result, an engage quality to all his work. He energizes his scholarship by using it to grapple with public events, while simultaneously using that scholarship to give shape and meaning to those events.

Finally, he brings to all his work a strong quality of moral judgement. He continually reminds us, by precept and example, that the study of politics is about public purposes and public values; about the use of authority for collective ends. He knows that the most powerful scholarship is driven by moral purpose; and that scholarship without purpose is both sterile and a fiction. Scholarship is about making judgement, and normative themes pervade his work. He is, as he reminds us, the son and grandson of clergymen, with a profound instinct to name and correct error. He is, in whatever he addresses, democratic and humanist, which he combines with a deep concern for the conditions of order and civility. He has a Tory sense of the need to nurture and sustain community and much of his work reflects a sometimes agonized search for the bases on which, in an era of politicized and governmentalized diversities, we can construct a viable Canadian community. In this sense he is a nationalist, but one skeptical of atavistic and exclusionary expressions of nationalism. In recent years he has argued the need for developing more explicit linkages between democratic political theory and federalism. But Don Smiley would be the first to say he is not a political philosopher; he is immersed instead in seeking to understand the empirical forces which shape Canadian federalism.

So let us turn to Smiley's work and the enduring themes of Canadian federalism which it has explored. He began his writing on federalism in the early 1960s, just as the postwar consensus on the Keynesian welfare state, and on the role of the federal government as the primary instrument for developing and implementing it was coming to an end. He started just as the Quiet Revolution was bursting on Quebec, calling into question not only the postwar order, but also, as he pointed out the Confederation settlement itself, which had been predicated on the ability to sustain a distinction between "culture" and "economy." He was one of the first to see that the equation "modernization equals centralization"—which most writers on federalism since the 1930s had argued—was wrong, and that the growth of provincial responsibilities and fiscal strength was itself a response to "modernization" (1962; 1984). Since then his work has chronicled the "compounded crisis" in Canadian federalism, touching on all the major questions of the day, and exploring with careful skepticism the chief political solutions being debated, whether they be special status for Quebec or intra-state federalism.

Much of this analysis has been deeply pessimistic. In the first edition of *Canada in Question*, he tells us that he stopped work on his manuscript twice, on the grounds that he felt the federation was not likely to survive long enough to see his book published. The next two editions conclude with chapters asking whether there is a basis for political community in Canada. By the 1980 edition, the three axes of Canadian federalism—French-English relations, centre-periphery relations, and Canada-US relations—have become a "compounded crisis," for which he sees little prospect for solution. In this again, he was reflecting much of the academic tenor of the times—*Canada in Question* was joined by other titles such as *Must Canada Fail?* (Simeon, ed., 1977), *Unfulfilled Union* (Stevenson, 1979), and *Canada and the Burden of Unity* (Bercuson, ed., 1977). More recently, as we shall see later, he has mellowed to become much more optimistic about the future of the federal system.

In many ways Don's work epitomizes the chief strengths of Canadian work in political science, and of the study of federalism in particular. But I will also argue, in a spirit of gentle criticism, that some of these strengths have a negative side as well. To be so engaged in wrestling with contemporary events is sometimes to limit the scope of analysis, and to constrain the ability to develop more general theory. It limits the ability to draw on comparative experience, or to contribute to the comparative literature. The eclecticism which is one of his great strengths can sometimes blur the central lines of analysis. So there are some difficulties with the work—but they are difficulties not unique to him, but common to much if not most of Canadian political science.

Central Themes in Smiley's Work

To read Smiley's work is to touch on virtually all the themes that have characterized the modern study of federalism in Canada. Not only has his work closely followed the changing political agenda, but also it has reacted to the emergence of new theoretical orientations. By his own admission, he is an academic scavenger, and his work has integrated the insights of several other disciplines, notably law, history and economics. His early work was solidly rooted in the institutional and public administration perspective of political science, but in the 1960s and 1970s he sought to incorporate the insights of more behavioral approaches, the most important result of which was his superb analysis of party conventions and the definitive chapters on the confederal Canadian party system in *Canada in Question*. Similarly, while explicitly rejecting Marxist approaches, he has integrated much of the work of political economists, most importantly in what he has said about province-building, centre-periphery relations, and especially the interaction between the domestic dynamics of federalism and Canada's relationship with the United States.

But the core of his theoretical approach has always been institutional: focussing on the relations between institutions and processes and public policy, as he put it. The literature has caught up with him. In stressing the centrality of institutions in early editions he seemed to imply that he was swimming against the behavioral tide; but by 1981 Alan Cairns' "Governments and Societies of Canadian Federalism" (1977) had reinstated the state-centered approach as the dominant theoretical perspective on Canadian federalism. Smiley describes his Third Edition of *Canada in Question* as an extended footnote to this article. By the most recent edition, retitled *The Federal Condition in Canada* (1987) Smiley was able to draw as well on a much larger comparative literature—including writers like Skocpol and Nordlinger—who had "brought the state back in" and who stressed the autonomy of state institutions and those who operate them. But this perspective on state and society is an old one in Canada, and it was the one in which he had been working all along.

Executive Federalism

Smiley has made notable contribution to almost every aspect of federal studies. I will touch on only a few of the most important here. "Executive federalism" is the concept most closely associated with his name; it has become the standard description of the operation of Canadian federalism. The term was coined in his study for the Royal Commission on Bilingualism and Biculturalism, *Constitutional Adaptation and Canadian Federalism* (1974), which brilliantly analyzed the shift from the postwar pattern of cooperative federalism under federal policy and financial leadership to the pattern of relations between two powerful orders of government locked into a kind of competitive interdependence orchestrated by their central political and bureaucratic officials. He found the primary explanations in the way changes in the role of government interacted with the institutional setting, in the changing character of federal and provincial political and bureaucratic elites, and in social changes, notably the Quiet Revolution in Quebec.

Much of our subsequent literature has concentrated on trying to understand, assess and evaluate this process. Again, Smiley has been at the forefront of these efforts. Critiques of executive federalism have taken three forms, each of which he has been among the first to contribute to. It has been attacked on democratic grounds as a closed, elitist process which blurs citizen participation and legislative accountability. His acerbic "Outsider's Observations" on the process in the 1970s (in Simeon, ed., 1979) touched on all these themes. Much of the current critique of the Meech Lake process can be drawn directly from that article. Executive federalism has also been attacked on the grounds that it is an ineffective device for the resolution of intergovernmental and interregional conflict—indeed on the grounds that it institutionalizes, reinforces, and exacerbates such conflict. This was a central theme in Smiley's writing early on. The third critique is a more functional one—that shared decision-making, divided authority, and the claim of provinces to participate in national decision-making undermine the coherence of policy and the ability to formulate effective national economic strategies in the face of global pressures.

Thus Smiley's analysis and critique of executive federalism has been a central contribution. The dilemma, as he put it in 1970, was that "Canada cannot effectively be governed under circumstances in which the most important public policies are made by...joint federal-provincial decision." But at the same time, "Canada is in the most elemental way a federal country."

These concerns with the fragility of intergovernmental relations as the central mechanism for political and policy accommodation led Smiley to become one of the first to explore what came to be known as "intra-state" federalism—the search for more effective means to accommodate Canada's diversities within the institutions and practices of the central government. In the first edition of Canada in Question the "structural defects" of the federal incapacity to represent all parts of the country was held fundamentally to undermine the ability of the federal government to speak authoritatively for the country, and to account in large part for the challenges provinces were able to mount. Hence in a number of writings, most recently the Macdonald Commission study with R. L. Watts (1985), Smiley has explored alternative devices for injecting the "federal principle" into the centre, including an early proposal for electoral system reform, Senate reform, and others. He has asserted that to be successful, any such reform must engage not simply peripheral federal institutions, but the core centres of federal authority, the cabinet and bureaucracy.

As this suggests, Smiley's own starting point is basically a centralist one, looking to the federal government as the primary definer of national collective interests, and as the protector of smaller, weaker regions. He analyzed the "attenuation of federal power" (1967)—another of his phrases to become common currency—with a clear-headed understanding of its causes, but with deep regret. In earlier writings he strongly attacked those who advocated a decentralizing response to provincial pressures. For example, he criticized a federal proposal to place limits on the federal spending power in 1968. He was critical of the younger generation of scholars who he saw as giving indiscriminate support to Quebec nationalism, and as accepting uncritically the idea of Canada as a loose collection of provinces. He dismissed both those who were prepared to accept a substantial special status for Quebec, and who talked about "a special status for all" in a decentralized Canada. Both, he argues, assume that there is no national community, and no collective national purpose to be achieved through the federal government. He was, as he put it, on the side of those who wished to resist the disintegration of the Canadian community, and that clearly meant the need to stress national values, national commitments, and the integrity of the national government. Only a "new national policy," he argued in 1975, could roll back the related threats of "American continentalism and provincial particularism." He later came to be more sympathetic to at least some constitutional recognition of Quebec's distinctive character as the only means to assure its voluntary continued membership in the federation, and this no doubt explains his willingness to support the Meech Lake Accord. And he was of course too much the democrat to suggest that Quebec could ever be held in Confederation against its will.

Much of Smiley's work therefore has been devoted to exploring what that national purpose might be—and therefore what might constitute the basis of the Canadian political community. The "attenuation of federal power" had turned into the "decline of Canadian nationhood." Like Pierre Trudeau, he early on concluded that it could not lie in definitions of Canadian nationality based on an exclusive conception of ethnicity and culture. His early examination of the "two themes" of Canadian federalism embodied in the Rowell-Sirois and Tremblay Reports (1965) had shown that was impossible. In his contribution to Peter Russell's 1965 book (Russell, 1965), he argued that nationalist symbols could never be the cement for Canada; the Canadian political nationality must be founded on the pursuit of agreed, concrete policy objectives, many of which he tried to set out in his later work, especially that on the search for a new national policy. Yet at the same time, he had recognized that it was precisely the expanded role of government which had underpinned the growth of state-based nationalism in Quebec, and rendered the confederation settlement, predicated on the ability to distinguish between economy and culture, obsolete. Now culture, policy and economy were inextricably entwined, and federal-provincial conflict was shaped by the expansion of government at both levels. As each level expanded into the available space, there appeared to be no principled grounds for achieving a new governmental division of labour. Indeed, Smiley came to argue that federalism itself helped contribute to the growth of government in Canada. And in his 1981 volume, one of his conditions for the re-establishment of political community in Canada now came to be a "discriminating limitation" on the powers of the state. His fear of the divisive effects of the use of untrammelled state power no doubt accounts for his hostility to the 1980 constitutional initiative undertaken by Pierre Trudeau. But the other side of the tension reemerges in his assessment of the Mulroney government's record on federalism. Smiley admits that there has been a reduction in regional and linguistic conflict, but argues that it has been achieved at the price of "a profound absence of national direction" (1987: 187) characterized chiefly by a free trade agreement which he argues will diminish Canadians' ability to use government for public purposes. Thus, his preoccupation with the political conditions of Canadian nationhood continues.

A final fundamental theme which pervades Smiley's work is the notion of the "compounded crisis"—the structuring of

Canadian federalism along the three axes of French-English relations, centre-periphery relations, and Canada-US relations. As he points out, for much of the time we have carried out each of these sets of debates in quite different frameworks, and thus have not brought them together—for example in exploring the link between domestic regional conflict and continentalism. The need to theorize the nature of the link has once again become prominent in the Meech Lake and Free Trade debates, with some arguing that both the provincialism in Meech Lake, and the voluntary constraints accepted in Free Trade are bound together by a common desire to constrain and limit the central government, and by a lack of commitment to national purposes carried out by a national government.

Only in his most recent book has Smiley paid much attention to a fourth axis, which has also both shaped and been shaped by the federal system, not only recently but throughout the postwar period. This axis includes interests and identities which are non-territorial, and therefore which cut across or transcend the territorially-defined interests which are institutionalized in federalism. Early editions of *Canada in Question* gave fairly short shrift to the Porter-Horowitz arguments against the sterility and conservatism of federalism, and their call for a reorientation of Canadian politics around class rather than territorial lines. At the conclusion of *The Federal Condition*, however, he makes a parallel argument, by suggesting not that class will displace territory, but that a variety of other cleavages such as gender may challenge the federalist emphasis on territory. Again this is strongly evident in the present in the Meech Lake debate.

This is only one respect in which his new book differs from previous editions of *Canada in Question*. It is considerably narrower in scope, and little remains of the attention to political economy, fiscal federalism, and specific policy issues. The focus is now more explicitly institutional. But the most important change is that the pessimism is gone. All previous editions were organized around the theme that the Canadian political nationality was fragile; that the compound crisis placed extraordinary strains on the system; and that there were profound failures both in the institutions of national government and the institutions of federalism which seemed to make the country ungovernable. While many institutional reforms were canvassed, most were regarded skeptically, and Smiley displayed little confidence that any of them would work.

Now he is discussing, as he puts it, "a relatively stable system of government," and indeed a relatively successful one. Moreover, while much of the earlier work suggested that federalism is indeed an historically rooted and necessary feature of Canadian politics, there was little principled defence of federalism except as a necessity. Now there is an explicit attempt to assess federalism in terms both of democratic theory, and its policy consequences, with the optimistic conclusion that the Canadian variant of federalism "contributes both to the preservation of certain key democratic values and to effective public policy."

But not only does he suggest that the federal system has changed, he also argues that the earlier pessimism and sense of institutional failure may itself have been wrong. "I, and most other observers, very much overestimated the strength of Quebec nationalism and provincialist influences elsewhere in the country," and underestimated the capacity of the system to respond. Similarly, Cairns' "Other Crisis of Canadian Federalism" (1975) is now held to have gone too far: it exaggerates the extent to which all governments are unitary actors, and all federal-provincial interactions are zero-sum, and all governments inevitably are engaged in seeking to expand their powers. Thus, the problem he poses is not to explain why federal-provincial conflict has diminished or how the system has become more responsive; instead we were wrong in the first place. There are a number of problems with this formulation; they help illuminate some of the weaknesses in Smiley's work and in our study of federalism more generally.

First, we pay a price for the engaged quality of our work, and for the closeness with which it hews to rapidly evolving public events. We continually get captured by them—which student of federalism has not devoted much of the last year to thinking, talking and writing about Meech Lake, for example. We have little time and energy to step back. All of us concerned with current policy continually risk being out-run or outdated by events, and risk being swayed from our analysis by them. Smiley is no exception. He just managed to slip a postscript on the federal wage and price control program into his second edition, suggesting it may arrest provincialist trends and energize class cleavages. But he was not able to include the election of the PQ. The Quebec Referendum result and the climactic constitutional battles of 1980-81 did not make it into the 1980 edition; nor did

Meech Lake get into the 1987 edition. Our engagement with events keeps us always trying to catch up; we risk confusing transitory events with long-term changes.

Moreover the stress on the intricacies of our own political system, and on the specific terms of the Canadian debate, means that we seldom address ourselves to the comparative dimension, though I think this is changing. Would it have changed our thinking about Canadian federalism if we had paid more attention to the fact that all western countries in the 1960s and 1970s were preoccupied with increasing fragmentation and regional protest; that everywhere there was a concern about the erosion of the postwar consensus, about "ungovernability," and about perceived institutional failure? On the other hand, it is also extraordinary to note how few references to Canadian writers on federalism are found in the comparative literature, and I do not think this is entirely the result of their parochialism.

There are also costs to the theoretical and disciplinary eclecticism most of us engage in. Especially when trying to comprehend the whole system, multi-dimensional analysis is essential; no single-cause model or theory explains the evolution of the federal system. Smiley's breadth enriches almost every page of his work. But there is also the possibility that this eclecticism can lead to theoretical muddiness, to a feeling that we are not quite clear what is to be explained, or just what the causal factors are. By encompassing any and all approaches we often end up with inconclusive lists of factors, or analysis of the form "on the one hand this, on the other hand that." There is too little emphasis on hypothesis-testing.

In particular, we have not have done a very good job theorizing about change in the federal system. It may very well be that we did exaggerate the strength of Quebec nationalist and provincialist challenges to the system, and that we underestimated its resilience in the 1960s and 1970s. Indeed that is almost certainly the case, a consequence of our tendency to get caught up in events and of the social scientists' general tendency to have a vested interest in failure and instability, which are so much more interesting to write about than boring success.

But another perspective is to say that major change has taken place—a diminution of Quebec nationalism, of the intensity of regional cleavages, of intergovernmental hostilities, and so on. The question then becomes what explains this change—and are the variables the same as those we would use to explain earlier shifts—from relative federal dominance, low conflict, and cooperative federalism in the postwar period to the competitive federalism, high conflict and decentralizing trends of the 1960s and 1970s?

Clearly institutional models alone are insufficient, since these changes have ocurred—with the exception of the adoption of the Charter—within an essentially unchanged institutional framework. So are theories which stress the power drives of incumbent elites as the determining factors since, if these are universal traits, they cannot explain change or explain why one set of elites is more able than another to mobilize support at any particular time. That depends on societal factors, which the elites can and do try to mobilize and exploit, but which they cannot control except in very limited ways. Nor can change be fully explained by the attitudes and intentions of the leaders: Joe Clark had just as much commitment to national reconciliation, and faced just as friendly a group of premiers as did Brian Mulroney, but he was unable to bridge the Ontario-Alberta differences in 1979. All these kinds of factors are important, and the virtue of the state-autonomy or neo-institutional school is to draw our attention to them.

But to fully explain change we are driven to revive our interest in societal forces and in political economy. It is these forces— domestic and international—which provide much of the energy and raw material which elites mobilize. It is impossible to understand major shifts in the federal system without exploring such factors as global economic forces as they interact with the regionally differentiated domestic economy and territorially defined institutions: the rise of global energy prices was surely the single most important factor shaping centre-periphery conflict in the 1970s, and their decline is one of the primary reasons for the diminution of regional conflict in the 1980s. Nor can we understand federalism without looking at changes in the domestic society and economy—the mobilization of new groups, changing societal values, and the like. For example, the rise of executive federalism and the rise of state-based Quebec nationalism were driven by fundamental changes in the role of the state; the decline of Quebec nationalism, or at least its shift to "market nationalism," is explained in large part by disillusionment with the role of the state. Provincialist pressures are mobilized when these kinds of larger changes energize the provincialist dimensions of Canadian interests and identities; nationalizing forces predominate when the larger changes mobilize the national, pan-Canadian dimensions of our identity. So if we want to understand the evolution of federalism we must look beyond the institutional and elite models.

My point here is not to repudiate the state-centered model, nor to argue that Smiley and others have ignored the societal dimension in state-society relations. It is to suggest that we may have gone overboard in our emphasis on state-centered models and that we have made little progress in theorizing state-society linkages. Of course federalism is about governments, since it is by definition an institutional system. But to argue that the explanation of the relations between these governments can be understood simply in governmental terms is wrong. Smiley's work has included discussion of many of these larger forces. Students of federalism may hope that his next book will set out more clearly the theoretical underpinnings and implications of his extraordinarily rich contributions to our understanding of the federal condition in Canada. He may find it time to put society and economy back in.

One of the best things about Smiley is a kind of presbyterian pragmatism, respect for the empirical, and suspicion of the grand, sweeping, simplifying assumption, combined with an extraordinary curiosity. This is what makes him the model for all those who work in Canadian federal studies. We all share his weaknesses, but very few of us can match his strengths.

References

Bercuson, David, ed., *Canada and the Burden of Unity*. Toronto: Macmillan of Canada, 1977.

Cairns, Alan, "The Governments and Societies of Canadian Federalism", in *Canadian Journal of Political Science*. 1977: 10, pp. 695-725.

Cairns, Alan, "The Other Crisis in Canadian Federalism", in *Canadian Public Administration*. 1977: 22, pp. 175-195.

Russell, Peter, ed., *Nationalism in Canada*. Toronto: McGraw-Hill, 1965.

Simeon, Richard, *Must Canada Fail?*. Kingston and Montreal: McGill-Queen's University Press, 1977.

Simeon, Richard, ed., *Confrontation or Collaboration: Intergovernmental Relations in Canada Today*. Toronto: Institute of Public Administration of Canada, 1979.

Smiley, D.V., "The Rowell-Sirois Report, Provincial Autonomy and Post-war Canadian Federalism", in *Canadian Journal of Economics and Political Science*. 1962: 28, pp. 54-69.

Ibid., "Public Administration and Canadian Federalism", in *Canadian Public Administration*. 1964: 7, pp. 371-388.

Ibid., "Federalism, Nationalism and the Scope of Public Activity in Canada", in *Nationalism in Canada*. pp. 95-111.

Ibid., "The Two Themes of Canadian Federalism", in *Canadian Journal of Economics and Political Science*. 1965: 31, pp. 80-97.

Ibid., *The Canadian Political Nationality*. Toronto: Methuen, 1967.

Ibid., *Canada in Question: Federalism in the Seventies*. Toronto: McGraw-Hill Ryerson, 1972, 1976.

Ibid., "An Outsider's Observations of Federal-Provincial Relations among Consenting Adults." in *Confrontation or Collaboration*. pp. 105-113.

Ibid., *Canada in Question: Federalism in the Eighties*. 3rd. edition, Toronto: McGraw-Hill Ryerson, 1980.

Ibid., "Public Sector Politics, Modernization and Federalism: The Canadian and American Experiences", in *Publius*. 1984: 14, pp. 39-59.

Ibid., *An Elected Senate for Canada? Clues from the Australian Experience*. Kingston: Intstitute of Intergovernmental Relations, 1985.

Ibid., *The Federal Condition in Canada*. Toronto: McGraw-Hill Ryerson, 1987.

Smiley and R. L. Watts, "Intrastate Federalism in Canada" in *Research Studies of the Royal Commission on the Economic Union*. Toronto: University of Toronto Press, 1985.

Stevenson, Garth, *Unfulfilled Union*. Toronto: Macmillan of Canada, 1979.

THE INTERPLAY OF POLITICAL INSTITUTIONS AND POLITICAL COMMUNITIES

Roger Gibbins, University of Calgary

> In the beginning Canada was a political creation. From the pieces of Britain's North American empire a handful of mid-Victorian colonial legislators fashioned a new state. Lacking a common culture, a common past, or a common interest, they created a common political system to bind themselves together. Since that time the greatest task of national government has been to develop and nourish a Canadian political community.[1]

My intent in this paper is to explore, in an admittedly rather abstract fashion, what Carty and Ward identify as the "greatest task" of the national government—the development and nourishment of a Canadian political community. The paper will first discuss the interplay between political institutions and political communities as that interplay has been developed in the writings of Donald Smiley. I will then move to a more specific look at Smiley's reaction to the Constitution Act of 1982, and a more speculative look at the Meech Lake Accord placed against the backdrop of Smiley's work.

Before launching into the body of the paper, there is an important caveat to be made. Although the paper draws from, and is even more emphatically informed by, the rich corpus of Donald Smiley's work, I make no claim to have successfully distilled the essence of that work. There is much that Professor Smiley has written about the linkage between political institutions and political communities that I have not fully absorbed, and undoubtedly in some cases have not even encountered. There is also a wealth of material that I have encountered and to a degree have absorbed, but which cannot be carried in the rather frail and limited vehicle provided by this paper. The paper, then, uses Professor Smiley as a point of departure in a somewhat more wide-ranging exploration of the interplay between political institutions and political communities.

While my success in capturing the analytical detail of Professor Smiley's work remains open to debate, I am more confident that I have caught its spirit—that political institutions are of central importance to the sustenance of political communities; that this is particularly the case in federal states; and that, in the specific case of the Canadian federal state, serious strains within the political community can be traced to flaws in institutional design and constitutional structures. That spirit has animated my own work since I took my first undergraduate political science class at the University of British Columbia in the fall of 1966. Not coincidentally, my instructor in the course was Donald Smiley.

The Theoretical Backdrop

In his 1977 presidential address to the Canadian Political Science Association, Alan Cairns crystallized a state-centred approach to the study and understanding of Canadian federalism. In stressing the "degree of autonomy possessed by governments and the ongoing capacity of the federal system to manufacture the conditions necessary for its continuing survival,"[2] Cairns brought to the fore the role of governments in structuring social relationships within federal states. Cairns' emphasis on "governmental societies" has more recently been reflected back on Canadian scholarship through the recent work of E.A. Nordlinger.[3] Writing in 1984, Smiley endorsed Nordlinger's *On the Autonomy of the Democratic State* as a seminal analysis,[4] and concluded that

> ...the state-centered view of liberal democracy is a valuable prism through which we might investigate federalism and state-society relations in democratic nations more broadly, and provides a congenial base for what one might pretentiously call a neo-institutionalism, which suggests that the structures and processes that prevail within the state apparatus are important determinants of the macro-distribution of power within these nations.[5]

Smiley, however, is by no means a recent convert to the importance of political institutions in structuring communities and citizen identifications within federal states. Writing in 1967, Smiley argued that the initial, even somewhat wary, creation of a national community in 1867 rested upon the institutional structure and resources of the new national government:

The Dominion was to be a deliberate creation which could be established, in the perspectives of the Fathers of Confederation, only through the instrumentality of a strong and vigorous central government. This meant both that the federal authorities would assume the decisive leadership in the task and that the dominant loyalties of the people, insofar as they were those of a political allegiance, would be focussed on the Dominion rather than its constituent parts. What was involved was, in George Etienne Cartier's words, the creation of a new 'political nationality.'[6]

As Smiley pointed out through reference to W.L. Morton, "Confederation was, indeed, to be a new nationality, but it was to be a political nationality, not an absolute one which would absorb the old cultural and linguistic nationality of the French into that of the British."[7] Yet Smiley went on to argue that "if Confederation is to continue, Canada must be seen as a single political community."[8] Canadians, moreover, must share a commitment to that community; they must also see it as "...more than an arena in which the divergent cultural, regional and economic interests contend for position and in which the established cultural groups coexist and cooperate in as limited a number of common purposes as is possible without their formal separation into independent sovereign states."[9] In his own centennial year project Smiley concluded that "if Canada cannot become a political community—one community not two—it is not worth preserving."[10]

The ongoing Canadian problem, however, is how to provide political expression for that over-arching community, that "one community not two," within the constitutional framework of a federal state. Even if that community is, as W.L. Morton asserts, "a community of political allegiance alone,"[11] it is still a community which requires political articulation if, as Smiley argues, Canadians are to have more than an instrumental attachment to the community. Yet the Canadian political landscape is littered with failed attempts at articulation. John Diefenbaker's appeal to "One Canada" fell on deaf, if not antagonistic, ears in Quebec. Joe Clark's notion of a "community of communities" showed initial promise, but then failed to flower as Clark's leadership of his country and party withered on the vine. More recently, Pierre Trudeau's vision of the national community, one embodied in the 1982 Constitution Act, is being dismembered by the architects of the Meech Lake Accord. Here, however, I am jumping ahead in the story.

Given the entrenchment of a large cultural-linguistic minority within the Canadian federal state, it has become difficult in political rhetoric even to speak of the 'national' community. Certainly the very idea of an over-arching 'national' community has been a threatening one to French Canadians, in the traditional sense, and remains a threatening one to Québécois in the more contemporary sense, evoking as it does images of anglo-conformism. (As an aside, this may explain why 'nation-building' in Canada has traditionally been seen in economic rather than in sociological, cultural, or even political terms.)[12] Dualist views of the country, much less more nationalist perspectives from Quebec, make it very difficult to talk about the 'Canadian community,' as indeed do the more general compact theories of Confederation favoured by many provincial premiers.[13] One is left instead with two communities, French Quebec and a residual anglophone population dispersed across ten provincial and two territorial communities.

Even more problematic than our inability to speak of a 'national community' is our inability to speak of a 'national' government. Since at least the report of the Tremblay Commission in the early 1950s, Quebec nationalists have rejected any claim that Ottawa is the site of the 'national' government, or have argued that, to the extent that institutions based in Ottawa constitute a national government, it is a national government for the English-Canadian community and not for any pan-Canadian community more broadly defined. Thus in Canada the *national* government becomes the *federal* government.

This transformation is important because it calls into question the ability of the federal government to speak for, or to articulate, the Canadian political community. Within the context of executive federalism and the growing importance of the First Minister's Conference, it also brings the ten provincial governments into play. The effective national government, if the term retains any meaning at all, expands to embrace not only parliamentary institutions sited in Ottawa but also the interplay between the federal cabinet and its ten provincial counterparts. Thus the right of the federal government to speak for, and to articulate, the Canadian political community is called into question not only by nationalist thought in Quebec, but also by the more general claim of provincial governments that they too speak for Canada, that if the

Canadian community is to receive political articulation it must come about through a choir of eleven governments rather than through the solo voice of any one. The prime minister might orchestrate, but his voice should not be heard over that of the choir. When Pierre Trudeau asks "who speaks for Canada?," the answer is "we all do, in our fashion."

All of this means, I would argue, that our written constitution becomes a critically important means of articulating the Canadian political community, and that constitution-making has become the definitive Canadian act of nation-building. In a sense, the constitution serves as a canvas upon which we can paint, or at least sketch in, visions of the national community which transcend the bounds of language, ethnicity and region. Certainly Pierre Trudeau in the early 1980s approached the constitution as a painter might approach a canvas, sketching in as he did a distinctive vision of the national community. As I have argued elsewhere,[14] western Canadian premiers brought a much more limited national vision to the canvas and, as a consequence, left much less of an imprint on the final product. René Levesque unquestionably had a national vision in mind, but it was a national vision of Quebec rather than of Canada, and a vision that was ultimately swept aside by that of Pierre Trudeau.

The constitution, then, provides one of the few means at our disposal for articulating a sense of the Canadian community. If Canada is first and foremost a political community, then it should not be surprising that it is through the constitution that the community is finding expression. Constitution-making, then, becomes an ongoing process of community expression. That process is important in turn because of its potential to alter the choir of governmental voices through which Canada finds articulation as a political community. Will changes to the constitution heighten the impact of some voices while dampening the impact of others? Will changes affect not only the interplay of governments but also the ability of the federal government to orchestrate that interplay, to impose some order upon provincial voices?

This discussion may seem to be taking us rather far afield. In fact, however, it brings us directly to the convergence of Donald Smiley and two milestones in Canadian constitutional life: the Constitution Act of 1982 and the Meech Lake Accord of 1987.

The Constitution Act 1982

> The claims of political allegiance can be defended only if they are illuminated by some vision of political community.[15]

There is little question that the Constitution Act 1982 gave expression to a vision of the political community, one shaped by the one man who had so dominated the country's political stage over the previous fifteen years.[16] In the Charter of Rights and, more specifically, in the constitutional entrenchment of language rights, the Act embodied a vision closely identified with the leadership and Liberal governments of Pierre Elliott Trudeau.[17] As a consequence it was also a liberal and individualistic vision. As Carty and Ward explain:

> At one time or another most provinces have represented the nation as the sum of its provincial components or, at least, of its regions... But all such claims, whether based on the assumption that the nation is composed of cultures, regions, or provinces, deny a fundamental principle of liberal democracy: that citizens are individually and equally incorporated into the political community.[18]

The Constitution Act, on the other hand, did recognize that fundamental principle; it provided a vehicle for the individual rather than collective incorporation of citizens into the Canadian federal state. However, Smiley argues that in so doing, the Constitution Act failed Canadians.

In Smiley's unequivocal view, the Constitution Act was nothing less than a betrayal of Quebec:

> The pressures of both government and opposition parties in Quebec provincial politics from 1960 onward has been for an enhanced range of autonomy for the authorities of that province and corresponding restriction on the power of the federal government over Quebecers. The Constitution Act 1982 *restricts* the powers of the Legislature and government of Quebec and was brought into being by a procedure which *was opposed* by that Legislature and government. Furthermore, the constitutional reform which was effected in the spring of 1982 was an integral

part of a general initiative from Ottawa towards a more highly centralized federal system. The pledges of constitutional reform made to the Quebec electorate by the federal Liberal leaders have *not* been honoured, and it is not too much to say that this electorate has been betrayed.[19]

Nor was this betrayal offset, if indeed it could be offset, by corresponding strengths in the Act. The constitutional settlement, Smiley argues, did not address what Alan Cairns has termed the "other crisis" in Canadian federalism, a virulent form of regional discontent associated with an unfocussed quest for intrastate reform. Smiley also rejects the argument that, over the long run, the Charter will serve as a nationalizing device, drawing together a linguistically-divided and territorially-diverse political community. Rather, he argues, "...the Charter is inherently a fragmenting rather than unifying measure; while one may make some rhetorical mileage by asserting that the Charter binds Canadians together in their common possession of certain rights, the defence of rights centres on conflict rather than co-operation."[20] Smiley's pessimism stems in part from the constitutional debate leading up to the Charter, one that "emphasized special claims rather than those rights possessed by all Canadians."[21]

Smiley also criticizes the Constitution Act on procedural grounds, rejecting the notion that the Act was legitimate because the principal federal advocates came from Quebec. Pointing out that "the Quebec community, alone of the provinces, did not participate in the double majority of the November consensus,"[22] Smiley appears to argue that constitutional change is not legitimate unless approved by one's political representatives in both the federal government and the provinces; consent by one cannot substitute for dissent by the other.

Whether this leaves any meaningful role for the federal government in the process of constitutional change is an issue of some considerable importance. The point to be stressed here, however, is that the vision of the political community that was embedded in the Constitution Act has not carried the field, and that its failure to do so extends beyond Smiley's important criticisms of the Act per se.[23] While Trudeau's national vision was certainly one that appealed to many Canadians, it also faced some major limitations. Firstly, the bicultural-bilingual ideal embedded in the vision was too elusive for most Canadians; it failed to provide a suitable hook upon which they could hang their own national identity. Secondly, Trudeau's vision failed to carry Quebec, or at least failed to do so decisively; although the 1980 sovereignty-association referendum was defeated, the PQ government was re-elected and, more importantly, refused to endorse the Constitution Act. Thirdly, Trudeau's vision failed to win a following in the West, in part because of lingering regional opposition to bilingualism per se, but more importantly because Trudeau and his government had become so thoroughly discredited in the region that Western Canadians would have rejected the Second Coming of Christ if Trudeau had supported it.[24] Fourthly, the Trudeau vision of the national community was rejected by provincial governments who quite rightly suspected that it provided the 'mythological' underpinnings for the centralizing thrust of the post-1980 Trudeau government, or what Smiley describes as the Third National Policy.[25] Also, the primary appeal of the Trudeau vision was to linguistic *minorities* rather than to the dominant linguistic *majorities* in Canadian political life, the francophone majority inside Quebec and the anglophone majority outside Quebec. Lastly, because this vision of the political community reflected so much one man and one party, it was open to attack on partisan grounds once Trudeau retired and once the Liberals had been defeated. While this may not have posed a problem had the constitutional process been brought to a close in 1982, Quebec's refusal to endorse the Act left the constitutional field open to a new constellation of political actors and partisan considerations.

As a consequence of all of the above, the Constitution Act was flawed as a constitutional embodiment of a truly national vision. While the Act was put into play, the requisite national consensus on the underlying vision of the political community has not been achieved. Thus the stage was set for the Meech Lake Accord which altered not only the constitutional superstructure but also the underlying definition of the Canadian political community upon which that superstructure rests.

Meech Lake

There is no question that the Meech Lake Accord addresses what Smiley identified as the fundamental flaw of the Constitution Act. While space does not permit the details of the Accord to be discussed here, I would argue that the Accord does belatedly meet the federal government's 1980 promise for a renewed federalism. It is, moreover, a renewed federalism in which the powers of the Quebec National Assembly have been further expanded and protected. Of central *symbolic* importance is the Accord's constitutional recognition of Quebec as a distinct society; of central *political* importance is the fact that the National Assembly and government of Quebec have embraced the Accord. Thus if ratified, the Accord should return Quebec to the Canadian constitutional family, and the 'betrayal' of 1981/82 should be rectified if neither forgotten nor forgiven.

One should presume, therefore, that Professor Smiley would endorse the Meech Lake Accord, as clearly it is in step with constitutional developments and ideologies in Quebec. Certainly his initial opposition to special constitutional status for Quebec has softened over time.[26] Smiley has also supported other elements of the Accord. Writing in 1985 about appointments to the Supreme Court, Smiley argued that "the involvement of the provincial governments is appropriate and even urgent if the legitimacy of the court is to be maintained."[27] Professor Smiley, moreover, has been a cautious supporter of Senate Reform, although not necessarily of the type embodied in the temporary provisions of the Accord.[28]

I would argue, however, that the Accord is fundamentally at odds with the importance Smiley has attached to both the federal government and the Constitution in promoting the Canadian political community. The process through which the Accord was born, the content of the Accord itself, and the ratification process all fail to provide any effective articulation of *Canada* as a political community. While the vision of Trudeau's which shone through the Constitution Act was admittedly a contentious vision, it was indisputably a national vision. Bluntly put, the Accord displays no such vision because the federal government and Prime Minister Mulroney failed to bring any national vision to the bargaining table at Meech Lake and the Langevin Block. More kindly put, any national vision to be found in the Accord is simply overwhelmed by the nationalist vision of the Quebec Liberal party, and by a provincialist vision shared by all ten premiers.

In the process leading up to Meech Lake, there was little public debate of constitutional issues, or at least very little outside the province of Quebec. Certainly there was nothing even faintly reminiscent of the prolonged debate leading up to the Constitution Act, a debate that embraced not only federal and provincial politicians, constitutional lawyers, newspaper columnists, academics, *Saturday Night*, editorial pages across the country, and a wide array of interest groups, but also a significant proportion of the Canadian public in countless townhall meetings and public hearings across the country over a span of more than ten years. Prior to the announcement of the Meech Lake Accord, the public debate that had been stilled by the Constitution Act was not revitalized. In fact, the governments of Canada orchestrated the constitutional process so that the public was not only excluded but was also unaware that constitutional changes of the magnitude incorporated in the Accord were even under discussion.

In itself, this process was not all bad as there is good reason to expect that an extended public debate over Quebec's position within the Canadian federal state would have generated national dissensus rather than consensus. However, when the Accord was then presented as a seamless web, when Canadians were told that the Accord could be debated *but would not be changed no matter what Canadians had to say*, the Accord began to crumble as the constitutional foundation for nation-building. Indeed, I would argue that the seamless web strategy coupled with a prolonged ratification period was a recipe for disaster. Writing in 1983, Smiley stated that "my judgments about the implications for national unity of the Constitution Act and the procedures by which it was effected are on the whole adverse."[29] I would argue that the same judgment could be applied to the Meech Lake Accord.

Through its recognition of Quebec as a distinct society, the Accord may well embody a vision of the Canadian political community that is of considerable appeal to Quebec, or at least to the francophone population of Quebec. In this respect, the Accord may also reflect important sociological and political realities in Canada, for in many respects outside the constitutional realm Quebec is indisputably a distinct society. However, it is not at all clear that the Accord captures either the reality of Canada-outside-Quebec, or that it embodies a vision of the *Canadian* political community that will capture the central symbolic elements of English Canada. I would argue that the Accord reflects the reality of the constitutional process in which a Prime Minister determined to make a deal came up against ten premiers determined to protect, and if possible expand, their own jurisdictional turf.

In his 1977 presidential address to the Canadian Political Science Association, Alan Cairns argued that

...the support for powerful, independent provincial governments is a product of the political system itself, that it is fostered and created by provincial government elites employing the policy-making apparatus of their jurisdictions, and that such support need not take the form of a distinct culture, society, or nation as these are conventionally understood.[30]

Cairns went on to argue that, for provincial governments, "their sources of survival, renewal and vitality may well lie within themselves and in their capacity to mould their environment in accordance with their own governmental purposes."[31] In the constitutional process culminating in the Constitution Act 1982, provincial governments were successful only to a limited degree in molding the constitutional environment in accordance with their own purposes. However, in the constitutional process culminating in the Meech Lake Accord, provincial governments were much more successful, in part because the federal government appears to have abandoned the field in search of its own electoral advantage. Whereas in the run-up to the Constitution Act 1982 the federal government had a constitutional vision designed to counter "the perceived disposition of Canadians to emphasize their provincial rather than national allegiances,"[32] there is no evidence that the Mulroney government had any vision at all.

Initially, it appeared that the provincialist vision embodied in the Meech Lake Accord would be accepted by the country, even though I would argue that it reflected the interests of governments more than it did the interests of citizens. However, the ratification process opened up the Accord to sustained attack led by a broad political coalition which emerged in fighting trim from the Constitution Act. In the early 1980s women, Aboriginals, linguistic minorities, and ethnic communities, among others, had fought successfully to ensure that they were incorporated in the new constitution, that their rights were included. However, once everybody was in, the second round in the battle for rights began as the "Charter Canadians"[33] jockeyed for advantageous position. The extended ratification process for the Meech Lake Accord provided an arena in the struggle for hierarchy, a struggle to ensure that one's own rights came near the top of the Canadian constitutional totem pole, that Quebec's "distinctive society" would not subordinate the rights of women, linguistic minorities, or other constitutional claimants.

In short, such groups, which had been successful in the early 1980s, are now reluctant to accept a government monopoly on constitution-making. If the constitution is to be opened up, they will insist on being constitutional players. They are determined to leave their imprint on the Meech Lake Accord, as they left their imprint upon the Constitution Act and the Charter of Rights. They have their own vision of the Canadian political community to pursue, one based more on rights than on the distinction between national and provincial identities.

Conclusions

I began this paper with Carty and Ward's statement that "the greatest task of national government has been to develop and nourish a Canadian political community." Interpreted somewhat more broadly, this statement reflects the state-centred approach to the study of federalism favoured by such writers as Cairns, Nordlinger, and Smiley, all of whom agree that governments within the federal states have considerable opportunity to shape the surrounding society. From this perspective, constitution-making takes on a critical importance because of its potential to restructure the relationship among governments in federal states, and thus its potential to restructure the underlying social order. Clearly the Meech Lake Accord set out to restructure the relationship between the federal and provincial governments in Canada. Equally clearly, it has the potential to restructure the nature of Canadian society.

As we meet today, the fate of the Meech Lake Accord remains in doubt. *If* the Accord is eventually ratified, the *interstate* sinews of the Canadian federal state should be strengthened in ways that should meet with Professor Smiley's approval.[34] At the very least, the open sore left when Quebec failed to sign the Constitution Act of 1982 will be closed, although the scar may remain. I would argue, however, that in this respect the Accord will play a radically different nation-building role than that played by constitutional documents in the past.[35] Battered and bruised by the attacks of linguistic minorities, feminists, Aboriginals, Territorians, and Senate reformers, the Accord may be stripped of any consensual legitimacy by what is turning out to be a prolonged and increasingly acrimonious ratification debate. More importantly, the Ac-

cord promotes a vision of Canada in which provincial governments and thus provincial communities will play a much more
significant role than they played in the past. To the extent that
the Accord articulates a national political community, it is a
community divided, a community composed of distinct societies,
a community in which our identities as Québécois, British Colum-
bians or Albertans are brought to the fore, and in which a
Canadian identity recedes.[36]

Writing in 1967, Smiley argued that "the Dominion was a
deliberate creation which could be established, in the perspectives of the Fathers of Confederation, only through the instrumentality of a strong and vigorous central government."[37]
Without question, the architects of Meech Lake have abandoned
nation-building through a strong federal government, opting instead for strengthening provincial governments and, through
those governments, provincial communities across Canada. Not
coincidentally, Meech Lake comes at a time when the federal
government, in its pursuit of a Free Trade Agreement with the
United States, is also abandoning earlier attempts at nation-building through the creation of a strong east-west economy. Taken
together, Meech Lake and the Free Trade Agreement entrust the
future of Canadians to their provincial and continental communities by constraining the nation-building capacity of future
federal governments. Small wonder, then, that both are supported by nationalists in Quebec and provincialists in the West
still reeling, emotionally if not economically, from Ottawa's energy initiatives of the early 1980s.[38]

If ratification fails, the Meech Lake Accord will come to play
a very different nation-building role, one that has come to be
identified with the *intrastate* federalism of Alan Cairns. The
defeat of the Accord would be a victory for the Charter
Canadians, a victory for those determined to remove constitution-
making from the secretive councils and political hands of the First
Ministers. It would also be a victory for champions of a strong
federal government, combatants who could be expected then to
redirect their fire upon the Free Trade Agreement. However, the
defeat of the Accord would also leave our amending formula in
shambles; we would have experienced a situation in which the
eleven First Ministers acting in concert were unable to carry the
country. More importantly, the defeat of the Accord could radically destabilize Quebec politics. In this specific but very impor-

tant sense, an enhanced sense of national unity would be an unlikely product of the Accord's defeat.

From a narrower disciplinary perspective, we are witnessing a struggle between the federal visions of Donald Smiley and Alan Cairns. In this setting, it is difficult to predict the outcome, and even more difficult to take sides.

Notes

1   R. Kenneth Carty and W. Peter Ward, "Canada as Political Community," in R. Kenneth Carty and W. Peter Ward (eds.), *National Politics and Community in Canada* (Vancouver: University of British Columbia Press, 1986), 1.

2   Alan C. Cairns, "The Governments and Societies of Canadian Federalism," *Canadian Journal of Political Science*, X (1977), 698.

3   E.A. Nordlinger, *On the Autonomy of the Democratic State* (Cambridge, Mass.: Harvard University Press, 1981).

4   D.V.Smiley, "Federal States and Federal Societies. With Special Reference to Canada," *International Political Science Review*, V (1984), 443-454, 450.

5   D.V.Smiley, "Federal States and Federal Societies," 453.

6   D.V. Smiley, *The Canadian Political Nationality* (Toronto: Methuen, 1967), 2.

7   W.L. Morton, *The Critical Years: The Union of British North America 1857-1873* (Toronto: McClelland and Stewart, 1964), 177.

8   Smiley, *Canadian Political Nationality*, 26.

9   *Ibid.*, 31.

10   *Ibid.*, 128.

11   W.L. Morton, "The Dualism of Culture and the Federalism of Power," *A New Concept of Federation: Vers une nouvelle Confédèration* (Proceedings of the Seventh Seminar of the Canadian Union of Students, Ottawa, 1965), 121.

12   Of relevance here is Smiley's discussion of Canada's quest for a "National Policy." Smiley argues that "National policy in the Canadian context is developmental: it is action by the national government both to stimulate economic activity and to shape the structure of the economy"; see "Canada and the Quest for a National Policy," *Canadian Journal of Political Science*, VIII (1975), 40-62; 46.

13   Dualist views of the country are discussed in Smiley, "Federal States and Societies," 444-45.

14 Roger Gibbins, "Constitutional Politics and the West," in Keith Banting and Richard Simeon (eds.), *And No One Cheered: Federalism, Democracy and The Constitution Act* (Toronto: Methuen, 1983), 119-132.

15 Smiley, *Canadian Nationality*, 134.

16 This vision is discussed at some length by Smiley and Watts: "He [Trudeau] insisted that the francophone community of Canada was not to be equated with Quebec alone and, on this basis, that the government of Quebec did not have the exclusive right to speak for French Canadians. He wanted Canada to become, in a fuller sense than before, a French-English community throughout; to this end, wherever concentrations of official-language groups made this at all practical, English-speaking and French-speaking Canadians needed to have rights and resources to sustain their respective languages and to deal with public authorities in those languages. The federal view found it essential that francophones should become more powerful than before in the federal government, both in the cabinet and at the senior levels of the public service;" Smiley (with Ron Watts), *Intrastate Federalism in Canada* (Toronto: University of Toronto Press, 1985, for the Royal Commission on the Economic Union and Development Prospects for Canada), 153.

17 Although the federal government was embarked on the road to official bilingualism well before Trudeau became Liberal leader and Prime Minister in 1968, I would argue that in the public's mind the policy is nonetheless closely associated with his leadership and tenure in office, an association helped by the passage of the Official Languages Act in 1969.

18 R. Kenneth Carty and W. Peter Ward, "The Making of a Canadian Political Citizenship," in Carty and Ward (eds.), *National Politics and Community*, 75.

19 Smiley, "A Dangerous Deed: The Constitution Act, 1982," in Banting and Simeon (eds.), *And No One Cheered*, 74-95; 75-6.

20 *Ibid.*, 80-81.

21 *Ibid.*, 81.

22 *Ibid.*, 79, and see 78.

23 I would also argue, given the opportunity, that Smiley's assessment of the Act's nation-building potential is too harsh. Here my views tend to coincide with my other UBC mentor, Alan Cairns.

24 Speaking in Edmonton on April 9, 1988, to nearly 2,400 delegates to the annual convention of the Alberta Progressive Conservative Party, Premier Don Getty drew attention to Pierre Trudeau's opposition to the Meech Lake Accord. "I knew the Accord was good," said Getty. "After Mr. Trudeau's intervention I'm certain it's one hell of a deal!" *Calgary Herald*, April 10, 1988, A2.

25 Smiley, *The Federal Condition in Canada* (Toronto: McGraw-Hill Ryerson, 1987), 178-184.

26 Compare *The Canadian Political Nationality* to "A Dangerous Deed: The Constitution Act," esp. 74-75.

27 Smiley, *Intrastate Federalism in Canada*, 153.

28 *Ibid.*, chap.7; and Smiley, *An Elected Senate for Canada? Clues from the Australian Experience* (Discussion Paper No. 21, Institute of Intergovernmental Relations, Queen's University, Kingston, 1985).

29 Smiley, "A Dangerous Deed," 83.

30 Cairns, "Governments and Societies of Canadian Federalism," 699.

31 Ibid.; this perspective is shared by Smiley who writes that in his opinion "only the state-centred view of Canadian federalism can explain the assertiveness and aggressiveness of the provinces other than Quebec. There is an opinion abroad that English-speaking Canadians and the governments they dominate are inherently and incurably centralist. This is a radical misreading of the Canadian federal experience," from "Federal States and Societies," 447.

32 Smiley, "A Dangerous Deed," 74.

33 In this context, the term "Charter Canadians" stems from Alan Cairns.

34 The intrastate/interstate distinction has played an important role in Smiley's work. This distinction has been further refined by Alan Cairns—see *From Interstate to Intrastate Federalism* (Kingston: Queen's University, Institute of Intergovernmental Relations, 1979), 11-13—who differentiates between "provincialist" and "centralist" versions of intrastate federalism. Smiley has incorporated this latter distinction in his own work, asserting that provincialist versions seek an enhancement in the powers of the provincial governments "to control certain operations of the federal government," while "centralist intrastate federalism is based on the contrary premise that the power and legitimacy of the national authorities are unduly weak and can be strengthened only by making the central government more representative and responsive to non-governmental provincial interests;" from Smiley, *Intrastate Federalism*, 17; and see "A Dangerous Deed," es67-68. Within this framework, any intrastate elements of the Meech Lake Accord are clearly provincialist rather than centralist.

35 The advocates of interstate federalism frequently argue that political institutions should, and indeed must reflect the reality of Canadian political life, and in particular the reality of strong provincial governments. Intrastate advocates are more likely to stress the role of institutions in shaping rather than reflecting political reality. Thus, for example, proponents of an elected Senate might argue that such reform would reduce and not merely reflect regional tensions within the body politic. The Meech Lake Accord, I would argue, is primarily a reflective document, designed to reflect rather than to shape the contours of Canadian political life.

36 Lipset and Rokkan discuss how the processes of political development and nation-building detach individual loyalties from sub-national communities and attach them to the nation state. It may be, however, that citizen identifications remain somewhat fluid, that the evolutionary pattern is not necessarily a flow of citizen loyalties towards the nation state, and that constitutional initiatives such as Meech Lake may succeed in re-attaching citizen loyalties to sub-national/provincial communities.

37 Smiley, *Canadian Nationality*, 2.

38 Premier Don Getty, in the speech cited above (note 24), argued that the Free Trade Agreement would ensure that "no one is ever going to shove anything down Alberta's throat again." Under the agreement, Washington would provide the political protection from central Canada, and from the Government of Canada, that parliamentary institutions have failed to provide in the past. The agreement, then, is to be welcomed by Albertans not because it protects Canadian sovereignty but because it restricts that sovereignty.

EXECUTIVE FEDERALISM: THE COMPARATIVE CONTEXT

Ronald L. Watts, Queen's University

Donald Smiley and the Concept of Executive Federalism

Like the other participants at this conference, I too would like to express my personal pleasure at this opportunity to participate in a tribute to Don Smiley. I have been enriched not only by the insights Don has provided me through conversations and his writings about Canadian politics and federalism, but by the warmth of his personal friendship. I owe a debt, too, to Alan Cairns for encouraging Don and me to collaborate together on a study of intrastate federalism in Canada for the Macdonald Commission. To be a co-author with Don was indeed a unique privilege.

Among the concepts which Donald Smiley has contributed to the analysis of Canadian federalism have been the development of the distinction between "interstate" and "intrastate" federalism and the coining of the term "executive federalism." Having collaborated with Donald Smiley in a study of the former, including its comparative dimension, for the Macdonald Royal Commission,[1] it seemed to me appropriate to take this occasion when Donald Smiley is being honoured to examine his concept of "executive federalism," particularly with reference to its utility as a concept in the comparative study of federations.

The concept of "executive federalism" refers to the process of negotiation between the executives of different governments within a federation. The importance of this aspect of inter-governmental relations was first identified by Donald Smiley in the late 1960s in a study for the Royal Commission on Bilingualism and Biculturalism[2] and developed and elaborated in the successive editions of *Canada in Question* which appeared between 1972 and 1980, each devoting a full chapter to the subject.[3] Its most recent iteration is in *The Federal Condition in Canada* published just last year.[4]

In the meantime, the concept has gained wide currency within the political science literature on Canadian federalism. A catalogue of references to the term "executive federalism" would itself require a full article, but one might just note extensive references to it by Richard Simeon, first in *Federal-Provincial Diplomacy: The Making of Recent Policy in Canada* (1972) and in many of his later works; by Alan Cairns, Timothy Woolstencroft, Michael Jenkin, Garth Stevenson, and Hugh Thorburn; by several contributors to the special edition of *Publius* on "Crisis and Continuity in Canadian Federalism" in 1984 including Milton J. Esman, Mark Sproule-Jones, Jonathan Lemco, and Peter Reigenstreif, as well as Donald Smiley himself; and by Roger Gibbins and Stefan Dupré.[5] Nor is the term limited to the academic realm. It has been frequently commented upon in such commission reports as those of the Pépin-Robarts Commission and of the Macdonald Commission.[6] It has even been referred to specifically by Prime Ministers, as when Mr. Trudeau, at a Liberal Party of Canada fund-raising dinner in Vancouver, November 12, 1981, argued: "Executive federalism is characterized by the idea that the role of Parliament in governing the country should diminish while premiers should acquire more influence over national public policy. In effect, this theory means that Canada's national government would be a council of first ministers..."[7] The appropriateness of the processes of executive federalism and the degree to which they bypass deliberation in the legislatures and by the public on major constitutional issues has, of course, been one of the major issues in the debate on the Meech Lake Accord. The concept of "executive federalism" which Donald Smiley identified nearly two decades ago clearly now permeates our discourse about Canadian federalism.

Donald Smiley himself has defined executive federalism "as the relations between elected and appointed officials of the two orders of government in federal-provincial interactions and among the executives of the provinces in interprovincial interactions."[8] In his earliest analyses of the influences leading to the predominance of "executive federalism" in Canada, Donald Smiley emphasized the influence of social factors and particularly the growing interdependence of governments which made it increasingly difficult for governments within the federation to fulfill their responsibilities in isolation from each other.[9] In successive iterations of the concept, culminating with his most recent analysis of it in *The Federal Condition in Canada*, Donald Smiley has come to emphasize, in a way which he did not initially, the degree to which "executive federalism" in Canada has been the logical outcome of the shape of our institutions, particularly the marriage of federal and parliamentary institutions and of the evolution in intragoverment organization of cabinet dominance within each government in Canada.[10] Thus, he sees two fundamental factors contributing to executive federalism. The first has been the unavoidable interdependence of the responsibilities of the two constitutionally ordained orders of government within the federal system. This requires a continuous process of federal-provincial consultation and negotiation. The second factor has been our parliamentary conventions which have made the cabinet, "the central energizing executive" as Thomas Hockin has referred to it, the "key engine of the state"[11] within each of the governments. Federal-provincial interdependence and our parliamentary practices combined have made the predominance of executive federalism an inevitable outcome.

The result has been the pattern of executive federalism in Canada which Donald Smiley and others have portrayed. This pattern has been marked in recent decades by three developments: the proliferation of federal-provincial conferences, committees and liaison agencies; the prominence of intergovernmental summitry as exemplified by the First Ministers' Conference; and the concentration within each government of responsibility for intergovernmental relations in the hands of coordinating agencies and specialists. The importance of this pattern of executive federalism has stemmed not only from the frequency with which first ministers, ministers, and senior officials have interacted, but also from the critical role which this interaction has played in the following: the range of programs and services provided by Canadian governments to their citizens; the discussion of economic policy including trade relations with the United States; and the revision of the Constitution itself, most notably in the period leading up to the Constitution Act of 1982 and again in the Constitutional Accord of 1987.

There have been considerable differences of opinion among Canadian political scientists about the impact of executive federalism and the degree to which it has contributed to intergovernmental cooperation or conflict. Over nearly two decades of writing on the subject, as the character of executive federalism itself has evolved, Donald Smiley's own assessment has not remained constant. Writing at the beginning of the 1970s, he pointed to the not inconsiderable achievements of executive federalism in Canada. These included improved intergovernmental communication, the mitigating of regional disparities, the establishing of an integrated tax structure, and the reducing of barriers to mobility of Canadian citizens through the development of hospital and medical insurance plans and the Canada Pension Plan. At the same time, he drew attention to influences at work which were threatening to attenuate the levels of federal-provincial integration.[12] By the end of the decade, Donald Smiley was much more critical. He argued that the institutionalization of executive federalism through the shifting within each government of federal-provincial relations from line departments to more politicized intergovernmental agencies where the symbolic jurisdictional and electoral stakes were much higher and where intergovernmental specialists were more concerned with their jurisdictional turf, had served to intensify intergovernmental conflict.[13] Some authors, such as Timothy Woolstencroft and John Warhurst, have argued that Donald Smiley overstated the impact of the intergovernmental relations specialists and the damage they had done.[14] Most recently, in *The Federal Condition in Canada* (1971), Donald Smiley himself has taken a somewhat more mellow view.[15] He has noted that the intensity and bitterness of conflict in Canadian federal-provincial relations between the 1960s and 1984 was the product of two interrelated sources: the polarization of participants between supporters of contradictory views of the nature of the Canadian political community as nation-centred or province-centred, a polarization fostered by Pierre Trudeau's personal influence; and the integration of executive power within each government, focused on maximizing the scope of its jurisdiction. With the considerable change in the cast of participants in intergovernmental relations since 1984, he saw some prospect for less intense conflict. To that end he has suggested that making the structures and processes of executive federalism more factored, more routine, and more incremental might help, as would the acceptance as a norm in intergovernmental relations of competition as well as cooperation, pointing to the contributions which Stefan Dupré and Albert Breton had made to his views on these matters.[16]

The Comparative Context

Most of the literature on "executive federalism" has focused on this as a particularly Canadian phenomenon. But if the two major factors contributing to the predominance of "executive federalism" in Canada have been the growing interdependence in the responsibilities of the two orders of government and the increasing dominance of the parliamentary executives within each order of government, one might note that these factors are not unique to Canada. What light then might an examination of other federations which have combined federal and parliamentary institutions shed? Such a combination was a Canadian innovation in 1867—in its imperial formulation as Douglas Verney has referred to it in his paper [found in this text]—but since then a number of other federations have followed Canada's example in this respect: Australia in 1901, the Federal Republic of Germany in 1949, and some of the newer Commonwealth federations including at the current time India (1950) and Malaysia (1963). Indeed, few Canadian political scientists seem to be aware how much the federal constitutions of independent India and Malaysia owe to the model of the British North America Act, 1867, by way of the Government of India Act of 1935.

Although most of Donald Smiley's writing on "executive federalism" has been about its evolution and operation in Canada, he has himself on at least one occasion examined its comparative significance. In his article, "Public Sector Politics, Modernization and Federalism: The Canadian and American Experiences," which appeared in *Publius* in 1984,[17] he drew out the contrasting patterns of intergovernmental relations in Canada and the United States. He argued that at the root of these diverging patterns lay the differences between the presidential-congressional system and the Westminster model for organizing power within the national governments and within the states and provinces. Thus, where intergovernmental conferences and committees and direct federal-provincial confrontation have characterized intergovernmental relations in Canada, in the United States, the Congress has been the central arena in which matters affecting intergovernmental relations have been determined, and this appears to have inhibited direct confrontation of federal and state governments.[18]

If that comparison helps to put "executive federalism" in Canada in perspective, there may be some utility in casting the comparative net wider. The growing interdependence of governments within federations has been common to virtually all federations in an era of increased governmental intervention within societies. Furthermore, with greater governmental activism in most societies there has been an increased importance in the role of the executive in most contemporary political systems. But the form of the constituent governments has varied from federation to federation. Here we may identify two broad categories: the parliamentary and non-parliamentary federations.

Among the examples of parliamentary federations are Canada, Australia, the Federal Republic of Germany, India, Malaysia, Pakistan until 1958, and Nigeria until 1966. In these federations both the central and provincial or state governments have had prime ministers and ministers chosen from among the members of the legislature and continuously and collectively responsible to it. In practice this fusion of the executive with the legislature has meant that so long as the cabinet has the support of a stable majority in the legislature, it becomes the key energizing element within that government, a position reinforced by the tight party discipline induced by the alternative prospect of dissolution.

The second category—non-parliamentary federal systems—is represented by those federations in which within each order of government the executive and legislature are separated. Examples are the presidential-congressional form in the United States and the collegial executive in Switzerland. In both the central and cantonal governments in Switzerland, the executive is a council of five to nine members (seven in the Federal Council) usually elected by the legislature for a fixed term of office, in most cases four years, and with the chairmanship rotating annually. This arrangement was seen as an improvement on the American model in avoiding the concentration of executive authority in a single person and in enabling a representation of different geographical groups and parties within the executive council. Thus, in the United States and Switzerland, the executives within each level of government, whether individual (the President or Governors in the U.S.) or collegial (the Federal or Cantonal Councils in Switzerland), are elected for a fixed term, and the "separation of powers" makes the legislatures, legislative committees, executives, bureaucracies, judiciaries, and in the Swiss case the electorate through the invocation of the legislative referendum, into multiple distinct centres of political power. Furthermore, "the separation of powers" has provided limits upon the degree to which the executive within each government can dominate policy-making.

What have been the implications of these two different forms of executive organization within federations? Can we identify patterns of intergovernmental relations common to each of the two broad categories? If Donald Smiley's explanation of "executive federalism" in Canada is valid, and I am inclined to the view that it is, then further in-depth comparative research might be illuminating. Such research might examine the two categories of federation under the following seven headings: the locus of intergovernmental consultation and negotiation; the intragovernmental organization of intergovernmental relations; the role of political parties; the role of interest groups; the scope of intergovernmental interaction; the character of intergovernmental financial relations; and the degree of intergovermental confrontation or cooperation. Here let me sketch some apparent patterns.[19]

The Locus of Intergovernmental Consultation and Negotiation

In all the parliamentary federations the major instrument for the resolution of intergovernmental conflicts has been consultation and negotiation between the executives and the representatives of the different governments within these federations. Indeed, John Warhurst has applied the term "co-operative-executive federalism" to the similarities in this respect between Canada and Australia.[20] Nevil Johnson, in characterising the primary characteristic of West German federalism, has expressly referred to "executive federalism."[21] In an earlier study, I have myself included an analysis of the variety of formal institutions for intergovernmental consultation and negotiation established in the newer Commonwealth federations such as India, Malaysia, Pakistan up to 1958, and Nigeria up to 1966.[22] In all these parliamentary federations, the locus for intergovernmental consultation and negotiation has been a variety of intergovernmental conferences, committees, and summitry, and these interactions have had a quasi-diplomatic character resembling those between sovereign powers.

In Australia these relations have been expressed through a variety of formal and informal councils and conferences held annually or more frequently; through numerous formal and informal agreements, policies and programs, often financed jointly by participating governments, resulting from these meetings; and through extensive day-to-day contacts between officers and ministers in different governments. Surmounting all these relationships has been the Premiers' Conference (the Australian equivalent of our First Ministers' Conference). But the Australians moved to institutionalize and constitutionalize these arrangements earlier than we did in Canada, for as long ago as 1927 the Loans Council, composed of Commonwealth and state representatives and with powers to bind governments at both levels, was established by a constitutional amendment.[23]

In Germany, the form of the distribution of jurisdiction and the existence of the Bundesrat have provided powerful incentives for interaction between the executives of the federation and the laender, an interaction accentuated by the identification of "common tasks" in the constitutional reform of 1969. Intergovernmental relations have been characterized by the existence of several hundred federation-laender committees composed of specialists from federal and land departments, by the "missions" of the laender in Bonn, by councils for economic planning—the *Finanzplanungsrat* and the *Konjunkturrat* for example—and by meetings from time to time of the chancellor and the ministers-president of the laender.[24]

The newer parliamentary federations within the Commonwealth have also established a variety of institutions to facilitate consultation and cooperation between governments. Some of these have actually been specified in the federal constitutions, although more often they have been established simply by agreement as the need arose. To catalogue them all would require more space than is available here, but one might note the way in which such bodies as the Planning Commission, the Finance Commission, the National Development Council, the National Integration Council, the Central Council of Health, the river boards, the Inter-State Transport Commission, and the Drugs Consultative Committee have operated in India; and how the National Finance Council, the Land Council, the Rural and Industrial Development Authority, and the Tariff Advisory Board have operated in Malaysia.[25]

By contrast to the predominance of "executive federalism" in these parliamentary federations, intergovernmental relations in the United States and Switzerland have been more fragmented and executive coordination of these relationships has been much more limited. In both federations intergovernmental interaction has been expressed through a variety of vertical and diagonal relationships between the many distinct centres of political decision-making within each federation. Administrative agencies at one level of government have been freer to negotiate with the agencies or legislators at another level of government to work out specific functional schemes or projects. Furthermore, the national legislatures, where party discipline has been relatively weak, have played a more prominent role in resolving intergovernmental issues through the establishment of programs supported by grants-in-aid or subventions and administered by state or cantonal officials. The resulting administrative and political interlacing of governmental activities has led Morton Grodzins to use the image of "marble cake" federalism in describing the United States,[26] a description which is equally applicable to Switzerland.[27]

The Intragovernmental Organization of Intergovernmental Relations

Within parliamentary federations, as a group, an apparently common pattern has been the tendency for matters relating to intergovernmental relations to be placed under the coordination or control of staff agencies and specialists exclusively concerned with intergovernmental affairs.

John Warhurst of the University of New England in Australia has recently examined the parallel trends in this respect in Australia and Canada.[28] He has tracked the growth in Canada over the past 25 years and in Australia over the past 14 years of specialized agencies within their governments for managing intergovernmental relations. He has also analysed the similar impact which intergovernmental relations specialists have had in both federations as an intergovernmental arm for their first ministers. They have served as agents for information collection and distribution, as agents intervening in the bilateral negotiations of other ministries, and as coordinators of diverse views within their own governments.

The German laender have also developed bodies of intergovernmental specialists to staff their ministries for intergovernmental cooperation and to staff their "missions" in Bonn. Normally there has been a specific minister heading the state ministry for cooperation with the central government who also heads the state's mission in Bonn.[29] Until 1969 the federal government included a Minister for the Bundesrat and the Affairs of the laender, whose main duty was to look after relations with the second chamber and to encourage cooperation between the federal government and the laender. But because this minister had no executive powers and those who had held the appointment had had relatively slight political weight, this particular method of coordination was abandoned in 1969, leaving executive departments within the federal government to deal directly with the special intergovernmental representatives of the laender.[30]

In the non-parliamentary federations, the diffusion of political power within each level of government has limited the ability of their executives to play a dominant coordinative role over the whole range of intergovernmental interactions. Participation in intergovernmental relations has been fragmented among a variety of functional administrative agencies and legislators within each level of government, each negotiating or lobbying in a relatively uncoordinated way with administrators and legislators in other governments. The complex character of these interactions in the United States has been described by Daniel Elazar,[31] and Samuel Beer has drawn attention to the influence of the intergovernmental lobby upon Congress.[32] In Switzerland too the channels of communication between the cantons and the federal government take a variety of forms, facilitated not the least by the constitutional provision permitting members of cantonal legislatures and executive councils to sit concurrently in either house of the federal legislature. Normally something like a fifth of the members of each house in the Swiss Federal Parliament represents such a cumulation of roles.[33] It is of interest that similar arrangements fro dual membership existed in Canada during the early years after Confederation, a period in which, as Garth Stevenson has noted in his paper, the first examples of cooperative federalism occurred in Canada.

The Role of Political Parties

In parliamentary federations tight party discipline has been encouraged by the fact that cabinet stability is dependent upon it. This has reinforced the cohesiveness and consolidation of cabinet control over administrative and political relations with other governments and has provided less room for administrators or individual legislators to lobby or seek support for their projects in other levels of government except with cabinet approval. In the case of Canada and Australia, it has also led to the federalization of the political parties themselves with the federal and provincial or state wings of the same party often taking distinctively different positions. Political parties have, therefore, had a limited capacity for effecting the resolution of intergovernmental conflicts through intraparty relations.[34] Thus, it has been through inter-executive negotiations rather than intraparty deliberations that intergovernmental differences have most often been resolved. Here the Federal Republic of Germany serves as something of an exception owing to the impact which its unique form of intrastate federalism, the Bundesrat, has had upon the interaction of parties at the federal and land levels.[35]

In the United States and Switzerland, the fixed executive has produced relatively undisciplined political parties since the life of the executive is not dependent upon the continued support of a majority in the legislature. This has had a dual effect on the character of intergovernmental relations. First, the political parties have been in a weaker position to exert monolithic control over the operation of various administrative offices and agencies. Second, the administrators have had to lobby, that is play a political role themselves, in seeking support not only within their own government, but within the legislatures of other governments, for the joint and shared-cost programs which they espouse.

The Role of Interest Groups

The predominance of "executive federalism" in the parliamentary federations has limited or affected the scope for interest group activity in relation to matters under intergovernmental negotiation. There is a considerable literature on this aspect of Canadian federalism.[36] A similar impact appears to have occurred in Australia. In Germany too, as one commentator has noted, the predominance of the executive has led interest groups to concentrate their main efforts upon influencing the executive.[37] But there is a major difference from the pattern in Canada and Australia. Because of the significantly different form which the constitutional distribution of authority between the federal government and the laender takes, whereby for large areas of jurisdiction legislative authority is assigned to the federal government and administrative responsibility for the same matters is assigned to the laender, there appears to have been a tendency for the interest groups to focus their attention upon the federal executive. This contrast should not be overdrawn, however, for the interest groups appear also to have been conscious of the role which the land executives play in the negotiations preceding the passage of legislation through both houses of the federal Parliament.

By contrast with the parliamentary federations, the "multiple crack" hypothesis formulated by Morton Grodzins through his analysis of the operation of American federalism[38] would appear to have much greater applicability to the non-parliamentary federations. In both the United States and Switzerland, federalism combined with the lack of executive dominance has increased rather than reduced the opportunities for the involvement at many points of interest groups in policy-making.[39]

The Scope of Intergovernmental Interaction

If one takes into account the variety of political and administrative as well as executive interactions occurring in the non-parliamentary federations, the frequency of intergovernmental relations has become so extensive in both types of federation as to make it difficult to argue that these interactions are more frequent in one form of federation than in another. No doubt this reflects the increased interdependence of governments within all federations as governments have become more active within society. The picture of "classical federalism" in which each level of government performed the responsibilities assigned to it by the constitution in relative isolation from the other, if it ever was a reality, has long since disappeared. But the character and scope of the agreements and programs produced by this intergovernmental interaction has differed.

By and large there has been a tendency in the parliamentary federations for individual projects for functional cooperation to be subsumed under more general arrangements or schemes for coordination. Furthermore, in the Federal Republic of Germany this has frequently taken the pattern of formal intergovernmental agreements, treaties, and conventions. Indeed, it has been estimated that in the first dozen years of its existence about 340 formal agreements were entered into between the federal government and the laender and among the laender themselves.[40] In the non-parliamentary federations, on the other hand, intergovernmental relations appear generally to have been factored into a much greater variety of distinct projects and programs often taking little account of other projects and programs. For instance, in the United States, governmental cooperative arrangements have tended to be along primarily programmatic lines involving the interaction of congressional subcommittees, federal agencies, state bureaucrats and legislators, city officials, and interest groups in a complex web of relationships for each specific program.[41] The pattern of intergovernmental relations in Switzerland appears also to be largely incremental in character and based on a complex variety of participants in the establishment of each program.[42]

The Character of Intergovernmental Financial Relations

The differences in the character of intergovernmental agreements and programs produced in the two types of federations are reflected also in the character of their internal financial relations. Two general features appear to mark off the parliamentary federations from the non-parliamentary ones. The first is the extent to which federal transfers to the provinces, states or laender have a substantial portion which is unconditional in nature. This contrasts particularly with the United States, where even when general and special revenue sharing were at their peak, at least 80 per cent of the transfers were conditional in form, and with Switzerland where a high proportion would be in this category.[43] The second is the degree of emphasis put upon equalization arrangements in Canada, Australia, and the Federal Republic of Germany, the last of these involving a substantial element of transfers directly between the laender. By contrast in the United States there is no general system of equalization payments. What equalization is achieved is simply the cumulative effect of the variable matching grant formulae for different programs.[44] In Switzerland a specific system of financial equalization has been developed, but this represents a comparatively small element in the total system of financial transfers.[45]

These differences may be accounted for by two factors. First is the coordinated way in which governments in federations where "executive federalism" has predominated have pressed their cases in the negotiations over financial arrangements. The second relates to the notion that public accountability for the expenditure of unconditional transfers can in parliamentary federations be provided by the responsibility of cabinets to their own legislatures. By contrast, in the United States the emphasis on the principle of fiscal responsibility and accountability, i.e. that the governmental authority which raises the revenue should specify how it is to be spent, has led to Congress's continued insistence upon a predominance of conditional programmatic transfers. This contrasts with the federations characterised by "executive federalism" where the emphasis on provincial, state or land financial autonomy, and the assumption that expenditure accountability is achieved through the responsibility of their cabinets to their own legislatures and through them to their electorates, has resulted in a substantial portion of transfers being unconditional in form.

One further contrast is in the areas in which issues relating to fiscal arrangements have been fought out. In the United States, for example, the struggle over the allocation of funds for various grant-in-aid programs and for specific projects has been in Washington, i.e. within Congress. In the parliamentary federations, the battles have been fought out within the intergovernmental mechanisms of "executive federalism" where the provincial, state, and land governments have been major actors.

The Degree of Intergovernmental Confrontation or Cooperation

Critics of "executive federalism" in Canada, including on occasion Don Smiley himself, have emphasized the degree to which it has exacerbated intergovernmental competition and confrontation.[46] On the other hand, John Warhurst, examining both the Canadian and Australian experiences, argues that this conventional wisdom about "executive federalism" exaggerates its negative effects and underestimates the positive contribution which intergovernmental specialists have made to the efficient management of these federations.[47] Nevertheless, a comparison of these two federations with the non-parliamentary federations of the United States and Switzerland indicates that in general "executive federalism" in the parliamentary federations has been marked by a considerably higher degree of intergovernmental conflict and confrontation. Experience in the newer parliamentary federations in the Commonwealth after the party solidarity of their independence movements had fragmented, points in the same direction.

The Federal Republic of Germany stands out, however, as a significant exception to this apparent pattern. How is this to be accounted for? One explanation may be in the greater socioeconomic homogeneity of West German society. But clearly there are also institutional factors. The administrative distribution of powers between federal and land governments, whereby something like 60 percent of federal legislation falls into a category where administrative responsibility is constitutionally assigned to the laender, provides strong pressure on both levels of government to be cooperative.[48] Furthermore, the particular form of intrastate federalism represented by the Bundesrat has encouraged federation and land executive cooperation. It has also provided for an integration of the activities of the federal and land wings of the political parties because every land election is in effect a mini-election for the national upper house.

The example of the Federal Republic of Germany raises a question about the impact of variables other than the existence of parliamentary institutions which have affected the character of "executive federalism" in federations. Four variables which affect intergovernmental relations and which we should not overlook are the number of constituent provinces or states in the federation, the form of the distribution of powers, the extent and character of intrastate federalism, and the inclusion or not in the constitution of a set of fundamental individual or group rights.

One would expect the number and relative size of the constituent provinces or states to have some impact upon intergovernmental relations. A few large constituent units are likely to have more clout both in relation to the federal government and to each other than individual states in a federation composed of many units. But the impact of this factor as an independent variable is hard to measure. Nonetheless, it is perhaps not insignificant that Canada and the Federal Republic of Germany are composed of ten provinces or laender and Australia of six, while the United States consists of 50 states and Switzerland of 26 cantons. Thus, the fewer units in each of the parliamentary federations would appear to have reinforced the strength of "executive federalism" in the former group. Nor does the experience of India with 21 states, or of Malaysia with 13, supply any clear contradiction of this impression.

The form of the distribution of powers may also be a significant factor affecting intergovernmental relations, as we have already noted in referring to the predominantly "administrative" character of the distribution of authority in Germany. Switzerland also has considerable elements of a similar "administrative" distribution of authority, and this has produced an incentive for more intense intergovernmental collaboration. The emphasis in the United States and Australia, like Canada, is more on a "legislative" distribution of powers whereby both legislative and executive authority for a particular matter are assigned to the same government. But the relatively restricted extent of exclusive federal authority and the extensive scope of concurrent jurisdiction set out in the constitutions of both the United States and Australia distinguishes them from the very restricted scope of formal concurrent jurisdiction in Canada. Indeed, except for the example of the "administrative" allocation of responsibilities in relation to criminal law and the very short list of concurrent jurisdiction in sections 94A and 95 of the Canadian Constitution, the Canadian Constitution contrasts with those of the other federations in the degree to which it has attempted to assign exclusive jurisdiction on nearly all matters to one order of government or the other. Given the degree to which, as Garth Stevenson has suggested in his paper, concurrent jurisdiction over immigration was a factor encouraging early examples of cooperative federalism in Canada, the otherwise restricted constitutional provision for concurrent jurisdiction by comparison with nearly all other federations has been significant. At the very least, this feature has done nothing to mitigate the impact of "executive federalism."

It has often been argued in Canada that a factor contributing to the strength of "executive federalism" has been the weakness of our institutions of "intrastate federalism." Indeed, the advocates of an elected senate, including the Macdonald Commission, have argued that such a body might provide an alternative to the premiers for expressing a regional voice in national affairs. Certainly, of all the contemporary federations Canada does the least institutionally to provide an adequate regional expression of views in national affairs through intrastate federalism. But Australian experience suggests that even the existence of a "Triple E Senate," a title for which the Australian Senate would amply qualify, has done little there to blunt the dynamic of "executive federalism" which flows logically from the combination of parliamentary and federal institutions. There are good reasons for improving the quality of intrastate federalism in Canada, but the Australian example suggests that "centralist intrastate" reforms as a way of moderating "executive federalism" are likely to have very limited efficacy.[49]

Ironically, it is in the Federal Republic of Germany, where there is a "provincialist" intrastate institution in the form of the Bundesrat, that "executive federalism" has been harnessed into a more cooperative mode. This institution, combined with the "functional" form of the distribution of powers, has contributed to an integration of the federal and land political parties in a way which in turn has produced an emphasis on intergovernmental cooperation rather than confrontation.

Conclusions

This preliminary comparative survey of federations suggests that Donald Smiley has been right to emphasize the extent to which "executive federalism" is a logical dynamic resulting from the combination of federal and parliamentary institutions. It also suggests that as long as this combination remains among "the pillars of our constitutional system,"[50] "executive federalism" as identified by Donald Smiley will characterize Canadian inter-governmental relations.

This conclusion suggests two major implications. First, intras-tate reforms may moderate its operation and impact but will not eliminate "executive federalism." If this is recognized, the task in Canada, as long as we have both parliamentary and federal institu-tions, will be to harness "executive federalism" in order to make it more workable through such steps as Stefan Dupré and Donald Smiley himself have advocated.[51]

Second, many of the criticisms of "executive federalism" and of the Meech Lake process referred to at the conference in honour of Donald Smiley, and the contemporary pressures for more participatory politics expressing pluralism discussed in the essays by Cairns, Thorburn, Verney, Black, and Gibbins raise a fundamental question: are the parliamentary and federal institu-tions which lie at the root of "executive federalism" becoming so dysfunctional as to require abandonment or radical modification? Yet there seems to be in the discussion a reluctance to carry the analysis back to these fundamental roots. Is this reluctance be-cause we political scientists recognize that, despite the concerns about "executive federalism," Canadians at large are not yet ready to pursue these implicit criticisms of our political institutions to their logical foundations?

Notes

1 D.V. Smiley and R.L. Watts, *Intrastate Federalism in Canada* (Toronto: University of Toronto Press, 1985).

2 D.V. Smiley, "Constitutional Adaptation and Canadian Federalism since 1945," *Documents of the Royal Commission on Bilingualism and Biculturalism 4*, (Ottawa: Queen's Printer for Canada, 1970), 3.

3 See D.V. Smiley, *Canada in Question: Federalism in the Seventies*, (Toronto: McGraw-Hill Ryerson Limited, 1972), Ch. 3; *Canada in Question: Federalism in the Seventies*, (2nd ed.; Toronto: McGraw-Hill Ryerson Limited, 1976); *Canada in Question: Federalism in the Eighties*, (3rd ed.; Toronto: McGraw-Hill Ryerson Limited, 1980), Ch. 4.

4 D.V. Smiley, *The Federal Condition in Canada*, (Toronto: McGraw-Hill Ryerson Limited, 1987), Ch. 4.

5 Richard Simeon, *Federal-Provincial Diplomacy: The Making of Recent Policy in Canada*, (Toronto: University of Toronto Press, 1972), esp. 5. See also: Alan Cairns, "The Other Crisis of Canadian Federalism," *Canadian Public Administration*, 22 (1979), 175-195; Timothy Woolstencroft, *Organizing Intergovernmental Relations*, (Kingston: Institute of Intergovernmental Relations, Queen's University, 1982); Michael Jenkin, *The Challenge of Diversity: Industrial Policy in the Canadian Federation*, (Ottawa: Supply and Services, 1983); Garth Stevenson, *Unfulfilled Union: Canadian Federalism and National Unity*, (revised ed., Toronto: Gage Publishing Limited, 1982), 190-196; Hugh Thorburn, *Planning and the Economy: Building Federal Provincial Consensus*, (Toronto: Canadian Institute for Economic Policy, 1984); *Publius: The Journal of Federalism*, 14 (1984); Roger Gibbins, *Conflict and Unity: An Introduction to Canadian Political Life*, (Toronto: Methuen, 1985), esp. 243-257; J. Stefan Dupré, "Reflections on the Workability of Executive Federalism" in Richard Simeon ed., *Intergovernmental Relations*, (Toronto: University of Toronto Press, 1985), 1-32, and "The Workability of Executive Federalism in Canada" in Herman Bakvis and William M. Chandler eds., *Federalism and the Role of the State*, (Toronto: University of Toronto Press, 1987), 236-258.

6 Task Force on Canadian Unity, *A Future Together: Observations and Recommendations*, (Ottawa: Supply and Services, 1979), esp. 94-99; Task Force on Canadian Unity, *Coming to Terms: The Words of the Debate*, (Ottawa: Supply and Services, 1979), esp. 58-59, 64; *Report of the Royal Commission on the Economic Union and Development Prospects for Canada*, (Ottawa: Supply and Services, 1985), e.g. Vol. 3, 260-264.

7 Quoted in Gibbins, *Conflict and Unity*, 252.

8 Smiley, *Canada in Question*, (3rd ed.), 91.

9 See, for instance, Smiley, *Canada in Question*, (1st ed.), 55-58.

10 See especially Smiley, *The Federal Condition in Canada*, 83-89, and Smiley, "Public Sector Politics, Modernization and Federalism," *Publius: The Journal of Federalism*, 14, (1984), 39-59, esp. 52-55.

11 Thomas A. Hockin, *Government of Canada*, (Toronto: McGraw-Hill Ryerson Limited, 1976), 7.

12 Smiley, *Canada in Question*, (1st ed.), 66-72.

13 Smiley, *Canada in Question*, (3rd ed.), 111-116, and Donald Smiley, "An Outsider's Observations of Federal-Provincial Relations Among Consenting Adults" in Richard Simeon (ed.), *Confrontation and Collaboration: Intergovernmental Relations in Canada Today*, (Toronto: The Institute of Public Administration of Canada, 1987), e.g. 110.

14 Timothy Woolstencroft, *Organizing Intergovernmental Relations*, 79-80; John Warhurst, "Managing Intergovernmental Relations" in Bakvis and Chandler (eds.), *Federalism and the Role of the State*, 268.

15 Smiley, *The Federal Condition in Canada*, 97-99.

16 Dupré, "Reflections on the Workability of Executive Federalism," and Albert Breton, "Supplementary Statement" in *Report of the Royal Commission on the Economic Union and Development Prospects for Canada*, Vol. 3, 486-526.

17 Smiley, "Public Sector Politics, Modernization and Federalism," 39-59, esp. 52-56.

18 For other analyses in the same issue of *Publius*, see Milton J. Esman, "Federalism and Modernization: Canada and the United States," *Publius: The Journal of Federalism*, 14 (1984), 21-38, esp. 28-31 and Jonathan Lemco and Peter Regenstreif, "The Fusion of Powers and the Crisis of Canadian Federalism," *Publius: The Journal of Federalism*, 14 (1984), 109-120, esp. 116-118. See also Ronald L. Watts, "Divergence and Convergence: Canadian and U.S. Federalism" in Harry N. Scheiber (ed.), *Perspectives on Federalism: Papers from the First Berkeley Seminar on Federalism*, (Berkeley, California: Institute of Governmental Studies, University of California, Berkeley, 1987), 179-213, esp. 187-191.

19 For an earlier comparative analysis of the two types of federations see Ronald L. Watts, *Administration in Federal Systems*, (London: Hutchinson Educational, 1970), 15-20.

20 John Warhurst, "Managing Intergovernmental Relations," 259-276 at 259.

21 Nevil Johnson, *State and Government in the Federal Republic of Germany: The Executive at Work*, (2nd ed.; Oxford: Pergamon Press, 1983), 168.

22 R.L. Watts, *New Federations: Experiments in the Commonwealth*, (Oxford: Clarendon Press, 1966), 219-224 and 241-247.

23 See R.S. Gilbert, *The Australian Loan Council in Federal Fiscal Adjustments 1890-1965*, (Canberra: Australian National University Press, 1973), and C. Sharman, *The Premiers' Conference*, (Canberra: Australian National University Press, 1977).

24 See Johnson, *State and Government in the Federal Republic of Germany*, (2nd ed.), 136-141; Klaus von Beyme, *The Political System of the Federal Republic of Germany*, (Aldershot: Gower Publishing Company Limited, 1983), 167-169.

25 See Watts, *New Federations: Experiments in the Commonwealth*, 219-224, 241-247; R.L. Watts, *Multicultural Societies and Federalism*, (Ottawa: Information Canada, 1970), 51-60. See also Amal Ray, *Federal Politics and Government*, (Delhi: The Macmillan Company of India Limited, 1979), 30-39.

26 Morton Grodzins, "The Federal System" in A. Wildavsky, (ed.), *American Federalism in Perspective*, (Boston: Little, Brown and Company, 1967), 257.

27 See Jurg Steiner, *Amicable Agreement versus Majority Rule: Conflict Resolution in Switzerland*, (Chapel Hill: 1974), 126-27; Max Frankel, University of North Carolina Press, "Swiss Federalism in the Twentieth Century" in J. Murray Luck (ed.), *Modern Switzerland*, (Palo Alto, California: The Society for the Promotion of Science and Scholarship, Inc., 1978), 332-334.

28 John Warhurst, "Managing Intergovernmental Relations," 259-276.

29 Von Beyme, *The Political System of the Federal Republic of Germany*, 168-69.

30 Johnson, *State and Government in the Federal Government of Germany*, (2nd ed.), 136.

31 Daniel J. Elazar, *American Federalism: A View from the States*, (3rd ed.; New York: Harper and Row, 1984), 51-102. See also N. Glendenning and Mavis Mann Reeves, *Pragmatic Federalism: An Intergovernmental View of American Government*, (Pacific Palisades, California: Palisades Publishers, 1984), 68-124.

32 Samuel Beer, "The Modernization of American Federalism," *Publius: The Journal of Federalism*, 3 (1973), 49-96, and Samuel Beer, "Federalism, Nationalism and Democracy in America," *American Political Science Review*, 72 (1978), 9-21.

33 Steiner, *Amicable Agreement versus Majority Rule*, 126-27; Frankel, "Swiss Federalism in the Twentieth Century," 333-34.

34 On this subject in relation to Canada see Donald Smiley's own comments in Smiley, *Canada in Question*, (3rd ed.), 146-148, and Smiley, *The Federal Condition in Canada*, 101-124.

35 William M. Chandler, "Federalism and Political Parties" in Bakvis and Chandler, *Federalism and the Role of the State*, (Toronto: University of Toronto Press, 1987), 149-170, esp. 155-156.

36 On this aspect in relation to Canada see Donald Smiley's own survey of the literature in *Canada in Question*, (3rd ed.), 148-153.

37 Von Beyme, *The Political System of the Federal Republic of Germany*, 89.

38 Morton Grodzins, *The American System: A New View of Government in the United States*, (Chicago: Rand, McNally & Company, 1966), 274-276.

39 On this characteristic of Switzerland see Steiner, *Amicable Agreement versus Majority Rule*, 110-127, and G.A. Codding, *The Federal Government of Switzerland*, (Boston: Houghton, Mifflin Company, 1961), 130-132.

40 Johnson, *State and Government in the Federal Republic of Germany*, (2nd ed.), 138.

41 Watts, "Divergence and Convergence: Canadian and U.S. Federalism," 188.

42 Steiner, *Amicable Agreement versus Majority Rule*, 128-225.

43 J.S.H. Hunter, *Federalism and Fiscal Balance: A Comparative Study*, (Canberra: Australian National University Press), 1977, 86-91; R.J. May, *Federalism and Fiscal Adjustment*, (Oxford: Oxford University Press, 1969), 104-106; Watts, "Divergence and Convergence," 206-7.

44 Hunter, *Federalism and Fiscal Balance*, 169.

45 May, *Federalism and Fiscal Adjustment*, 104.

46 Smiley, "An Outsider's Observations on Federal-Provincial Relations Among Consenting Adults," 109-110; see also Stevenson, *Unfulfilled Union*, 190-196.

47 Warhurst, "Managing Intergovernmental Relations," 268.

48 Smiley and Watts, *Intrastate Federalism in Canada*, 45-47, distinguishes between "legislative federalism," where the allocation of legislative and administrative jurisdiction between governments largely coincide and "administrative federalism," where for a substantial range of functions administrative responsibility is assigned to an order of government other than that allocated legislative jurisdiction. Chandler, "Federalism and Political Parties," 156-161 makes the same distinction using the terms "jurisdictional" and "functional" regarding the distribution of authority.

49 For the distinction between "centralist" and "provincialist" intrastate federalism see Alan C. Cairns, *From Interstate to Intrastate Federalism in Canada*, (Kingston: Institute of Intergovernmental Relations, Queen's University, 1979), 11-13, and Smiley and Watts, *Intrastate Federalism in Canada*, 17-22.

50 *Report of the Royal Commission on the Economic Union and Development Prospects for Canada*, vol. 1, 14-23.

51 Dupré, "The Workability of Executive Federalism in Canada," 236-258, esp. 249-256; Smiley, *The Federal Condition in Canada*, 97-99.

POSTFACE

ON POLITICAL SCIENCE AND POLITICAL POWER

Donald Smiley

Friends. All of you have been very kind to me this weekend. Among those of you who have been students of mine I get this kind of consensus, "Smiley interested me in matters which came to be at or near the centre of my professional concerns. Let it be said, however, that I believe his methodology, if it can be called that, is loose and his conclusions often perverse and do not follow from his premises. But he *did* encourage me when I was starting." I take a good deal of satisfaction out of this kind of judgement. I do not believe it is the business of a university teacher to create disciples and I like very much the tribute that Emily Carr in her autobiography paid to Lawren Harris, "He did not seek to persuade others to climb his ladder. He steadied their own, while they got foot-hold."

I am the son and grandson of clergymen and thus I have this ancestral urge to begin my remarks this evening with a text and end with sort of an altar-call. My text is from the first chapter of James Joyce's *Portrait of the Artist as a Young Man*. It refers to Stephen Daedalus, an introspective and insecure Irish boy of perhaps eight, away from home for the first time in the harsh environment of a Jesuit boarding-school. "It pained him that he did not know well what politics meant and that he did not know where the universe ended." What a beautifully constructed sentence that is!

Like Stephen, I do not know well what politics means, if it means anything at all. And like him my deficiencies here may be attributable to me not knowing where the universe ends—or begins. That is, I do not have confident answers to fundamental questions of life and existence. And again like Stephen I am pained by this ignorance although not, I hope, mortally wounded.

Of all the things I experience I find time to be the most puzzling and an event like this seminar impels me to consider time and its passing. A comtemporary philosopher suggests that while most of us have no difficulty understanding a square metre we cannot get our minds around a square hour. Here is a personal anecdote on the theme. In 1981 as a member of a group of Canadian political scientists I visited India. During part of this trip we stayed at the guest-house of Osmania University in Hyderabad. Early one evening we were waiting for transport to take us to an event elsewhere in that city. The bus was somewhat delayed and in North American fashion some of us became impatient. I remember a courtly old gentleman who was head-servant of the guest house putting his hand on the arm of one of my Canadian colleagues and saying this, "Be calm sir, sometimes time in India goes fast and sometimes time in India goes slow but time in India never all the time goes the same time." Now what in hell did *that* mean? Was the Indian teasing? Or was he trying to introduce the Canadians to some kind of Asian metaphysics which we had little capacity to understand? Or was it a bit of both? But I am still intrigued by the notion that sometimes time goes fast and sometimes time goes slow.

So in our life and work the way we perceive and deal with the passing of time is important. Most of you here tonight are younger than I am but I shall refrain pressing my views on you as did my sainted mother on me and my sister with the unanswerable argument "When you have lived as long as I have you'll know that I am right." On a somewhat less serious note the distinguished Scottish political scientist and MP John Mackintosh told us this story a few weeks before his death in 1977. Mackintosh was dining at the head-table of an ancient Oxford college. The conversation was lagging and John thought he could revive it by launching into a criticism of Westminster's stinginess towards British universities. For some reason this kind of talk irritated the elderly Bursar who finally burst out, "My dear Mackintosh you seem quite to be unaware that the last century in university finance has been a most unusual one."

If we were to examine the development of a political scientist over time to try to discover what made that person tick *qua* scholar we might focus on two things. The first would be early political socialization, the second how he or she had been formed—or deformed—by the graduate school experience.

I am a member of the last generation of English-speaking Canadians whose childhood was in an environment pervasively British and relatively free of United States influence. The British-ness was pervasive even in Southern Alberta, said to be the most Americanized part of Canada, and within my family which had no direct links with the British Isles, it was still commonly called "the Old Country." In every schoolroom there was a Mercator map—courtesy of the Cadbury Chocolate people—with the Empire in red and less favoured parts of the world in white. We were intensively instructed in Shakespeare and Milton and Scott and Dickens and we celebrated the end of prairie winter by memorizing Browning's, "Oh, to be in England/Now that April's there." We learned the major events of English constitutional history and were introduced to the rawer elements of politics by way of *Julius Caesar* and *Barchester Towers*. In our home the high point of Christmas Day was the Empire broadcast when we shared our Yuletide celebrations with other British subjects throughout the world, all this coming to a climax with the King's message.

There is I suppose something to regret in the passing of these British influences from Canadian life. But what is I believe to be celebrated is the elimination of the Tory dimension of the British tradition. Toryism by definition was both exclusivist and authoritarian. Its fundamental assertion was the assertion of the superiority of Anglo-Saxondom, at least the non-American parts of it, and by inference of individuals with Anglo-Celtic roots. Thus I have never been able to understand the sympathy with Toryism shown by some members of the contemporary Canadian left. Perhaps Dennis Lee explains this:

> The myth of Tory origins
> Is full of lies and blanks.
> But what remains when it is gone
> To tell us from the Yanks?

There is I would argue something more than the Tory "lies and blanks" to mark us from the Americans, at least in the political sense. This is a distinctively Canadian tradition of liberalism best embodied in the recent university community in the lives and writings of S.D. Clark, Alex Corry and John Holmes. Ronald Manzer in his perceptive 1985 book on Canadian public policy is onto something very fundamental in his conclusion "...liberalism is not the core it is the essence of the Canadian public philosophy."

So *if* Toryism is to be celebrated in this country—and I see little reason why it *should* be—let good taste and a sense of the appropriate confine such ceremonials to the well-appointed premises of Massey College and/or the Albany Club. John Holmes said this with his characteristic wisdom: "Nostalgia is seductive. The Grantian version of our bucolic Canadian paradise lost is somewhat reminiscent of the Reaganite lament for the world of Booth Tarkington and the land of Oz." I have been privileged for the past twelve years to have been a member of a university community wholly the product of a liberal Canada without this country's Tory encrustations. Most of the time, invariably almost in York's Department of Political Science, we conduct our common affairs in a context of civility, tolerance, and professionalism. But beyond that, our emergent liberal traditions are manifested in the sensitivity of the York community to the special needs and interests of disadvantaged groupings—the physically handicapped, women, the sons and daughters of recent immigrants.

To return to my early political socialization, there was much talk in my childhood of William Aberhart, Richard Bedford Bennett, and William Lyon Mackenzie King. The first two of these had their headquarters just down the road in Calgary. My boyish evaluation was that all three were sanctimonious and self-serving scoundrels promoting values and interests hostile to those of decent people like myself. I have learned nothing in the past 55 years or so to cause me to alter that judgement.

Now on to graduate school, to Northwestern University in the early and mid 1950s. This period was at or near the peak of the behavioral revolution in political science. The ambience was positivist and empiricist. There was, we were taught, an unbridgeable gap between fact and value and it was the imperative of any defensible political analysis to make clear the distinction between "is" and "ought." I was schooled in this in its most erudite and persuasive form by George Sabine, then in his 70s but still mentally and physically active. Those of you who know Sabine's magisterial *History of Political Theory* will remember that in this scholar's view the decisive event in the history of political philosophy was David Hume's critique of natural law.

Now positivists and empiricists are accused of being insensitive to the meaning of what they experience, of being like the person who asserted "of course I believe in infant baptism, I've seen it done." But any positivist true to his faith, or lack of it, is open-minded about new and seemingly unlikely possibilities and properly open-mouthed when they do in fact turn up. Thus when I lived in British Columbia I was on the lookout for the Sasquatch, the hairy snowman. Since coming to Ontario I have been similarly open-minded about the existence of red Tories. I have not yet encountered either creature. There are, it seems, relatively well authenticated snow-tracks of the Sasquatch. No such evidence of the existence of the red Tory has been found and my tentative judgment is that this being is entirely a convenient mythic contrivance of certain Canadian political scientists.

Another quality of political science as I experienced it in graduate school was the intense disciplinary self-awareness. At the centre of the graduate curriculum was the compulsory Scope and Methods seminar. This was what its title implied, an examination of the tasks and boundaries of the political science enterprise and of how knowledge about politics might be acquired and tested.

I deplore the lack of self-awareness about political science among my colleagues and graduate students today. For example, I have not been able to engage any of them in a debate about what kind of a political act it is to be, or to become, a professional political scientist. Somehow I would have hoped this praxis-question to be of concern to members of one or the other of the sects into what has been called "professorial Marxism" is divided. Another kind of question arises. If, demonstrably, political scientists have little influence in shaping the political process, how does the political process shape political scientists? Balzac wrote in the dedication to one of his novels "...most of our professors live on Germany, England, the Orient, or the North as insects live on a tree, and like the insect become part of what they live on, borrowing their importance from the importance of their subject." *That* is sobering. During the Irangate hearings last summer Dan Rather delivered himself of this one-liner: "There are two things which no decent person would want to see made—sausages and laws." But how then are the voyeurs of the law-making process influenced by what they observe?

For myself, and putting aside my positivist training, I am convinced that the heart of politics is the conjuncture, the interface, if you like, between power and justice. (Politics, as I use the term, includes the discourse about political matters, even that discourse at the most esoteric levels.) It is the intermingling of fact and value, of the "is" and the "ought," of the empirical and the normative, which makes politics the most damnably difficult and ambiguous of human enterprises. The justice-agenda as it is now being worked out in the Canadian political process is exceedingly complex, and the Charter of Rights and Freedoms requires us to confront justice matters in a more direct and principled way than before. Almost every week some new grouping arises to claim that its special needs should receive the recognition of the community as of right—the latest to come to my attention is an association of parents of triplets, quadruplets, and quintuplets.

But despite the importance of politics, we deal here with second-order, rather than the most fundamental questions of existence. Those latter are within the province of art and religion and philosophy and perhaps the intimacies of friendship and family relations, but not of politics. The imperative of politics is justice. But love-unlimited, unconstrained love—is the ultimate imperative in human relations. And whatever politics is about, it is not about love.

The evening's proceedings have impelled me to speak personally in a highly self-indulgent way. I will end my remarks by some account of the Dutch dimension of my experience which has become increasingly important to me. If I were a superstitious person, and perhaps I am, I might believe that Something, Somebody, Somewhat out there was trying to tell me about things I should know.

During the latter days of the Second World War, I was a young artilleryman in eastern Holland. Until three years ago I had not returned to that country and the few weeks there in 1945 had faded into the mists of almost forgotten memory. However in 1985 along with some 3,000 other Canadian Army veterans I came back to the Netherlands for the Fortieth Anniversary of the Liberation. If there had been any oral historians about to record the sharing of our reminiscences, it would have been shown that most of us had become fiercer and braver warriors by 1985 than ever we were four decades before. In fact, there would be all the materials here for a revisionist account of the European campaign that would downplay the roles of such as Eisenhower, Montgomery, Patton, and Rommel and give prominence to those of such hitherto unrecognized participants in these historic events as me. However, I have little hope that future research will render any markedly different judgment on my soldierly capacities than did the late Sergeant Bob Goddard, one of the great and formative influences in my life, who said on an English parade-ground about mid-1942, "Gunner Smiley, you're the best argument I've seen for a negotiated peace."

During the 1985 events I stayed with a wonderful family in Holten, a town of about 15,000 people which owes its prosperity to the production of dairy surpluses for the European Community. Just outside the town is the Holterburg—"holter" is the Dutch name for mountain—which is the highest point on Dutch soil. On the Holterburg is a lovingly kept war cemetery where are buried more than 2,000 Canadians, almost all of them killed in the last six weeks of the European war. One beautiful spring morning there was a very moving memorial service in the cemetery attended by the Canadian veterans and their spouses and several hundred Dutch people of all ages, including most notably veterans of the Dutch Resistance. Standing on this holy ground a person like myself would have been a clod if he did not ponder why he had been spared to the brink of old age while his comrades buried there had been cut down while barely out of their adolescence.

But if I was being pressed to consider fundamental questions I would have to puzzle out something about the basic nature of universities. After all, apart from four years in the 1950s, I had been within one university community or another since 1945. The essential nature of institutions, like that of individuals, is manifested only when there is a direct challenge to their integrity or survival. And again there was a Dutch clue, a clue involving not only the university but the conjuncture between power and justice which I mentioned earlier.

While rummaging around the remainder table of a book sale last fall I came across a short paperback entitled *Thank You Canada*. It is a collection of photographs and documents of the Nazi Occupation and of the Liberation of the Netherlands made by a group of Dutch citizens and presented to the government of Canada on the Centennial of Confederation. With your indulgence I am going to read the operative parts of the translation of a speech in this book made in the Great Hall of the University of Leiden to the students and professors of the Faculty of Law, and apparently many other persons in the university as well, by R.P. Cliveringha, Professor of Commercial Law, on the morning of November 26, 1940.

Today you see me appear before you at an hour when you were accustomed to see another man. Your teacher and mine Meyers.

The cause of this is a letter which he received this morning from the Ministry of Education, and which had the following contents, "Acting under the instructions from the Reichs Kommisar for the Occupied Dutch Territories, on matters concerning non-Aryan public servants and persons holding similar positions, I let you know that, as from today, you are released from your office as Professor in the University of Leiden. The Reichs Kommisar has decreed that, for the time being, those concerned will receive their salaries as usual..."

If I had no other aim than to accentuate our mood, I could not have done better than to end here and leave to you the impression of the icy silence that would then fall. Nor shall I attempt to lead your thoughts in the direction of those who have issued the notice I have just read to you... This compatriot, this noble and true son of our people, this father of his students, this scholar, is relieved from his office by the foreign enemy who now rules us.

I said I would not speak of my feelings and I shall keep my word...However in this faculty, which in accordance with its objective, is dedicated to the exercise of justice, the following remark must not remain unsaid. In accordance with Dutch tradition the constitution declares every Dutch citizen eligible to every position, and it declares him to possess, whatever his religion, the same civil rights and rights of citizenship. According to Article 43 of the Convention of Geneva the occupying forces are bound to respect the laws of the country 'sauf empêchement absolu.' We cannot but feel that there is no obstacle whatever to prevent our conquerors leaving Meyers where he was. This implies that we must see the dismissal of Meyers from his office and similar actions that have been taken against others as unlawful acts...

Meanwhile we shall continue our work as best we may...And in the mean time we shall wait and trust and hope, and always keep alive in our minds and hearts the image and the personality and the appearance of the man whom we will always believe to belong here in this place, where, God willing, he will return.

I was, and am, very moved by this speech and resolved to find out more about the man who made it and the circumstances under which he had spoken. Cliveringha was arrested by the Occupation authorities before the end of the day. Two days later the underground student newspaper *de Geus* circulated this speech in a special edition and added the following:

> We hope that the students will unhesitatingly show they reject the reopening of the university under conditions which would in any way place them under foreign supervision by continuing to strike. Especially the students of Leiden would be put to shame if lectures resumed while Professor Cliveringha is suffering the hardships of German imprisonment for their sake.

Because of the actions of students and faculty the University of Leiden was closed by the Germans for the duration of the Occupation. The occupying authorities had some plans that Leiden be re-opened as a Nazi institution and it seems that lists of acceptable Dutch professors were drawn up. Fortunately nothing came of this scheme to desecrate one of the world's great universities.

Cliveringha and Meyers were interned throughout the Occupation but under relatively favorable circumstances. Both returned after the war to the University of Leiden, where Cliveringha served as rector before his retirement in 1958. A third professor of law, a Professor Cheffels, met a less happy fate. When the news of Meyers' dismissal came down there was a hurried meeting of the teachers of law. It was agreed that this action must be met by a forthright protest on behalf of the Faculty. Cheffels argued that, because unlike Cliveringha he had no family, he should make this protest. Cliveringha as the most senior professor of law would have none of this. Cheffels was, it appears, a more politically active person than his colleague, a member of the Liberal party of Holland and a liaison between students and faculty in the strike which began in November 1940. He was soon interned by the Nazis and perished in Bergen-Belsen.

But what manner of man *was* Cliveringha? Last month I visited the University of Leiden to give a seminar in the Faculty of Law and had some chance to pursue this question. I got the impression that Cliveringha was an unlikely hero. He was a conventional man in both his bearing and his style of living. His scholarship was in technical areas of Dutch commercial law. He was, it appears, an apolitical person, possibly politically naïve. He was associated with the Dutch Liberals but not in any very active capacity. The Nazis allowed him to have his private law library brought to his place of internment and from time to time he somewhat bemused his captors by presenting them with long legal memoranda arguing that their conduct was contrary to the Dutch Constitution and the requirements of international law. By the end of the war his action in November 1940 had made him a Dutch folk-hero and he had opportunities to take a prominent role in the political reconstruction of his country. These seem to have had little attraction for him and he returned to his former work at the university.

Less than three weeks ago, on April 21 to be exact, I visited the Great Hall of the University of Leiden. It is truly an impressive and historic room. There are two podiums—podia?—the higher of which is reserved by venerable tradition for speakers who are of professorial rank in the University. Behind that podium are the Cliveringha stained glass windows portraying in compelling symbolism the challenge of 1940 by the voice of law and justice to political power expressed in as brutal a form as it has ever been experienced. I stood for a few brief seconds in the place where this challenge was made. I knew that as in the war cemetery at Holten I was indeed on holy ground.

APPENDIX

BIBLIOGRAPHY OF WORKS BY
DONALD SMILEY

Prepared by Paul Rynard
with the assistance of Andrea Demchuk

Books and Monographs

Canadian Labour and the Law, University of Alberta MA thesis, 1951.

A Comparative Study of Party Discipline in the House of Commons of the United Kingdom and Canada and in the Congress of the United States, microfiche, doctoral dissertation series, Ann Arbor Michigan: University Microfilms, 1954.

Editor, *The Rowell-Sirois Report: An Abridgement of Book One of the Royal Commission on Dominion-Provincial Relations*, Carelton Library Series 5, Toronto: McClelland and Stewart, 1963.

Conditional Grants and Canadian Federalism: A Study In Constitutional Adaptation, Canadian Tax Paper 32, Toronto: Canadian Tax Foundation, 1963.

Devices of Articulation: The Theory and Practice of Cooperative Federalism, Research Report 1 of the Royal Commission on Bilingualism and Biculturalism, Ottawa: 1966.

The Canadian Political Nationality, Toronto: Methuen, 1967.

Rationalism or Reason: Alternative Approaches to Constitutional Review in Canada, for the "Priorities for Canada" Conference, Niagara Falls: the Progressive Conservative Party, October 12, 1969.

Constitutional Adaptation and Canadian Federalism since 1945, Document 4 of the Royal Commission on Bilingualism and Biculturalism, Ottawa: Queen's Printer, 1970.

Canada in Question, Federalism in the Seventies, Toronto: McGraw-Hill Ryerson, 1st edn. 1972, 2nd edn. 1976.

The Sovereignty-association Alternative: An Analysis, Ryerson lectures in economics, Toronto: Ford Motor Company Ltd., 1978.

The Freedom of Information Issue: A Political Analysis, Research Publication 1, Toronto: The Ontario Commission on Freedom of Information and Individual Privacy, 1978.

Freedom of Information and Ministerial Responsibilty, Research Publication 2, Toronto: The Ontario Commission on Freedom of Information and Individual Privacy, 1978.

The Association Dimension of Sovereignty-Association: A Response to the Quebec White Paper, Discussion Paper 8, Kingston: Institute of Intergovernmental Affairs, Queen's University, 1980.

Canada in Question, Federalism in the Eighties, 3rd ed., Toronto: McGraw-Hill Ryerson, 1980.

The Canadian Charter of Rights and Freedoms, 1981, Toronto: Ontario

Economic Council, 1981.

The Austrailian Senate: Clues for Canada?, 1984.

An Elected Senate for Canada? Clues From the Australian Experience, Discussion Paper 21, Kingston: Institute of Intergovernmental Relations, Queens University, 1985.

with Ronald L. Watts, *Intrastate Federalism in Canada*, Research Study 39 for the Royal Commission on the Economic Union and Development Prospects for Canada, Toronto: University of Toronto Press, 1985.

The Federal Condition in Canada, Toronto: McGraw-Hill Ryerson, 1987.

Articles and Chapters in Books

"Two-Party System and One-Party Dominance in the Liberal Democratic State," *Canadian Journal of Economics and Political Science*, 24 (1958), 312-322.

"Local Autonomy and Central Administrative Control in Saskatchewan," *Canadian Journal of Economics and Political Science*, 26 (1960), 299-313.

"Equipping the Functional Specialist for Administrative Responsibilities in the Public Service," *Canadian Public Administration*, 3 (June 1960), 171-178.

"Rowell-Sirois Report, Provincial Autonomy and Post War Canadian Federalism," *Canadian Journal of Economics and Political Science*, 28 (1962), 54-69.

"Public Administration and Canadian Federalism," *Canadian Public Administration*, 7 (1964), 371-388.

"Block Grants to the Provinces: A Realistic Alternative?" *Report of the Proceedings of the Eighteenth Annual Tax Conference*, Toronto: Canadian Tax Foundation, 1965.

"Two Themes of Canadian Federalism," *Canadian Journal of Economics and Political Science*, 31 (1965), 80-97.

"Federalism, Nationalism and the Scope of Public Activity in Canada," in Peter Russell (ed.), *Nationalism in Canada*, Toronto: McGraw-Hill, 1966, 85-111.

"Contributions to Canadian Political Science Since the Second World War," *Canadian Journal of Economics and Political Science*, 33 (1967), 569-580.

"The National Party Leadership Convention in Canada: A Preliminary Analysis," *Canadian Journal of Political Science*, 1 (1968), 373-397.

"The Case Against the Canadian Charter of Human Rights," *Canadian Journal of Political Science*, 2 (1969), 277-291.

with R.M. Burns, "Canadian Federalism and the Spending Power: Is Constitutional Restriction Necessary?," *Canadian Tax Journal*, 17 (1969), 467-482.

"Canadian Federalism and the Resolution of Federal-Provincial Conflict," in Dwivedi, Frederick, Kyba, Patrick, Vaughan (eds.), *Contemporary Issues in Canadian Politics*, Scarborough: Prentice-Hall, 1970, 48-66.

"The Constitutional Entrenchment of Human Rights," a brief presented to the Special Committee on the Constitution of the Senate and the House of Commons, Ottawa: Queen's Printer, 1970.

"McRuer Report, Parliamentary Majoritarian Democracy and Human Rights," *Journal of Canadian Studies*, 5 (May 1970), 3-10.

"Consent, Coercion and Confederation" in Abraham Rotstein (ed.) *Power Corrupted: The October Crisis and the Repression of Quebec*, Toronto: New Press, 1971, 32-8.

"The Structural Problem of Canadian Federalism," *Canadian Public Administration*, 14 (1971), 326-343.

"The Managed Mosaic," in Viv Nelles and Abraham Rotstein (eds.), *Nationalism or Local Control*, Toronto: New Press, 1973, 69-72.

"The Federal Dimension of Canadian Economic Nationalism," *Dalhousie Law Review*, 1 (October, 1974).

"Federal-Provincial Conflict in Canada," *Publius, The Journal of Federalsim*, 4 (1974), 7-24.

"Must Canadian Political Science Be a Miniature Replica?" *Journal of Canadian Studies*, 9 (Autumn 1974), 31-42.

"Canada and the Quest for a National Policy," *Canadian Journal of Political Science*, 8 (March 1975), 40-62.

"Courts, Legislatures and the Protection of Human Rights," in M. L. Friedland (ed.), *Courts and Trials*, Toronto: University of Toronto Press, 1975.

"The Political Context of Resource Development in Canada," in Anthony Scott (ed.), *Natural Resource Revenue in Canada, A Test of Federalism*, Vancouver: University of British Columbia Press, 1976, 61-72.

"French-English Relations in Canada and Consociational Democracy," in Milton J. Esman (ed.), *Ethnic Conflict in the Western World*, Cornell University Press, 1977, 179-203.

"Territorialism and Canadian Political Institutions," *Canadian Public Policy*, 3 (1977), 449-457.

"Canadian Federalism and the Challenge of Quebec Independence," *Publius, The Journal of Federalism*, 8 (1978), 199-224.

"Federalism and the Legislative Process in Canada," in W. A. W. Neilson and J. C. MacPherson (eds.), *The Legislative Process in Canada*, Montreal: Institute for Research on Public Policy, 1978, 73-87.

"An Outsider's Observations of Federal-Provincial Relations Among Consenting Adults," in Richard Simeon (ed.), *Confrontation and Collaboration: Intergovernmental Relations in Canada Today*, Toronto: Institute of Public Administration of Canada, 1979, 105-113.

"Rights, Power and Values in the Canadian Community," in R.St.J. Macdonald and John P. Humphrey (eds.), *The Practice of Freedom*, Toronto: Butterworth, 1979, 1-24.

"Reflections on Cultural Nationhood and Political Community in Canada," in R. Kenneth Carty and W. Peter Ward (eds.), *Entering the Eighties: Canada in Crises*, Toronto: Oxford University Press, 1980, 20-43.

"The Challenge of Canadian Ambivalence," *Queen's Quarterly*, 88 (Spring 1981), 1-12.

"Federalism and the Canadian Party System," in M. K. Akenyemi (ed.), *Approaches to Federalism*, Logos: Nigerian Institute of International Affairs, 1981, 106-122.

"Freedom of Information: Rationales and Proposals for Reform," in John D. McCamus (ed.), *Freedom of Information: Canadian Perspectives*, Toronto: Butterworth, 1981, 1-21.

"The Canadian Charter of Rights and Freedoms with Special Reference to Quebec-Canada Relations," in William R. McKercher (ed.), *The U.S. Bill of Rights and the Canadian Charter of Rights and Freedoms*, Toronto: Ontario Economic Council,1983, 218-225.

"A Dangerous Deed: the Constitutional Act, 1982," in Keith Banting and Richard Simeon (eds.), *And No One Cheered: Federalism, Democracy and the Constitution Act*, Toronto: Metheun, 1983, 74-95.

"Central Institutions," in Stanely Beck and Ivan Bernier (eds.), *Canada and the New Constition: The Unfinished Agenda*, Vol. 1, Montreal: Institute for Research on Public Policy, 1983, 19-90.

"Public Sector Politics, Modernization and Federalism, The Canadian and American Experience," *Publius, The Journal of Federalism*, 14 (1984), 34-59.

"Federal States and Federal Societies, with Special Reference to Canada," *International Political Science Review*, 5 (1984), 443-454.

"The Three Pillars of the Canadian Constitutional Order," a review of the Report of the Royal Commission on the Economic Union and Development Prospects for Canada, *Canadian Public Policy*, 12 (1986), 113-121.

Short Articles(5pp and under) and Academic Commentaries

"One Partyism and Canadian Democracy," *Canadian Forum*, 38 (July, 1958), 79-80.

"The Alienation of the Politician," *Canadian Forum* 39 (March, 1960), 271-273.

"Consensus, Conflict and the Canadian Party System," *Canadian Forum*, 40 (January, 1961), 223-224.

"Research Program of the Institute of Public Administration of Canada," *Canadian Public Administration*, 4 (March 1961), 41-43.

"Canada's Poujadists: A New Look at Social Credit," *Canadian Forum*, 42 (September, 1962), 121-123.

"Canadian Federation After the Unwanted Election," *Canadian Forum*, 45 (December, 1965), 193-195.

"Political Images," *Canadian Forum*, 48 (July, 1968), 75-76.

"The Political Thought of Pierre Eliot Trudeau," cassette tape (Erindale College, 1971).

"Consent, Coercion and Confederation," *Canadian Forum*, 50 (January, 1971), 330-333.

"Managed and Mosaic," *Canadian Forum*, 52 (April, 1972), 38-40.

"From Progress to Parochialism," *Canadian Forum*, 52 (September, 1972), 18-19.

"Pretensions of the Provinces," *Canadian Forum*, 53 (May, 1973), 6-8.

"Are More Stringent Controls Needed for Multinational Corporations in

Canada?" panel discussion for the Committee for An Independent Canada, cassette tape (Erindale College, 1975).

"Pervasive Government Involvement in Privat Sector Lacks Coherence," *Financial Post* (November 23, 1974), 68.

"The Non Economics of Anti-Inflation," *Canadian Forum*, 55 (March, 1976), 11-14.

"As the Options Narrow: Notes on Post-November 15, Canada," *Journal of Canadian Studies*, 12 (July 1977), 3-7.

"Distressing Confusion," *Canadian Forum*, 59 (Nov. 1977), 24-6.

"Quebec Independence and the Democratic Dilemma," *Canadian Forum*, 58 (January, 1979), 11-12.

"Update: The Canadian Federation in 1978," *Publius, The Journal of Federalism*, 9 (1979), 237-241.

"Political Science in Canada," *Proceedings and Transactions*, 4th Series (Royal Society of Canada, 1980), 271-275.

"Comment," commentary on articles (same issue) by Pratt and Tupper ("The Politics of Accountability") and Stevenson ("Political Constraints and the Province Building Objective"), *Canadian Public Policy*, 6 (1980), 277-279.

"Political Metaphysicians," *Canadian Forum*, 60 (October,1980),13-14.

"The Right Honourable John A. Diefenbaker, 1895-1979," *Proceedings and Transactions*, 4th Series, 19 (Royal Society of Canada, 1981), 79-83.

"The Left and the New Trudeau," *Canadian Forum*, 61 (November, 1981), 18-20.

"A Note on Canadian-American Free Trade and Canadian Policy Autonomy," in Marc Gold and David Leyton-Brown (eds.), *Trade-offs on Free Trade, the Canada-U.S. Free Tade Deal* (Toronto: Carswell, 1988), 442-445.

Book Reviews

Essays in Federalism, by G. S. Benson, M. Diamond, H. F. McClelland, W. S. Stokes and P. Thomson, *Canadian Journal of Economics and Political Science*, 28 (1962), 617-9.

Richard Jones, *Community in Crisis: French-Canadian Nationalism in Perspective*, *Canadian Historical Review*, 49 (1968), 68-70).

Pierre Trudeau, *Federalism and the French Canadians*, *Canadian Historical Review*, 49 (1968), 413-4).

John S. Moir (ed.), *Character and Circumstance: Essays in Honour of Donald Grant Creighton*, *Canadian Journal of Political Science*, 4 (1971), 292).

Ramsay Cook, *The Maple Forever: Essays on Nationalism and Politics in Canada*, *Canadian Historical Review*, 53 (1972), 75-8).

George Carter, *Canadian Conditional Grants since World War Two*, *Canadian Public Administration*, 15 (1972), 499-501).

John Saywell, *Quebec 70: A Documentary Narrative*, *Canadian Historical Review*, 54 (1973), 92-3).

"The Dominance of Withinputs?: Canadian Politics," *Polity*, 6 (1973), 276-

281.

David Cameron, *Nationalism, Self-Determination and the Quebec Question*, *Canadian Journal of Political Science*, 9 (1976), 138-139).

A. E. Safarian, *Canadian Federalism and Economic Integration*, *Canadian Public Policy*, 3 (1977), 126-7.

Leo Panitch (ed.), *The Canadian State: Political Economy and Political Power*, *Canadian Journal of Political Science*, 11 (1978), 656-659).

F. R. Scott, *Essays on the Constitution*, *Canadian Forum*, 58 (Oct. 1978), 445.

Carlo Caldarola (ed.), *Society and Politics in Alberta: Researh Papers*, and Larry Pratt and John Richards, *Prairie Capitalism: Power and Influence in the New West*, *Canadian Public Administration*, 23 (1980), 175-178).

R. Bothwell, I Drummond and John English, *Canada since 1945: Power, Politics and Provincialism*, *Canadian Forum*, 61 (Nov. 1981), 33-4.

J.M.S. Careless (ed.) *The Preconfederation Premiers*, *Canadian Forum*, 60 (Feb. 1981), 28.

George C. Perlin, *The Tory Syndrome: Leadership Politics in the Progressive Conservative Party*, *Canadian Journal of Political Science*, 14 (1981), 148-150).

J. A. Corry *Memoirs of J. A. Corry: My Life and Work a Happy Partnership*, *Canadian Forum*, 61 (Mar. 1982), 30.

Charles Taylor, *Radical Tories: The Conservative Tradition in Canada*, and Joseph Levitt, *A Vision Beyond Reach: A Century of Images of Canadian Destiny*, *Canadian Forum*, 63 (June 1983), 33.

Paul Davenport and Richard Leach (eds.), *Reshaping Confederation: The 1982 Reform of the Canadian Constitution*, *Canadian Journal of Political Science*, 18 (1985), 169-170).